MORAL PHILOSOPHY

What is moral philosophy? That is the question with which this important volume grapples. Its starting point is the famous critique made in 1958 by Elizabeth Anscombe, who argued that moral philosophy begins from a mistake: that it is fundamentally wrong about the sort of concept that the word 'moral' represents. Anscombe rejected moral philosophy as it was then (and mostly now still is) practised. She offered instead a blueprint for the task moral philosophers must embrace if they are to speak intelligibly to society about good and bad, right and wrong, duty and obligation. The chapters in this book are inspired by Anscombe's classic text. One of the most powerful voices here, among many authoritative voices, is that of Philippa Foot – Anscombe's lifelong friend – who asserts that 'any account of practical reason evacuated of an understanding of what human beings need to flourish is inadequate and must be rejected.'

ANTHONY O'HEAR, OBE, is Professor of Philosophy at the University of Buckingham. He is an Honorary Director of the Royal Institute of Philosophy and Editor of the Institute's journal Philosophy.

RACHAEL WISEMAN is Senior Lecturer in Philosophy at the University of Liverpool. She is author of the Routledge Philosophy GuideBook to Anscombe's Intention (2016)

TALKING PHILOSOPHY

General Editor: James Garvey

The Royal Institute of Philosophy has been, from the very start, a fundamentally outward-facing organization. In 1924, Sydney Hooper – main mover behind the establishment of the Institute – realized that outreach to a wide interested public was a vital part of the value (whether social, cultural or intellectual) that philosophy at its best can impart. The Institute's first executive committee actively promoted that broad pedagogical message through accessible civic talks, and included in its ranks many of the most eminent luminaries of the day: not just professional philosophers but also sociologists, physicians, politicians, evolutionary biologists and psychologists. The Institute, from its foundation, has thus been rooted in an egalitarian community of people devoted to the principles of learning, debating and teaching philosophical knowledge in the broader service of what Hooper called 'the most permanent interests of the human spirit'. Talking Philosophy maintains this noble tradition. A book series published under the joint auspices of the Institute and Cambridge University Press, it addresses some of the most pertinent topics of the day so as to show how philosophy can shed new light on their interpretation, as well as public understanding of them.

Books in the series:

Moral Philosophy
The Philosophy of Mind
Ethics

MORAL PHILOSOPHY

EDITED BY

ANTHONY O'HEAR

University of Buckingham

WITH A FOREWORD BY

RACHAEL WISEMAN

University of Liverpool

CAMBRIDGE
UNIVERSITY PRESS

University Printing House, Cambridge CB2 8BS, United Kingdom

One Liberty Plaza, 20th Floor, New York, NY 10006, USA

477 Williamstown Road, Port Melbourne, VIC 3207, Australia

314–321, 3rd Floor, Plot 3, Splendor Forum, Jasola District Centre, New Delhi – 110025, India

103 Penang Road, #05-06/07, Visioncrest Commercial, Singapore 238467

Cambridge University Press is part of the University of Cambridge.

It furthers the University's mission by disseminating knowledge in the pursuit of education, learning, and research at the highest international levels of excellence.

www.cambridge.org
Information on this title: www.cambridge.org/9781009111393
DOI: 10.1017/9781009109413

Previously published as Royal Institute of Philosophy Supplement: 54, *Modern Moral Philosophy*, 2004, Paperback ISBN 9780521603263
This edition first published 2022

A catalogue record for this publication is available from the British Library.

ISBN 978-1-009-11139-3 Paperback

CONTENTS

FOREWORD

RACHAEL WISEMAN

G. E. M. Anscombe's 'Modern Moral Philosophy' was published in 1958 by the Royal Institute's journal, *Philosophy*.[1] Sixty-years on, ethicists are still getting to grips with her deep and subtle critique of moral philosophy and have barely begun to work through its implications for the subject as we know it. This volume, and the 2002–3 Royal Institute of Philosophy lecture series that was its genesis, takes its name from Anscombe's essay. Though not a set of commentaries, the radical character of the moral philosophy the collection contains – presented in many cases quietly, cautiously and without swagger – is best seen against the background of Anscombe's intervention. For this reason, I begin this preface with an examination of Anscombe's essay and its import.

It tends to be taken for granted that we have an intuitive grasp of the subject matter of moral philosophy – that our mastery of ordinary language allows us roughly to identify the phenomena that it is the task of the moral philosopher to explain and understand. When a philosopher says that she is interested in moral as opposed to

[1] G. E. M. Anscombe, 'Modern Moral Philosophy, *Philosophy*, vol. 33, no. 124 (1958), 1–19.

conventional obligation we seem to understand the sort of distinction she is making. When she declares that she wants to give an account of moral as opposed to prudential reasons we think she makes her topic clear. The distinction between the moral and the instrumental necessity of an action is one that we suppose can be grasped by simple common sense. The moral philosopher begins by indicating her topic with a few illustrative examples and then moves on to make a philosophical investigation of the area she thereby identifies. She may find that the boundary has been inaccurately drawn, or even that the existence of a hard border is after all chimerical. She may even discover that the area identified by the concept *moral* is empty. However, her starting point is an intuitive grasp of the subject at hand.

Anscombe argues, in 'Modern Moral Philosophy', that moral philosophy starts from a mistake. The error, as Anscombe's mentor Wittgenstein might have put it, is in the 'first step that altogether escapes our notice'.[2] We do not understand the character of the distinction that we draw when we oppose moral obligation, moral reasons and the moral necessity of an action to conventional obligation, prudential reasons and an action's psychological necessity. The moral philosopher, according to Anscombe, has not identified a fuzzy-edged area of investigation; she has identified no area at all. The problem, Anscombe thinks, is that the moral philosopher is mistaken about the sort of concept that the word 'moral' represents. We can compare this

[2] Ludwig Wittgenstein, *Philosophical Investigations* (Macmillan Publishing Company, 1963), §308.

diagnosis to the one that Anscombe makes at the beginning of *Intention.* There she says that we do not understand the character of the concept that the word 'intention' represents and so do not understand the sort of distinction that we are drawing when we contrast expressions of intention with predictions or involuntary actions with intentional ones.[3] So too, thinks Anscombe, with the concept *moral.* Anscombe says that philosophers ought to stop using the word 'moral' until they are clear about the character of the concept it represents, and until they are clear about this, the very *subject matter* of moral philosophy remains elusive.

Anscombe sketches a genealogy to explain the deep confusion into which 'modern moral philosophy' has fallen. Aristotle located the concepts of goodness and badness in the context of a pattern created by the *human form of life.* Specifically, he explained the meaning of 'good' and 'bad' by reference to what a man or woman needs to be excellent of their kind. According to Aristotle, to speak of a good human is not to say that some individual has two properties, goodness and humanity, but rather to say that some individual is a good instance of the kind, *human.* 'Good', in 'Elizabeth is good' is attributive and not predicative, as Peter Geach would put it.[4] The sentence says that Elizabeth is good *qua* human. To be good *qua* knife is to be sharp; to be good *qua* oak tree is to produce acorns. What is it to be good *qua* human? Aristotle's answer is as profound as it is familiar: to be good *qua* human is to act well, in accordance

[3] G. E. M. Anscombe, *Intention* (Blackwell: Oxford, 1956), 1.

[4] Peter Geach, 'Good and Evil', *Analysis*, Vol. 17, No. 2 (1956), 33–42.

with practical reason informed by an understanding of what humans need to flourish.

Among the things that humans need to flourish are goods that can be attained only through cooperation and collaboration in the context of conventional, political and institutional norms. As such, much of practical reason governs interaction with others and concerns the relation between the individual and her polis. The Aristotelian ethical framework makes no fundamental cleavage between egoism and altruism, morality and prudence, self-interest and justice, integrity and happiness. From its perspective the goodness that is the topic of ethics is, as Foot calls it in this volume, natural goodness: it is goodness that is understood in relation to human nature. The 'ought' that appears in 'You ought to keep your promise' represents the same concept as that in 'You ought to watch your weight', 'You ought to go to bed at a reasonable hour' or 'You ought to do what the teacher says'. Each concerns one's acting well *qua* human.

Intervening between us and Aristotle is the rise and fall of Judeo-Christianity as the dominant worldview. According to Anscombe's genealogy, Judeo-Christian ethics begins from Aristotle's picture but adds that vicious acts, as well as being bad for a human, are unlawful. This brings onto the scene an 'ought' that is generated not by the internal features of human life but by a Divine command. Noncompliance with such a command is seen as not merely bad for a human but also wrong because it is disobedient. Over the many centuries during which this worldview dominated, the language of good (*qua* human) and bad (*qua* human) and that of right (lawful) and wrong (unlawful) became intertwined. As the actions that God commands are those that a good human would go in for, this makes no practical difference: that which is contrary to natural goodness is that which is unlawful, so to speak of vice as unlawful or virtue as right makes no trouble. But, Anscombe says, we are now living after the collapse of Judeo-Christianity as the dominant worldview, and in this context the mixing of these language games is no longer benign. We must expunge from our ethical language those parts that depend for their meaning on the existence of a Divine authority in whom we no longer believe. This, however, is something that atheistic modern moral philosophers have not done. Rather than recovering the language of natural goodness, virtue and practical reason, they have instead sought to preserve a concept that is an heir of the Christian concept of *unlawful.* In doing so they enshrine talk of '*moral* obligation and *moral* duty . . . and of what is *morally* right and wrong, and of the *moral* sense of "ought"' but cleave it from the form of life that would provide its content and the metaphysical background that would lend it force'.[5]

This brings us to Anscombe's final piece of diagnosis: a system of morals that is characterised by pseudo-commands is one that will necessarily degenerate toward the rejection of moral absolutes and the adoption of consequentialist and conventional thinking. How could we 'bind'

[5] Anscombe, 'Modern Moral Philosophy', 1.

ourselves to *musts*, *shoulds* and *oughts* that are opposed to those of prudence and self-interest, while being empty of content and lacking in force? It is inevitable that the visible rewards of 'doing evil that good may come' will prevail and so-called moral principles – the shadows of Divine commands – will become rules of thumb that an educated person will know when prudentially to ignore.

This background should put us in a position to understand the three theses with which Anscombe begins her essay:

> The first is that it is not profitable for us at present to do moral philosophy; that it should be laid aside at any rate until we have an adequate philosophy of psychology, in which we are conspicuously lacking. The second is that the concepts of obligation, and duty – *moral* obligation and *moral* duty, that is to say – and of what is *morally* right and wrong, and of the *moral* sense of 'ought', ought to be jettisoned if this is psychologically possible; because they are survivals, or derivatives from survivals, from an earlier conception of ethics which no longer generally survives, and are only harmful without it. My third thesis is that the difference between the well-known English writers on moral philosophy from Sidgwick to the present day are of little importance.[6]

Anscombe's essay rejects moral philosophy as it was and – to a large degree – is still practised. It provides a blueprint for the task that philosophers must embrace if they are to provide philosophy and society at large with the concepts

[6] Anscombe, 'Modern Moral Philosophy', 1.

needed to speak intelligibly about good and bad, right and wrong, duty and obligation. The character of the concept *moral* is not illuminated by a search for a special sort of binding, motivating, obligation. What is needed is a description of the structure of practical reason and of the sorts of considerations that count, for humans, as deep, serious and even worth dying for. This is to begin moral philosophy again, from the position of knowing only that we do not yet know the character of the concept we are seeking to understand. This brings us to the present volume and its place today.

The essays in this collection are each animated by the provocation of Anscombe's classic text and the theses it defends. It is this context that gives unity to an otherwise disparate set of topics: authority, promising, co-operation, practical inference and human nature to name just a handful. Authors tend not to focus on topics that might standardly appear in a volume of moral philosophy. No importance is placed on the distinction that is drawn between metaethics and normative ethics on Anscombe's picture, and so you will not find in this collection the usual stand-offs between realist, anti-realists, irrealists and quasi-realists; in the stead of disembodied 'ideally rational agents' are ordinary human beings at work in the world; there is little in this volume about 'states of affairs', so-called trolley-problems or altruism; when rights, duties and obligations are discussed, you will find authors carefully tread and do not assume that such things come in two flavours: moral and non-moral.

Even those writers least sympathetic to Anscombe's theses (Crisp, Pink, O'Neill) write in the context of the challenge that her essay poses to the very intelligibility of the project of moral philosophy. While those authors seek to domesticate aspects of Anscombe's project by rendering it less unfriendly to modern moral philosophy, others (Foot, Muller, Thompson, Chappell, Price, Teichmann, Oderberg, Lovibond) set to work on answering the questions raised by Anscombe's essay. How are we to understand the unity of the concepts represented by 'ought', 'should', 'must', etc.? How can it be rational to act against one's own self-interest? Isn't there a genuine conflict between flourishing and goodness in so-called tight corners? What role should consideration of the expected consequences of an action play in the exercise of practical reason? What place is there for pleasure in a theory of ethics? Can there be absolute prohibitions without Divine Command? What is the character of the concept *human*? What is the form of practical (as opposed to theoretical) reason?

These questions set the agenda for the subject area formally known as 'moral philosophy'. Work under this agenda echoes Anscombe's call for a return to the language of virtue in the context of an understanding of the genealogy just sketched. This understanding makes this research quite different from that done under the heading 'Virtue Ethics', a label Foot herself explicitly rejects in this volume (2). 'Virtue Ethics', now one of the triad of normative moral theories (alongside Deontology and Consequentialism), takes the 'first step' against which Anscombe warns. It takes as its subject matter *moral* virtues and *moral* character and in doing so takes for granted just those conceptual dichotomies that 'Modern Moral Philosophy' throws into doubt. Though both Virtue Ethicists and – as we might call them – Unmodern Moral Philosophers are working with Aristotelian concepts (virtue, practical reason, character), only the latter are doing so with the understanding that our 'modern' psychology, our 'modern' theories of practical reason and our 'modern' conception of human life are all barriers to genuine insight into the sort of characteristic that a virtue is.

It is worth emphasising this point not least because a failure to do so has left philosophers slow to recognise the radical character of Philippa Foot's quiet and unshowy contribution to the dual topics of rationality and goodness, the relation between which she reflects on in this volume. Few philosophers have understood the seriousness of Anscombe's challenge to moral philosophy as well as Foot, who was Anscombe's colleague and lifelong friend. It is testament to this understanding that Foot dedicated her life's work to the problem of rational action 'in the tight corner' (4). In this volume Foot illustrates the problem using a letter written in 1944 by a farm boy from the Sudetenland:

> Dear parents: I must give you bad news: I have been condemned to death. I and Gustave G. We did not sign up for the SS, and so they condemned us to death . . . Both of us would rather die than stain our consciences with such deeds of horror. I know what the SS have to do. (2)

What Foot recognises is that modern instrumentalist theories of practical reason have to say that the farm boy's choice is irrational: they have to say that in choosing to die rather than do some terrible thing, he acts against reason. Foot saw that this must be wrong. An account of practical reason that cannot recognise that the farm boy acts well, in accord with practical reason informed by an understanding of what humans need to flourish, is inadequate and must be rejected. An enquiry into the nature of practical reason, Foot holds, must be already oriented toward a substantive account of the human good. To approach practical reason in this way is to follow Anscombe in refusing the distinction that the 'modern moral philosopher' seeks to make when she contrasts moral and prudential reasons.

Foot is not the only author in this volume to have made a substantial contribution to this research agenda. Her student Michael Thompson's influential and important monograph *Life and Action* builds on the claim defended in this volume (in 'Apprehending Human Form'): that it is a mistake to think the life-form concepts are empirical concepts derived from experience.[7] As Thompson puts it in this volume: 'Against [the empiricist] I would like to claim that the concept *life form* is more akin to such logical or quasi-logical notions as *object*, *property*, *relation*, *fact*, or process' (63). In saying this, Thompson makes it possible to see that life-form judgments – judgments with species concepts like *human* in the subject-position – are not statistical generalizations (akin to 'Most humans have 32 teeth') but norms against which individual members of the species might be recognised as deficient or defective. Anselm Muller's 'Acting Well' (this volume) is part of a life's work influenced, as he says, by Anscombe and

[7] Michael Thompson, *Life and Action: Elementary Structures of Practice and Practical Thought* (Harvard University Press, 2008).

Philippa Foot. Like Foot, Muller refuses to countenance an analysis of *human action* that does not take as its starting point *acting well.* Donald Davidson's analysis of action, for many years utterly dominant in English-language philosophy, is now seen by many as inadequate, precisely because it is unable to serve the agenda set by 'Modern Moral Philosophy'. Roger Teichmann, Sophie Grace Chappel and Sabina Lovibond continue to contribute philosophy of psychology and metaphysics in service of a different sort of ethics.

It is good that this volume should be reissued this year, which is the centenary Anscombe's and Foot's births. Their work, and this volume, shows us the way in which history of philosophy is part of philosophy. The stories that tell ourselves and each other about where we came from and how we got here are not inconsequential to the philosophical theories we develop. What counts as intuitive and common sense reflects our muddled, contingent, careless assumptions about the genealogy of our concepts. As philosophers it is as much our job to examine those assumptions as it is to innovate and theorise. This sort of work is unglamorous and slow and rarely issues in theses that translate into slogans. But Foot's essay in this volume reminds us of its importance. Modern moral philosophy, and the society in which it still flourishes, begins from a 'prejudice in favour of the rationalizing force of self-interest' (13). This prejudice is one that we must collectively expunge before appeals to what is 'reasonable', 'practical', 'prudential' and 'realistic' usher our species into a future that is hostile to the human form of life.

References

Anscombe, G. E. M. *Intention*. Oxford: Blackwell, 1956, 1.

Anscombe, G. E. M. 'Modern Moral Philosophy', *Philosophy*, 33 (124) (1958), 1–19.

Geach, Peter. 'Good and Evil', *Analysis*, 17(2) (1956): 33–42.

Thompson, Michael. *Life and Action: Elementary Structures of Practice and Practical Thought*. Cambridge, MA: Harvard University Press, 2008.

Wittgenstein, Ludwig. *Philosophical Investigations*. New York: Macmillan Publishing Company, 1963), §308.

PREFACE

ANTHONY O'HEAR

The papers contained in this volume are based on the Royal Institute of Philosophy's annual lecture series for 2002–3. Many readers will be aware that the title of the series refers to a famous paper by Elizabeth Anscombe with the same title, which was itself published, appropriately enough, in the Royal Institute's own journal *Philosophy* in 1958. While this collection is not a commentary either on 'Modern Moral Philosophy' or on Anscombe's work more generally, it is a testament to the influence and potency of that article. Many of our contributors acknowledge its influence on them, and several take up the challenges Anscombe threw down in her original piece. In some quarters and in some ways moral philosophy was changed by Anscombe's article and, in the opinion of many, for the better. The collection as a whole reflects this state of affairs.

It is a pleasure to acknowledge the contributions of all those who gave lectures in the series, and who, collectively and unintentionally, have produced a remarkable, coherent volume. On behalf of the Royal Institute, I thank them all. But I am sure that no one would think it invidious if I were to single out one contribution in particular, that, namely, of Philippa Foot. Mrs Foot has herself been a towering presence in moral philosophy over several decades, and, as she herself acknowledges, particularly in the early days, was greatly influenced by Anscombe. It was, therefore, especially fortunate for the Institute that she gave us considerable help in organising the series in the early stages. But over and above that, her own lecture was not just a model of what such a lecture could be; it was, she assures us, the last public lecture she will give. The Royal Institute considers itself privileged to have provided the setting for so significant an event.

LIST OF CONTRIBUTORS

Philippa Foot
Anselm Müller
Michael Thompson
Roger Crisp
Tim Chappell
A. W. Price
Sabina Lovibond
Thomas Pink
Avishai Margalit
David Oderberg
Roger Teichmann
Joseph Raz
Gavin Lawrence
Onora O'Neill

Rationality and Goodness

PHILIPPA FOOT

The problem I am going to discuss here concerns practical rationality, rationality not in thought but in action. More particularly, I am going to discuss the rationality, or absence of rationality (even, as one might put it, the contra-rationality or irrationality) of moral action. And 'moral action' shall mean here something done by someone who (let us suppose rightly) believes that to act otherwise would be contrary to, say, justice or charity; or again not done because it is thought that it would be unjust or uncharitable to do it. The question is whether in so acting, or refusing to act, this person will be acting rationally, even in cases where he or she believes that not only desire but self-interest would argue in favour of the wrongdoing.

In starting out like this I shall be addressing the concerns of one whom I might label 'the moral doubter': one who has problems about the rationality of acting morally rather as many Christians have problems about the existence of evil in the world. This person wants to be convinced and may be particularly attached to morality, but has a worry about why 'in the tight corner' anyone has reason to do what there seems to be reason enough not to do, or again not to do what there seems reason enough to do. My moral worrier may not be in any doubt about what is right and wrong, and is therefore different from an immoralist such as Thrasymachus in Plato's *Republic*, who insists that justice is not a virtue but rather 'silly good nature.'

Concentrating on justice, I am going to assume that if anything is a moral virtue justice is, and so for the moment shall bypass that part of the immoralist dispute. Thrasymachus, in the *Republic*, Callicles in Plato's *Gorgias*, and Nietzsche too in his own way, all argue that justice is not an excellence of character. But I assume that it is. People act well when they act justly, badly when unjustly. A further assumption will be about what justice is: that men and women are properly called *just* in so far as they are disposed to do certain things, such as keeping contracts and respecting the lives and property of others; unjust when they lie, cheat, bear false witness. To have the virtue of justice they must, of course, do these things for the right reasons, but the choice of a virtue word such as 'justice' does not commit me to what is nowadays called a virtue theory of ethics.[1]

My problem, therefore, is about the rationality of acting on a moral judgment where there seem to be indubitable reasons for *not* doing what morality requires, but no ulterior reason for being just.

[1] I am thinking here of the undoubtedly interesting work of philosophers such as Rosalind Hursthouse, Christine Swanton, and Michael Slote who insist that dispositions, motives, and other 'internal' elements are the primary subjects and determinants of moral goodness and badness. I myself have never been a 'virtue ethicist' in this sense. For me it is *what is done* that stands in this position.

These are the terms in which the problem of the rationality of acting justly confronts me. When does it do so? Not of course whenever a judgment has been made to the effect that justice demands that certain things be done or left undone, because there are often obvious enough reasons to act justly rather than unjustly. There are penalties for instance. The law may speak for justice. Or a good reputation may be at stake. But quite apart from the fact that a stern moralist such as H. A. Prichard will insist that these are not the right reasons for following justice; what if the rewards and penalties are predominantly, or even all, on the other side?

It will be useful at this point to introduce an example, and I choose one from the book called *Dying We Live* from which, in my book *Natural Goodness,* I took the case of anti-Nazis condemned to death, ones I partly invented and called 'the Letter Writers'.[2] Here I give as an example one very brief letter printed in *Dying We Live,* which was from a young man identified only as 'A Farm Boy from the Sudetenland.' On Feb 3, 1944, he wrote as follows:

> 'Dear parents: I must give you bad news—I have been condemned to death. I and Gustave G. We did not sign up for the SS, and so they condemned us to death. . . Both of us would rather die than stain our consciences with such deeds of horror. I know what the SS have to do.'[3]

[2] H. Gollwitzer, K. Kuhn, and R. Schneider (eds.) *Dying We Live* (London: The Harvill Press), 1956 11. See Philippa Foot, *Natural Goodness* (Oxford: Clarendon Press, 2001) 94–6, 102.

[3] *Dying We Live,* 11.

The farm boy from the Sudetenland chose to be hanged rather than become a member of the SS, though joining would no doubt have gained him many rewards, and at the very least would have saved his life. Was this, I ask, a rational choice? How can we defend such a proposition? On what theory of practical rationality—of the rationality of choices—can this be made out?

This seems to be an example of the 'tight corner' that will test us. It will be obvious, for instance, that on neither of the two most favoured theories of practical rationality around today will it be possible to show the course taken by the farm boy and his friend to be a rational rather than a non-rational, irrational, contra-rational choice—whichever form you choose for the description of a choice made in the face of strong reasons against it—in the absence of an explanation as to why it itself was rational.

The two modern theories that I am thinking of can both be called instrumentalist.

There is 1) The Humean, or neo-Humean, theory of practical rationality that refers all rational decisions to the base of the agent's present desires. There is nothing here to call on for the case of the farm boy from the Sudetenland. It is true that he said he would rather die than join the SS. But for us to take his decision as therefore rational would be either simply to affix practical rationality automatically to actual choices, or else to suppose, quite unrealistically, that his present desire for life, and his fear of death by hanging had disappeared. If there is a way in which a moral judgment 'silences' desires incompatible with acting well, this is not it.

2) Alternatively, practical rationality is often seen as belonging to whatever action is reasonably supposed by the agent to be for his own good on the whole, the fact that he may *at present* be indifferent to future happiness or unhappiness now being treated as irrelevant. Such a theory allows us, of course, to weigh on the side of morality all the furthest effects of acting badly, including such penalties as biting remorse, or the diminishing of the capacity for some innocent joys. But however far we press such (real) advantages of acting well over acting badly there will always seem to be some special pleading here, and a tendency to assume *a priori* what is supposed to be based on empirical fact. In truth a 'self-interest', or as we may call it a 'prudential' theory of practical rationality cannot deal honestly with the case of the farm boy from the Sudetenland. So long as the concept of future good is seen in terms of happiness or satisfaction it cannot help us here.

I want to stress how serious is the difficulty that we are now in. This is clear if we think about the use of the word 'should' in making moral judgments. Our farm boy from the Sudetenland was, in effect, saying to himself 'I *shouldn't* have anything to do with the SS. I *should* refuse to join them, because of the terrible things they do.' But how is it that 'should' and 'shouldn't' belong here? *These words speak of reasons for doing a certain action or not doing it.* So how can they be used unless the problem of reason for acting morally has already been solved? Isn't the use of the ordinary words 'should' and 'shouldn't' in question? Of course if their function in expressing moral judgment is thought of as not the ordinary one, but rather a mere expression of attitudes, feeling, commitments etc. —if *that* is offered as an account of their meaning—then it is, I suppose, possible to think that in moral contexts the necessary connection with reasons for action will have disappeared, in favour of mere persuasion or the expression of feeling or attitude. But I myself will have no truck with expressivist accounts of the special 'shoulds' of moral judgment, or indeed with anything but the ordinary use of the words 'should' and 'shouldn't,' found in moral judgments as elsewhere.

Two replies to the difficulty that I have just raised about the use of 'should' may, however, be given: both of which are attempts to down play the connection between what should be done and what there is reason to do.

A) It may be pointed out that there are uses of 'should' and 'shouldn't' that when fully expressed speak only of what by certain existing *rules* is forbidden or enjoined. This is true, but in moral judgments such words are obviously not to be explained like that.

B) It may be pointed out that 'should' even when it does imply reason for action may imply a *pro tanto* reason rather than a reason all things considered. But have we yet got the right to speak even of *pro tanto* reasons for acting in such a situation as that of our Farm Boy in his terrible situation? And in any case it was clearly an all-things-considered judgment of reason that would have been implied had the 'shouldn't' terminology been used by the Farm Boy when he spoke of joining the SS.

We therefore have fair and square on our hands the problem of rational action 'in the tight corner': the problem of the rationality of doing what morality enjoins where desire and long term self interest both speak on the other side. It is a problem that I myself have wrestled with unsuccessfully over the whole of my philosophical life: at one time (in a rather notorious article called 'Morality as a System of Hypothetical Imperatives') going so far as actually to deny the rationality of action required by justice when opposed both to prudence and desire.[4]

The reason that I think I can do better this time round is that I have been much impressed by the resources that I see as offered in two papers of my friend Warren Quinn: one of the most brilliant of contemporary moral philosophers, by whose sadly early death we are much deprived. The two papers that I want to discuss tonight are both published in the collection of Quinn's writings called *Morality and Action*.[5] They are 1) 'Rationality and the Human Good' and 2) 'Putting Rationality in its Place'. The argument of each is intricate, and I shall take what I want from them without going into all the moves that Quinn himself, a most rigorous and meticulous thinker, saw as necessary for the defence of his main thesis.

Let me simply summarize what I take to be most important and most *a propos* of Quinn's arguments. The structure of his argument is notably idiosyncratic. For the rest of us usually try now this now that way of showing that it must be possible to show that it is rational to act justly even in the tight corner, *starting off with some old (or new)*

[4] *The Philosophical Review*, volume 81, Number 3 (3 July, 1972).

[5] W. Quinn, *Morality and Action* (Cambridge, Cambridge University Press, 1993).

theory of practical rationality, into which 'moral' action will somehow be made to fit. Quinn suggests a reversal of the direction of these thoughts. He suggests that so far from supposing that moral action must be in some way 'irrational' if it cannot be made to fit with a preconceived idea of rationality, we should rather count any theory of rationality deficient if an action known to be shameful (like joining the SS) would be tolerated or even recommended by its canons.

How does Quinn argue this remarkable case? What he does is to take a particular theory of practical rationality—or strictly two—that he labels neo-Humean, corresponding to the two instrumentalist theories that I mentioned above. One is a neo-Humean theory identifying practical rationality with policies designed to maximize fulfilment of an agent's desires; the other a prudentialist theory in which practical reason aims at the agent's well being. In each case the theory is characterized by an absence of moral input: all desires, are as such on the same footing, and well-being is also understood in morally neutral terms.

Quinn points out that on either theory it would be possible for *morally disgraceful* actions to be tolerated or even recommended under the heading of the practically rational. And then he makes the crucial move of asking why, if this were true, we should think practical rationality so important? We think of practical rationality as a kind of master virtue. But what would be so important about it if it would license or even mandate disgraceful actions? How in such a case could it keep its supposed status as the master virtue? Why should *its* criteria have to be met in a satisfactory theory of moral virtue?

The asking of this question seems to me to be a move of great originality in the context of modern moral philosophy, which has for long assumed that the direction of command must go the other way: that morality must somehow be brought under the mantle of practical rationality, rather than a theory of practical rationality having to fit in with moral judgment. That command goes the other way is what Quinn himself argued in the two articles that I am considering. To be sure in these articles he was explicitly concerned only with instrumentalist theories of practical rationality: arguing that *they* should be seen as discredited by their undoubted dissonance with moral judgment. But if one theory of practical rationality can be so discredited, so can another. That is why the reach of his argument is so great.

Quinn is talking about precedence. But it is important here to be clear about just what it is that has precedence over what: the answer being that the rationality of acting morally has precedence over any assumption about practical rationality that would put this in doubt. If an instrumental or prudential theory of rationality tells us that to follow the dictates of justice can be contrary to rationality, *it is that theory of rationality that is defective.* And this is a very important conclusion indeed, which should bring to an end desperate attempts to 'rationalize' the action of the Farm Boy from the Sudetenland in refusing to join the SS by showing it to be instrumental to maximum happiness or maximum fulfilment of desire. If, according to a particular theory of rationality, a good action such as his seems dubiously rational, then so much the worse, not for the moral judgment, but rather for that theory. This is what I meant when I said that Quinn was suggesting a change in direction of authority or command.

Here, however, I must warn against a possible misunderstanding of what is being said: the mistake of thinking that Quinn was supporting the old idea that 'moral considerations are overriding,' having *a priori* precedence over considerations of self interest or of the fulfilment of desire. This was not implied by anything that he said. In arguing that by any *acceptable* theory of practical rationality morally shameful actions must be judged to be irrational (nonrational) he was saying, of course, that where the actions *really were* shameful then this must be the verdict about their rationality. And he developed examples in which the considered verdict really was on the side of morality. But that, I must insist, did not imply any a priori difference of status between moral and other considerations *going towards* an all-things-considered judgment. Nor would that thesis have been anything but a mistake. It is often said that 'moral considerations are overriding', but I think that belief in that edifying sounding pronouncement is due to a confusion. For what are 'moral considerations'? A moral *consideration* is some fact such as that a promise has been given, an utterance is truthful or mendacious, or a course of action likely to be seriously helpful or harmful to others. These considerations do indeed give good *pro tanto* reasons for acting in a particular way; that is reasons relative to a certain fact. But as these reasons are not always conclusive, in speaking of them we are not yet committed to saying how all-things-considered it would be good or rational to act. For in some circumstances, as for example when in the hands of an implacable enemy, the proper thing to do would surely be to lie one's way out of the situation if one could: to lie, if necessary, through one's teeth. A consideration of self-interest here trumps a moral *consideration.* And similarly a moral *consideration* may be trumped by a consideration about mere desires. For it is surely over scrupulousness to think that a promise about some unimportant matter, lightly given and so understood, should always stand in the way of an unexpected chance to do something one *very much* wants to do. (For instance visiting an especially marvellous circus.) A moral consideration may be such as to be everywhere conclusive but *as such* it does not have trumping power, any more than does a consideration of self-interest or desire. So what is it that gives the impression of a special authority belonging to moral considerations? It is, I think, that we tend here not to compare like with like: to compare what I shall call (here inventing a term) 'verdictives' on the moral side, with mere *considerations* on the side of self interest or desire. Let me explain. By a 'verdictive' I mean an expression that carries with it finality of judgment: that implies an all-things-considered rather than a *pro tanto* reason for action. A statement that a certain action would be 'an act of injustice' is in this sense, a verdictive, as in the statement that the action would be 'cruel', or that it would be 'wrong'. To use any one of these three words is to imply that a moral consideration, which as a mere consideration does not imply a conclusive judgment, does in fact win out. What causes confusion is that when we speak of 'a moral judgment', and the power of a moral judgment we usually think of a 'verdictive' on the moral side; whereas we are apt to choose as its rival on the side of prudence, or of desire, what is not a verdictive but a mere consideration, such as the observation that we should lose something by doing the action that is being weighed. And so it is not surprising that a consideration that we call 'moral' comes to seem especially authoritative in the matter of what should (all-things-considered) be done. That this is a false impression is, however, made clear enough when we start comparing like with like, verdictives with verdictives and *pro tanto* reason-giving consideration with their ilk. And the, perhaps surprising, fact is that some words by their meaning, actually imply the victory of a prudential or desire-based consideration and *as such* are what I have called verdictive words. An over-scrupulous attention to a trivial promise, or truth-speaking in the hands of an implacable enemy, would rightly, surely, be branded precisely as over-scrupulous, or foolish, in a *verdictive* judgment.

We should remember therefore that we have before us three ways in which actions may be shown to be rational or contra-rational: in judgments about justice, self-interest, or the fulfilment of present desires. And the, perhaps rather surprising, conclusion has been that so far from one having precedence over the other they are, so far as the present argument has gone, on a par.

The correct picture, as I see it, is of three categories of reasons of logically equal status. Each one of them provides a test of practical rationality that is naturally expressed by saying that each can show either *pro tanto or* all-things-considered reasons for acting or not acting in certain ways.

But when an all-things-considered verdict has been reached any one of the three must be regarded as final. Told that we should give up smoking we may ask Why should I?' and be told that we should because smoking is bad for health, or that we could spend the money on something we really want. But we do not ask 'Why should I do what is in my interest to do?' nor 'Why should I do what will best satisfy my desires?' and what Quinn's argument implies is that we can no *more* make sense of the question 'Why should I be moral?' than we can make sense of the question 'Why should I act self-interestedly? Or 'Why should I do what will get me what I most desire?'

This is surely an important result. It may, however seem trivial. For in coming to this conclusion what have we really accomplished? We have set three kinds of considerations that we want to *call* 'intrinsically reason-giving' side by side. Where previously there seemed to be two, and the need to bring a third (morality) under one of the others—to bring the rationality of moral action under the rationality of self interested action, or that of the maximum fulfilment of present desire—we now *say that* moral considerations have their own reason giving force. Given an all things considered judgment about what, for instance, the virtue of justice requires we are to *say that* that judgment carries with it an unquestionable 'should' and unquestionably gives us good reason to act.

It may be objected, however, that this is merely a decision about a verbal package. For as yet we have nothing to tell us *why* we so unite these three classes of judgments. Have they indeed really *been* united, except verbally? How, if at all, is a 'should' backed up by considerations of desire-fulfilment linked conceptually with a 'should' backed up by prudential considerations? And how is either of these 'shoulds' connected with the 'should' that morality is now said to carry with it? We are open to the criticism of mere verbal triviality unless we can answer such questions and, crucially, can say how we should judge the claims of some fourth set of 'rationalizing considerations' to join the other three. Suppose, for instance, that we think about the reason any person may or may not have to favour his friends, or members of his family, in the distribution of certain goods or services. Can such a special distribution be mandated, or even licensed, without it being shown that the action comes into one of our three already established categories? By what principle would the putative granting of independent rationalizing status be judged?

I believe that these questions can be answered if we call in aid the idea of natural goodness as I defined those words in my *Natural Goodness.*[6] It is, I think, by reference to facts about the way things of different species live their lives that we can see the unity of the three rationalizing categories that we set side by side for human beings. And I think it could also become clear why a certain amount of 'partiality' for relations and friends could be justified or even mandated, in other words how a fourth kind of rationalizing consideration, and perhaps others, could be added to the three we have already discerned.

[6] Philippa Foot, *Natural Goodness,* especially chs. 1–3.

I must, therefore, very briefly, explain the meaning that I gave in my book to the words 'natural goodness'. Natural goodness, as I define it, can belong only to living things; but belongs to all of them: to plants, as well as to animals and human beings.

To approach this discussion of 'natural goodness' as, in its applications to the operations of living things, it will have to do *inter alia* with human actions, I should like to start with some remarks about the way in which animals (meaning here non-human animals) live their lives, although had I wanted to I could have begun with natural goodness and defect in plants. Let us think about the operations of animals. These cannot, of course, be dictated by reason as human choices can be. It does not even make sense to say that an animal sees reason to do one thing rather than another, or that it acts rationally or non-rationally. And yet we can see in animal life analogues of at least our three types of rationalizing considerations in human life. Animals, like us, have appetites and other kinds of desires, which on the whole they do well to satisfy, either directly as when in the presence of food or water, or indirectly as when, being hungry, they go foraging for food. They also do, by instinct or as learned behaviour, things that are necessary for their survival, or for reproduction, not immediately but even a whole season away. We can see these things as the analogues of human desire fulfilment, and of prudential behaviour, while many social animals behave in set ways that are the analogues of our moral and non-moral rules.

It belongs to what Michael Thompson has called 'the natural history stories' of particular species—or as he says 'life forms'—that they do such things in particular ways.[7] And from these natural history accounts of species we can derive 'should' propositions about the ways in which an animal of a particular species should or should not behave, as when we might say that a deer *should* flee from a predator whereas in the same situation a hedgehog *should* roll itself into a ball. When we say that animals, generally, do what they should in satisfying immediate appetites, taking steps to later fulfilment, and acting in ways first and foremost useful for their own survival and reproduction, we are giving the background against which a certain kind of behaviour can be judged, not of course as things work out in the particular case, where proper behaviour may by chance be disastrous, but as belonging to the 'how things should be' of an individual of this kind. There is a general connection, depending on the conformation of animals of a particular species and their natural habitat, with what, crucially, counts as flourishing in living things that are as they are.

There are obvious analogues here to just the features of members of the human species with which we have been dealing in thinking about practical rationality in men and women. When things are in order—are as they should

[7] It is Michael Thompson who has developed the concept of a *life form* on which I relied heavily in *Natural Goodness.* See M. Thompson 'The Representation of Life' in R. Hursthouse, G. Lawrence and W. Quinn (eds.) *Virtues and Reasons* (Oxford: Clarendon Press, 1995) and his contribution 'Human Nature and Practical Reason' in the present volume.

be—in human beings, they too should, in general, eat when they are hungry, must lay up food for the winter as squirrels do, and like the birds must build shelters for their young. Moreover some kinds of animals have social hierarchies that are as necessary to the flourishing of individuals, as are our own social conventions, codes of behaviour and laws. Where animals have hierarchies and a kind of social order, humans have norms that include moralities and this has sometimes been seen as a ground of suspicion of morality itself, and is perhaps one reason why it has been thought desirable to bring morality under the aegis of self-interest. Self-interest has been seen as part of *nature*, whereas morality has been seen as mere convention, as by the Sophist Callicles in Plato's Gorgias. When Socrates said that it was worse, because more disgraceful, to do than to suffer injustice Callicles said that this was only according to *nomos* (by society's convention), whereas according to *phusis* (that is by nature) the reverse was the case. But in terms of a 'life form' account of natural defect and goodness the mistake in this attempt to downgrade morality is not hard to see. The making of laws, and obedience to them, is as much part of human life as flying is of bird life or hunting in packs a part of the life of wolves. Good rules, including moral codes, are not *mere* conventions but things that are needed in human life. And only *incorrect* moral judgments (such as the belief that there is nothing wrong with slavery, or that homoerotic behaviour is 'wrong') deserve to be downgraded as 'mere opinion', and contrasted with that which has its basis in nature.

There are, therefore, similarities between species-based goodness in animal and human life, but of course there are enormous differences as well, and that not only in the great variety of forms that human societies can take. For flourishing in human beings is not just a matter of what happens in a human life where this could be described in physical terms as 'growth', 'survival', and 'reproduction,' but contains a necessary mental element. We might, for instance, say that a human family is an emotional as well as a biological unit, and think in those terms when considering matters having to do with human sexuality and fertility, seeing that reproduction does not have the *same* role in determining goodness and defect in humans that it has in animals.

Moreover, if we are thinking of *human* flourishing we must also take account of the way a person's life looks to him or her, and must of course consider happiness. This is one great difference in the forms taken by that which I have called natural goodness in animals and in humans. Another, and the one that is more directly relevant to our present discussion, is of course that human beings act on reasons as animals do not. Animals do not act on reasons, and therefore they cannot fail to do so, being neither rational nor imperfectly rational in what they do. Human beings, by contrast, all too often either do not see what there is reason for them to do, or else, through 'weakness of will', fail to shape their behaviour accordingly. They may be as they should be, or again defective, in respect of acting on reasons just as they can be defensive in physical conformation, in sight or hearing, or in memory or concentration. Natural goodness in reason following is as much a form of goodness in humans as is proper instinctive behaviour in animals.

And what humans have reason to do is determined by the exigencies of their form of life, as are (*mutatis mutandis*) certain forms of behaviour in particular species of animals. In the end it is the *need* for moral action—the part that justice and other virtues play in human life—that makes it possible for actions such as those of the Farm Boy from the Sudetenland to be rational actions in spite of the terrible consequences that he faced.

Why, then, does there seem to be a special problem about the rationality of what the Farm Boy did? It comes of course from the fact that in choosing death they were in an especially obvious way going against their own self-interest; death being their fate and the example having been set up, in my description of those I called 'the Letter Writers', so as to ignore even thoughts of the remorse they might later have felt had they participated in the murderous deeds of the SS. Deprived of expedients by which the tightness of the tight corner could perhaps be mitigated, we may be tempted to take refuge in the thought that it will not be easy for anyone to change the mind set that he has rightly come to see as essential for his happiness in more normal times: not being able all of a sudden to become as ruthless as is necessary for his own good. This, I should say, is simply a 'cop out.' Our problem is what to think about the rationality of a certain action, not about the ease or difficulty of doing it in a certain situation. Nor is it any use saying that to give in to the Nazis would be 'against the values' that a truly just person would have made his own, and that acquiescence would therefore be rejected by such a person. *For it is part of the virtue of justice that is itself in question when the rationality of the Farm Boy's refusal is raised.*

Rather than take refuge in any such argument as that from an agent's existing 'values' I suggest that we should go farther back; asking for the source of the rather desperate desire that we have to reconcile duty and happiness. Why we may ask does practical rationality seem to be in doubt when someone does what is clearly against his own interest? How it is that an appeal to self-interest seems to stand out on its own as the prime and unquestionable source of reasons for action? To be sure, it seems to exhibit an acceptable *form* of practical reasoning rather than a mere summary of judgments that we make; but are there not other such forms? Do we not give equal recognition to practical reasoning that tacitly or explicitly gives priority to a our friends or family over the general good? And do we not find forceful an argument from the need in human societies for an institution such as promising to the reason that there is to keep a promise even where, in the particular instance, the act of breaking it would do no one any harm? These too may be seen as belonging to our own forms of practical reasoning. We may however leave room for the possibility of non-human rational beings whose practical reasoning is different from ours. There could be Martians who, though rational, are more like ants or bees than we are and operate a more impersonal level than we do. Perhaps they are double-dyed utilitarians who think that even the prospect of satisfying one's own *present* desires gives reason for action only when it is believed to be in the *general* interest to do that. Or perhaps they simply do not use arguments from an agent's long term self-interest to back up judgments about what it is rational for him to do. I should remark in closing that I would not myself be able to say much about the idea of beings with different forms of practical reasoning from our own. I am only using this fantasy to try to weaken our prejudice in favour of the rationalizing force of self-interest.

Acting well

ANSELM WINFRIED MÜLLER

Introduction

I am very happy indeed to contribute to this series of lectures, especially because I owe most of my training in philosophy to Elizabeth Anscombe, whose work has given the series its name. I am deeply indebted to the marvellous generosity of her teaching, to the example she set me of an unrelentingly thorough and serious thinker, to the unobtrusive way she introduced me to Wittgenstein's later philosophy. Through Elizabeth Anscombe I also made the acquaintance of my friend Philippa Foot, whose work in moral philosophy has, over decades and more than anyone else's, influenced my own. I hope it will be possible to recognize in what I am going to say here not indeed the excellence but at least traces of the beneficial influence of both these philosophers.

This lecture is on *acting well.* It has two parts, matching the two notions that go to make up its title. Its aims is to show that these notions are interdependent in the sense that grasp of the notion of *acting well* is not a matter of grasping and putting together antecedently intelligible notions of acting and of goodness. More particularly, I hope to establish the following two theses:

> *Thesis 1*, implying a version of 'descriptivism': To grasp the notion of *acting* as it occurs in 'acting well/badly', you have to know not what might be common to all cases of acting, but rather which *standards of evaluation* the use of 'acting' invokes.
>
> *Thesis 2*, capturing the truth in 'non-descriptivism': The notion of *goodness* as it occurs in 'acting well' is in part determined by the fact that, in attributing goodness to a way of acting, we standardly signal *readiness to act* in this way.

As a kind of hinge, the idea of a *good reason* will turn out to be responsible for this dependence, in both directions, between the two components of the notion of acting well. On the one hand, the *notion of acting* implies a standard of evaluation that relates to motives, or types of reason, for doing things. (This will be made plausible in Part 1 of the lecture and presupposed in Part 2.) On the other hand, in approving of a reason of this type, we standardly accept a related pattern of *practical inference*; and therefore we may be held to be *prepared to act* in a certain way when we call it a good way of acting. (Hence the account of *acting well* that emerges in Part 1 needs to be supplemented by the considerations of Part 2.)

Part 1: On the Grammer of *Acting*

1.1 *A remarkable difference between action and acting shows in the way questions of time and of quality relate to the latter*

Among the many uses of the verb 'to act', there is one that joins to it evaluative terms like 'well' and 'badly'. We should count with this use[1] also the cases where an adverbial phrase tells us what the goodness or badness in question consists in ('She acted from revenge', 'He acted generously')[2]. It is this use of the word (and this use only!) that I am going to have in mind when speaking of *acting* in what follows.

The first thing to observe concerning this concept is that, in spite of etymological appearances, it has surprisingly little to do with *action*, *act*, or *activity*. Acting in the sense I am examining need not be a matter of acting in a sense that requires the agent to be active. And where it is, we must still distinguish the one from the other. To see this, consider how questions of *time* and of *quality* relate to acting (in my preferred sense).

[1] Cf. the *Shorter OED*, which lists this type of case under the heading 'To perform on the stage of existence'. Now the use of 'acting' in the sense of 'performing', 'simulating', etc. is indeed very similar, from a formal point of view, to the use of 'acting' that is my topic. Roughly speaking, both kinds of acting must be explained in terms of their respective teleologies rather than in terms of observable constituents. On the other hand, it must not be thought that the notion of acting I am going to be concerned with depends on a metaphor that is peculiar to the English language. Neither 'agir' in French nor 'handeln' in German are used for performance on the stage. Yet both words exhibit the kind of grammar that I am after.

[2] Cf. 1.5 (c).—Sometimes an adverbial phrase seems to indicate a *neutral* motive ('to act from curiosity'). In fact, however, an innocent motive of this kind makes for one way of acting *well*. Cf. 1.4 (e). On the other hand, 'acting' also combines with phrases like 'as the law demands' or 'in accordance with the highjacker's orders'. These express standards of evaluation other than that revealed in the use of 'acting well/badly'.

(a) Obviously, you may act well in performing a particular act, or action—say in warning somebody of some danger. But while the question 'When?', as applied to the action, is easily answered by specifying day and hour when the words of warning were spoken, it is not so clear that a time in this sense is being specified when it is said that you *then* acted well. The 'then' here seems to relate to an *occasion* rather than a date.

This becomes more evident as we consider a variant of the example: *You acted well in warning him twice.* Obviously, this does not amount to saying that you acted well at two times. On the other hand, you can be said to have acted well *then*—not indeed at the time of the first, *or* the second, warning; but on the occasion when, say, that stubborn fellow was so determined to invest all his money in shares that he needed to be warned twice.

If this example does not convince you, consider yet another variant: *You acted well in not warning him.* There is no action whatever in this case that acting well might have consisted in, so there is no question of dating any such action. Nevertheless, there is a *then* here, too: In not warning him, you acted well on that occasion.

So much about a characteristic difference in the way that time comes into acts and actions, on the one hand, and into acting, on the other. Now about evaluation.

(b) From the case where you acted well in not warning him, it is clear that acting well, or badly, does not necessarily *consist in* action. It may instead consist in refraining, refusing, omitting, or just not doing. But even in a case where you act well in performing some action, you may not do so *by* performing it—your acting well need not consist in your action.

Suppose it is your business to administer grants on behalf of some foundation. On some occasions, justice may require you to treat two equally qualified applicants equally without demanding that you should offer *or* that you should deny them the grant. In such a situation you will be acting well by either offering or denying both of them a grant. If, for instance, you offer them the grant, you will be acting well in doing this; but your acting well will not consist in this. It will not consist in *any* action or combination of actions but, rather, in the very same thing that your denying the grant to both candidates would consist in, viz. your treating them *equally.* And it is easy to verify that, similarly, if you were to treat the two *unequally,* no *action* of yours would constitute your acting badly.

In other words, the goodness or badness of the *way you act* is not, in this kind of case, a quality of any act, or action (nor, for that matter, of any sort of inaction). And we may well begin to wonder whether it ever is.

1.2 *The notion of acting relates to a standard of evaluation*

What then is it that is being evaluated as good (or bad) in phrases like *acting well* (or: *badly*)? What is it to act (in the sense that I am discussing) if it is not to perform an action, or actions?

In a way, the answer has to be: Nothing—or: Almost nothing. There isn't anything that acting could be said to be in the way in which repairing a car can be said to *be* the same thing as: modifying, replacing, and arranging the components of a car that does not operate properly, in such a way that it will again operate properly.

Let us call the concept of an X *teleological* if, to understand its application, you have to have an idea of a standard by which to evaluate an X and/or its qualities. The notion of *repairing a car*, for instance, is teleological in this sense. For part of possessing it consists in a grasp of what repairing a car *should* be like. But the notion of repairing a car seems to harbour a 'neutral' component as well, a grasp of whatever it is that good and bad car repairs have in common.—Can we discern analogous components in the concept of *acting*, too?

There is reason to think that it has at least a teleological component. Indeed, the notion of acting may seem to be nothing but teleology.

For where is its *neutral* component? You may produce a video that shows a person repairing a car as opposed to repairing a motor bike, or to climbing a staircase. But what could *acting* be 'opposed to'? How would you go about producing a video that showed a person acting? If any video can do the job, then any video can—as long as it features some sane adult human being. That is, the neutral component of the concept of acting reduces to the *voluntariness* that is characteristic of the way human beings operate. There is nothing else that different 'cases of acting' have in common.

Can we then say, at least: 'It is distinctive of the notion of *acting* that its only neutral component is the idea of *voluntariness*'? No. For this is equally true, e.g., of the notion of *dressing* as it occurs, not in 'getting dressed' but in 'poorly dressed' or 'generally dresses well'. Think once more of a video that shows at least one sane adult human being and, therefore, a stretch of voluntary behaviour. Whatever goes on in this video, I claimed, it necessarily represents a human being acting well or badly. The very same video, however, might be said to represent a human being dressing well or badly. (If you insist that an uncensored version of the video may show a person with *no* clothes on, we can treat his condition as a limiting case. Why not count a naked person as well dressed for a few kinds of occasion but not for the rest?)

So, what is common to acting well and acting badly is no different from what is common to dressing well and dressing badly. To articulate the difference between the notions of acting and of dressing we have to turn to their respective evaluative dimensions. In particular, you do not know what an occurrence of 'acting' in expressions like 'acting well', or 'badly', contributes to their meaning unless you are aware of the *standard of evaluation* that the word 'acting' imports. To use this word correctly you need to grasp 'what acting *should* be like'. In other words: *Acting* is a teleological notion in the sense I have explained.

1.3 *The quality of the way one acts in Φ-ing depends on the quality of relevant reasons.*

Let us now get clearer about the nature of the standard of evaluation that this notion introduces. Anything a person does can be evaluated from indefinitely many points of view, each of them corresponding to a standard of evaluation. We may, e.g., ask how that person *behaves*, implying *good manners* as the relevant standard. What then is the standard we invoke by asking whether he *acts* well or badly?

Simplifying a little, we may say: *In Φ-ing (i.e. in doing or not doing anything) you act well as long as you Φ for good reasons.*[3]—I have no knock-down argument to support this answer. But I hope that the following considerations will make it sufficiently plausible.

Acting well is a manifestation of virtue, and virtue is a matter of the quality of one's motives. Motives, however, are reasons (cf. (b) below). Hence it would seem that you act well if you act on reasons that virtue demands or suggests or condones.

Further, small children, insane persons, and animals are not said to act well or badly. The capacity to act well thus seems to depend on the possession of *reason*. Now the primary relevance of reason to the way in which a sane adult lives and operates seems to be that he does things for reasons. So it is plausible to assume that the quality of the way he acts depends on the quality of the reasons on which he acts.

It may be objected that, for one to act well, it is not enough that one should do things for the right reasons: one must also do the right kind of thing. To this I reply that a

[3] I am going to call this standard *ethical* (1.5).—Admittedly, other evaluative standards, too, may be articulated *in connection with* the verb 'to act'. A person may be said to have acted illegally, or in accordance with the chairperson's instructions, etc. Nevertheless, in qualifying the verb 'to act' by means of 'well', or 'badly', *tout court*, one does seem to be invoking a single standard: the ethical one. Cf., however, 1.5 (c) on evaluative subdimensions.

person's acting on the right reasons not only reveals his good motives. Rather, these very reasons also serve to make sure that the right kind, and only the right kind, of thing is being done. This, indeed, is their primary job. They would seem to *be* the right reasons *because of* what is done or what happens where they are acted on.

For *reason* is a relational concept (cf. 2.2): nothing is a good reason, *tout court*—a good reason for *whatever* way of acting you care to envisage. To act on a good reason is to do the kind of thing that that reason is a good reason for doing.

Cannot we say, however, things like 'From a good motive, Robin Hood did the wrong thing' ?—Of course, we can. But if the claim is true, then his motive (to help the poor) would have been a good reason only for, say, going to the courts on their behalf, or organizing a strike, not for robbing the rich. If, on the other hand, one were to hold that his motive was a good reason for doing what he did, i.e. robbing the rich, then one would *eo ipso* be claiming also that he did do the right thing.[4] Hence for something to be a

[4] From the fact that a motive is a reason it does not follow that a good motive is a good reason. The two notions import somewhat different evaluative dimensions. In particular, we do sometimes speak of a good motive, *tout court.* One may assess the quality of a motive for Φ-ing by answering the question if it invokes an inferential pattern (cf. 2.2–3) that is, as such, of the virtuous sort—whether or not it yields *Φ-ing* as a valid practical conclusion under the *given circumstances.* Nevertheless, *motive,* like *reason,* is a relative notion. To help the poor, or concern for them, though perhaps a *good motive tout court,* can be one's motive only *for* doing what one at least thinks may be *of value to them*—not for just anything you fancy doing.— The 'function' of practical reasons has

good way of acting, it is after all enough that it should be a case of acting on good reasons.[5]

Pointing to the relational nature of reasons will similarly dispose of another objection—the objection that

two aspects: (1) what I have called their primary job: to get the right things done; and (2) to qualify the agent's character. This is borne out by the two ways in which we evaluate what a person does when a good motive leads him, through non-culpable ignorance, to do the wrong thing. For we would tend to say that, in such a case, he acted *well* in one way: by acting for the right reasons, or from a good motive—aspect (2); but *not well* in another: in not doing what these reasons were reasons for doing—aspect (1).

[5] These considerations may enable us to simplify Aquinas' tripartite requirement for the goodness of acting. In the *Summa Theologiae* he specifies, apart from goodness 'secundum genus, prout scilicet est actio', three kinds of goodness: 'secundum speciem [. . .] circumstantias [. . .] finem' (I/II, q. 18, a. 4). But as long as you act in accordance with the right reasons, you will not fail to secure all three of them. (1) Obviously, where you do something for a good purpose (*finis*), this enters the ethical quality of what you do, *via* the right reasons for doing it. (2) Equally, the situation (*circumstantiae*) can be relevant to the value of your Φ-ing only to the ectent that your reason, all things considered, for Φ-ing ought to take account of that situation (q. 18, a. 5 ad 4: 'non enim circumstantia faceret actum malum, nisi per hoc quod rationi repugnat'); so good-making circumstances, too, will be reflected in good reasons. 3) Finally, there is no way of doing the wrong kind of thing (*species*) for the right reasons and, in particular, for a bad purpose, if reasons are relational in the way I have explained; so the kind of thing you do in acting well is also looked after in my account of acting well. Nor, for that matter, are absolute prohibitions excluded by this account. Torture, e.g., is always wrong if there is, all things considered, good reason not to torture anyone, *whatever* reasons may be adduced in favour of doing so.

the role of *practical reason* is not merely to provide one with reasons for action but also to form notions of (possible) situations and ways of acting. What the objection says is true enough. However, in identifying something, R, as a practical reason one is relating (in accordance with a certain pattern: 2.2–3) a way of acting to a situation. And this does involve conceptions of that way of acting and of that situation—conceptions, or aspects, under which, and in virtue of which, they are being claimed to be related when R is said to be a reason for Φ-ing.

Suppose, e.g., my situation is characterized, *inter alia,* by a promise I have made to Φ. It will then, indeed, be the task of practical reason to identify the situation as one that involves that promise; to classify various things I might do, Ψ_1, Ψ_2, etc., as Φ-ing and thus keeping the promise; to identify aspects of the situation that might give me reason not to keep the promise, or not to Φ, or not to do any of Ψ_1, Ψ_2, etc. But all this takes place in the service of a judgment concerning reasons for action—which, in the absence of countervailing reasons, will turn out to be the judgment that *because of the promise I ought to Φ* (cf. Müller 1992).

In this way, the truth contained in each of the two objections is already taken care of by the relational character of reasons. And I shall proceed on the assumption that it is indeed reference to the quality of one's reasons for doing what one does that distinguishes 'acting' from other teleological verbs and verbal phrases. The *goodness of reasons* is the standard of appraisal invoked by the relevant use of 'acting'—just as the *fitness of a car* to be driven efficiently and safely is the standard invoked by this use of 'repairing a car', or the *appropriateness of one's clothes*, by the use of 'dressing', or *good manners*, by a certain use of 'behaving'.

Why then did I speak of simplification when I formulated this assumption at the beginning of the present section?—There are three points that fail to be reflected in that formulation but need to be considered in a decent account of *acting well*.

(a) The first of these points is the distinction between *pro tanto* reasons and reasons *all things considered*. A *pro tanto* reason R for Φ-ing is one that by itself favours Φ-ing but is provisional or defeasible in that Φ-ing may, in a specific kind of situation, be excluded, in spite of R, by other *pro tanto* reasons. Only where these other reasons ought not to prevail, is R definitive as well—a reason all things considered (Foot, 2001, pp. 57f.).

Hence, what I say about the quality of a way of acting has to be understood to mean two things. First: if and only if R is a *pro tanto* reason to Φ, is Φ-ing on R a way of acting well (or even: the only way to act well) as far as the description of the situation goes (viz. its description as an R-type situation). And second: If and only if, in a given situation, R is a reason all things considered, is Φ-ing on R a (the) way to act well.

(b) A second point that needs to be considered is the relationship between motives and other reasons. Suppose you get your tools out in order to repair my car, and repair my car in order to be of help. There is a modest hierarchy of purposes here. The one that is mentioned first is your reason for getting the tools out but not a motive, while the second constitutes a reason as well as, possibly, a motive. I say 'possibly' since in mentioning *help* we may not yet have reached the top of the hierarchy: you may wish to help me *in order to put me in your debt*—in which case this is more properly called your motive in helping me, in repairing my car, and in getting your tools out (as well as, of course, your reason for doing these things). Thus, among reasons there are those that are conditioned by *ulterior* reasons, and those that are not (for which the word 'motive' seems to be reserved). I'll be chiefly concerned with the second kind of reason, since it is their quality that is responsible for the quality of ways of acting.[6]

(c) There is a third respect in which the account I have given of acting well in terms of good reasons lacks

[6] It may seem that I also need to consider the case where a *bad* reason occurs *below* the top of a hierarchy of purposes. Suppose, e.g., that Robin Hood forces the gate open in order to steal cattle in order to help the poor. In spite of the latter purpose, which we assumed constitutes a good motive, the ethical quality of what he does is vitiated by the immediate reason on which he acts, the purpose of stealing cattle.—Even so it is right to say, as we have already seen, that the 'good motive' itself amounts to a bad *reason for stealing* and, in view of this, also *for opening the gate.* It is, once more, the relational character of reasons that we must attend to. Here it allows us to stick to the claim that, to assess the quality of a way of acting, we need to examine the agent's *ultimate* reason only.

precision: the connection between goodness of a way of acting and goodness of reasons is not always as straightforward as the simplifying formula suggests. For it is not always the quality of your reason in favour of Φ-ing that is responsible for your acting well, or badly, in Φ-ing (cf. 1.4 (c–e)). And, more generally, we must distinguish between a variety of ways in which the quality of reasons may be constitutive of the quality of ways of acting. I'll spend the next section specifying some of these ways (cf. also Muller 1998, pp. 101–28).

1.4 *The quality of a reason may be constitutive of the quality of a way of acting in a variety of ways*

(a) The most obvious way in which reasons may be relevant to your acting well is provided by *mandatory* reasons. You have a mandatory reason for Φ-ing where, in the absence of countervailing reasons, you will act badly unless you are moved, by that reason, to Φ—as when a promise provides you with a reason for doing what you promised.

Most frequently mandatory reasons are reasons-against. Consideration of what Φ-ing would amount to in the circumstances may require you to refrain from Φ-ing. Veracity, e.g., requires you, not: to say things because they are true, but rather: not to say what you don't believe to be true because saying them would amount to saying what for all you know is not true.

From an act utilitarian perspective, there is just one (ultimate) reason that you may act on without acting badly, and that is a mandatory reason. For on this view you ought to be motivated in your conduct by nothing but the prospect of an optimal impact of this conduct on some aspect of the world; and this consideration would not, in general, leave room for options.[7]

Now my general analysis of acting is, so far, compatible with the utilitarian perspective. But it is also compatible with the more plausible view implied in the way we ordinarily talk about acting well. On this view, irreducibly different kinds of reason for doing something may be responsible for the goodness of the way somebody acts—reasons of justice, of respect, of gratitude, etc. The idea that ultimately there is just one reason that you have to act on in order to act well in any situation, is quite alien to our moral language.

Not only, however, do we recognize the moral relevance of different reasons. In addition, our criteria for judging whether people act well relate to their reasons in a number of different ways.

(b) As Anscombe (1963, § 33) pointed out, an account of practical reasoning must take into account non-mandatory as well as mandatory reasons for doing

[7] Kant, too, seems to recognize only one reason for acting as constitutive of acting well: In order for you to act well in Φ-ing your sole motive for Φ-ing must be respect for the moral law. In the case of imperfect duties, however, you will not be acting badly if you fail to Φ from this motive on any particular occasion.—We may observe that the one and only reason you must act on in order to act well is a *purpose* if act utilitarians are right but not if Kant is to be believed. On my own account, ultimate reasons are not restricted to but may include purposes (Müller 1998, pp. 113f.).

things. And for you to act well in Φ-ing because of R, it is not necessary that R should be a mandatory reason: it may just be a good reason, as when X's generosity towards you is your reason for dedicating a book to X. Here you may act well, instead, by writing X a letter for the same reason. Moreover you may even not act badly in not acting on this reason at all. In both these respects a reason can be non-mandatory, or *invitatory*.

(c) So far, I have considered reasons, mandatory or invitatory, for Φ-ing whose goodness makes us say that in Φ-ing you acted well. But good reasons for Φ-ing may not be what formally makes your way of acting virtuous, even where the goodness of your Φ-ing requires such reasons. Let me illustrate what I have in mind by the example of acting courageously.

There is no special *kind of reason for which* you have to (enter a house on fire) in order to count as acting courageously. Rather, on the presupposition of good reasons—reasons of *any* kind, but proportionately weighty—in favour of Φ-ing, you act courageously in Φ-ing for these reasons if you do so in spite of *pro tanto* reasons against Φ-ing that arise from the (apparent) danger to you, or from the discomfort of Φ-ing. Acting well here primarily consists in not being moved by reasons of this kind to *desist* from Φ-ing (reasons that are not, all things considered, good enough reasons for desisting from Φ-ing).

(d) Courage is the taming of fear. But fear, it would seem, need not be a response to reasons for being afraid; it may just be a sort of 'animal' reaction to something perceived or imagined. Equally, and perhaps more obviously, the kind of desire that is tamed by temperance, need not be a response to any reasons; it may be appetite.

So there will be cases where acting well requires a kind of temperance, or courage, that opposes not reasons but rather sensual attractions, or repulsions, that are liable to lead you astray. Here, acting well is neither a matter of acting on a kind a reason, as with (a) and (b), nor a matter of refusing to act on a kind of reason, as with (c).

In these cases, acting badly will consists in following the attractions of what pleases the senses, or the repulsions of what deters them. But how can this be a way of acting badly—something we find with humans only and not with (the other) animals—since reason has no hand in it? Well, just because reason fails to intervene, it is a bad way of acting. Or, more accurately: To follow sensual attractions or repulsions is to act badly where there are definitive reasons against doing so; and in these cases it is to act badly *because* there are such reasons—reasons that should, and fail, to be acted on in those cases.

Correspondingly, you act well, in this kind of case, by letting yourself be guided by these reasons in spite of sensual attractions, or repulsions. Such attractions and repulsions take the place, in (d) type cases, of the kind of reason you must disregard, in (c) type cases, in order to act courageously (or temperately). Moreover, (d) type cases do, of course, involve the operation of *reasons* for acting that require you, all things considered, to disregard those attractions, or repulsions.

These, then are the ways in which (d) type cases depart from as well as match the pattern of acting well that I provisionally characterized in terms of *Φ-ing for good reasons* at the beginning of 1.3.

(e) Finally there seems to be a kind of acting well for which it is enough that you should *not act badly*. Do what you like: you will be acting well in Φ-ing provided certain conditions are met, notably: (1) there are no mandatory reasons, all things considered, for you to refrain from Φ-ing; and (2) you don't Φ for bad reasons. In this sense you may be acting well by vacantly gazing into the sky on a given occasion, even when there are no good reasons for doing so.

We may view this as a limiting case of acting well; one that we can 'engage in' without taking any of the trouble that may be involved in acting well in the ways identified by categories (a) to (d).[8] Even so, the connection with good reasons is not entirely lost. But these now enter the picture solely by way of the conditions I have just articulated in (1) and (2) above, and thus even less directly than in the kind of case I have described under (d).

[8] One might put this point paradoxically by saying: Not only is it possible to act well without *acting*—viz. without performing any actions; it is also possible to act well without *goodness*—viz. without acting on any good reasons that might make for ethical quality of what one does. Alas, it does not seem possible to spend one's whole life acting well in this comfortable way!

I am not claiming that the list I have just given of ways in which the quality of reasons affects the quality of acting is exhaustive. Nor am I going to make much use of it in what follows. Having drawn due attention to the variety of structures that my account of *acting well* has to accommodate, I will proceed as if mandatory reasons (1.4 (a)) were the only kind of case to consider. If I am able to handle this kind of case, it will not be difficult, I believe, to extend my explanation to other patterns.

1.5 *Moral evaluation is a component in the evaluation of acting, not the whole of it*

An account of acting well in terms of good reasons provokes the question how it relates to the obvious idea that acting well is just what morality requires you to do. My answer is that moral evaluation *is* evaluation by reference to the quality of reasons for doing things. On the other hand, not all evaluation of this kind is moral evaluation.

We may however say that all such evaluation is ethical in nature since *ethos* is essentially the way the will is disposed with regard to the acceptance and rejection of reasons for doing things.[9] A person's moral character can

[9] The realm of the ethical will then comprise prudential as well as moral considerations.—Should it be taken to include further types of reasons as well, like what is sometimes called expressive rationality? Can reasons arising from the subject's wishes and ideals be reduced to prudential and moral considerations?

then be seen to be an important part of this disposition, and to act morally is an aspect of acting well.

'But aren't moral reasons in a completely different category from prudential ones, the former being concerned with the well-being of other people, the latter with the agent's own interests, wishes and preferences?'—I admit that the distinction ordinary usage tends to draw in this way has a point. And people are likely to invoke, as well as evoke, only moral standards when using the expression 'acting well'. On the other hand, there are good reasons for calling the dichotomy into question and, in particular, for doubting that it can be based on a plain distinction between agent's and others' interests. Here are some of these reasons:

(a) There are cases, in particular cases connected with human relations, where there is no doubt that there are good reasons to Φ but we would be hard pressed to decide whether these reasons should be called moral or rather prudential.

Think, e.g., of parents who take great care to send their daughter to a good school. Suppose there is no bad motive behind what they do; they do it for the sake of the expected benefit to the daughter; and in the circumstances there is no overriding reason against sending her to a good school. There seems to be no question that they act well in doing as they do. But if you insist on classifying it as either done for moral, or for prudential reasons, you will find that an equally convincing, or equally unconvincing, case can be made for either option.

(b) Justice is no doubt an important part of morality. And the rights that are protected by justice and respected by the just are often viewed as representing particularly important interests of the right-holders. But is this in fact their job?

We may observe that some rights *precede* the interest people may have in whatever those rights are rights to do or enjoy. The right to wear a particular title is a case in point. It also shows that a right does not signal importance.

Quite apart from this, however, reasons of justice tend to be connected only more or less indirectly with the well-being of others. To see my point here, you may think of the demands of justice that arise from rights like these: the right of parents to bring up their children undisturbed by the interference of others; voting rights; the right of way of an ambulance; the right of an airport official to check your luggage for weapons. (The latter right is an excellent reason for you to open your bag. The rationale for this is quite neutral with regard to the question whether the bomb that may be found in your bag was placed there by you with the intention of threatening the pilot and hijacking the plane for purposes of your own, or rather smuggled into your luggage by some third person out to kill you by blowing up the whole plane. The question 'Whose interest, yours or theirs?' is clearly beside the point.)

Courage is an even more notorious example of a virtue that is of prudential as much as moral value. The common denominator of courageous action is a disposition to reject considerations of self-protection when other considerations should be given more weight—whether these other considerations concern one's own or others' well-being or, indeed, some good that cannot be defined in terms of interest at all.

(c) Prudent behaviour and morally good behaviour are mutually related by a single *system* of reasons that are attuned to each other. Indeed, the evaluative dimension of acting may be thought of as containing the standards of prudence and of morality as subdimensions—just as, from a somewhat different angle, it may be thought of as containing the evaluative sub-dimensions indicated by virtue words. Requirements of prudence stop short of demanding what is immoral, and we do not call imprudent what is disadvantageous but required by morality.

To see the significance of this, contrast the relation between prudence and morality with the relation between conformity to law and morality. In Nazi Germany, the fact that it was immoral to betray the hiding place of Jews is quite compatible with the fact that existing laws gave people mandatory *legal* reasons for betraying them. Equally, the other way round, the fact that it was illegal to hide the Jews could not prevent moral reasons in favour of doing so from being morally good reasons. Legal reasons and moral reasons thus belong to separate systems.[10]

[10] The example reminds us that the notions of law and of morality do not relate to a common dimension of evaluation (1.5 (c)). It is nevertheless correct to speak of *unjust laws,* thus placing legal systems under the claims of morality. Also, a just legal requirement *generally* provides the

It is not the same with prudential reasons and moral ones. As I have pointed out, they are rather interconnected in much the way that moral reasons are among themselves. Let me illustrate the latter case by *charity and justice.* Charity may give you a *pro tanto* good reason to give money to X; but you will not be called uncharitable if you refuse to help because you need the money to pay a debt. And now look at *charity and prudence.* Again, you will not be called uncharitable if you refuse to help because you need the money to satisfy your own basic needs.

To put the point more formally: In most cases, moral reasons for Φ-ing will not count as morally good reasons, all things considered, in circumstances where Φ-ing would imply gross neglect of one's own interests. And, likewise, the fact that there are mandatory reasons of a moral nature against Φ-ing tends to prevent an ordinary prudential reason in favour of Φ-ing from being a good reason, all things considered, even from a prudential point of view.[11]

1.6 *Do the grounds on which a way of acting is called good exhaustively determine the meaning of 'acting well'?*

Most of the time so far I have been talking about acting *well.* But my purpose in doing so has not really been to explain

individual with a moral reason to comply. Similarly, observance of civilities *may* be a matter of politeness, or respect, and thereby a moral requirement.

[11] Here we encounter the problem of the unity of the virtues. Cf. Dancy 1993, pp. 136f., Appendix III; Muller 1998, pp. 160–8, and 2003.

goodness but rather to clarify the grammar of 'acting', or, more precisely, to clarify one characteristic use of the word.

As a first step, I argued that we are not going to understand this use if we ask: What is it to act? What kind of action or performance or activity is shared by the person who acts well and the one who acts badly? By what criteria do we decide whether somebody acts? It seemed more promising to ask: What kind of evaluation is being invoked where people are said to act well, or badly—as opposed to, say, dress, or work, or use their time, or repair a car, well, or badly? And it is for this reason that it was necessary to examine the idea of acting *well*.

The result can be summarized by saying: The concept of acting relates what human beings do, to a standard of good reasons for doing and not doing things. Some kinds of good reason arise from people's rights, others from the agent's or other people's interests, or wishes, or the need to handle danger, others again from the requirements of human relationships, or from other aspects of the situation. They all go to make up a system of reasons, and the various standards of goodness they define form evaluative subdimensions within the ethical dimension specified by the notion of acting.

If we wish to know more about the kind of goodness involved in acting well, the natural question to ask is: What is the unifying *ground* that brings the different kinds of reason into a system? Or, perhaps: In virtue of what are reasons ethically good reasons? This is one of the questions that Philippa Foot sets out to answer in *Natural Goodness* (2001; cf., in particular, pp. 17f.). Her view can be summarized by saying: *Good reasons are the ones that have to be acted on where a society of human beings is to get on well*—a view that I believe to be correct. It provides us with *something like* a criterion for answering questions of the form: Is R a good reason for Φ-ing?

There is, however, a further question that can be raised concerning the implications of the use of 'good' as applied to ways of acting, viz.: What is one *doing* in *saying that, in Φ-ing, Soandso would be acting well*, i.e. acting for the right reasons? It may seem that this question, too, will have been answered as soon as we have specified criteria that govern the ascription of goodness to people's ways of acting. This idea, however, I now wish to challenge.

Part 2: On the Grammer of *Well*

2.1 *Can Pure Descriptivism account for the practicality of ethical judgments?*

One of the major merits of Philippa Foot's recent book (2001), as well as of Jonathan Dancy's work (1993), is an insight that can be expressed by saying: Facts may give people reasons to do things independently of their desires or 'pro-attitudes'.

On the basis of this insight, Foot believes herself to be in a position to reject the non-cognitivist explanation of the practical significance of moral judgment; to reject, that is, the subjectivist assumption of 'a gap between moral judgments and assertions' or, more precisely, 'the idea that truth conditions give, and may exhaust, the meaning of the latter but not the former'. Her account of reasons is to save us from 'the mistake of so construing what is "special" about moral judgment that the grounds of a moral judgment do not reach all the way to it' simply because you may not be '*ready to* take the decision to act' in accordance with that judgment (2001, p. 8).

From the fact that reasons may be, and in the case of ethical considerations are, of a purely factual nature, Foot derives a position that may be called Pure Descriptivism. On this view, reference to speakers' desires or dispositions to act is no part of a proper account of acting well any more than it is part of a proper account of seeing well or reproducing well or any other such merit of an organism.

2.2 *To understand the meaning of 'reason', we should turn not to the way good reasons are identified hut to their role in practical inference*

In order to find out whether Pure Descriptivism is true, let us consider an ethical judgment which says that, on a given occasion, or generally, in Φ-ing one is/would be acting well. Is its meaning adequately described by stating its truth grounds—its truth (or perhaps: assertibility) conditions?

On the simplifying assumptions made at the beginning of section 1.3, the truth conditions can be stated as follows: In Φ-ing you act well *iff* there is a mandatory reason for you to Φ. But when is there a mandatory reason to Φ?

In one way this question is answered by stating the kind of criterion that was suggested in 1.5: R is a mandatory reason to Φ just in case a human society does not *get on well* unless people act on R. Following Anscombe, Foot calls what is thus required for the good of human beings, an 'Aristotelian necessity' (2001, pp. 15–17 and 46).

If, however, we wish to know what it *means* to say that R is a (mandatory) reason to Φ, an answer like the one just given in terms of human good seems unsatisfactory. It is unsatisfactory, in particular, because *you do not seem to need the idea of an Aristotelian necessity or anything very similar in order to understand the notion of a mandatory reason.* Only philosophical reflection leads you to this kind of account, and thereby to an account of acting well. Moreover, we may suspect that the relevance of Aristotelian necessity to an explanation of good reasons, let alone of acting well, is not even accepted by a majority of moral philosophers. So even if this explanation is implicit in our common understanding of *good reasons* and of *acting well*, the implication is not, at any rate, a very obvious one.

Let us therefore approach the question from a different angle. Instead of asking how good reasons are identified, let us ask what it is to treat something as a good reason.

I shall take it without further argument that R is a (good) reason to Φ if it would be right, or good, or correct to make a particular kind of *move or step* that takes one from consideration of R to Φ-ing. In this, I am largely following Aristotle, who represents acting on a reason as making an *inference* from the statement of that reason. Over the last decades, investigation into practical reasoning by a number of philosophers has given shape to the idea that acting on reasons may be represented as a kind of inference from premises that articulate the reasons.

On this view, reasons for doing things are on a par with reasons for believing things. In both areas, your reasons are good reasons only if the premises of your conclusion are true and the pattern of inference valid. On some accounts, the premises of a practical inference must include an expression of desire, an imperative, a *Fiat*, or some such. But this requirement is unnecessary if we follow Dancy and Foot in holding that facts may by themselves provide one with a reason for doing something (cf. 2.1).

In a practical inference, you draw the conclusion not by believing something (not even by believing that you ought to Φ), but by doing something (by Φ-ing). This is why a practical inference cannot, strictly speaking, be formulated. The inferential character of acting on reasons is, however, brought out in the way we report on it: 'He needed my help, *so* I helped him'; 'I have promised to Φ, *so* I'll Φ'. In the first case, for instance, I cannot be asserting—as the grammar of the sentence might suggest—that what the premise says *is* a basis for the (judgmental) conclusion that I helped him; I am rather asserting that it *was* a basis for the (practical) conclusion that I drew in helping him.

2.3 *The validity of an inference, theoretical or practical, may be recognized either theoretically (acknowledgement) or practically (acceptance)*

Since practical (as well as theoretical) reasons can be understood in terms of inference, we may say: The judgment 'In Φ-ing one is/would be acting well', or 'To act well you have to Φ' is true if *some valid pattern of practical inference takes you from true premises to Φ-ing.*

Let us now ask: What is it to *recognize* that, to act well, one has to Φ? We know: a subjectivist is going to answer that it consists in favouring, or universally prescribing Φ-ing, or in being ready to Φ, or in having some similar disposition of the will. Like Foot, I reject this position. On my view, recognition that to act well one has to Φ involves the *belief* that some valid pattern of practical inference takes one from true premises to Φ-ing.

This, however, does not settle the question what is meant by 'well' in this kind of context. Let me explain why I think an account of acting well has to go beyond the purely descriptivist explanation.

Given that Φ is the thing to do in the circumstances, nevertheless, for you to act well in Φ-ing it is not enough that you Φ. You also have to be motivated in the right way, i.e. you have to arrive at your Φ-ing in a valid move from true premises: you have to Φ for the right reasons. So in recognizing the ethical value of *your* Φ-ing, one is recognizing the soundness of *your* inference. And in recognizing that, given those kind of circumstances, Φ-ing is a good way of acting, one is indirectly recognizing the validity of a particular kind of inference; more precisely: one is recognizing that *there is* a valid pattern of inference that takes one to Φ-ing from a statement of some of those circumstances (where 'circumstance' is to be understood in the wildest possible sense).

Now, recognition of a certain pattern of inference as valid may take the form either of judging that it is valid, or of applying it—i.e. of drawing the conclusion when the premises are satisfied. Let us call the first: theoretical recognition, or *acknowledgement*, and the second: practical recognition, or *acceptance*.

It should be noted that this distinction does not apply to practical inference only. The validity of patterns both of theoretical and of practical inference can be recognized theoretically as well as practically. We may interpret Lewis Carroll's famous dialogues on theoretical inference (Dodgson 1965) in terms of the distinction between acknowledgement and acceptance that I wish to apply to practical inference: Whenever Achilles perceives that some variant of *modus ponens* can be validly applied to the premises that he has written down by then to yield the desired conclusion, he expects the Tortoise to recognize this application as valid and hence the conclusion as true. Yet he lets himself be fooled by the Tortoise into contenting himself with theoretical rather than practical recognition. He allows the Tortoise to manifest recognition by way of a *conditional statement* ('Hypothetical Proposition') to the effect that *if* those premises are true so is the conclusion, i.e. by judging that the pattern of inference can be validly applied. In this way, Achilles allows the Tortoise to agree to yet another premise instead of insisting that the recognition of validity be manifested 'practically', by agreeing to the inference itself—by accepting it, by *inferring*.

2.4 *How is it possible for the shameless person to believe he has reason to Φ and yet have no intention of Φ-ing?*

In the case of theoretical inference, the distinction between acknowledgement and acceptance seems rather academic, or even spurious. Replace the Tortoise by anybody placed in a real life situation, and ask yourself: How would we react if he professed to recognize the validity of, say, *modus ponens* but refused to consent to Q although he agreed that P and that if P then Q? It is not obvious what we should make of this. But so much seems clear: We would *not* say: 'Well, he is convinced that *modus ponens* is valid and that, given *P* and *If P then Q*, one ought to believe that Q; only he just doesn't take the step that he knows he ought to take.'

Yet this is exactly the kind of thing we may have to say when confronted with an analogous discrepancy between acknowledgment and acceptance in cases of practical inference. A shadow, it seems, is cast on the practicality of practical reasons, even mandatory reasons, by the possibility of *shamelessness*.

My shameless person is one who does not Φ, or want to Φ, while yet agreeing that to act well you have to Φ and that, therefore, he ought to Φ.[12] On the account I have given of acting, this amounts to a situation where an agent acknowledges the soundness of an inference that issues in Φ-ing but does not accept it—he does not actually draw the

[12] In fact, this is a definition rather of 'generalized' shamelessness. For what I describe may take the form not only of conscious *imprudence* but also of other branches of moral recklessness as well as conscious *imprudence*, or irrationality. Nor do I distinguish the person who 'doesn't care a damn' from the one who regretfully resigns himself to not acting well.—There is a vague difference between regretful resignation and weakness of will, corresponding to a vague difference between ineffectual wishing and ineffectual wanting. Weakness raises problems of its own that I wish to avoid here.

practical conclusion. He does admit that the promise he has made is, under the circumstances, a mandatory reason to do as he promised, but he does not act on it.

This, however, is only part of the story. For here, too, we won't content ourselves with just saying: 'Well, he is convinced that the practical inference is valid; only he just doesn't take the step that he knows he ought to take. He is convinced that the promise he made gives him reason to do as promised; yet why should we on that account expect him actually to Φ just because he promised to?'

Our response will be different not because we have a 'pro-attitude' to promise keeping, but rather because the language of recognition he uses ('good reason', 'sound inference', etc.) is made for use by a community of speakers who recognize by accepting, and he is a member of this community. Hence *mere* acknowledgement is a *defective*, or *deviant*, form of recognition. Our expectation of recognition by performance, or readiness to perform, in this way manifests the meaning of phrases like 'I have reason to Φ' and, to this extent, the very meaning even of the shameless person's own concession that he has reason to Φ.

This claim may become more intelligible when we contrast the shameless with a bunch of Martians doing research on our species. Let us imagine them to be intelligent enough to spot not only our practice of giving and accepting reasons for doing things but also the significance of our acting on good reasons—of our acting well— for human well-being. These Martians may, for instance, discover not only that humans do in fact follow a rule of practical inference by which they pass from promising to Φ to Φ-ing; but also that humans ought to be motivated to Φ when they have promised to Φ—i.e. that this step from promise to performance is part of a system of rules that is suited, beneficial, even indispensable to human life—much the way the very special shape of a human hand is suited to human life (cf. the remarks about criteria for *good reasons* towards the end of 1.5 and in 2.2).

Now this piece of Martian anthropology—and here is the point of the comparison—would not be recognition. For, unless the Martians are much like us, there is no reason why in their system of practical inferences, if they have one, the keeping of promises should have a place—as it does in ours. The shameless, however, are in a different position. Being human themselves, they know they have reason to Φ when they have promised to, in the way we all do; they know it not as a result of anthropological observation and theory, but rather by way of an awareness of being required to take the step from 'I have promised to Φ' to Φ-ing, i.e. as a matter of recognition. However, such recognition would hardly differ from anthropological knowledge unless in its merely theoretical form it counted as defective.

But what kind of connection should we expect to obtain between acknowledging something as a reason, and acting on it, once we have admitted that shamelessness, though perhaps irrational, is nevertheless possible?

The demand for such a connection is what Foot calls 'Hume's practicality requirement', the demand that morality be 'necessarily practical, serving to produce and prevent action' (2001, p. 9). Though she accepts the demand, she does not think it entails the gap between factual and moral judgments that non-cognitivist accounts would insist on. Rather, the practicality requirement 'is met by the (most un-Humean) thought that acting morally is part of practical rationality' (p. 9). But is it met by this thought?

True, if morality is part of practical rationality, the question 'Why should I act well?' is off the agenda. But after reading *Natural Goodness*, the shameless person will not ask this question. He will agree that it is against reason not to Φ when one has promised to Φ. But the reasons for action that he acknowledges seem not to be 'practical enough', as it were, 'to produce and prevent action' *in him*.

What then is the force of practical reasons? To see this, let us take a fresh look at the use of reason statements. What is one doing in saying that there is reason to Φ, that R would be a good reason for Φ-ing, etc.?

2.5 *The notions of acting well and of a reason to Φ are acquired not by grasping criteria but by learning patterns of response*

Suppose again you have promised Φ, and there are no good reasons against keeping the promise. In this situation you will not act well unless you Φ—unless, to be more precise, you Φ because you promised to. Your promise requires you to Φ, it provides you with a mandatory reason to Φ. But what is the nature of this requirement? What account should be given of the use of whatever locutions express it?

In trying to answer these questions, we should remember two well-known points to be learnt from Wittgenstein: (1) In studying the meaning of an expression we must attend both to conditions that *permit or typically prompt* the employment of that expression and to the standard *role*, or *function*, of its use. (We may call this Wittgenstein's 'duality point'.) (2) Our account of a concept must be consistent with the possibility of its being acquired and, indeed, with its being acquired the way it *actually is acquired*. (The 'acquisition point'.)

To take account of the acquisition point, let us attend to the way in which children come by the notion of being required to Φ by a reason to Φ. They seem to acquire this notion by learning the use of such sentences as: 'It is her toy, *so* you must give it back to her'; 'I ought to help him *because* he needs my help'; '*If* one has promised to Φ, one must Φ'. In other cases, the reason may be expressed by phrases like 'You will hurt yourself', 'You wouldn't want that done to yourself, would you?', 'What if everybody did it?'. All these locutions serve somehow to tie a kind of response to a kind of circumstance or consideration. A child will have mastered the concept of a reasoning for doing things to the extent that he has grasped the nature of that tie. And this grasp will show, primarily, in an ability adequately to handle the verbal devices by which the tie may be marked. Prominent among these devices are expressions such as *so* and *therefore*, *ought* and *reason*, *because*, *if-then*, and—no doubt the most popular with children—*why must I...?*

How can the use of these expressions be acquired? What kind of environment and behaviour is it that goes with relevant occurrences of 'so', 'therefore' etc.? What is the child typically exposed to on his way to mastering the notions of a reason and of acting well?

We may begin by noting—and this is crucial to my argument— that the last thing the child is typically exposed to is the presence or presentation of *criteria* for something's being a good reason. He does not learn what are the conditions that permit or typically prompt the use of a proposition of the form 'Such-and-such is a reason to Φ'.

The child will indeed learn to recognize which kind of circumstance or consideration provides one with reasons for doing what kind of thing. He will also learn to recognize situations in which it is proper to say of people that they did act on this or that reason. But the resulting knowledge of what 'reason', or the practical 'therefore', signify will be no more than knowledge of an expandable list, a collection of convictions like: *If a thing is not yours this is a reason to return it to its owner*, and: *If he needs help this is a reason to help him.*

These convictions are acquired in a context that does not provide anything like truth grounds for them. As I have pointed out already, even an adult's understanding of items on the list does not, in general, involve more than a rather foggy idea of their truth grounds, i.e. of the connection between something's being a reason for something, and human well-being. In this sense, then, one does not even need to know *what it is for something to be a reason* in order to master the use of 'reason'!

So what is it, apart from common truth grounds, that different reason statements, different items from the list, have in common? What is it for the child to grasp the nature of the tie between reason and response, what is it for him to acquire the ability to handle the verbal devices which mark that tie?

It is for him to learn to act on reasons—to perform the practical inferences that are suggested to him by means of 'so' and 'therefore' and the rest. He is introduced to the general *idea* of a reason, in the first instance, by being trained to *treat* certain circumstances and considerations as reasons in what he *does*. In terms of the duality point, this suggests an essential preponderance of the role of reason statements over their truth grounds in an account of their meaning.[13]

If the idea of a reason must be conceived of on these lines, what kind of experience is apt to enable the child to acquire it? Obviously, people's trying to get him to do what they tell him there is reason to do will play a major role. This may amount to his being trained, first, to react in a characteristic way to a particular *perceivable feature* of the environment; later, to show the same reaction when *told* that this feature is present; and so on. I need not go into this: we are here on familiar Wittgensteinian and Anscombian ground. At any rate, learning the idea of a reason seems to consist in recognizing the requirement to Φ that a *reason* places on one, as somehow replacing *more immediately* enacted, and felt, forms of requirement. With regard to learning what 'reason to Φ' means, moral (and prudential!) upbringing is thus inextricably woven into the teaching of language.

But is it really necessary that we begin to learn the idea of a reason by learning to act on reasons ourselves? May we not come to grasp this notion by being exposed to, say,

[13] The point holds of theoretical no less than of practical reasons. This is why logic should be taught as the art of valid inference rather than as a science of logical relations.

the way others respond to being presented with reasons?—The account I have sketched is meant to be an account of what seems in fact to happen, and an account that thereby makes us ready to shift attention from questions of truth grounds to questions concerning the role of reason statements. There is indeed no logical necessity about the way we come to grasp this notion—although not every imaginable way of doing so would count as *learning*.

What is important is, of course, the notion that is in the end acquired. And of this we can say: Speakers of a language could have no grounds for *asserting* (or denying) propositions of the form 'R is a reason to Φ' unless there were a general practice, among the same speakers, of *acting* on reasons that are mentioned in this way. So you do not display a grasp of the notion of a reason unless you tend to respond to what you deem a good reason by acting on it, or at least show (as the shameless person does!) *awareness that this is the most fundamental way of displaying that grasp.*

Knowledge of the 'nature of the tie' between reason and response, and mastery of the words that express it, is thus manifested primarily, with regard to any reasons one is aware of, by readiness for the appropriate response itself.

2.6 *The practicality of an ethical judgment may be usefully compared to the practical character of a probability statement*

It may be helpful at this point to draw attention to an analogy, in respect of the duality point, between reason statements and probability statements.

It is characteristic of probability estimates that they are standardly based on certain types of *evidence* as well as meant to express and inspire degrees of *expectation*,[14] Imagine, however, a type of instruction by which a child acquires the use of 'probable' as a way of creating guarded expectation without, at first, learning by what evidence to support a claim of probability. He may be trained, on the one hand, to expect that P, though not as a certainty, when others say that probably P; and, on the other hand, to qualify his own expressions of intention as 'probable' when he does not wish to be committed. We might even teach the child (if his guardians do not object!) to take bets and to call 'probable' those outcomes that he is prepared to bet on.

It seems possible, then, to be introduced to the *role* of probability statements without acquiring any grasp of relevant *criteria*. Of course, this is not in fact the end of the matter. (Nor could it, maybe, exhaust the meaning of 'probable' or any other word as a word of any *language*.) Predictions that are not expressions of intention do have to rely on evidence. When they are qualified as merely probable, perhaps to a certain degree, evidence is provided by frequencies, equipossibilities etc. And this type of evidence has the status of criteria: the nature of such evidence must be counted as affecting our concept of probability.

Nevertheless—and this is my main point here—the word 'probability' does not lose its connection with guarded expectation as a result of its use being tied to more or less

[14] Indeed, neglect of the duality point seems to be a major reason why we find conflicting theories of probability.

well-defined criteria. On the contrary, by losing that connection, it would lose its point: it would no longer serve a purpose that is not already served by 'frequency', 'equipossibility', etc.

There is something wrong with the person who admits that on the available evidence it is extremely unlikely that P, and yet builds his decision in a matter of vital concern to him on the assumption that P. Imagine rules of a language that tied the use of 'probable' to the usual kind of empirical evidence and applied Kolmogoroff's calculus to 'probability' values but did not confer on 'probability' statements the standard role of expressing and inspiring degrees of expectation and of practical reliance. We could not say that in this language 'probable' meant what it means in English.

If a speaker of English used the word 'probable' in the truncated way I have just now described, he could indeed be said to make probability statements—but only because of the connection of his special use with the standard use. The very notion of probability justifies us in expecting, on the part of a person who can be said to believe that probably P, the kind of behaviour that exhibits a corresponding degree of reliance on P.

In an analogous way, I submit, the connection of a reason statement with the subject's readiness to act in accordance with it is not superseded as a result of bringing into the notion of a reason for Φ-ing, reference to criteria by which to decide whether such-and-such is in fact a good reason to Φ. Otherwise, a judgment of the form 'R is a reason to Φ' would not serve any purpose that was not served by 'Things go well in a human society only if its members respond to R by Φ-ing'. Hence, while only a vague idea of criteria is necessary for possession of the concept of a reason, no idea of criteria at all could be sufficient: it could not mark the difference between those two judgments.

So the shameless person, who admits to having every reason to Φ but doesn't Φ is not just acting against reason. Rather, his use of 'good reason', 'acting well' etc. is a truncated one, intelligible only against the background of a standard use that goes with corresponding practical dispositions. To put it differently: What justifies us in expecting people to be *ready to act on* what they profess to *recognize* as reasons? Obviously, the justification is provided not by mere experience but rather by the very notion of a reason, and hence by the meaning of what they say in talking of 'good reasons', 'acting well' etc.

Without the practice of acting in accordance with reason statements, these statements could at best be conclusions from a reflection, accessible also to Martians, on what kinds of practical inference *would* serve the well-being of human creatures.

In sum, then, the analogy with probabilities confirms my claim that the use of a reason statement standardly signals acceptance of a pattern of practical inference at least as much as it signals awareness of truth grounds of the statement.

Indeed, the truncated use of 'reason', or 'acting well' may be even more problematic than that of 'probable'. For, as I have pointed out, the meaning of 'good reason' contains no more than a pretty hazy reference to criteria (2.5).

In order to be correct, the use of 'acting well' doesn't need to wait to be informed by the correct descriptivist theory of what is responsible for the goodness of good practical reasons. It is characterized, rather, by the following three ingredients:

(1) *An expandable 'list' of applications:* We are acquainted with standard types of circumstances and considerations that characterize as cases of acting well whatever is done as an appropriate response to them. We have learnt to tie the ascription of ethical goodness to the presence of reasons that correspond to the requirements of prudence, justice, generosity, courage etc.
(2) *Something like a criterion:* In saying that in Φ-ing on account of R you are acting well, we are implying two things: (a) The practice of responding to R-type reasons by Φ-ing satisfies the *conditions whatever they are* for R's being a (good) reason to Φ. (b) This practice is *somehow* connected with the *good of human beings.*
(3) *General acceptance:* In a general way, most of us *tend to respond* by Φ-ing to what they think is a reason to Φ, and thus to intend well.

It may be asked what gives the notion of *acting well* its unity? The occurrence of various patterns of response on a single list such as specified under (1) will hardly do. By (2a) no more than a promise of unity is added to (1). So should we be content with (2b)? Must we not say that the idea of a reason for doing things, and with it that of acting well, would simply crumble unless they were held together by the rather homogeneous way in which (3) tells us good reasons *operate* in motivating people?

If this were so, the shameless person would present us with a semantic problem. For, *ex hypothesi*, he does not share the acceptance of certain types of reason. So what account are we going to give of *his* use of 'reason', 'ought', and 'acting well' in these areas? If we cannot count on the unifying function of (2), we may well start to wonder whether there isn't, after all, something to the idea that the shameless person uses these phrases in a sort of inverted comma sense— not necessarily with irony, or cynicism, but as it were 'quoting' an attitude that isn't his own but is, in accordance with (3), the standard attitude necessary to hold the 'items on the list' together. In this case, his use of 'acting well' might indeed be said to be more problematic than the deviant, merely descriptive use of 'probable' that I imagined earlier on. But in whatever way that use should be accurately characterized, it will at any rate turn out to require a background of untruncated use by other speakers of the language.

It may be objected that Wittgenstein's duality point applies to every expression, not just to 'probable', 'reason' and a few others.— I agree that the meaning of an expression is characterized, quite generally, by the roles its use can play in a sentence as well as by criteria. But these roles can be more or less specific.

Thus the way in which expressions occur in the sentence 'This hospital has 412 beds for patients' is pretty open-purpose as far as practical consequences are concerned. By contrast, the contribution of 'reason' to a sentence like 'His condition gives you reason to help him' is, in typical circumstances, more or less single-purpose. In the first case, we envisage practical consequences, typically, where a particular purpose is as it were added to what is being said. Not so in the second case.

2.7 *Although the acceptance standardly signalled by a reason statement is not expressed by the corresponding proposition, it ought to figure in accounts of the use of 'reason' and 'acting well'*

Has it, however, really been shown that it is the *notion* of a reason to Φ that has to be explained by reference to the reason's characteristic practical relevance? Even if in judging that R gives one reason to Φ one standardly signals acceptance of the inferential step from R to Φ-ing, it does not follow that such acceptance is in any way constitutive of the meaning also of the proposition 'R gives one reason to Φ'. And if acceptance doesn't enter the meaning of the proposition (i.e. of the assertoric sentence) it doesn't enter the notion of a reason either. As Peter Geach has repeatedly insisted on, we must take care not to confuse a proposition with the judgment, or statement, which it may serve to express.

Let *P* be, for instance, the proposition that the humanity of a foetus is a reason not to procure its abortion. And suppose that some doctor, X, asserts that it is not true that P. Or suppose he asserts that, if a foetus' being a person is guaranteed by its humanity, then P. Obviously, on neither supposition does X *assert* that P: the proposition that P is rather a component (perhaps a truth-functional argument) in what he is asserting. *A fortiori*, X's assertions do not commit him to *accepting* the humanity of a foetus as a reason not to abort it.

We need not, however, be denying or ignoring the Geach point in accounting for the meaning of a proposition, or a predicate, in terms of the function that is characteristic of its assertoric occurrence. We may, on the contrary, accept the point and say: Whatever X says with the help of *P* receives part of its meaning from the meaning of this proposition; yet the proposition *P* itself must be understood in terms of *its primary function*—in terms of the meaning of the reason statement made by an assertoric utterance of *P*; and among this statement's components and constructive devices it is, obviously, the notion of a reason that confers practicality on it—on the statement that P. (How are we going to account for the special kind of acceptance standardly expressed in a reason statement unless we attribute this aspect of its meaning to the meaning of such expressions as 'reason'? Cf. 2.4–6.). Hence the proposition that P as well as whatever may be said with the help of *P* does depend *for* its meaning on the practicality of the notion of a reason.

This conclusion may sound a little hollow: truth-functional compounds of *P* do not seem to show any trace of practicality. But this appearance is misleading.

In the spirit of Michael Dummett's account of meaning (1991, esp. p. 103), we may characterize the meaning of an expression as its *inference potential*. For an expression contributes to the meanings of propositions and speech acts by contributing to the selection of those inferential connections in which the propositions and speech acts validly occur. It follows that the meaning of 'reason', as it occurs in the proposition that P and its compounds, does include the practicality of reasons. For otherwise this aspect of meaning could not as it were surface as soon as, in virtue of some valid (theoretical) inference, *P* comes to be asserted.

To see this, let us suppose that X becomes convinced that

(N) A foetus' being a person is in fact guaranteed by its humanity.

With this judgment he joins, as a further premise, his antecedently accepted view that

(O) If a foetus' being a person is guaranteed by its humanity, then the humanity of a foetus is a reason not to abort it.

and arrives at the conclusion that

(P) The humanity of a foetus is indeed a reason not to abort it.

If my previous arguments are correct, *P* standardly serves to express acceptance of the reason it mentions.[15] But the statement that P, which expresses this acceptance, is validly inferred from O (in conjunction with *N*). Hence that aspect of the notion of a reason which accounts for the practicality

[15] Cf. 2.4–6. This acceptance is, primarily, readiness actually to pass from the consideration that the genetic make-up of a human foetus is of such-and-such a kind to a refusal to perform abortions. In stating that P, one asserts that *this practical inference* is valid.

of the statement that P, must be acknowledged to be already present in *O*. The occurrence of 'reason' in *O* must be understood in such a way that it can be seen to account for the deductibility from *N* together with *O* of the assertion that P—an assertion characterized by the practicality of a reason statement.[16]

These considerations suggest the following conclusion: Not only does the judgment that there is reason to Φ standardly signal readiness to Φ; rather, the very notion of a reason to and consequently that of the goodness of acting well, have to be explained by reference to reasons' characteristic practical relevance.

[16] What I have called the inference potential of 'reason' is manifested in the kind of theoretical inference of which the above derivation of the statement that P is a simple illustration. Consider now the special kind of inference, theoretical or practical, whose validity is expressly stated in terms of 'reason', as in a statement of the form 'R is a reason to believe that Q', or in a statement (like *P*) of the form 'R is a reason to Φ'. The inference potential of 'reason' is here manifested, it seems, in the kind of *consequence* that may or should be drawn from the statement. For, having deduced that

(P) The humanity of a foetus is a reason not to abort it

X may apply this reason statement to the particular case that is given by

(Q) Y is a human foetus

and draw a practical conclusion that consists in not aborting Y. However, it may be urged that the reason statement *P* should here be understood not as a premise that combines with Q to yield the practical conclusion, but rather as reminding X of a *pattern of practical inference* (2.2) that prescribes the move from accepting Q to not aborting Y.

Conclusion

In Part 1, I claimed that, roughly speaking, in Φ-ing one *acts well* if one Φ-es for the *right reasons.* If this is correct we must bring in the use of reason statements ('Such-and-such is a reason to Φ') in order to explain the use of statements, and indeed propositions, of the form 'In Φ-ing one would be acting well'. Given the duality point, there are two aspects to this. On the one hand, the *grounds* for saying that in Φ-ing one would be acting well must be sought in the grounds for saying that such-and-such is a reason to Φ. On the other hand—and this is the upshot of Part 2—the latter statement standardly expresses *acceptance* of a reason. Mention of such acceptance will therefore have to play a major role in an account of the meaning of 'well' as this expression occurs in claims of the form. 'In Φ-ing one would be acting well'.

I am claiming, then, that in one way the idea of goodness is the same, when you speak of a plant growing or reproducing well, an animal seeing well, and a human being acting well; and, equally, of course, when you speak of Soandso growing well, seeing well, and acting well. There is, however, a way, too, in which '*acting* well' is 'special' (cf. Foot, 2001, p. 8) in that the use of the expression is not purely descriptive.[17]

[17] Are not other evaluations, like 'complying with the law' or 'behaving well' (in the sense of 'showing good manners'), special in much the same way?—In some ways, they are. But they also differ significantly. (1) For one thing, you may use the 'ought' that is at home in a system like law or etiquette from an 'external point of view' (Hart, 1961, e.g. pp. 86f.), i.e. without in any way recognizing a requirement *on you;* by

This is because *acting* invokes a dimension of evaluation different in kind from the dimensions invoked by *growing* or *seeing*. In relating to standards of reasons, the notion of *acting* refers one to standards of practical inference. And, in any given language, assessment of an inferential pattern that is part of the same language cannot be recognized as approval unless the speakers of this language are in general disposed to be moved, by the assessment, to practise that pattern of inference. Hence the use of expressions like *good reason* and *acting well* standardly implies or signals readiness to pass from a certain kind of reason to doing what it is thought to be a reason to do.

contrast, the ethical 'ought' could fail to signal recognition in the mouth of a Martian only, not in yours (2.4). (2) This is because, under the simplifying assumption of 1.3, the kind of reason to Φ that qualifies your Φ-ing as a way of *acting well* is an ultimate reason, *tout court*; while considerations of legality or civility are not—even though they may be treated as such, and actually be ultimate reasons *from the point of view* of the law, or etiquette, i.e. within this or that conventional system (cf. however fn. 10). (3) Hence, compliance with laws or rules of etiquette is not (at least not rightfully) a matter of *motivation*, and therefore does not, by itself, determine the quality of a person's character, or of the person, as is the case with acting well. (4) Finally, and less importantly, when one learns to distinguish, from acting well, such things as good manners, obedience to one's parents, conformity to the law or a code of honour, etc., one does so by learning relatively clear *criteria* that mark off these various standards of evaluation; so the problem that we found with accounting for the meaning of 'acting well' in terms of truth grounds alone (2.2 and 2.5–6) may be felt less urgently with regard to expressions that signal non-ethical dimensions of evaluation.

If this is right, we may have to reopen the question that Foot (2001, p. 8) hopes to close by arguing that truth conditions exhaust the meaning of moral judgments. We may have to admit, after all, 'that the grounds of a moral judgment do not reach all the way to it'. For if reason statements are calculated to express acceptance of a type of practical inference, this cannot fail to have repercussions on the analysis of the notion of *goodness* contained in the notion of *acting well.*

This may sound like good news for the subjectivist. But it is neither meant nor apt to give him comfort. The fact that ethical statements signal acceptance does not show that they do not also signal acknowledgement. On the contrary, their practical use is taught and practised on the understanding that *there is* something, independent of any attitude of the subject's, in virtue of which a reason is a good reason for Φ-ing; and that this something is closely connected with human well-being.

Acknowledgement and acceptance of reasons are tied to each other particularly closely in the case of theoretical reasons. If mere acknowledgement that a pattern of inference is valid makes sense here at all, it is at any rate secondary to recognition in the form of acceptance. Hence, the meaning of 'reason to believe' cannot be explained without reference to something like subjects' readiness to believe. But nobody on that account holds a subjectivist theory of theoretical inference. Equally, if we have to understand 'reason to Φ' partly in terms of subjects' readiness to Φ, this does not in the least commit us to any kind of ethical subjectivism.

Let me end by pointing out a paradoxical feature of the argument of Part 2: We started off with the sound descriptivist observation that statements of fact may give one reason for doing things independently of one's aims and desires. It now turns out that this very observation leads us to concede a non-descriptive component in the meaning of ethical judgments. For just because such judgments point to the facts that by themselves afford reasons to act on, they standardly involve, in a sense that I have tried to explain, the acceptance of certain patterns of practical inference. And the primary manifestation of such acceptance is performance. With regard to the judgment that to act well one has to Φ, or that there is reason to or that R is a mandatory reason to Φ, this means: even though this judgment must be assumed to be supported by something like truth grounds that justify us in acknowledging Φ as the practical conclusion of a valid inference, it also standardly signals readiness to draw this conclusion, and, more generally, to act well.

Works referred to

Anscombe, G. Elizabeth M., *Intention* (Oxford: Blackwell, 1963).

Dancy, Jonathan, *Moral Reasons* (Oxford: Blackwell, 1993).

Dodgson, Charles L., 'What the Tortoise Said to Achilles', *The Works of Lewis Carroll*, R. L. Green (ed.) (London: Paul Hamlyn, 1965), 1049–51.

Dummett, Michael, *The Logical Basis of Metaphysics* (London: Duckworth, 1991).

Foot, Philippa, *Natural Goodness* (Oxford: Clarendon Press, 2001).

Hart, Herbert L. A., *The Concept of Law* (Oxford: Clarendon Press, 1961).

Müller, Anselm W., 'Mental Teleology', *Proceedings of the Aristotelian Society* 92 (1992), 161–83.

Müller, Anselm W., *Was taugt die Tugend? Elemente einer Ethik des guten Lebens* (Stuttgart: Kohlhammer, 1998).

Müller, Anselm W., 'Which Mean? Why Unity? Two Problems in Aristotle's Account of Ethical Virtue and One Solution', *Was ist dasfiir den Menschen Gute? Menschliche Natur und Giiterlehre/What is Good for a Human Being? Human Nature and Values,* J. Szaif and M. LutzBachmann (eds.) (Berlin: de Gruyter, 2004).

Apprehending Human Form

MICHAEL THOMPSON

My immediate aim in this lecture is to contribute something to the apt characterization of *our representation and knowledge of the specifically human life form*, as I will put it—and, to some extent, of things 'human' more generally. In particular I want to argue against an exaggerated empiricism about such cognition. Meditation on these themes might be pursued as having a kind of interest of its own, an epistemological and in the end metaphysical interest, but my own purpose in the matter is practical-philosophical. I want to employ my theses to make room for a certain range of doctrines in ethical theory and the theory of practical rationality—doctrines, namely, of *natural normativity* or *natural goodness*, as we may call them. I am not proposing to attempt a positive argument for any such 'neo-Aristotelian' position, but merely to defend such views against certain familiar lines of objection; and even here my aims will be limited, as will be seen.

In order to bring my empiricist target into focus it will be necessary to consider *the representation of things as alive* quite generally, and at its most rustic and fundamental level, before moving to our proper study, viz. the representation of matters specifically human and practical.

Some elementary forms of representation of life[1]

Suppose that you are an expert on some particular type of terrestrial organism. Let's say, to fix ideas, that you are an expert on the jellyfishes and their relatives in the phylum *Cnidaria.* A writer of science fiction, populating the seas of Jupiter in her imagination, would be hard pressed to come up with a range of life forms as strange as this collection of transparent drifting gelatinous creatures. Their peculiar labour and life plan is to render themselves as little distinct as possible from the surrounding aqueous medium, as if to realize some oceanographer's idea of a ghost.

Let our thoughts now place you on some distant reef. Armed with your extensive knowledge of the phylum, you set out, inevitably, to study the local gelatinous fauna. And now you come upon a very peculiar 'jelly', as they call them, one with novel parts and features. For a jelly so tiny it has an unusually large number of secondary mouths, as they call them; its tentacles are disproportionately short; its upper part, or 'bell', is extremely thin, spreading out over rest of its mass like an umbrella.

The specimen in question at first strikes you as a bit of a freak, perhaps. You wonder whether it might not be a

[1] The next three sections and the first part of the next to last section adhere closely to the claims of my essay 'The Representation of Life', *Reasons and Virtues*, R. Hursthouse, W. Quinn and G. Lawrence (eds.) (Oxford: Oxford University Press, 1995), though the discussion is structured differently and much abbreviated. I hope that it is independently intelligible and persuasive.

defective instance of a species familiar to you, perhaps the cross jelly. You consider that maybe its development has been compromised by some complex chemical pollutant abroad in these waters. But now you come upon another individual jelly similar to it, and another; the reef is full of them, and so, you find, is another many miles to the south, beyond the reach of any similar source of potentially compromising chemistry.

At some point in the gathering of this storm of experience, condensation will occur. You will find yourself with a new object of explicit and independent thought: you will, that is, be in a position to recognize a novel species of jellyfish, a hitherto unknown form of gelatinous life, a new way for physical particles to be trapped in a vortex of life-processes. You will thus, for one thing, be in a position to introduce a new general name, a name for a living kind or form. Let's suppose you introduce the name 'umbrella jelly' for them.

Armed with this new name and concept you will be ready to frame new judgments. The simplest range of new judgments would of course be those bringing given individual organisms under this life form, as bearers. We might call such claims *life form attributions*, or judgments of type A. Their general form will be something like this: *X is a bearer of life form S*, or *X is a member of species S*, or, in suitable contexts, simply *X is an S* or *Lo, an S*.

But your increasingly abundant experience as you study these reefs will put you in a position to frame certain distinctive *general judgments* as well. These judgments will not be about individual jellies taken singly or *en masse*, but, we might say, directly about the newly conceived life form itself—about *umbrella jelly* or 'the' umbrella jelly. The verbal expression of these general judgments will deploy your new general name in a sort of subject position; but the predicates attached to it will be otherwise attachable to representations of individuals. In these general propositions, you might, for example, describe the peculiar so-called life-cycle associated with life-in-this-novel-form. This cycle moves from an egg stage to a polyp stage to what is called the medusa stage, as it does in every form of jelly-life. But the familiar basic pattern has numerous peculiarities in the case of the umbrella jelly. You will take note of these in the monograph that you are, let's suppose, beginning to compose.

We may call the judgments you are assembling in your monograph *natural historical judgments*, or judgments of type B. Their general form will be something like this: *the S is/has/does F*, or *S's are/do/have F*, or *S's characteristically are/have/do F*, or *it belongs to an S to be/do/have F*, or *this is (part of) how S's live: they are/do/have F*. What particular verbal materials are used to join 'S' and 'F' in speech is of no importance; what matters is that the resulting nexus of signs, perhaps taken together with features of the context, expresses a distinctive form of general judgment.

Note, for example, that these general propositions about the life form have unusual temporal properties. Of any individual jelly here and now, you will speak in the usual temporal way. You will judge that it 'is' in some one of these phrases and 'has been' in another, and you might form the expectation that it 'will later on be' in another. But of *umbrella jelly* as a general kind, or form, of life, you will speak in the first instance completely atemporally. In your monograph about the life form, you will say that on its first appearance the thing 'is' an egg, then later it 'is' a polyp, then later it 'is' a medusa. Or again: of *this* umbrella jelly *hie et nunc*, you will say that it 'is developing' into a medusa; of 'the' umbrella jelly you will say that it 'develops' into a medusa. Though temporal relations are somehow registered, everything is put into a special kind of present tense, grammatically speaking.[2] Your monograph will employ similar general atemporal judgments in its elaboration on the peculiar structure of the bell that characterizes the mature medusa phase of 'the' umbrella jelly. If the medusa of this kind is characterized by a fixed number of tentacles and mouths, you might assign a Latin name to each of 'them', and go on to characterize 'its' position and structure, again atemporally and generally, as doctors do for each of the

[2] Of course we have plenty of use for a past tense version of natural historical propositions, for example in the description of extinct life forms. But I think that this is a secondary conceptual development (see the paper mentioned in note 1 above, section 4.1). It seems we could enjoy the capacity for just this form of judgment though the formation of past tense expressions of it is grammatically excluded or nowhere envisaged. In this respect natural historical judgment is unlike, say, present progressive judgment (*X is doing A*), which presupposes the possibility of forming the opposing past perfective (*X did A*). I should perhaps rather speak of a 'relative atemporality' than of 'atemporality' simply. Consider that in *statements of exemplification* a past particular fact can here be used to illustrate a 'present' generalization: 'S's characteristically do F,' I might say, '-for example, this S did F just yesterday.' The forms of generality described in logic textbooks do not admit of this phenomenon.

human bones and dentists do for each of the human teeth. You view the various parts as akin to individuals in this enterprise, even though each can have indefinitely many instances.

We may call the complete class of true such general judgments the *natural history* of the umbrella jelly. Your little monograph will inevitably contain only the tip of this iceberg, which of course might be extended into the deepest biochemical detail. But in the ideal with which you are operating, your propositions belong to a totality, a connected whole, a system. In it each general atemporal proposition will explain others and be explained by others. Relations of dependence among the propositions would be marked by what are called teleological or functional connections. Your particular propositions, e.g. 'The medusa of the umbrella jelly has one hundred and forty four tentacles', are understood as out-takes from this possible connected system.

It is important to emphasize that the particular out-taken propositions, the natural historical judgments, are not mere reports of what is always or mostly or even often the case with jellies of this kind. You are not aiming at anything like a synopsis of what has happened. To paraphrase Elizabeth Anscombe, one hundred and forty four is probably not the *average* number of tentacles that mature umbrella jellies have had at any time.[3] The point becomes clearer if we consider that your monograph might contain some such

[3] G. E. M. Anscombe, 'Modern Moral Philosophy,' *Ethics, Religion and Politics* (Minneapolis: Minnesota University Press, 1982), 26–42, 38.

natural historical proposition as this: 'Upon fertilization, the mature umbrella jelly lays hundreds of eggs'. But you can hardly fail to have reflected that the population must for generations have remained more or less stable, at least within a few orders of magnitude. It is clear, then, that only a tiny fraction of umbrella jelly eggs have ever realized the story you told about how 'the egg' develops into 'the polyp' and then 'the medusa'—a narrative which might seem a bit Pollyannaish from a certain point of view, but which is forced on you by the form of representation in which you are engaged. If even a sizable proportion of them had for some time followed, in reality, your account of what 'happens' to such a thing, in the natural history, then in a few generations the seas would have become completely clogged with gelatinous goo. Things would be structurally the same if your enquiry had found that tens of thousands or even tens of millions of eggs are produced. In your articulation of the natural history of the umbrella jelly your thoughts exhibit a certain *form of generality*, as one might say, but it is clearly very far from any familiar Fregean or statistical or *ceteris paribus* form.

Vital description and reciprocal dependence

Your enquiry is moving you closer and closer to the distant ideal of complete comprehension of the general atemporal natural history of the umbrella jelly, a complete account of how they live, or how life-in-this-form hangs together. But note that this monographic knowledge will at the same time position you to give increasingly rich temporal descriptions of what is going on with any one specimen here and now. We might call these judgments about particular organisms by the name of *vital descriptions,* or judgments of type C: their typical forms would simply be *this S (or X) is/has/does,* G and its past and future versions—or more explicitly, *it is a phenomenon of this S's life that it is/has/does* G, together with *its* past and future forms.

For example, the better your natural historical knowledge of the umbrella shaped bell that the umbrella jelly grows—and the better you understand, say, its peculiar mode of contraction—the more clearly you will be able to tell when this individual jelly here and now before you in the reef *is moving itself up or down the water column* and when instead it *is being moved by currents.* And with improved atemporal monographic knowledge, you will be able to distinguish individual cases of bell-contraction that are a part of self-movement from those that are immediate defensive reactions to perceived predators.

Or again, even though it might be that the individual medusa you are now observing is not engaged in any process of reproduction, and has not yet engaged in any such process, still your general monographic knowledge might position you to say, of these parts here and now, that they are reproductive organs. No connection with reproduction can be found in this individual case; and there never will be any if you now take a notion to dissect the specimen. It is only by appeal to the natural history of this form of life taken generally, and thus mediately by appeal to what you have observed in other individual jellies, that you are in a position to frame this judgment—*these are reproductive organs*—about the specimen given to you here and now.

This sort of case brings out what seems on reflection to be a general and thoroughgoing reciprocal mutual interdependence of *vital description of the individual* and *natural historical judgment about the form or kind.*

At the outset, in your first vital descriptions of the first strange jelly you encountered, you did not make even latent reference to 'umbrella jelly kind' as such, which you hadn't properly conceived. But you did, I think, make latent demonstrative reference to 'this kind of jelly' or 'this form of jelly life'—the kind or form of jelly before you. Even at the outset you thought things like *these are the tentacles* and *this is the bell* and *these are the reproductive organs.* You thus implicitly thought that these bits, however deformed in the individual case, occupied the position or role of tentacles and bell and reproductive organs in 'this form of life'. Of course you thought wrongly that 'this form of life' was the cross jelly form of life. And so you thought some false things about 'this form of life' and thus also some false things about the parts of this individual— for example, that they were stunted and otherwise deformed.

Even such apparently purely physical judgments as that the organism starts here and ends here, or weighs this much, must involve a covert reference to something that goes to beyond the individual, namely its life form. It is only in the light of a conception of this form, however dim that conception might be, that you could intelligibly suppose, for example, that the tentacles are not parasites or cancerous excrescences or undetached bits of waste. Similarly, the recognition judgment—that this is the same organism as was sighted earlier—must presuppose a conception of the inner character of the life form supposed borne by what is sighted on the different occasions.

I will return to this idea of a reciprocal dependence between judgments about the individual organism and judgments about its form, and also to the correlative connection that *facts* about the individual can bear to *facts* about its form.

These three sorts of judgment about the umbrella jelly and umbrella jellies might be compared to three parallel forms of judgment about human speech—an analogy Darwin himself draws.[4] As we distinguish various species, or natural forms of life, so also we distinguish various languages, or customary forms of discursive interaction. We classify individual organisms as *bearers* of particular life forms; and so also we classify people as *speakers* of particular languages (type A). A naturalist like you, we saw, will make numerous general and atemporal judgments about any given life form under investigation, and will attempt to join them into a system. And so also a linguist will make numerous general atemporal judgments about a given language she is studying, attempting to join *them* into a (quite different) sort of system (type B). She will characterize its lexicon for example, and assign particular meanings to particular

[4] Charles Darwin, *The Origin of Species* (1876), P. H. Barrett and R. B. Freeman (eds.) (New York: New York University Press, 1988), 386. He is discussing the principles of hierarchical classification, defending a genealogical or historical conception as ideal.

words—words which admit indefinitely many individual 'tokenings', as *tentacle 137 of the umbrella jelly* admits indefinitely many instantiations.[5] Finally, a naturalist like you will engage in much vital description of given organisms here and now, framing judgments about what they are up to and what parts these are and so forth. And so also our linguist will be positioned to say what words this person is now using, what sentence he is now asserting, and what, in fact, he is now telling his interlocutor (type C).[6]

5 The linguistic analogy might make clearer the priority of a sort of 'atemporal' use of the present tense in these two connections (life form and language). Part of our linguist's task, it is natural to suppose, is to give propositional representation to the knowledge that her informants possess as competent speakers of the language under investigation. But it does not seem that this 'implicit' knowledge operates with an opposition between what is past and what is present in the use of language. It is not part of linguistic competence to know anything that a linguist might report in a past tense use of her sort of generality. Thus our linguist's inevitable use of some sort of grammatical present in the representation of this competence should not be taken as committing her to the attribution of robustly temporal contents.

6 The linguistic analogy suggests a slight rectification of vocabulary. I have been making a somewhat crude use of the words 'life form', 'species' and 'kind' (of living thing) as more or less equivalent. This seems to me justified for present purposes, and I will retain it, but sharper metaphysical implements would incline us to split things up, as we certainly would in the case of language: the concept *life form*, might be kept strictly parallel to the concept *language* or *form of discursive interaction*; the concept *species* might then be understood as parallel with the concept *linguistic community*, finally the concept of a given *kind* of living thing would be parallel to that of a given

But note again the element of reciprocal dependence: once our linguist gets into the system, many of her tensed remarks about individuals will presuppose generic atemporal thoughts about the language in question. For example, any description of a given speaker *hic et nunc* as telling another *that snow is falling* or *that snow fell yesterday* will presuppose a general assignment of meanings to words. Here too, then, there is a sort of dependence of tensed judgments about individuals on untensed general judgments. In each case, vital and linguistic, the connection between the given individual (or pair) and the property ascribed to it is mediated by the presence in it (or them) of a determinate *form.*

We might say, then, if we care to push the linguistic analogy off a cliff, that a life form is like a language that physical matter can speak. It is in the light of judgments about the life form that I assign meaning and significance and point and position to the parts and operations of individual organisms that present themselves to me. As *French* or *English* are to the people and brains of which they take possession, so are things like *umbrella jelly* and *cross jelly* to the physical particles of which *they* take possession. And just as there is no speech—no discourse, no telling and believing people, no knowledge by testimony—without a language that is spoken, which is to say, without a framework for interpreting what is going on between the speakers, so there is no life without a life form, which is to say, without

'speaker-kind,' i.e., the concept *speaker of L* for a given language L. The first of these is the principal object of my attention in this essay.

a framework for interpreting the goings-on in the individual organism.

Judgments of natural goodness and standard

But let us move to two further forms of judgment we frame about living things. Note that you will as time goes on be in a position to make judgments of defect and deformity in individual umbrella jellies. Having given names to all one hundred and forty four tentacles of the umbrella jelly in your monograph, you will be able, e.g., to say when an individual jelly is missing a tentacle, or when a tentacle is present but broken. You will be able to say when one of the many mouths is malfunctioning, when contractions of the umbrella-like bell are well or badly effected, and so forth. We might call these judgments *judgments of natural goodness and badness*, judgments of type D. Their canonical form would be something like this: *this S is defective/sound, as an S, in that it is/has/does H.* If some forms of defect or deformity are frequently seen, you might invent special concepts to capture them, as we speak of *lameness* and *blindness* in human beings and *etiolation* in green plants.

Note that what sorts of things are aptly judged good or bad, defective or sound, in the parts and operations of a given umbrella jelly will differ, in detail at least, from what counts as good or bad in jellies of other kinds—still more from what counts as good or bad in the workings of oak trees, bacteria or squid. When you thought, of the first specimen you sighted, that it was a cross jelly, you thought it was woefully deformed. And if it had been a cross jelly, it would have been woefully deformed. But now, with further observation, you can see that that original specimen was quite sound, except perhaps for a few broken tentacles. It is just that it belonged to a *different kind*, and was thus subject to a different standard.

In speaking of 'different standards for different species or kinds or forms', I have implicitly suggested that you will by degrees also come to form *general* judgments with evaluative content, a fifth form of judgment, type E. You will be positioned to say when in *general* an umbrella jelly is formed well or badly or operating well or badly, in respect of some part or capacity. We might call such general judgments *judgments of natural standard.* Their general form would be something like this: *an S is defective/sound in a certain respect if it is/has/does G.* The system of general judgments of natural standard about umbrella jellies will closely track the system of atemporal natural historical judgments about the same kind or form. Indeed, judgments of natural standard might be said simply to transpose our natural historical judgments into an evaluative key: the monograph you have been composing might be viewed as indirectly articulating the ideal, standard or perfect operation of a bearer of this kind of life. A natural history, as we saw, does not describe what happens on average or mostly; its relation to facts about individuals is evidently much more complex.

Your observations, which are at bottom always observations of individual organisms, will thus lead in the end to a possible *critique* or *evaluation* of individual organisms and their parts and operations. And they will lead to the articulation of general *standards of critique* applying to organisms of the kind in question. This sort of critique of the individual is everywhere mediated by the attribution to it of a specific form; to bring an individual under a life form is, we might say, at the same time to bring it under a certain sort of standard. It goes without saying that this sort of critique or evaluation of an individual is not the only sort possible: a dog might be profoundly deformed as a dog, but prize-winning at a general congress of St. Bernards; a tree might be woefully deformed as a Japanese black pine, but prize-winning at a bonsai exhibition.

Note that here again your position is much like that of our imagined linguist. With time she too will take on a critical role. She will be able to declare whether particular statements made by her informants are true or false, if it happens that she knows about the matter under discussion (type D). And if she arrives at the point of a so-called truth theory for her object language, she will be able to say when *in general* a sentence of the language is true or false (type E).

The role of observation in the framing of judgments falling under these diverse types

I have been describing the progress of your mind as it arrives at particular judgments of five types, A through E. The judgments take as their theme either individual organisms—*X* or *this S*—or else the general 'life form' or 'kind' or 'species', *S*, that these individual organisms exhibit, bear, or fall under. As I have written them, these are mere schemata of judgment, colourless abstract forms. In the course of your study of those jellies on those reefs, you made numberless particular judgments falling into these forms, filling in the blanks in a variety of ways. We might compare these abstract shapes with the shapes printed in a fresh children's colouring book. Faced with a tide of umbrella jellies, you coloured them in, so to speak.

The point I want to emphasize is that you did this filling-in or colouring-in—which was both factual and evaluative, temporal and atemporal, general and particular—*entirely on the basis of observation*, observation performed on a couple of distant reefs. You deployed your senses in connection with certain external objects and as a result were able to fill these abstract judgment frames with manifold contents. One class of such judgments, the natural historical judgments, you included in your monograph. This colouring-in or blank-filling would of course have gone quite differently if you had been a fern expert faced with some unusual ferns, or a primatologist faced with unclassifiable individual primates, or a bacteriologist faced with a peculiar colony of microbes. The differential impact of outward things, living things, upon your senses and instruments would account for the different concrete judgments framed in each case.

Let us apply these thoughts to our real topic, which is the specifically human form, a product of evolutionary history quite as strange in its way as the umbrella jelly. And it seems plain that this empiricist or observationalist picture of things holds for much of what is known about things specifically human. We certainly deploy our five forms of judgment in this connection: 'human' can be put in place of 'S';

your name can replace 'X'. And we happily fill in the other blanks in these judgment-forms on the same sort of ground we met with in the case of the umbrella jelly: we do it, that is, on the basis of observation, or intelligent experience with individual members of the kind. It is clear that the ordinary operations of a doctor or a dentist, for example, will involve implicit or explicit deployment of all five forms of judgment. And it is equally clear that the distinctive knowledge of a doctor or a dentist is purely empirical, or founded on observation, formally no different from your knowledge of the umbrella jellies.

The empiricist propositions

If we take the cases so far canvassed as typical, the overwhelming role of observation in supplying our abstract forms with determinate content might lead us to accept the following propositions. I will call them *the empiricist propositions*:

> The concept *species* or *life form* is itself an empirical concept. Concepts of particular life forms (*cross jelly, umbrella jelly, white oak, horseshoe crab, human*) are invariably empirical, or observation-dependent, concepts.
>
> Singular representations of individual organisms are invariably empirical representations.
>
> Substantive knowledge of any given individual organism (propositions of types A, C and D) can only arise from observation. Substantive knowledge of the character of a given species or life form (propositions of types B and E) can only arise from observation.

The empiricist propositions might be opposed in a number of ways, but my purpose is to oppose them with something like the following *anti-empiricist propositions*:

> The concept *life form* is a pure or a priori, perhaps a logical, concept.
>
> The concept *human*, as we human beings have it, is an a priori concept attaching to a particular life form.
>
> A mature human being is typically in possession of a non-empirical singular representation of one individual organism. Individual human beings are sometimes in possession of non-observational knowledge of contingent facts about one individual organism.
>
> Human beings are characteristically in possession of some general substantive knowledge of the human life form which is not founded empirically on observation of members of their kind, and thus not 'biological'.

The empiricist propositions are rarely affirmed explicitly, but I think they are—or many of them are—implicit in much of our thinking about life and human life. A comparative survey of opposing pairs of propositions from the two lists will show that each disputed point raises potentially absorbing metaphysical and epistemological issues, just by itself. But, as I have said, I am moved to consider the merits of the empiricist propositions by the place that some of them occupy in ethical theory.

Normative naturalism

More particularly I want to consider the place the empiricist propositions implicitly occupy in much of the received criticism of ethical doctrines which appeal to notions of *natural normativity* or *natural goodness.*

By such a doctrine I mean, in the first instance, a theory of the type sketched in the concluding paragraphs of Elizabeth Anscombe's 'Modern Moral Philosophy' and lately developed in the last part of Rosalind Hursthouse's book *On Virtue Ethics*, and still more recently in Philippa Foot's book *Natural Goodness.*[7] These works are of course united in a number of ways, for example in the use they make of the concept of virtue. I will focus, though, on the special significance they attach, within ethical theory, to the idea of the *human*—that is, to the concepts of a *human being* and of the specifically human life form and of so-called human nature.

The idea of the human that these writers propose to make central to ethical theory is not the abstract idea of a rational being or a person; it is not what Kant meant in speaking of 'humanity'. Like human beings, the Martians and other so-called humanoids of science fiction would be 'persons' and 'rational beings', for sure, but they wouldn't covered by the concept of a human being that is in question. That concept expresses something more specific: it would not even cover those so-called 'twin humans' whom philosophers sometimes imagine. These are (on some versions) creatures exactly similar to us, living on a planet, Twin Earth, which developed independently of ours, but which nevertheless came to be like Earth in any respect you care to mention. The twin humans are bearers of a different life

[7] *On Virtue Ethics* (Oxford: Oxford University Press, 1998); *Natural Goodness* (Oxford: Oxford University Press, 2000).

form, viz. *twin human*, just as the languages they speak are different languages, even if it is part of the story that they are qualitatively the same as the languages we speak.

The concept *human* as our naturalist employs it is a concept that attaches to a definite product of nature, one which has arisen on this planet, quite contingently, in the course of evolutionary history. For our naturalist, this product of nature is in some sense the theme of ethical theory as we humans would write it. But there is in the larger literature a kind of fear or dread of any appeal to this sort of concept in ethical theory, and this is what I want to address. The contemporary moralist is anxious to leave this concept behind, and to develop his theory in terms of 'persons' and 'rational beings', but if the naturalist is right the concept in question is everywhere nipping at his heels. There is in practical philosophy a kind of alienation from the concept *human* and the sort of unity of agents it expresses.

A typical difficulty that the normative naturalist means to resolve is this: how are we to account for the intuitive difference between considerations of justice and prudence, on the one hand, and those of etiquette and femininity, on the other? If I criticize an action as unfeminine or as a violation of etiquette—as 'not done' or not *comme il faut*—my appeal is at best, it seems, to convention only; in so speaking I am acting precisely as an arm of convention. If now I criticize an action as unjust or imprudent, or if I praise it as just or prudent, custom or convention may well be part of the story. But I seem to be aiming at something more. My evaluation purports to have what philosophers sometimes call 'normative authority'; it purports to speak directly to the genuine 'reasons' that the agent 'has'. It has been a puzzle how we are to understand what these phrases mean, what this further purport is. For our naturalist this further purport is a matter of the supposed goodness and badness of the operations of will and practical reason that would be exhibited in the action judged of. And goodness or badness in the operation of these powers is to be understood, in point of logical position, on the model of goodness or badness of sight, or the well-formedness or ill-formedness of an umbrella jelly's tentacle. Unlike judgments of etiquette or femininity, judgments of prudence and justice claim a place on our five-fold chart. The judgments in which I criticize the actions of individual persons as unjust or imprudent, or criticize the people themselves as unjust or imprudent people, will thus be *special forms* of what I called judgments of natural goodness or badness, type D on our list, as judgments of blindness and etiolation are. A formulation of general normative principle, or of a basic general form of reason for action, where such a thing is formulable, will be a specific type of judgment of natural standard, a specific form of a type E judgment. The reasons that we 'have' are the ones we take account of when we are *reasoning well*.

That these evaluative judgments pertain to intellectual powers like will and practical reason must introduce numerous peculiarities into their description. But, on naturalist hypotheses, they nevertheless fall onto the same plane in logical space as claims about what makes for good sight. That there is a specific difference could hardly argue against the presence of a common genus.

Life form relativity

Consider, though, that no one thinks that the fact that an individual organism does or doesn't make certain colour-discriminations, just by itself, shows that its visual capacity is defective or sound. In different sighted species, different discriminatory powers count as good sight. In the life of the umbrella jelly no sight is necessary at all. Similarly, what would seem lame in a hare is sound movement in a tortoise. Knowledge of what counts as good sight, or as a sound capacity to move, is thus *substantive knowledge of the specific life form in question.*

For a normative naturalist our fundamental practical evaluative knowledge is, as we have seen, substantive knowledge of what makes for a good will and a good practical reason in a specifically *human being.* What would be virtue in the bearers of another intelligent form of life we don't know. We have no more insight into what would count as a 'reason for action' among Martians, for example, than we have into what would make for good eyesight among them, supposing they have eyes. The mind goes blank at the approach of the question. Thrasymachus and Callicles, in Plato's dialogues, argued in different ways that justice as we ordinarily understand it is mere convention only, and that to take its considerations seriously is a vice in human beings. The so-called just agent is a human bonsai, or worse. Anscombe, Hursthouse and Foot all earnestly deny this, insisting that it is the unjust agent who is twisted and unsound. But I think they should grant that those immoralist teachings might be exactly right for our imagined Martians. Perhaps, that is, our writers should confess to *immoralism about the Martians.* Can't we suppose a sufficiently alien life form to exhibit some quite other way of getting on—that the practical life that is characteristic of their kind has some fundamentally different structure, even though it is mediated by objective judgment and conceptual representation, as ours is? The peculiar structuring imposed by considerations of justice will have no place in it.[8] *Our* practical knowledge, though it is general, is not so general as to rule this out. In this respect normative naturalism breaks with the received Kantian and Humean conceptions of practical rationality, each of which appears to claim possession of a table of principles of sound practical reasoning that would apply indifferently to humans, twin earthers and Martians alike.

These points bring out that any given normative naturalist theory will have two levels, one formal, as we might put it, and the other substantive. Critiques of normative naturalism often leave it unclear to which level their arguments are pitched. Only the first level is at issue here. This formal aspect of the theory might be accepted as much by an 'immoralist' like Callicles or Gide as by an orthodox Aristotelian—namely the naturalist interpretation of the content of judgments of goodness and badness in practical thought as coming under our fourth and fifth headings as more determinate forms. Callicles, in the play he makes with the opposition between what belongs to *nomos* only and what belongs properly to *phusis*, would seem to be explicitly a

[8] The special logical character of 'considerations of justice' is addressed in my essay 'What is it to Wrong Someone?' in *Practical Reason and Value*, R. J. Wallace, P. Pettit, S. Scheffler and M. Smith (eds.) (Oxford: Oxford University Press, forthcoming.).

normative naturalist in this sense. Or, to put the point another way, the *formal* aspect of the theory could be accepted without alteration by bearers of radically alien forms of 'intelligent life'; it is after all essentially a matter of logical analysis. The *substantive* part of the theory, by contrast, would be addressed to human beings in the first instance, fellow bearers of the form our writers bear, and would amount to the isolation of a table of virtues or basic types of reason for action appropriate to human beings. It is an attempt to make articulate an aspect of something that is present equally in writer and reader, namely what I am calling the specifically human life form. It is here that the struggle with the naturalist immoralist will be pursued: this is a struggle, as we might say, over different conceptions of specifically human life; or, to approach the matter from another direction, it is a dispute over which forms of upbringing damage the human individual—casting a spell on him as Callicles puts it and putting him into mental shackles and so forth—and which upbringings rather yield a sound human practical understanding.

Often in writings on practical philosophy, we find moral principles developed, or substantive formulations of reasons adopted: 'It is impermissible to do A', we read, or 'One has reason to do B'. The question of the scope of this generality, or of the form of generality contained in such judgments, is rarely posed. Suppose, for example, that our writer is rendering verdicts on sundry variants of Philippa Foot's 'trolley problem'. Is she developing the normative consequences of the particular local ensemble of practices under which we bearers of Western modernity live? Or is she proposing a cosmic scope for her propositions, speaking to Martians as well as to me? Doctrines of natural normativity may be understood as holding that the *highest* form of generality that can attach to such claims is the form of generality that is also found in our natural historical judgments or judgments of natural standard.

Biologistic complaints

This then is the sort of theory at issue. My thought, though, is that if the empiricist propositions are taken for granted, this naturalist line of thought will inevitably seem somehow absurd. It might seem, for example, to constitute a sort of vulgar evolutionary ethics: a system, in any case, which doesn't know how to distinguish a mere 'is' from the genuine moral or normative 'ought' (for 'is's are what all of our forms of judgment, A through E, might seem in truth to record). And such a theory might seem to give a wrong position to natural facts in the formation of ethical judgment, to turn ethics into a sub-discipline of biology, and thus to deny what is legitimately called the 'autonomy of ethics'. It might seem to lend an 'unconvincing speaking part', as David Wiggins puts it, to facts about our nature. It might seem to express an unsound desire to give a sort of external 'grounding' to ethics, as John McDowell has put it, a grounding ethics doesn't need and can't have.[9] It might,

[9] David Wiggins, 'Truth, Invention and the Meaning of Life,' in his *Needs, Value and Truth*, 2nd ed. (Oxford: Blackwell, 1991), 87–138, 134 note 53; John McDowell, 'Two Sorts of Naturalism,' in R. Hursthouse, W. Quinn and G. Lawrence, (eds.) *Op. cit.*, 149–80, see, e.g., 150–1.

finally, seem to medicalize moral badness, to reduce it to a sort of psychological and volitional ill health.

Each of these complaints rests, I think, on at least one of the empiricist theses, all of which are, I think, false. The threat of 'biologism', as we might express their common theme, only holds if the concept *human*—which for the naturalist is the highest concept of practical philosophy, one which all of our genuinely normative predication implicitly involves—is an empirical and biological concept, and only if all substantive knowledge about the human life form is empirical and biological knowledge. If that is right, then the critique of normative naturalism as biologistic presupposes a biologistic conception of the representation of life, a conception encoded in our empiricist theses, a conception according to which truth about the human form must come into the practical intelligence 'from outside'. Perhaps, that is, it is not the normative naturalist who is importing a coarse empiricism into the discussion, but her critic.

Against the empiricist propositions

Let us begin with the empiricist thought that the concept of a life form is an empirical concept like the concept of a quantum state or a mammal. Against this, I would like to claim that the concept *life form* is more akin to such logical or quasi-logical notions as *object, property, relation, fact,* or *process.*

A first and rather intuitive sign of this, I think, is to be found in the extreme plasticity of the five forms of speech and judgment we discussed at the outset. A life form, we might say, is something a representation of which can take the position of 'S' in those and perhaps some other related forms. But it is intuitively clear that we can get readings of 'S' that are utterly different from one another in material content. The umbrella jelly, the hayscented fern, the spirochete, the human being, slime molds, turnips, tarantulas: how much more different can things get? Yet in all cases our five forms of judgment find a foothold. We see nothing unintelligible in imagining even more violently different forms of life arising on other planets, or even under different regimes of fundamental physical law. It seems that a very abstract grammar finds a place in the description of all these things, the grammar we found by reflecting on your study of the umbrella jelly. This intellectual structure is not a response to a common empirical feature of things, but is somehow carried into the scene. It is in this respect, I think, that the grammar of the representation of life is akin the grammars of thing and property, thing and relation, and thing and process, each of which too can assume wildly various sorts of content and coloration.

The a priori character of the idea of a life form becomes clearer, I think, if we reflect once again on the reciprocal dependence between natural historical judgments, the general atemporal judgments about life forms, S, and the temporal or tensed vital descriptions of individual organisms X.

One's first naive thought is that a typical vital description of an individual living thing is just a matter of studying what is going on with the individual taken by itself. I set my sights on a definite region of space, one occupied by an organism, and declare what is there. It is then by intelligently assembling these form-independent vital descriptions of individuals that I first build my way up to any general claims about a life form I might suppose these individuals bear—which is of course exactly how things *would* stand if I were proposing to frame general propositions of a statistical nature or a proposition bearing Fregean generality.

But, as I have already suggested, almost everything we think of an individual organism involves at least implicit thought of its form. Consider, to emphasize the point, that determinate phenomena of life can be quite differently constituted, physically speaking, and that, on the other hand, similarly constituted things can add up to quite different phenomena of life. The wings of a dragonfly and the wings of a sparrow have little in common; and the wings of a young dragonfly or sparrow would still have been wings even if, thanks to prompt predators, they never got to the point of actually being used in flight. By contrast, the division of an amoeba and the division of a human cell have a *lot* in common; the essentials are described in some detail on the same pages of the average introductory text. But while amoeba division is reproduction of amoeba-kind, human cell division is not the reproduction of humankind. The description of something as *a wing*, or of a process as one of *reproduction*, is thus not a matter of the material constitution of the thing taken just by itself—no more than the description of a person as telling someone something is a merely physical description of sounds or vibrations in the air. In another language the same sounds might amount to telling someone something different; and the same thing might be told elsewhere in quite different sounds. Applications of the concepts *wing* and *reproduction* to individuals are everywhere implicitly mediated by an appeal to the underlying life form which the individual exemplifies, an item potentially described in a system of general propositions of the type discussed above.

This 'externalism' would seem to pervade the description of things precisely as alive: the living being, as living, points beyond itself in a quite particular way; the idea of a life form, as something atemporally describable, and as something at least potentially borne by many individuals, seems to be contained in the idea of life as a process that unfolds in time.[10] On reflection, that is, it appears that our

[10] This point is laboured with numerous examples in my essay 'The Representation of Life', part 3. The language of 'externalism' is perhaps inapt, suggesting as it might that the vital description of an individual depends somehow on facts about other 'external' individual bearers of the life form in question. The look beyond the individual in the framing of a vital description is not to the 'community' of bearers of the life form but to the life form itself. (The parallel distinction should be observed in the interpretation of Wittgenstein: an appeal to features of the 'practice' into which the use of a word is inserted, or of the 'form of life' of which it is a part, is very different from an appeal to facts about the 'community' of bearers of that practice or form of life considered *in extenso*. A form must in general be distinguished from the manifold of its bearers.)

I am not sure that it is a priori that a life form must have (or have had or be going to have) more than one bearer, though I think we know of no other way for the duality in question to be realized in nature as we know it to be—in particular I think we know no other way for such a thing to be constituted than by a system that includes, *inter alia*, a phenomenon of reproduction. (A theological theoretical infrastructure, for example, might lead one to entertain other possibilities.) What seems to be excluded a priori is the idea of a life form that is essentially bound to just one material bearer—a 'logically private' life form, so to speak.

whole five-fold grammar comes into deployment together. If this is right, then we are very far from an account of the concept *life form* as an abstract precipitate of observation, which is the claim contained in our first empiricist proposition. The concept of a life form, or the specific form of generality associated with it—or the apprehension of the concomitant form of unity of *things happening here* with *things happening there*—are everywhere at work in any materials of experience from which it might be abstracted. We arrive at an explicit conception of it by reflection on certain of the forms of thought of which we are capable—as we arrive, for example, at the general concept *relation*. The opposition of *individual organism* and *life form* is, as we might say, a more determinate form of the opposition of *individual* and *universal* in general, and shares the a priori character the latter.[11]

[11] It might be suggested, in view of the linguistic analogy developed above, that a similar argument could show that the concept *language* is a pure or a priori concept. It may be so, but it seems clearer that the superordinate concept of a 'practice' or 'social practice' possesses the desired apriority, as is shown again by the distinctive turn taken by the intellect in apprehending such a thing, in particular by the distinctive form of generality contained in the propositions that describe it. See my 'Two Forms of Practical Generality,' *Practical Rationality and Preference,* C. Morris and A. Ripstein (eds.) (Cambridge: Cambridge University Press, 2002).

It is of course clear that the *words* 'species' and 'life form' *might* be assigned a content that presupposes facts of terrestrial biology. In the literature on method in biology there is a contest among various 'species concepts,' and the contestants inevitably contain some empirical content. Consider, for example, Ernst Mayr's famous

Skip now to the third empiricist proposition, that every singular representation of an individual organism is somehow grounded on observation. This would be obviously false if it meant that I could not think of an individual organism except where it is presented to my senses. I might manage to single out an individual organism for thinking of through memory of past observation, or through a hypothesis founded on traces the thing has left, foot prints for example; or I might acquire the use of a proper name for the thing from other peoples' testimony; or from some combination of these things. The empiricist thought would

'biological species concept.' A 'species,' he says, is a group of interbreeding populations. This can be criticized on the ground that not every kind of organism breeds: dandelions don't for example. But it works in many terrestrial cases and where it does it gives clear answers to the question whether two organisms belong to the same or different species. But it seems to me to *presuppose* the vaguer more abstract conception we are after, a conception for which we might reserve the title 'life form'; it presupposes it because it presupposes vital description, e.g. in the use of the concept of breeding, and this is everywhere form dependent. But this more primitive concept would not lead us a priori to expect that sameness and difference of life form should be clearly specifiable, a task empirically informed definitions like Mayr's are attempting to execute.

The idea of a language might once again be used as a model here. We do not expect that the question whether two speakers speak the same or different languages should always have a clear answer. But this unclarity does not lead us to drop the idea of language in philosophy. We say, despite this inevitable vagueness, that it is only because they are speaking a common language, or inhabit a common discursive structure, that any determinate content can be assigned to the noises traded by the parties to a discussion.

be that all of these possibilities must rest in the final analysis in some sort of observation somewhere, that is, on some sort of passivity in relation to the organism in question.

Though it has the ring of truth about it, it seems plain that the proposition is false. It fails to take account of the peculiar singular representation mature humans are able to effect, a representation, namely, of themselves through the first person, or through the *I*-concept. This representation has a completely different status from any we might have envisaged in thinking about your intellectual labour upon the umbrella jellies. Its connection with the thing it is about does not arise from the user's sensuous passivity in relation to the intended object. A use of *I* or 'I' is connected to the thing it is about by the fact that the thing it is about is using it in thought or speech. As not resting on link to observation, the *I*-concept is in some sense a non-empirical or a priori representation. This of course does not keep it from acting, in each case of its use, as a singular representation of what is in fact an individual thinking organism, one which, say, occupies a certain amount of space.

Let us piece together these two facts—the apriority of the idea of a life form and that of the first person concept. It is then easy to see that each of us can readily come into possession of an a priori representation of what is in fact the human life form, thus defeating the second empiricist proposition. This holds despite the fact that this life form is one with a natural history like any other, characterized by a certain number of teeth and bones and an unusually large brain. Each of us can lay hold of this item in thought under the title 'my life form' or 'the life form I bear', descriptions which contain no empirical content at all. Just as I can think the empirical thought, *I have a wounded knee*, using a non-empirical representation as subject, so I can think the empirical thought, *the life form I bear has several other bearers in this room*, with this non-empirical subject term.

Someone might raise the objection that it might be open to doubt whether I actually bear any life form. So maybe the definite description 'the life form I bear' could fail to answer to anything, as the description 'the present King of France' does; though the concept is pure, perhaps it is empty. Certainly it doesn't seem to carry its referent onto the scene as each use of 'I' and the *I*-concept does. But this of course is to overlook that deployments of the idea of *my life form* will be in acts of self-conscious thought or speech. Thought and speech are phenomena of life if anything is. So the characterization of an individual organism here and now as thinking or speaking, like the characterization of it as eating or breathing or leafing out, is a life form-dependent description: take it away the life form and we have a pile of electrochemical connections; put it back in and we have hunger and pain and breathing and walking, indeed, but, in suitable cases, self-conscious thought and discourse as well. The life form *underwrites* the applicability of these diverse state- and process-types in individual cases.

Though it might seem an unwholesome Cartesian manoeuvre, it is I think harmless to re-express the a priori concept in question, or anyway to formulate another, in some such terms as these. Rather than speaking of 'my life form' we might speak of 'the life form of which this very thought is a manifestation' or 'the life form that underwrites the character of this very thought as thought'. So I might think, on empirical grounds, but truly, something like this: *the life form that underwrites the character of this very thought as thought has several other bearers in this room.* Though this is an empirical proposition, it contains a non-empirical representation which is in fact a representation of the human life form. My life form comes into this thought by its being manifested or exemplified in the thought itself, rather as I come into my *I*-thoughts by being the thinker of them.

In the self-conscious representation of myself as thinking, as in all my self-conscious self-representation, I implicitly represent myself as alive, as falling under life-manifesting types. And in bringing myself under such types I bring myself under a life form. I carry our five fold grammar onto the scene, and with it the life form position. Self-consciousness is thus always implicitly form-consciousness. I might now engage in the sceptical doubt whether this life form of mine has any *other* bearers, and I might not know much about how to fill in the blanks in our five forms—but I bring the basic duality of life form and individual bearer into the picture.

Whichever path we take, it seems to follow then that every reflective human being is able to lay hold of the human life form through something other than observation, and is thus able to conceive it through something other than a so-called biological concept.

Though these remarks, if they are right, suffice for a refutation of the second empiricist proposition, it might be thought that the characterizations I have offered are a bit sophisticated. They don't seem quite to capture the concept *human*, or quite what is expressed by words like 'human', *Mensch*, *homo* or *anthropos*, though they designate what is in fact the same thing. The concept *human* seems to be a simple and rustic concept, one not involving any subtle use of the first person or a covert reference to something like 'this very thought'. That is quite right, it seems to me, but can easily be remedied without introducing any empirical material into the story.

Everyone grants that it is in the nature of the first person concept to refer to the thinker of the thought in which it is deployed; that is the kind of concept it is; that is its 'character', in Kaplan's language.[12] It would be inept, though, to *analyse* the *I*-concept as the complex concept *the thinker of this very thought*. But only slightly inept: it is an equivalent concept, at least in ordinary extensional contexts; it can replace the *I*-concept in any such thought. *The thinker of this very thought is wearing shoes*, I might judge.

There was perhaps a similar slight ineptness in our account of the concept *human*. Here too we should simply say that it belongs to the character of the concept *human* to refer to, or lay hold of, the life form manifested in particular deployments of that concept; that is the kind of concept *human* is. It is, if you like, the 'first life form' concept. Its function is to bring into explicit thought the life form that mediates the relation between the thinking subject and the

[12] David Kaplan, 'A Logic of Demonstratives,' *Themes from Kaplan*, J. Almog, J. Perry and H. Wettstein (eds.) (New York: Oxford University Press, 1989).

act of thought in which this concept is deployed, i.e., the life form that underwrites the character of the latter precisely as thought. Its reference thus depends on the thought in which it appears, but it does not itself refer to that thought or to the thinker of it. This entails that in some sense Martians and twin humans might deploy the same concept, or work the same intellectual function, as we do, but that in deploying it they will be bringing their own different life forms under discussion. Similarly, a Martian might possess the first person concept, as I do, but his deployments of it will refer to himself and not to me.

I said that our normative naturalists are marked off by the central place they give to the concept *human* in practical philosophy, as its highest concept and the index of the generality of its most abstract principles. This feature of these doctrines has been greeted with alarm by the larger literature as introducing something empirical or even biological into ethical theory. If the present line of thought is sound, we can I think see that there is nothing in this. The concept *human* is a pure concept of the understanding devoid of even the least empirical accretion. We no more poison our practical philosophy by using it to set our theme therein, than we do our rational psychology by taking the *I think* as setting our theme *therein.*

In suggesting, for example, that the concept *human* marks the most extensive scope that I can intelligibly attach to my substantive general practical thoughts—e.g., to my judgments about what reasons 'one' 'has'—our naturalist is saying that the most extensive scope these thoughts can have is whatever scope may be had by *the life form that is manifested in these very thoughts*, and which underwrites their character as thoughts. That is: wherever we may find instanced *that by which this thought is thought*, there this thought may have application. In this exposition of the generality of fundamental practical propositions there is no appeal to any biological concept nor to any concept alien to practical thought: there is appeal only to what, as its formal element, constitutes practical thought as thought and as practical.

Materials are now in place for a prompt refutation of the two empiricist propositions that have to do with knowledge. We have seen that certain representations of individual organisms, of particular life forms, and of at least one abstract category, viz. *life form* itself, do not derive from observation—and thus for sure are not specifically biological representations. Can we now find substantive thoughts into which these representations are inserted, which likewise do not depend, for the knowing of them, on empirical observation?

The first of these empiricist propositions, the fourth on my list, says that all knowledge of vital descriptions about individual organisms is founded on observation.

Again it seems plain that this proposition must fall immediately. The self-knowledge you possess in self-conscious awareness of your psychological states would once again seem to supply an easy refutation. That you are in pain or are hungry or that you are thinking something are, after all, as much vital phenomena as that your heart is beating. They presuppose among other things the presence in you of a life form with pain- and hunger-potential and a power of thought (see below); yet you are able to bring yourself under these particular vital descriptions—I'm hungry, I'm in pain, I think there's something wrong with my liver—without adverting to any inner or outer observation of yourself much less of your life form or kind.

A more interesting type of case for our ultimately practical purposes was familiarly investigated by Elizabeth Anscombe: namely, my knowledge of what I am doing, where I am doing it fully intentionally.[13] This knowledge is, at least in many ordinary cases, again not founded on observation of the thing known. Consider for example my knowledge that I am taking the camera upstairs to put it away, if that's what I'm doing. I might declare this knowledge to you as I leave the kitchen table. Of course, this is the sort of thing I could be wrong about. Maybe an abyss has opened between me and the staircase, or maybe I'm confused, and the house I'm in doesn't have a second floor. Then it wouldn't be true and I wouldn't have knowledge. But in many ordinary cases my thought that I am taking the camera upstairs will be true, and it will be knowledge. But this knowledge will not be founded on any sort of observation, inner or outer, of my movements. For one thing, having just got up from the kitchen table, there has simply been too little to observe. Any number of things can happen after a man gets up from the kitchen table. As it is, though, *I'm taking the camera upstairs*, and I know this. It would indeed be strange to call this cognition a priori, but it seems

[13] *Intention* (Cambridge: Harvard University Press, 2000).

it would also be wrong to call it empirical or observation-recording. Of course, the self-same fact, the same worldly process, might be known by another human being through observation—once, say, I make it to the point of getting to the stairs, camera in hand. Here there are two forms of knowledge, but not two things known.

However that may be, our fourth empiricist proposition has evidently fallen. Let us turn then to the fifth, which is that all substantive *general* knowledge of the human or any life form must arise from observation. It seems to me that we can give a few easy counter-examples to this empiricist proposition as well, based immediately on the arguments we gave against the last one. The epistemologies of pain and hunger and thought and perhaps of intentional action are, we saw, non-observationalist in the first person. But consider again that pain and hunger and thought and concept-governed action are not the sorts of things that we can attribute to individual organisms as private peculiarities, like a small scar on the forehead, or a thought about the far corner of this room. Individual states and episodes coming under the general types *pain, hunger, conceptual thought* and *intentional action* must always be realizations of a *capacity* that is characteristic of the life form of the pained or hungering or thinking or intentionally acting individual organism. These are not things that could break out in a rogue individual where they have no place in the description of the life form it bears; no more than a case of long division could break out in a person unacquainted with any methods of calculation, whatever it may be that he is doing with his pencil. Of many kinds of organism I recognize by observation that they possess capacities for pain or hunger, that these phenomena are a part of how they live and get on—that there is, as Ludwig Wittgenstein would say, a 'place' for pain and hunger in such life. These are propositions of type B on our list. And of Martians I may perhaps recognize by empirical study, through my telescope, that they possess the powers of conceptual thought and concept-governed action; this is again a proposition of type B. But it seems I, as a human, may reach the same general facts about the specifically human form without a telescope. I can reach them by reflection on the logical conditions of particular facts about myself which are not themselves matters of observation. These general facts about the human would once again be expressed in propositions of type B. But I do not know these facts about my kind or form 'from the outside' or 'from sideways on'; they are for me not matters of a properly biological awareness. Of course, the self-same facts *would* be matters of empirical cognition for a Martian investigator, and in that case known very much from sideways on, as the correlative facts about *Martian* are for me. Here again there are two forms of knowledge, but not two things known.

These examples are perhaps in some respects *recherché*, but they are, I think, quite enough to kill off our fifth empiricist proposition. They show that we have ways of knowing some substantive propositions that bear the generality that is our theme apart from anything like biological observation; we have, if you like, ways of knowing things about our own life form 'from within'.

Conclusion

And this means—doesn't it?—that we have provided an opening, however narrow it may be, for the possibility of a naturalist interpretation of the content of normative judgment. We have provided an opening, that is, for the view that our fundamental moral and practical knowledge—our knowledge of good and evil and of what is rational and irrational in human action—is at the same time knowledge implicitly about the specifically human form, knowledge of how the well-working human practical reason reasons, yet in no way a biological or empirical knowledge or any sort of knowledge that derives from observation. For it seems that the character of knowledge as *knowledge of a substantive general proposition about a life form* does nothing to settle its character as empirical or biological—no more, as the case of intentional action shows, than the character of knowledge as *knowledge of a process unfolding in the world* does anything to settle *its* character as observational or otherwise empirical.

We have non-observational knowledge in self-consciousness of certain of our inner states, and a special practical knowledge of certain of the processes of which we are the subject, and moreover a knowledge by reflection of some of the powers characteristic of the form we bear; what is to be said against the idea that we might have another kind of practical knowledge—*ethical* knowledge, if you like—of certain norms that attach to us as bearers of a particular life form characterized by practical reason? As my thinking representation of what I am doing intentionally is an *aspect* of what this representation itself is about, so this latter cognition will be an aspect of the life characteristic of the developed human subject and will characteristically mediate her practical operations. Such cognition goes to constitute the form of life in question as one in which the things cognized are true. I speak, as usual, of what is 'characteristic': in individual bearers of the human form, some of this knowledge will often enough go missing, of course, as often some teeth are missing; or the knowledge will be present but nevertheless fail to make it into the determination of action.

In representing my propositions as possessing so-called normative authority, or as expressing something more than private taste or local custom—in reaching, that is, for the concepts *good* and *well* in this connection—I implicitly represent my propositions, the naturalist will say, as possessing the status just described. I represent them not simply as manifestations of the form I bear, as all my thoughts (and heartbeats) are, but as characteristic of the form I bear. I thus represent myself as in this respect in possession of a sound practical understanding *qua* bearer of this form. If all has gone well in the development of my understanding—improbably enough—then my propositions will in fact have this status. And, moreover, I will not be damaging my daughter, or casting spells on her, or binding her feet spiritually speaking, or turning her into a practical bonsai, if I coax *her* into accrediting them as well, by example and precept; for this, on any view, is part of how an organism of this type is brought into apprehension of practical truth. Of course we have no way of judging what practical thoughts and what range of upbringings might be characteristic of the human, and sound in a human, except through application of our fundamental practical judgments—judgments about what makes sense and what might count as a reason and so forth. And these are judgments each of us must recognize to be the result of his own upbringing and reflection.

As these very preliminary remarks suggest, a developed normative naturalism will no doubt assign our general practical knowledge a precise epistemological position that differs from any we contemplated above. It would take another essay, or a treatise, to develop the matter properly—in particular to resolve the very difficult problem of the mediation of a human's apprehension of fundamental practical truth by his induction into more local, specific, determinate so-called social practices, or shapes of *Bildung* or 'second nature'. My present point is only this, that the idea that recognition of the human form is everywhere empirical cannot be permitted smugly to operate as an *a priori* impediment to the development of a naturalist account.[14]

[14] Very much less, of course, can a manly wisdom about the bloody course of human history be set against the claim that, say, justice belongs 'according to nature' to the human practical understanding; no more than knowledge of the bloody—well, not exactly *bloody*—course of umbrella jelly history considered *in extenso*—in which what happens in your natural history has so rarely happened, almost everything having been thrown against rocks, starved, or eaten by predators—be brought as proof of Pollyannaism against your monograph. This point does not turn on epistemological subtleties, but on the logical form of the propositions in question.

The specifically human form does not come into our thoughts and intelligences as something alien, from without, through the medium of the senses, but as the form these things themselves manifest it is utterly transparent to them.[15]

[15] To paraphrase Gottlob Frege's summary remark about our apprehension of the numbers, *The Foundations of Arithmetic*, trans. J. L. Austin (Oxford: Blackwells, 1974), 115.

Does Modern Moral Philosophy Rest on a Mistake?*

ROGER CRISP

Someone once told me that the average number of readers of a philosophy article is about six. That is a particularly depressing thought when one takes into account the huge influence of certain articles. When I think of, say, Gettier's article on knowledge, or Quine's 'Two Dogmas', I begin to wonder whether anyone is ever likely to read anything I write. Usually the arguments of these very influential articles have been subjected to widespread analysis and interpretation. The case of Elizabeth Anscombe's 'Modern Moral Philosophy', published in 1958, is something of an exception.[1] That article has played a significant part in the development of so-called 'virtue ethics', which has burgeoned over the last three decades in particular. But there

* For comments on and discussion of previous drafts, or for other assistance, I am grateful to my audience at the Royal Institute and to Brendan Biggs, John Broome, Krister Bykvist, Jonathan Dancy, Peter Geach, Brad Hooker, Margaret Howatson, Matthew Leigh, Andrew Mason, Christopher Megone, Anthony O'Hear, Derek Parfit, Catherine Paxton, Tom Pink, Michael Ridge, Daniel Robinson, Julian Savulescu, J. B. Schneewind, John Skorupski, Philip Stratton-Lake, John Tasioulas, David Wiggins, and Bernard Williams.

[1] Anscombe, 1997.

has been less close attention to its arguments than one might have expected.[2]

Anscombe's first sentence is: 'I will begin by stating three theses which I present in this paper'. Let me start with three of my own. The first is that historical and philosophical analysis throw some doubt on her main thesis, which concerns the moral concepts. Second, I shall suggest, we appear to have more in common, ethically, with Aristotle and the Greeks than Anscombe—and certain other writers, such as Alasdair MacIntyre and Bernard Williams—believe.[3] Finally, however, I shall conclude that Anscombe's strategy of examining the moral concepts before using them in moral theory is helpful, and that the application of that strategy to the very notion of morality itself supports something closer to the 'consequentialist' position she attacks in her paper than to her own.

The moral concepts

Anscombe's own three theses are the following: (1) *the profitability claim:* it is not at present profitable for us to do moral philosophy: (2) *the conceptual claim:* the concepts of 'moral obligation', 'moral duty', what is 'morally right and wrong', and 'ought' in its moral sense should be discarded; (3) *the triviality claim:* the differences between English moral philosophers since Sidgwick are of little significance.[4]

[2] See, however, Baier, 1988; Diamond, 1988; Pigden, 1988; Richter, 1995.

[3] See MacIntyre, 1981, esp. chs. 1, 9, 12; Williams, 1985, 5–6, ch. 10.

[4] Anscombe, 1997, 26. All parenthetical references in the text are to this article.

The conceptual claim, I take it, is meant to provide some support for the profitability claim, the thought being that some preparatory work outside ethics will be needed to provide us with material for ethical thought, once the language of obligation has been discarded. The triviality claim, in essence, is that the most significant characteristic of the views of these modern philosophers is that they will permit the punishment of the innocent, in certain circumstances, and that this puts them at odds with the Hebrew—Christian ethic (35). Even if it were true that there were this significant difference, however, it is not clear why other differences might not also be significant, even if less so (for example, these philosophers will differ greatly on the circumstances in which such punishment is acceptable).[5] But it is anyway not clear that the Hebrew–Christian tradition has absolutely forbidden killing the innocent. Augustine, for instance, allowed that enemy soldiers may be killed in a war, even though they may be completely innocent.[6] I intend, therefore, to focus on the conceptual claim, and, as does Anscombe, on 'ought' in particular.

Anscombe's suggestion is that the views of modern moral philosophers (i.e. those since Butler) are stated using

[5] It might be said that punishment of the innocent, in certain circumstances, is an example of something that is wrong whatever the consequences, and that what characterizes this group of English philosophers is that they can make no room for that idea. But this is incorrect. Utilitarians, for example, believe it is wrong not to perform the action that maximizes utility, whatever the consequences (torture, the death of innocents, promise-breaking. . .).

[6] See Hartigan, 1966, 201–2.

moral concepts, such as 'ought', which have now lost the context within which they once made sense. There is a perfectly respectable use of 'ought'—we might call it the 'non-moral "ought"'—which relates straightforwardly to non-moral goodness or badness. For example,

> 'This engine ought to be oiled' means something like, 'Running without oil is bad for this engine'. But such concepts have now acquired a special so-called 'moral' sense—i.e. a sense in which they imply some absolute verdict (like one of guilty/not guilty on a man) on what is described in the 'ought' sentences used in certain types of context... [They] acquired this special sense by being equated in the relevant contexts with 'is obliged', or 'is bound', or 'is required to', in the sense in which one can be obliged or bound by law (30).

This legalistic sense of 'ought', Anscombe suggests, emerged from Christianity's 'law conception' of ethics, that is, a conception according to which 'what is needed for conformity with the virtues failure in which is the mark of being bad *qua* man... is required by divine law' (31).[7] I take it that, in

[7] Anscombe's conceptual claim was made by Arthur Schopenhauer, in his criticism of Kant in *On the Basis of Morality,* first published in 1841: 'Every ought is... necessarily conditioned by punishment or reward... But if those conditions are thought away, the concept of ought or obligation is left without any meaning: and so *absolute obligation* is certainly a *contradicto in adjecto*... Putting ethics in an *imperative* form as a *doctrine of duties,* and thinking of the moral worth or worthlessness of human actions as the fulfillment or violation of *duties,* undeniably spring, together with the *obligation,* solely from theological morals, and accordingly from the Decalogue' (Schopenhauer, 1995, 55–6; cf. 53–4,

fact, Anscombe would count as a law conception any view according to which there is a divine law governing our action, and would not wish to restrict that notion only to conceptions of ethics expressed in terms of the virtues.[8] For her view is that the claim of a modern utilitarian, for example, that we ought, morally, to maximize utility, may be taken to be equivalent to the claim that divine law requires us to maximize utility. And herein lies the problem: Most modern utilitarians would not accept the existence of any such law. All that remains is the 'psychological' force of the notion (primarily, presumably, some kind of 'anti-attitude' to those who do what it is believed they ought not), and very little else. 'Ought' is 'a word retaining the suggestion of force, and apt to have a strong psychological

56–8, 68, 103, 130). Professor Peter Geach has told me (in a private communication, for which I am most grateful) that, as far as he knows, Anscombe had little direct knowledge of Schopenhauer's work, but that he and Wittgenstein would certainly have talked to her about Schopenhauer. Indeed, it appears from a report by Waismann, cited by Pigden (1988, 32–3, n. 10), that Wittgenstein himself accepted certain elements of Schopenhauer's position. The terms used by Anscombe in connection with certain other philosophers (Butler ('ignorant'), Kant ('absurd'), Mill ('stupid')) cannot help but remind one of the tone Schopenhauer takes towards Hegel in his preface. There is some irony in the use of emotive language in an argument directed against, among others, the emotivists.

[8] John Tasioulas has pointed out to me that implicit within Anscombe's view there appears to be a dubious conception of law, thrown into serious doubt by the work of H. L. A. Hart, as an imperative issued by some authority and backed up by sanctions. Later in this paper I shall offer a more relaxed notion of a 'law conception' as a set of binding constraints.

effect, but which no longer signifies a real concept at all' (33). As Anscombe puts it, the modern usage of 'ought' is 'as if the notion "criminal" were to remain when criminal law and criminal courts had been abolished and forgotten... [W]here one does not think there is a judge or law, the notion of a verdict may retain its psychological effect, but not its meaning' (31, 33).[9] And, of course, Anscombe takes these claims to apply to all of the moral concepts she mentions, not only 'ought', and recommends:

> We should no longer ask whether doing something was 'wrong', passing directly from some description of an action to this notion; we should ask whether, e.g., it was unjust; and the answer would sometimes be clear at once (34).

Anscombe's position, then, is an artful one, given the philosophical milieu of the late nineteen-fifties. Essentially, she is accepting, in broad terms, much of what the emotivists and the prescriptivists said about the force of 'ought', but suggesting that once we see that this force is all that the concept gives us then it cannot serve in serious moral philosophy.

The return to Aristotle

Anscombe supports her argument through a contrast between modern usage and that found in Aristotle's *Ethics* (26–7). In particular, she suggests, the modern sense of 'moral' is nowhere to be found in Aristotle. Aristotle

[9] One is reminded here of the spooky scenario described in the opening pages of MacIntyre, 1981, in which science has been all but forgotten, with a few fragments remaining entirely out of context.

distinguishes between the 'moral' and the 'intellectual' virtues, but the intellectual virtues themselves have what we would describe as a 'moral' aspect, in so far as certain intellectual failures are seen by Aristotle as blameworthy. We might want to say '*morally* blameworthy'.

> Now has Aristotle got [the] idea of *moral* blame, as opposed to any other? If he has, why isn't it more central? There are some mistakes, he says, which are causes, not of involuntariness in actions but of scoundrelism, and for which a man is blamed. Does this mean that there is a *moral* obligation not to make certain intellectual mistakes? Why doesn't he discuss obligation in general, and this obligation in particular? If someone professes to be expounding Aristotle and talks in a modern fashion about 'moral' such-and-such, he must be very imperceptive if he does not constantly feel like someone whose jaws have somehow got out of alignment: the teeth don't come together in a proper bite.

Given the conceptual claim, and the claim that the problematic notion of obligation is absent from Aristotle's thought, we can understand Anscombe's recommendation that we return to an essentially Aristotelian form of virtue ethics—though, she says, we should begin with psychology rather than with straightforward first-order ethics, seeking to understand concepts such as 'action', 'intention', and 'virtue' more clearly than did Aristotle himself (30, 37).[10]

[10] Anscombe says that she sees 'no harm' in moving towards an Aristotelian conception, as opposed to a law conception, of ethics (40). But later in her article (43–4), she appears to express some doubt about the enterprise. For further discussion, see below, 85–6.

'Ought' and necessity

Let me turn to Anscombe's general position on the moral concepts. An important preliminary point is that, even if Anscombe were right about the special modern sense of 'ought', it would not follow that we should return to any particular first-order ethics, such as one with any close similarity in content to Aristotle's or indeed Anscombe's. For it might well be that many modern debates—such as those between Rossian intuitionists and utilitarians—could be carried on in the terminology of virtue (is gratitude, say, a self-standing virtue, or is every other alleged virtue to be subsumed under benevolence?). Anscombe's strategy is to suggest that, in returning to Aristotle, we drop the notions of 'ought', 'right', and 'wrong' entirely, and use only what Williams has called the 'thick concepts',[11] such as 'injustice' (40).[12] Her hope is that we shall also accept that an action's being unjust is a matter of fact, and always avoid injustice, because, on the assumption that the virtues could not conflict, we no longer have the conceptual apparatus to ask whether there may be cases in which injustice would be right (40–1). Again, even if Anscombe's history were right, we might wonder whether we could not raise the question in Aristotelian terms whether a virtuous person might not in certain circumstances procure the punishment of the

[11] Williams, 1985, 129.

[12] If anything like my account of 'ought' below is correct, it is doubtful whether one could unpack the content of thick moral concepts without reference to thin.

innocent, or, indeed, whether we might not invent some new moral concept in which this question could be asked.[13]

Now consider Anscombe's 'criminal' analogy. What might be going on in the culture in which judicial institutions have been forgotten? There would of course be no place for the use of the term within those very institutions. But it might well be used of those who commit certain actions which were once crimes, such as assault. If so, the most plausible initial interpretation would be not that 'criminal' no longer had any sense, but that it had changed its sense to become equivalent to something like 'morally bad individual'. So we should ask whether, even if Anscombe is

[13] Anscombe recognizes the former possibility: 'It may be possible, if we are resolute, to discard the term 'morally ought', and simply return to the ordinary 'ought', which, we ought to notice, is such an extremely frequent term of human language that it is difficult to imagine getting on without it. Now if we do return to it, can't it reasonably be asked whether one might ever need to commit injustice, or whether it won't be the best thing to do? Of course it can' (43). Anscombe goes on to repeat her point that we cannot decide such questions at present because 'philosophically there is a huge gap, at present unfillable as far as we are concerned, which needs to be filled by an account of human nature, human action, the type of characteristic a virtue is' (43–4). But this raises the question how Anscombe felt entitled to such certainty herself in this paper about what justice required. One is reminded again of that other project in virtue ethics which combines deep pessimism about the fragmentary resources of current ethics with a strong first-order recommendation to return to Aristotle: that of Alasdair MacIntyre, and especially his *After Virtue* (1981). Seeing these positions as in internal tension is of course consistent with accepting that moral philosophy—at least the moral philosophy of the mid-twentieth century—could have done more with virtue-concepts.

right about the past sense of 'ought', the term might not have taken on some new sense.[14]

Recall that Anscombe allows for uses of 'ought'—non-moral uses—which involve no reference to divine law, such as, 'This engine ought to be oiled'. As I have said, Anscombe sees this as equivalent to something like, 'Running without oil is bad for this engine'. But this seems to leave out any reference to action. That phrase, in the standard case, is better seen as amounting to, roughly, '[Given that you want this engine to function], you have a reason to oil it'. That is, it is something resembling what Kant would have called a hypothetical imperative. So we shall need to ask whether there is space in our conceptual scheme for something like a Kantian categorical imperative, an action-guiding analogue to Anscombe's 'absolute verdict'.

With these thoughts in mind, let me now address the contrast Anscombe attempts to draw between Aristotle and modern moral philosophy. Anscombe asks whether Aristotle has the notion of 'moral blame', as opposed to any other. Her example of non-moral blame is criticism of the workmanship of a product or the design of a machine, but this is problematic, since such blame could well be understood to be moral criticism of the worker or designer,

[14] It is a little surprising to find the Wittgensteinian Anscombe looking not to use but to etymology. A simple 'open question argument' (Moore, 1903, 15–17) throws the onus directly onto Anscombe: Whether 'ought' means 'required by divine legislation' seems an entirely open question, which fact at least suggests that the senses of each are different.

of her lack of conscientiousness or attention to detail, perhaps. A better example might be someone's blaming the weather for ruining their holiday. Such blame (if that is what it is) may have certain properties in common with some paradigm cases of moral blame: One may be angry at the weather, for example. But what is missing is the possibility of holding the object blamed responsible, on the assumption that the object has the capacity to act for reasons, and may now have to pay the penalty for not doing so appropriately in this case. Does Aristotle have this idea of moral blame? He does: Praise and blame fix the boundaries of the voluntary, which he seeks to elucidate in the first five chapters of the third book of the *Ethics*, and he frequently notes that the excesses and deficiencies of character that constitute the vices are to be avoided as blameworthy.[15] It is central to his conception of ethics.

But what of the law conception of ethics? Surely that is not to be found in Aristotle? Anscombe is of course right that Aristotle does not claim that we must be virtuous because it is required by divine law.[16] But her claim that

[15] See e.g. Aristotle, 1894 (*EN*) 1109b30–31, 1126b7. The contrast between 'moral' and 'intellectual' virtues in Aristotle noted by Anscombe (26–7) is between virtues of character and those of thought. Aristotle's 'morally good person' would be required to possess both.

[16] This is not to say that the notion was alien to the Greeks. Zeus came to be seen as the most prominent of the gods, and part of his role was to punish moral transgressions. This aspect of Zeus can be found even in Homer (C8 BCE) (Lloyd-Jones, 1983, 7, 77–8) (see also Hesiod, 1990, e.g. 9–10, 238–9). See in general Dover, 1994, 246–61, and in particular 255, which gives some useful examples from the orators in which

the law conception led to a change in sense of 'ought' such that the word became 'equated in the relevant contexts with "is obliged", or "is bound", or "is required to", in the sense in which one can be obliged or bound by law, or something can be required by law' (30) is less plausible.[17] For that sense can be found in Aristotle. Anscombe suggests that the Greek word '*hamartanein*' was the one most apt for expressing the concept of being bound. *Hamartanein* means something like 'to miss the mark', but Anscombe fails to consider whether Aristotle may have had in mind the sense of 'missing the *moral* mark', that is, 'being bound to hit a moral target but failing'. It can be used, in deliberate contrast with *adikein* ('to commit injustice or wrong-doing'), to mean *mere* 'error', but this is not usual: '[A]ny crime or sin can be called "error" in Greek'.[18]

It is true that there is little room in Aristotle's ethics for the notions of being permitted or excused, which Anscombe sees as correlative to 'being bound' and as likewise the 'consequence of the dominance of Christianity' (30). But that is a result not so much of the language in which he states his position, but of the content of that

certain positive laws are ascribed to divine prescription. For a particularly clear expression of a divine law conception of ethics, see Sophocles, 1990, 450—7. We should remember also of course that for Aristotle theology is 'first philosophy', so that there is a theological grounding for ethics as for everything else.

17 See Baier, 1988, 128.

18 Dover, 1994, 152. One finds a similar contrast—this time between 'wickedness' and the 'frailty' of the tragic hero—in Aristotle's account of tragedy (1965, 1453a8–10).

position itself.[19] As is the case with, say, utilitarianism, and not the case with the 'Hebrew–Christian ethic' to which Anscombe subscribes, it is not easy to find room in Aristotle's ethics for 'agent-centred options',[20] or for a clear and distinct conception of supererogation.[21] There is always something that one is required to do: to act as the virtuous person would act. Any deviation from that standard would be to 'miss the mark', and that of course is never permitted. And the fact that Aristotle uses *hamartanein* in the moral context, in which missing the mark is blameworthy, unless also involuntary, shows that he does—*pace* Anscombe (30–1)—have a 'blanket term… meaning much the same as our blanket term "wrong"'. Missing the mark, in the moral context, just is acting wrongly, according to Aristotle. And to say that someone has missed the mark is to express an 'absolute verdict' on them: They have acted wrongly, and are hence candidates for blame.[22]

[19] There are of course Greek concepts Aristotle could have used: *exesti* ('it is permitted'), for example.

[20] See Kagan, 1989, 3.

[21] Aristotle does speak of 'superhuman virtue' at *EN* 1145al9. But gods and heroes likewise cannot go beyond what is required by virtue at their level.

[22] Here it is worth noting the origin of 'right' in the Latin root 'reg-', 'to make or lead straight', and the fact that 'wrong' has had as one of its senses for at least a thousand years 'having a crooked course or direction; twisted', and has been used to mean 'marked by deviation' (which is perhaps why the *OED* chooses to elucidate its moral sense as 'deviating from equity, justice, or goodness'). For these and other relevant references in my text below, see *Oxford English Dictionary* (online version), s.v.

But *hamartanein* strikes me as not the most obvious word in Aristotle to study in search of the expression of claims about moral obligations. That word is *dei*, a standard word in Greek for 'one ought', 'one should', or 'one must'.[23] It is most plausibly seen as an impersonal form of *deō*, 'to need'.[24] So it is quite natural to translate Aristotle's doctrine of the mean as follows:

> For example, fear, confidence, appetite, anger, pity, and in general pleasure and pain can be experienced too much or too little, and in both ways not well. But to have them at the time one ought [or: it is necessary; or: one is required to; or: one is obliged to; or: one is bound to; or: it would be wrong not to; or: one should; or: one must; or: one has to; or: at the right time; or:. . .], about the things one ought [or: it is necessary. . .]. . . is the mean and best.[25]

Indeed, *dei* came to be used in the fifth century, in contrast to *chrē*, for 'objective' necessities or constraints.[26]

[23] Nor of course should one forget *chrē* (see below in the text), or *adikia*, 'justice', especially the notion of 'universal justice' employed at the beginning of *EN*, bk. 5; see Pigden, 1988, 33.

[24] The principal parts speak against the hypothesis that the word is a form of *deō*, 'to bind'. But given the similarity in sense in the impersonal, it is not surprising that there has been some dispute about this. It seems likely indeed that most of the Greeks themselves would not have known the source of *dei*. Interestingly, as Margaret Howatson has pointed out to me, Liddell and Scott (1940, s.v.) say that it is the impersonal from '*deō* (A), *there is need*'. *Deō* (A) is in fact 'to bind'. This is a slip; but it is an illuminating one.

[25] *EN* 1106b18–22.

[26] See Williams, 1993, 184, who refers to Bernadete, 1965. Bernadete notes also that *dei* emphasizes the setting of a particular action (287; cf. 292),

What about the word 'ought' itself? Its history is illuminating. It is a petrified imperfect of 'to owe', which has now taken a self-standing present ('You ought to P'), past ('You ought to have P-ed'), or future sense ('When the clock strikes, you ought to P').[27] 'Owe' replaced the Old English *sculan* (a form of 'shall', from which derives 'should' ('You should P')), which meant both 'to owe' and 'to have it as a duty'.[28] Now it is almost certain that *chrē* is related to *chreos,*

and that the *dei/chrē* distinction can be used as well to capture the distinction between 'objective need' and 'self-interest' (294, n.l; cf. also in this note the reference to Aristophanes, *Ecclesiazousae* 893—6, where an old woman uses *chrē* in her attempt to entice a young man to sleep with her, and *dei* when she goes on to appeal to a decree). For a source of further examples, see Goodell, 1914. Goodell also claims (102) that in Aristotle *dei* and *chrē* are interchangeable.

27 The *OED* for some reason does not mention the future sense.

28 See Mitchell, 1985, sects. 932–3, quoting S. Ono: 'It was towards the end of the eleventh century that the meanings [of *agan*] "to have to pay" and "to have as a duty (*to do*)" became prevalent. In the earlier period these meanings were usually expressed by *sculan*. I am grateful to Brendan Biggs for this reference, and for pointing out to me that the connection between possession ('owe') and necessity is found today also in the word 'have'. Like *dei* (Liddell and Scott, 1940, s.v.), 'shall' in Old English was used to express necessity of various kinds; cf. *OED*, s.v., B.I I.3: I am most obliged again to Brendan Biggs for translating and placing in context the passages of Old English there cited. Note for example the passage from *Gregory's Past* (dating from c. 897), according to which a bishop 'must remember himself, even if he is unwilling', which may plausibly be seen to concern an alleged moral obligation or duty.

('need' or 'debt').[29] This suggests a general conception of practical necessity or 'bindingness' running from the Greeks, through Old English, into the modern day.

Here, then, as far as the moral sense of *dei* and 'ought' is concerned, we have a metaphor for morality as something that 'binds' us, a matter of necessity, whose requirements are, like a debt, to some degree inescapable—something adherence to which can be demanded from us. A not implausible hypothesis is that this conception of morality as something binding emerged from the sense of morality as something external to one's self and its largely egoistic desires, putting constraints on one's actions, these constraints to be understood as a kind of 'law' (*nomos*).[30] The

[29] Cf. Goodell, 1914, 94. Note also Nietzsche's attempt to account for the origin of guilt in the legal notion of debt (1967, II.4, 8).

[30] On externality, cf. Wood, 1990, 209–10: 'Hegel describes the moral standpoint as the standpoint of the "ought"... Part of what he means is that moral duties are experienced as external limits on the subject's particular desires, projects, and mode of life'. And in this of course he was only agreeing with Kant, who took his characterization of morality as involving a conception of the categorical to be bringing out what we already believe. In other words, the Kantian conception of morality is, in one highly significant aspect, identical to that of the earliest Greeks, and attention to the various modern components in his position (especially, perhaps, autonomy) should not be allowed us to lead us into blanket claims about the modernity of Kant. Even in the case of autonomy, as J. B. Schneewind points out, Kant can be understood to be reviving a Socratic position (Schneewind, 1998, 548). On *nomos*, see e.g. Guthrie, 1971, ch. 4. Guthrie brings out well the connection with religion and divine law (55): '*Nomos* for the men of classical times is something that *nomizetai*, is believed in, practised, or held to be right; originally, something that *nemetai*, is apportioned, distributed, or

divine law conception of ethics, then, is one early expression of the notion of a binding morality, a notion which can be expressed, as in Aristotle and secular modern philosophy, without reference to divine law.[31]

There is of course a puzzle at the heart of this conception of morality: Why should anyone accept its constraints except in so far as doing so advances his or her own good? That was the central question in ancient ethics. The answer given by Socrates, Plato, and Aristotle is that the virtuous life and the happy life coincide.[32] In our present context, that can be seen not as a rejection of morality as binding, but as an attempt to show that there is no conflict between moral duty and one's own good, and as well, perhaps, to substitute for the view that desires provide their

dispensed. That is to say, it presupposes an acting subject—believer, practitioner or apportioner—a mind from which the *nomos* emanates. . . [S]o long as religion remained an effective force, the devising mind could be the god's, and so there could be *nomoi* that were applicable to all mankind. . . for Hesiod (*Erga*, 276, echoed in the myth of Protagoras, Plato, *Prot.* 322d) Zeus has laid down "a law for all men", that unlike the beasts they should possess justice'. I am particularly grateful here for the comments of Christopher Megone.

31 Cf. Dodds, 1951, 31–2: '[S]ooner or later in most cultures there comes a time of suffering when most people refuse to be content with Achilles' view, the view that "God's in his heaven, and all's wrong with the world". Man projects into the cosmos his own nascent demand for social justice'. As Dodds points out, there are clear signs of this in archaic thought.

32 I believe there is one exception: the moral requirement on Plato's philosophers to descend once again into the cave after contemplation of the sun; see Crisp, 2003, 67–71.

own reasons for satisfaction a more objective conception of the constraints of prudence: so one is bound both by the rationality of morality, and by the rationality of egoism, to pursue virtue. It is worth considering whether Anscombe, in her advocacy of Aristotle and the ethics of virtue, is suggesting a return to the project of an egoistic justification of morality. Consider the following passage:

> One man—a philosopher—may say that since justice is a virtue, and injustice a vice, and virtues and vices are built up by the performance of the actions in which they are instanced, an act of injustice will tend to make a man bad; and essentially the flourishing of a man *qua* man consists of his being good (e.g. in virtues); but for any *X* to which such terms apply, *X* needs what makes it flourish, so a man needs, or ought to perform, only virtuous actions; and even if, as it must be admitted may happen, he flourishes less, or not at all, in essentials, by avoiding injustice, his life is spoiled in essentials by not avoiding injustice—so he still needs to perform only just actions.(43)

But Anscombe goes on to say: '[I]t is a bit much to swallow that a man in pain and hunger and poor and friendless is flourishing' (44). Nevertheless, I suspect that Anscombe, as a Christian who did, I assume, accept certain divine laws, was inclined to swallow this, and to identify herself with:

> The man who believes in divine laws [who] will say perhaps 'It is forbidden, and however it looks, it cannot be to anyone's profit to commit injustice'; he like the Greek philosophers can think in terms of flourishing. . . if he is a Jew or Christian, he need not have any very

> distinct notion: the way it will profit him to abstain from injustice is something that he leaves to God to determine, himself only saying 'It can't do me any good to go against this law'.

If this is right, Anscombe's view that moral philosophers should turn to issues in moral psychology may be taken to apply only to those who deny the kind of divine law of which she is speaking in this passage. Christians know what to do, and their trust in God is sufficient to quiet any doubts they might have about apparent conflict between morality and their own good.[33]

So, to conclude this section, far from its being the case that Aristotle's ethics provides us with an alternative to the modern conception of 'ought', we have found the same metaphor underlying both ancient and modern thought—of morality as a set of constraints, requirements, or 'debts'. In my final section, I shall consider further what may be called the *binding conception* of morality.

Justifying morality

First, let me distinguish what I shall call *lived morality* from *philosophical ethics,* as the latter is usually understood.

[33] Oddly, Anscombe appears never to consider the view that claims that we have such obligations might be self-standing, requiring no justification from elsewhere, though she does consider, as alternatives to divine legislation, the norms of society, self-legislation, the laws of nature. Hobbesian contractualism, and the virtues. Perhaps, like the early Greeks, she also felt that a *nomos* had to be *nomizetai* ('dispensed'). But Aristotle, in his distinction between natural and legal justice in *EN* 5.7, might have alerted her to other possibilities.

A lived morality is a set of practices, norms, beliefs, emotions, and so on, that has developed in a particular society. If people never blamed one another, never felt guilt or shame, never believed that certain actions were right or wrong, there would be nothing to serve as an origin, or to provide conceptual material, for philosophical reflection. Philosophical ethics emerges out of lived morality, and, though any particular philosophical ethics may depart significantly in its content from the lived morality in which it is situated, a philosophical ethics, to be such, must be couched in the language of lived morality itself (right and wrong, the virtues and the vices, or whatever). The conception of morality as binding, that is to say, carries across from lived morality to philosophical ethics.

What is meant by describing a lived morality as 'binding'? I have already suggested that this metaphor involves the idea of morality as a set of to-some-degree-inescapable constraints, perhaps constraints on our pursuit of self-interest, adherence to which is demanded by morality itself and can be demanded also by others. To speak more generally, if a lived morality is accepted within some society, a central part of what is accepted is that there are reasons that individuals, to whom that lived morality applies, have to act, reasons that exist independently of the views or preferences of those individuals. So, if I say, 'It is wrong to torture babies', I am appealing to a lived morality according to which there are reasons to avoid torturing babies, reasons possessed even by those who do not recognize them and who may even have a strong desire to engage in such torture. These reasons need not be other-regarding. A lived morality may include norms of prudence governing how agents might best further their own well-being, and these norms may be independent of the agent's views and desires.

A central element, then, of a lived morality is the acceptance of subject-independent reasons for action.[34] There also appear to be certain aesthetic, rather than reason-related, elements. In our own lived morality, for example, we might describe someone as having an appalling character, or as having performed an appalling action, even if we believe that the agent was not responsible for this character or this action, that he could not have acted otherwise, and that he cannot change or even make recompense. Here one is unhappy to speak of this agent's having a reason, say, not to have this character, since the possession of a reason to P seems at the very least to require that P-ing be possible. But these purely 'aesthetic' elements are, I suggest, derivative from the action-guiding core of lived morality. If the (bad) states of character or the actions in question were of a kind that no one could ever avoid them, then moral criticism would seem out of place.

But the acceptance of subject-independent reasons is not sufficient for there to be a lived morality. The other central component is that of sanctions for non-compliance, and perhaps rewards for compliance. These sanctions, and

[34] By this, it may be that I am meaning something close to what Bernard Williams ('Internal and External Reasons', 1981, 101–113) calls 'external reasons'. Indeed it seems in part to be morality's commitment to such reasons that leads him to reject it as a 'peculiar institution' (1985, ch. 10).

the weight attached to them, can vary. Though we should not exaggerate the difference between ourselves and the Greeks, it is broadly correct to describe their culture as a 'shame-culture' and ours as a 'guilt-culture', where by 'shame' and 'guilt' I mean the experiences of those who are ashamed or guilty.[35] The other significant sanction, of course, is blame, the expression of which can be employed to cause either shame, or guilt, or both.[36] Binding moralities, as they have developed in human culture, have been primarily negative, using unpleasant sanctions to encourage adherence to the norms of the morality itself. But of course there is usually a place for what Hume calls 'peaceful reflection on one's own conduct',[37] as well as guilt; a sense of self-respect, as well as shame; praise, as well as blame.

[35] Cf. the similarly cautious acceptance of this claim in Lloyd–Jones, 1983, 25–6; see also Dover, 1994, 220, n. 3; Williams, 1993, 5–6. Because (some of) the Greeks felt guilty, it is no surprise to find the notion of a conscience emerging in Greek thought: see Dover, ibid., 220–3. Matthew Leigh has alerted me to the useful citations in Stobaeus, *Anthologium*, 3.24 (*peri tou suneidotos*), many of which are also helpful in understanding the Greek view of the link between shame and conscience. I take it that everything I say here is consistent with the view that early modern ethics places a peculiar emphasis on the notion of conscience.

[36] One might wish to distinguish blame directed at causing guilt from that directed at shame, perhaps through reference to the voluntary; see e.g. Williams, 1985, 177; Skorupski, 1993, 132, 135. But one should remain aware of the significant similarities between our reactions and responses to both the voluntary and the involuntary (see my discussion of character–traits, above).

[37] Hume, 1998, 9.25.31–2.

Why should I, and why should we, continue with lived morality? What justifies it? One might attempt such a justification internally: You should adhere to the moral principle that it's wrong to torture babies because it's wrong to torture babies, or because it is cruel to do so and cruelty is wrong.[38] But given the analogy already noted between lived moralities and positive legal systems, it may be worth contemplating at this point a more specific analogy between wrong-ness and illegality. Just as what is illegal within some state or other is what is forbidden by the law in that state, so what is wrong in any culture is what is forbidden by the lived morality within that culture.[39] Note that this is not a form of moral relativism as it is usually understood, since such relativism implies that those within a certain culture have a reason to abide by the moral requirements of that culture. The claim I am making leaves it quite open whether, in any particular case, there is indeed such a reason. The question is: Can lived morality, in general or in any particular

[38] It may be claimed that torturing babies is wrong because suffering is bad and something to be prevented. But the claim that we have a reason to prevent suffering does not employ moral terminology, and is to that extent an external justification.

[39] One may define 'wrong' such that it means, when ascribed to some action, that one does not have strongest reason to perform that action, and 'right' to mean that one does have strongest reason; see Sidgwick, 1907, 8–9, 23, and *passim*. This strikes me as a unwise philosophical stipulation. The notions of rightness and wrongness are too closely involved in lived morality—which will be at most only one source of reasons—for them to be suitable terms for what one has or does not have strongest overall reason to do.

instantiation, be justified from a rational perspective which does not itself assume there are moral reasons?

Here it may be objected that, though the idea of natural law seems implausible to many, it seems unproblematic to ask the question whether what is forbidden by a certain lived morality is 'really wrong'. That is indeed how things appear, but at this point may be introduced the plausible view that lived morality involves an error of objectification.[40] Lived moralities may be understood, like legal systems, as coercive social institutions that have evolved, culturally, and survive, because of the advantages they bring.[41] It is true, of course, that the conceptual content of morality is now extremely sophisticated, but all lived moralities essentially involve as sanctions feelings and attitudes which have their origin in far more primitive emotional responses: fear of social exclusion, fear of anger, a sense of powerlessness.[42] One might view these sanctions from the anthropological or non-normative perspective—as constituting the punishment of moral miscreants in the same sort of way that legal sanctions are punishment for legal

[40] See Mackie, 1977, ch. 1; Joyce, 2001. [41] See e.g. Katz, 2000.

[42] See the very illuminating discussion in Endnote 1, Williams, 1993, 219–223. This claim seems to me consistent with a very good deal of what David Wiggins calls 'a sensible subjectivism' in his essay of that title in 1998, ch. 5. We might well say, for example, that genuinely appalling things—such as the actions of Pol Pot—are things that appal us precisely because they are appalling. But we are entitled to ask what it is about appalling actions that grounds our reasons to avoid and indeed to condemn them.

miscreants, or indeed the sanctions of other practices such as etiquette are punishment for their violators.[43]

If we attempt to reflect upon lived morality as a practice, then, there is no need to do so in the sanction-involving terms of morality itself—rightness, wrongness, duty, blameworthiness, virtue and vice, and so on. That would be to run the risk of making the mistake of the natural lawyers.[44] Rather, we should ask whether we can find justifications for continuing with lived morality which are not themselves morally loaded.[45] And here, I suggest, one immediately attractive thought is that lived morality is justified by the benefits it brings to particular individuals.[46]

[43] Cf. Foot, 1978, 160.

[44] Consider the following questions asked by Daniel Robinson, in his recent and illuminating *Praise and Blame:* 'When one is praised or blamed, and thus assigned a moral property, is there anything whatever of an "objective" nature in the assignation?... Is there anything in external reality to which such ascriptions refer, or are they little more than terms tied to tastes and sentiments?' (Robinson, 2002, 6). My answer is that there is indeed something objective in the assignation of, say, blameworthiness, within some lived morality, just as there is something objective in the assignation of illegality within some lived legal system. But the property of blameworthiness is not self-justifying. It must seek its justification from elsewhere, and the argument in the text below will explain how this need not be an appeal to mere tastes and sentiments.

[45] I am here taking what Skorupski (1993, 125, 128) calls an 'external' view of morality, a view that he himself insightfully adopts in the paper cited.

[46] Hume can be read as holding a similar view: 'Common interest and utility beget infallibly a standard of right and wrong' (1998, 4.20.24–5). See Crisp (forthcoming). The view is also found in Mill: see Skorupski,

Now it is of course true that what one might call a 'welfarist' view can be stated in moral terms, utilitarianism being the paradigmatic example. But the view I am advocating here is one not within morality but about morality itself. And utilitarians themselves have been particularly careful to point out that utilitarian lived moralities are unlikely to be successful by the lights of utilitarianism itself. So it seems that the lived morality most likely to be justified will in fact be non-utilitarian, but its justification may well rest on advancement of well-being broadly understood.[47] Further, since it does seem unlikely that it would most advance the good were utilitarianism, or welfarism generally, to efface itself entirely, conflicts within lived morality, or questions lived morality currently leaves unanswered, would best be resolved by reference to the favoured welfarist view itself.

Having distinguished the internal and external perspectives on morality, I can now end on something like a note of agreement with Anscombe. Much contemporary ethics occupies itself with the question of which theory of the right is correct: consequentialist, deontological, virtue ethical, or whatever. I do think that this debate should come to an end, since it is analogous to a debate about whether

1993, 123; Crisp, 1997, 119–32. A hypothesis worth considering is that this is the 'standard' British empiricist view.

47 There are of course welfarist positions that do not rest on utility-maximization alone, such as those that give some priority to the badly off, or allow agents to give special weight to their own good.

certain actions are legal or illegal, independently of some legal system or other. But what is needed, in ethics at least, is not philosophy or psychology, but rather attention to which principles should govern the distribution of the goods supplied by morality itself.

References

Anscombe, G. E. M. 1997. 'Modern Moral Philosophy', repr. in Crisp and Slote, 1997, 26–44. Orig. pub. *Philosophy*, 33, 1–19.

Aristotle, 1894. *Ethica Nicomachea (EN)*, ed. J. Bywater. Oxford: Clarendon Press.

Aristotle, 1965. *De Arte Poetica*, ed. R. Kassel. Oxford: Clarendon Press.

Baier, K. 1988. 'Radical Virtue Ethics', in French, Uehling and Wettstein, 1988, 126–35.

Bernardete, S. 1965. 'XRH and DEI in Plato and Others', *Glotta*, **43**, 285–98.

Crisp, R. 1997. *Mill on Utilitarianism.* London: Routledge.

Crisp, R. and Slote, M. (eds.). 1997. *Virtue Ethics.* Oxford: Oxford University Press.

Crisp, R. 2003. 'Socrates and Aristotle on Happiness and Virtue', in Heinaman, 2003, 55-78.

Crisp, R. forthcoming. 'Hume on Virtue, Utility, and Morality', in Gardiner, forthcoming.

Diamond, C. 1988. 'The Dog that Gave Himself the Moral Law', in French *et al.*, 1988, 161–79.

Dodds, E. R. 1951. *The Greeks and the Irrational.* Berkeley: University of California Press.

Dover, K. J. 1994. *Greek Popular Morality in the Time of Plato and Aristotle.* Repr. Indianapolis: Hackett.

Foot, P. 1978. 'Morality as a System of Hypothetical Imperatives', repr. in *Virtues and Vices,* Oxford: Blackwell, 157–73.

French, P. A., Uehling, T. E., and Wettstein, H. K. (eds.) 1988. *Ethical Theory: Character and Virtue, Midwest Studies in Philosophy,* **13.** Notre Dame: University of Notre Dame Press.

Gardiner, S. forthcoming. *Virtue Ethics: Old and New.*

Goodell, T. D. 1914. 'XRH and DEI', *Classical Quarterly,* 8, 91–102.

Guthrie, W. K. C. 1971. *The Sophists.* Cambridge: Cambridge University Press.

Hartigan, R. S. 1966. 'Saint Augustine on War and Killing: The Problem of the Innocent', *Journal of the History of Ideas,* **27**, 195–204.

Heinaman, R. 2003. *Plato and Aristotle's Ethics.* Aldershot: Ashgate.

Hesiod. 1990. *Opera et Dies,* ed. F. Solmsen, 3rd edn. Oxford: Clarendon Press.

Hume, D. 1998. *An Enquiry Concerning the Principles of Morals,* ed. T. Beauchamp. Oxford: Clarendon Press.

Joyce, P. 2001. *The Myth of Morality.* Cambridge: Cambridge University Press.

Kagan, S. 1989. *The Limits of Morality.* Oxford: Clarendon Press.

Katz, L. D. (ed.) 2000. *Evolutionary Origins of Morality: Cross-disciplinary Perspectives.* Thorverton: Imprint Academic.

Liddell, H. G. and Scott, R. 1940. *Greek—English Lexicon.* 9th edn. Oxford: Clarendon Press.

Lloyd-Jones, 1983. *The Justice of Zeus.* Rev. edn. Berkeley: University of California Press.

Maclntyre, A. 1981. *After Virtue.* London: Duckworth.

Mackie, J. L. 1977. *Ethics: Inventing Right and Wrong.* Harmondsworth: Penguin.

Mitchell, B. 1985. *Old English Syntax.* Oxford: Clarendon Press.

Moore, G. E. 1903. *Principia Ethica.* Cambridge: Cambridge University Press.

Nietzsche, F. 1967. *On the Genealogy of Morals,* trans. W. Kaufman and R.J. Hollingdale, New York: Random House.

Oxford English Dictionary, http://dictionary.oed.com/http://dictionary.oed.com/

Phillips-Griffiths, A. (ed.). 1993. *Ethics.* Cambridge: Cambridge University Press.

Pigden, C. 1988. 'Anscombe on "Ought"', *Philosophical Quarterly,* **38**, 20–41.

Richter, D. 1995. 'The Incoherence of the Moral "Ought"', *Philosophy,* **70**, 69–85.

Robinson, D. N. 2002. *Praise and Blame: Moral Realism and its Applications.* Princeton: Princeton University Press.

Ross, W. D. 1930. *The Right and the Good.* Oxford: Clarendon Press.

Schneewind, J. 1998. *The Invention of Autonomy.* Cambridge: Cambridge University Press.

Schopenhauer, A. 1995. *On the Basis of Morality.* Rev. edn., trans. E. Payne. Providence and Oxford: Berghahn Books.

Sidgwick, H. 1907. *The Methods of Ethics.* 7th edn. London: Macmillan.

Skorupski, J. 1993. 'The Definition of Morality', in Phillips-Griffiths, 1993, 121–44.

Sophocles, 1990. *Fabulae,* ed. H. Lloyd-Jones and N. G. Wilson. Oxford: Clarendon Press.

Wiggins, D. 1998. *Needs, Values, Truth.* 3rd edn. Oxford: Oxford University Press.

Williams, B. 1981. *Moral Luck.* Cambridge: Cambridge University Press.

Williams, B. 1985. *Ethics and the Limits of Philosophy.* London: Fontana.

Williams, B. 1993. *Shame and Necessity.* Berkeley: University of California Press.

Wood, A. 1990. *Hegel's Ethical Thought.* Cambridge: Cambridge University Press.

Absolutes and Particulars[1]

TIM CHAPPELL

I heard an old religious man
But yesternight declare
That he had found a text to prove
That only God, my dear,
Could love you for yourself alone
And not your yellow hair.

(W. B. Yeats, 'For Anne Gregory')

How is it possible to love some particular person *for herself*, or *for himself*, alone? Love—especially erotic love—does not typically begin when we love someone 'for herself alone'. It very often begins with some strikingly superficial feature or property of the beloved: a certain grace of movement, maybe, or a glimpse inside a young man's shirt (Plato, *Charmides* 155d4), or the colour of Anne Gregory's hair in Yeats's poem. As Yeats sardonically points out, it is quite common for love never to get any further than this. It's hardly news that plenty of love affairs have rested on no deeper foundations than hair coloration.

[1] Thanks to Joel Katzav, Jeff McMahan, Anthony O'Hear, Eric Olson, Christopher Tollefsen, Helen Watt, Mike Wheeler, Garrath Williams, and a Royal Institute audience in London for helpful discussion of this paper, which is nonetheless not their fault.

The same point applies, though perhaps less dramatically and with less obvious potential for disaster, to the non-erotic varieties of love. Maybe I hang out with you because you shake a wicked cocktail, or can teach me how to catch rainbow trout. Maybe, in fact, this is the only reason I hang out with you. Non-sexual friendships of these superficial sorts—and perhaps I can show that there is some philosophical interest in that word 'superficial'—are as familiar and commonplace as sexual friendships of the sort that bothered Anne Gregory.

My question how we might love someone for himself is the question how we might get beyond relationships like these. Get beyond them is undoubtedly what we often want to do; not because we think such relationships are always bad, or that we should have no relationships like this. In advance of more precise description (for some of which see p. 7), there is no reason to think that superficial relationships are either a necessary defect in human living, or, indeed, possible to avoid. The point is only that they're not enough on their own. We can borrow Aristotle's overschematic, culture-relative, and incomplete division of the kinds of friendship (*Nicomachean Ethics* 1156b ff.), and say that advantage-friendships and pleasure-friendships are not enough for full *eudaimonia*. For that we need at least some enjoyment of the focal case[2] of friendship, *hê teleia philia* (1158a11)—the 'friendship of excellence' in which two

[2] On focal meaning see G. E. L. Owen, 'Logic and Metaphysics in some Earlier Works of Aristotle', in his *Logic, Science and Dialectic* (London: Duckworth, 1986).

people[3] love each other *ekeinôn heneka,* 'for the other's own sake' (1156b11, 1157b32).

Well, what's the problem about 'getting beyond' superficial relationships? We find ourselves led to say that the problem is that what makes these relationships superficial is not just that they involve loving the surface qualities or properties of a person (though they obviously do involve this). It's also that they involve loving the qualities or properties of a person, rather than the person himself.

But how are we to spell out this distinction between a person and his properties? If we add certain tempting assumptions about properties, it becomes hard to see what it could mean to talk about 'the person himself' aside from his properties. Witness Locke (*Essay* 2.23.2):

> If any one should be asked, what is the subject wherein Colour or Weight inheres, he would have nothing to say, but the solid extended parts; and if he were demanded,

[3] Aristotle does not say 'people'; he says 'men of virtue'. He thinks full friendship impossible for those who are not *agathoi* (1157a16–20), since 'bad men take no pleasure in each other, except where there is something in it for themselves'. This is simply wrong; you don't have to be an *agathos* to be capable of taking disinterested pleasure in other people. Possibly Aristotle has in mind the truth that there is more to take pleasure in when you contemplate a good person than when you contemplate a bad one. But then, as Aristotle himself tells us (1143b18), bad people typically take pleasure in the wrong things; including, perhaps, the contemplation of other bad people.

Aristotle too remarks that only a limited number of full friendships is possible: NE 1158a10.

> what is it, that that Solidity and Extension inhere in, he would not be in much better case, than the *Indian*... who, saying that the World was supported by a great Elephant, was asked, what the Elephant rested on; to which his answer was, a great Tortoise; but being pressed again to know what gave support to the broad-back'd Tortoise, replied something, he knew not what... The *Idea* then that we have, to which we give the general name Substance, being nothing but the supposed, but unknown support of those Qualities we find existing, which we imagine cannot subsist, *sine re substante*, without something to support them, we call that support *Substantia.*

For Locke, substance is what is left of a thing when you take away all the thing's properties. But we can have no idea what could possibly be left after this subtraction process; still less of how you might you get at it. Familiarly, Locke's metaphysics makes the thing itself systematically inaccessible to knowledge.

A Lockean approach to persons and their properties can likewise make the person himself systematically inaccessible to love. We can imagine ourselves reasoning as follows: 'Either I love you for some reason, or I love you for no reason. If I love you for no reason, then obviously my love is unreasonable. If I love you for some reason, then my reason for loving you must cite some property that you have. But then what I love is not *you,* but that property. It follows that loving a person "for himself" is either impossible or unreasonable.'

Perhaps a Humean will go further still, and deny that there is any 'person himself' to love in the first place, on the ground that any person is 'nothing but a bundle or collection of different perceptions' (Hume, *Treatise* 1.4.6): 'For my part, when I enter most intimately into what I call *myself*, I always stumble upon some particular perception or other... I never can catch *myself* at any time without a perception, and never can observe any thing but the perception.' The step from Locke's systematically inaccessible substances, to Hume's denial that there is any such thing as substance, is a notoriously easy one. One implication of taking this step is that it becomes not just problematic, but downright impossible, to speak of persons as distinct from their properties. So it also becomes impossible to speak of loving persons as distinct from their properties.[4]

No doubt part of the antidote to this philosophical malaise is to follow Elizabeth Anscombe's advice, and have no truck with the Lockean conception of substance as 'something hidden'[5] that gives rise to it (Anscombe, 'Three Philosophers: Aristotle', pp. 10–11)[6]:

[4] Presumably the next move in this dialectic is a Kantian one: *even though* we have no idea of the person in himself, loving the person in himself is a moral necessity. So the person in himself is transcendentally reinstated.

[5] Anscombe, *Three Philosophers* (Oxford: Blackwell, 1961), p. 17: 'The theory of accidents ... lends itself to representation as a cluster or veneer theory of properties; as if the substance were the underlying material, and the properties a ... barnacle-like cluster of dependent quasi-substances stuck on to the substance...'

[6] Cp. Christopher Martin, *The Philosophy of Thomas Aquinas: Introductory Readings* (London: Routledge, 1988), pp. 62–63: 'People often talk as if the accidents were that which can change, and the substance that which does not change... [this] leads people in the end to suppose that the substance

> Because Aristotle distinguishes between substance and quality, those who take a predicate like 'man' [in the sense of 'human'] to signify a complex of properties readily suppose him to be distinguishing between the being of a thing and the being of any attributes that it has. They then take the thing itself to have no attributes. It would be almost incredible, if it had not happened, to suppose that anyone could think it an argument to say: the ultimate subject of predication must be something without predicates; or that anyone who supposed this was Aristotle's view could do anything but reject it with contempt.

We may say with Anscombe that if this is where Locke's approach to substance gets us, then that is just so much the worse for Locke's approach. In metaphysics, we should prefer[7] a view of substance that (like Aristotle's) allows us to be aware of the substance itself, directly, in our immediate experience—and not just the properties of the substance. Likewise (or indeed as one application of this), we should

is a "bare particular", that has no accidents, that has no colour or shape, that is a "something I know not what" that is completely unknowable.' Contrast the Aristotelian view that particular substance is not only knowable by perception, but the primary object of knowledge by perception (e.g. *Metaphysics* 1018b31–34).

[7] Perhaps 'we should prefer' makes it sound as if this philosophical choice was a completely free one, a choice not made, for instance, under the formidable pressures of Newtonian and Cartesian scepticism that led Locke to say what he said about substances. The answer to this doubt is another story, which I can't tell in this paper. See my forthcoming *Western Philosophy: The Inescapable* Self (London: Orion Books, 2004).

prefer a view of the person that makes persons themselves directly available to be loved, and not just their properties. It isn't only the properties of the particular existing thing—not even only its essential properties—that are available to be known. We can and should hold to the commonsense belief that the particular thing that has the properties can itself be known. And then it can meaningfully be said that there is a difference between loving the person's properties, and loving the person.

If this proposal is right, then despite Locke we can have a good philosophical account of what it means to love a person 'for herself'. It simply means loving what she really is rather than what she sometimes happens to be. The commonly-heard exhortation to love people 'in themselves' or 'for what they are' is then not unreasonable, impossible, mysterious, or misconceived. It is something that—after, no doubt, a bit more logical tidying up—can become a working part of a coherent philosophical outlook.

For this line of thought, recognizing the primacy of substance is as important in ethics as it is in metaphysics. To take substance as primary for ethics is to take the person—the person as she really is—as the main end, or one of the most important ends, of moral activity.

This approach to ethics has some important consequences. Here is one. If the person—the person as she really is—is the main end, or one of the most important ends, of moral activity, that commits us to the task of trying to establish what the person really is.

In fact there are two tasks here: different, but interestingly related. The first is to answer the general metaphysical question 'What is a person?', a question whose central and fundamental importance for ethics still seems to me to be seriously underestimated. In 'Modern Moral Philosophy', Anscombe famously urges us not to waste our time trying to do ethics until we have an adequate philosophy of psychology to base it on (Anscombe, *Collected Essays* Vol. III p. 26). A clear account of what a person is looks to be another unavoidable prerequisite for ethics. You might, I suppose, call this a problem in philosophy of psychology too; or better, perhaps, a problem that needs to be extruded from psychology, and restated within metaphysics. More about that later.

Distinct from the task of answering the general metaphysical question 'What is *a* person?' with a statement of the nature of persons in general, there is also the task of answering the particular biographical and psychological question 'What is *this* person?': the task of understanding the nature or character of this particular individual substance (a task in which, of course, one presupposes one's answer to the first question). No one has described this second task better than Iris Murdoch in *The Sovereignty of Good.* According to Murdoch, 'attention', 'a just and loving gaze directed upon an individual reality', is 'the characteristic and proper mark of the active moral agent' (*Sovereignty*, p. 34). And what is 'attention'? Murdoch gives us an example of attention at work, in an imaginary relationship between a mother-in-law ('M') who is tempted to feel snobbery, jealousy and hostility towards her daughter-in-law ('D'), but is a good enough person to try to resist these temptations (pp. 22–23):

> M *looks* at D, she attends to D, she focuses her attention. M is engaged in an internal struggle. She may for

> instance be tempted to enjoy caricatures of D in her imagination... What M is... attempting to do is not just to see D accurately, but to see her justly and lovingly.

Attention to 'an individual reality' means *trying to get that person right.* The difficulty here is not merely our epistemic shortcomings, though no doubt they are part of the problem. It is also an ethical shortcoming, a recurrent and perennial temptation. This is the temptation to indulge in fantasy rather than reality, to settle for a caricature of the other person instead of keeping at work on trying to see what she is really like. We never escape this temptation completely. That is why the activity of attention 'is essentially something progressive, something infinitely perfectible', 'an endless task' (p.23).[8]

Since the activity of attention to the particular person is 'something infinitely perfectible', *some* level of failure in this activity is inevitable. But it has been powerfully argued by Murdoch herself, and by Gregory Vlastos too, that serious, systematic and wilful failure in this task is pathological. It involves the substitution of a fantasy world, and a fantasy other, for the real world, and the real other.

Characteristically, this pathology rests content with a mere shallow caricature of the particular person. The

[8] See also Murdoch p. 38: 'Goodness *is* connected with knowledge: not with impersonal quasi-scientific knowledge of the ordinary world, whatever that may be, but with a refined and honest perception of what is really the case, a patient and just discernment and exploration of what confronts one, which is the result not simply of opening one's eyes but of a certain perfectly familiar kind of moral discipline.'

person becomes a place-holder for the various properties that we love to hate (if what we feel is prejudice or contempt), or love to love (if what we feel is infatuation). We lose all interest in the person herself, both as distinct from our caricature of her, and as distinct from her properties. In Vlastos' words ('The individual as object of love in Plato', *Platonic Studies* (Princeton UP, 1973), p. 28),

> much erotic attachment, perhaps most of it, is not directed to an individual in the proper sense of the word—to the integral and irreplaceable existent that bears that person's name—but to a complex of qualities, answering to the lover's sense of beauty, which he locates for a time truly or falsely in that person.

One way to explain why this sort of relationship is pathological is to point out that it is, in a way, solipsistic. If this is how my relationships are then, for me as for the Russellian logical atomist, there is nothing but *me and my world*: I become a punctual self in a universe of punctual quality-instances.[9] There is only myself and the qualities that I

[9] See e.g. Russell, *The Philosophy of Logical Atomism,* pp. 200–201 in R. C. Marsh, (ed.), *Logic and Knowledge* (London: Allen & Unwin, 1956): 'The names that we commonly use, like "Socrates", are really abbreviations for descriptions... what they describe are not particulars but complicated systems of classes or series. A name, in the narrow logical sense of a word whose meaning is a particular, can only be applied to a particular with which the speaker is acquainted, because you cannot name anything you are not acquainted with... That makes it very difficult to get any instance of a name at all in the proper strict logical sense of the word. The only words one does use as names in the logical sense are words like "this" or "that"' [for items

experience, moment by moment, whether attractive or aversive. Other people cease to be realities, except as I construct them, out of my own momentary experiences, to fit my philosophical theories; or fantasies. I become the solitary 'agent of a universal satisfaction system',[10] the only real being in a cosmos centred on *me*.

Vlastos' (self-confessed) example of this pathology is Jean-Jacques Rousseau:

> 'There is no real love without enthusiasm,' he writes in the *Emile*, 'and no enthusiasm without an object of perfection, real or chimerical, but always existing in the imagination.' So if we do want 'real love', we must buy it with illusion. We must transfigure imaginatively the necessarily imperfect persons in whom we vest our love... 'Finding nothing in existence worthy of my delirium, I nourished it in an ideal world which my creative imagination peopled with beings after my own heart.'[11]

Vlastos' central thesis in 'The individual as object of love' is that Plato suffers from the same pathology as Rousseau.

of immediate subjective experience], Cp 'On the nature of acquaintance', at p. 138 in Marsh (italics added): 'For the present, let us assume *as a working hypothesis* the existence of other people, and of unperceived physical things.'

10 Bernard Williams, *Utilitarianism: for and against* (Cambridge: CUP, 1973, p. 118.

11 Vlastos, loc. cit. Vlastos's first quotation is from the *Emile*, at Vol. IV, p. 743, in the Pléiade edition (Paris, 1969). The second quotation is from *The Confessions*, at Vol. I, p. 427. Compare a poignant sentence from Book 3 of *The Confessions* (my italics): 'Je ne sentais toute la force de mon attachement pour elle *que quand je ne la voyais pas*.'

In fact, Vlastos suggests, Plato is betrayed into that pathology by his own philosophy[12] (loc. cit., p. 31):

> What we are to love in persons is the 'image' of the Idea in them. We are to love the persons so far, and only insofar, as they are good and beautiful. Now since all too few human beings are masterworks of excellence, and not even the best of those we have the chance to love are wholly free of streaks of the ugly, the mean, the commonplace, the ridiculous, if our love for them is to be only for their virtue and beauty, the individual, in the uniqueness and integrity of his or her individuality, will never be the object of our love. This seems to me the cardinal flaw in Plato's theory.

If Vlastos is right, we should reject as pathological any philosophical theory that makes it impossible to see the individual person, the human particular, as the particular substance that he or she is, and as a proper object of ethical concern in his or her own right: not merely as a congeries of possibly valuable properties. But, as Diotima's speech in the *Symposium* makes clear, this is just what Plato's theory does make impossible. Diotima's Platonism[13] leads us away from

[12] And, perhaps, *vice versa.* I won't speculate here about whether the philosophy caused the pathology, or merely expressed it. Maybe it did both.

[13] '*Diotima's* Platonism': no sensitive reader of the *Symposium* can possibly miss the evidence that Plato himself feels torn between Diotima's values and Alcibiades'. See Martha Nussbaum, *The Fragility of Goodness* (Cambridge: CUP, 1986), Ch. 6, 'The Speech of Alcibiades: a reading of the *Symposium*', at p. 167: Vlastos' 'criticism of Plato's perceptions… requires us to treat as Plato's only the view expressed in

the human and personal particular, toward a kind of absolute that is entirely superhuman—or inhuman—and entirely super-personal—or impersonal: towards *to polu pelagos tou kalou*— towards 'the whole ocean of the beautiful' (*Symposium* 210d3). For this theory no individual can possibly be valuable, except as a step on the road towards the vision of that ocean of transcendently hypostatized property.

This Platonism turns out to be just another way into the Lockean predicament; just another way of making it impossible for us to treat the individual person as what Kant called an *end in himself*: as something to care about directly, unconditionally, and in his or her own right.[14]

But Platonism is not the only philosophical theory that makes this impossible:

> [P]leasure, and freedom from pain, are the only things desirable as ends; and. . . all desirable things (which are as numerous in the utilitarian as in any other scheme) are desirable either for the pleasure inherent in themselves, or as means to the promotion of pleasure and the prevention of pain. (J. S. Mill, *Utilitarianism,* Ch. 2, at p. 257 in Mary Warnock, (ed.), *Utilitarianism* (London: Fontana, 1962))

the speech of Diotima as repeated by Socrates, and to charge [Plato] with being unaware of the rest of what he has written' in the *Symposium*.

[14] Cp. Mary Margaret McCabe, *Plato's Individuals* (Cambridge, MA: Princeton UP, 1994), for further argument that Plato's metaphysics gives properties a crucial ontological priority over individuals.

If pleasure and freedom from pain are the only things desirable *as ends,* it is a red herring for Mill to tell us that things desirable as ends *or means* are 'as numerous in the utilitarian as in any other scheme'. What matters is that Mill's scheme only recognizes two things that are to be desired or pursued *in their own right*: pleasure and freedom from pain. So nothing else has underived moral importance for the Millian moral agent; so, in particular, particular persons have no underived moral importance for the Millian moral agent. If I am right that particular persons must have underived moral importance in any adequate ethical theory, this objection is as fatal to Mill as it was to Plato.

At this point, no doubt, modern consequentialists will want it registered that they are not caught by this objection, even if Mill is. They will wonder (aloud) why, if this is what I want to argue, I haven't yet referred to the flourishing literature on consequentialism and friendship.[15]

[15] For instance: Bernard Williams, 'A critique of utilitarianism', in Smart and Williams, *Utilitarianism: for and against,* and 'Persons, Character, and Morality' in Williams, *Moral Luck* Cambridge: CUP, 1981); Peter Railton, 'Alienation, Consequentialism, and the Demands of Morality', *Philosophy and Public Affairs* 1984; Neera Badhwar Kapur, 'Why it is wrong to be always guided by the best', *Ethics* 1991; Dean Cocking and Justin Oakley, 'Indirect Consequentialism', *Ethics* 1995; Elinor Mason, 'Can an indirect consequentialist be a true friend?', *Ethics* 1998; Madison Powers, 'Rule Consequentialism and the value of friendship', in Hooker, Mason, and Miller, (eds.), *Morality, Rules, and Consequences* (Edinburgh: EUP, 2000).

They will point us (again) in the direction of a familiar distinction, already implicit in my last quotation from Mill, between treating individual goods as *means to the end* of utility, and as *constituents of the whole* of utility.[16] And they will remind us (wearily) that you can accept Mill's consequentialism without accepting his value theory (his 'theory of life', as he himself calls it in *Utilitarianism).* So, they will say, there is nothing to stop a modern consequentialist from saying that individual persons do have underived moral importance—are ends in themselves.

To take these points in turn. First, the reason why I haven't referred yet to the literature on consequentialism and friendship is simply because friendship is not my subject here. The pathology that I am talking about arises wherever a consistent utilitarian tries to take the person as she really is as the main end, or one of the most important ends, of moral activity. But it is not only in friendships that you take (or fail to take) another person as an end in himself. The problem that interests me is wider, and I think deeper.

One way of bringing this out is to observe that while there doesn't seem to be anything necessarily wrong with an instrumental *friendship,* there does seem to be something necessarily wrong with an instrumental *personal relationship.* Consider again the superficial friendships mentioned at the beginning. You and I might come together only for the

[16] This distinction is also deployed by John Ackrill in his classic paper 'Aristotle on Eudaimonia', in A. O. Rorty, (ed.), *Essays on Aristotle's Ethics* (Berkeley: University of California Press, 1980).

pleasure of fishing, or shaking cocktails; in that sense, our friendship might be a purely instrumental one. That needn't matter, so long as we recognize each other's intrinsic value *apart from* our instrumental friendship. It is easy for philosophical discussions of friendship to make it sound as if there's something wrong with any friendship that does not have a quasi-marital intensity. This 'righteous absurdity'[17], this prissy unrealisticness, perhaps arises from not distinguishing an instrumental attitude *to a friendship* from an instrumental attitude *to a person.*

Second, on the familiar distinction between means-end relations and part-whole relations. I think the value of this distinction for the consequentialist's purposes has been overrated, perhaps because of a confusion caused by the terminology. The difference between treating a person 'merely as a means' and treating him 'at the same time as an end in himself' does not rest on the distinction between means-end relations and part-whole relations. It rests on the difference between the various descriptions under which we might act towards another person. If I bring you flowers *as a means to promoting utility,* that is obviously treating you 'merely as a means'. If I bring you flowers *as an instance of promoting utility,* that is *also* treating you 'merely as a means'. Both actions have the same fault, which has nothing to do with the means-end/part-whole distinction. The fault is that both are done under a description that foregrounds *utility* and backgrounds *you.* Obviously not every further

[17] Williams' phrase in 'Persons, Character and Morality'.

thought about the ultimate reasons for any action or way of life, is a case of Williams' 'one thought too many'[18]. As Williams himself emphasizes, if we are not to lapse into mere obscurantism, at least some sorts of deeper reflection on action and life and purpose must be available to us. But the idea that this deeper reflection—at any level of depth—might take the usual consequentialist form of judging the value of particular persons against the value of an impersonal absolute called 'utility' (or whatever) is definitely a non-starter.

This brings us to the third issue, the important question whether modern consequentialism can, in fact, coherently recognize a plurality of different ends-in-themselves or intrinsic values—especially when the plurality is as extreme as the plurality of presently-existing persons. No matter what theory of value a consequentialist adopts, the basic consequentialist injunction is the command to maximize. Now it is not clear what it can even mean to maximize a variety of basically different intrinsic values. To maximize one of these values will presumably be *not* to maximize the others. To maximize them *all* seems an idea too multiply interpretable to have any particular content. To apply practical rationality to a plurality of intrinsic values in a way that has any chance of having a determinate shape, we need to suppose that practical rationality involves not only trying to promote some values, but also recognizing limits on what you can do while promoting one value, to another value that

[18] See Bernard Williams, 'Persons, Character and Morality', at p. 18 in his *Moral Luck*.

you are *not* promoting. But recognizing these limits means recognizing *constraints*—deontological absolutes[19]—about how

[19] This is about my only allusion to moral absolutes in the sense of unbreakable moral rules. Most of this paper is about a different absolute/ particular contrast from the contrast most discussed recently. That is the contrast between moral particularism—roughly, the view that any morally relevant property whatever can vary in its valence—and moral absolutism—roughly, the view that some morally relevant properties not only never vary in their valence, but also invariably provide a decisive reason for a specific type of action or abstention. I used to think that I knew I was an absolutist and not a particularist. Three very fine recent papers have made me doubt that I do know that: Mark Lance's and Maggie Little's 'Mad Dogs and Englishmen' (unpublished; presented at the British Society for Ethical Theory, Reading 2002), and the symposium between Garrett Cullity and Richard Holton in *Proceedings of the Aristotelian Society* (Suppl.) 2002. The Lance/Little paper suggests that a particularist can also be a generalist, someone who believes in general moral principles, provided these take the form of *ceteris paribus* laws; the Cullity/ Holton exchange suggests that a particularist can be someone who thinks that adding further moral information about a situation can change its moral character in non-monotonic ways. My question in both cases is the same: What, on these characterisations, counts as being an absolutist? The answers that I think this question must evoke leave no room for a more than technical distinction between absolutism and particularism.

Lance and Little take absolutism to involve thinking that there are some general moral principles that have no *ceteris paribus* clauses. If that *is* absolutism, then absolutism looks irresistible (cp. Cullity, loc. cit. p. 182, on the absolute wrongness of making someone suffer for your own enjoyment). Understood this way, the absolutism/ particularism dispute is too easily settled to be interesting. Presumably absolutism might be understood, instead, as a stringent view of what it takes for *cetera* to be *imparia* (e.g., denying that we can invoke the

you may treat any unpromoted value. And a normative theory that has a multiplicity[20] of constraints as a basic feature of its architecture is not a consequentialist normative theory at all. If this line of thought is right, then consequentialism cannot

ceteris paribus clause in the principle 'Murder is wrong' in any situation that *we* can think of, while admitting that a case where this clause could be invoked is theoretically possible). Here the difference between particularism and absolutism is only about degrees of stringency, which doesn't seem a very interesting difference either.

Meanwhile Holton and Cullity characterise the absolutist as someone who denies non-monotonicity on the evaluative side. Absolutism means thinking that once some moral descriptions are in (e.g. 'This is an act of murder'), no further moral descriptions that we might add can change the overall moral character of the situation or action that we're considering. Fine; but you could accept non-monotonicity on the evaluative side *while denying it on the factual side.* That is, you could hold that the correct *moral* description of something as murder settled the question of its wrongness (and settled it indefeasibly, as suggested above), while also holding that there is no finitely specifiable *factual* description which settles the question of whether a given act *is* an act of murder. Something like this may be Anscombe's own view in 'Modern Moral Philosophy': 'exceptional circumstances can always make a difference' to the correct factual description of a situation (p. 28), but there are cases where 'no circumstances, and no expected consequences, which do *not* modify' a given moral description of a situation can alter its moral character (p. 39). This distinction between two places where non-monotonicity might occur is real; but rather fine. If this is all there is to the distinction between particularism and absolutism, you are left wondering how big a deal that distinction actually is.

20 We need the word 'multiplicity' because, presumably, even the simplest form of consequentialism recognises as basic one single constraint: 'Don't fail to maximise the good'.

recognize a plurality of intrinsic values without ceasing to be consequentialism altogether.[21]

So I doubt that modern consequentialists do in fact have the wide-ranging freedom in the theory of value that they often claim they have. Whether or not they have this freedom, in practice they do not use it much. This comes out when we take another look at the literature on consequentialism and friendship. What's usually at stake in this literature is whether friendship, or some other test-case commitment, has much chance of coming out the winner when it is put in competition with something called 'overall utility'. The question would not even be posed this way unless modern consequentialists were, in practice, not making any important theoretical use of the possibility of a plurality of values. The whole point of appealing to indirect forms of consequentialism is to reinstate a possibility that has somehow gone missing in the *Ur*-theory: the possibility of valuing (or appearing to value) friends or particular persons as ends in themselves. There would be no need for this indirection in the first place, if the value of particular persons was not already being factored into the value of a single impersonal absolute utility. (This point remains in force even where the value of utility is said to be composed out of, *inter alia*, the values of particular persons; cp. my remarks above on part-whole *versus* means-end relations.)

[21] The argument of this paragraph is developed further in my 'Implications of Incommensurability', *Philosophy* 2001, and 'Practical Rationality for Pluralists about the Good', *Ethical Theory and Moral Practice* 2002.

For a different kind of evidence that modern consequentialism does not, in practice, recognize a plurality of different goods, we may return to Mill and Plato. Both hold what I shall call a receptacle view of the person. For Mill as for Plato, individual persons can matter, can have positive moral value, only insofar as they have the right properties—the morally valuable properties. On the receptacle view, persons are not intrinsic values, but merely possible receptacles for intrinsically valuable properties. Furthermore, these properties are not themselves in any deep sense a plurality of properties. For Plato, 'the right properties' means, first, participation in *to kalon,* and then whatever other properties conduce to participation in *to kalon.* For Mill, 'the right properties' means, first, actually experiencing pleasure and freedom from pain, and then whatever other properties conduce to such experience: such as, so to speak, being an efficient conduit or a retentive receptacle[22] for the experience of utility.

Thus both for Mill and for Plato, the individual person's value, aside from her possession (or at least her potential possession) of the right properties, is zero. In themselves, persons are simply neutral between positive and negative value. To put it another way, Mill and Plato see persons on the model of bank accounts for utility. It's a good thing when these accounts are in the black, a bad thing when they're in the red, and neither good nor bad, except relatively, when they are simply empty.

[22] The idea of persons as receptacles for pleasure is not new: see Plato, *Gorgias* 493e, on Callicles' version of the receptacle view.

My claim is that the receptacle view of the person, and of the value of the person, focuses our attention on the *in* essentials and ignores what really matters. What really matters is that each particular person, just as such, has underived and intrinsic value. Because it ignores this, the receptacle view—in any version, including Mill's and Plato's—is pathological. On the receptacle view, the ultimate object of our moral efforts is not other particular persons at all, but an impersonal absolute: the value that can be realized *in* persons. This picture is a close correlate of the solipsism I described above. This too is a moral world in which the only realities are myself and the qualities, good or bad, that I can bring into being. Once more I become the solitary 'agent'—or 'janitor'?—of a universal satisfaction system: the only real being in a cosmos that centres on me and the impersonal value that I can bring about.

This impersonal value also seems to be a kind of secular deity. It is a shadow or an after-image (*eidôlon*, idol) of the conception of ethics that ultimately directs our moral efforts beyond other particular persons towards an absolute—God—who, at least for the Christian, is precisely *not* impersonal, but personalized and particularized by incarnation.

This means that Mill's and Plato's accounts of the value of persons are, in the last resort, necessarily superficial, in at least two ways. They are metaphysically superficial, because these accounts focus on what's secondary, the properties of the individual person, while ignoring or bypassing the primary thing, the person herself. They are ethically superficial, for essentially the same reason: because they give ethical priority to what is at most ethically secondary.

I believe the receptacle view of the person is another instance of the superficiality or shallowness of consequentialism, alongside the instance that Elizabeth Anscombe noted in 'Modern Moral Philosophy'. (This was that consequentialists cannot use their own theory's resources to formulate moral rules applicable to particular action-types, since there is no knowing in advance what consequences actions of any particular type may have; consequentialists therefore have no theoretical basis for rules with any deeper justification than the conventions of their own society.)[23] Of course consequentialism is not *the same thing* as the receptacle view of the person. All the same, the receptacle that the person is, on the receptacle view, is usually and most

[23] Anscombe, 'Modern Moral Philosophy' p. 36: 'It is a necessary feature of consequentialism that it is a shallow philosophy... the consequentialist has no footing on which to say "This would be permissible, this not"; because by his own hypothesis, it is the consequences that are to decide, and he has no business to pretend that he can lay it down what possible twists a man could give doing this or that... the consequentialist, in order to be imagining borderline cases at all, has of course to assume some sort of law or standard according to which this is a borderline case. Where then does he get that standard from? In practice the answer invariably is: from the standards current in his society or his circle. And it has in fact been the mark of all these philosophers that they have been extremely conventional; they have nothing in them by which to revolt against the conventional standards of their sort of people; it is impossible they should be profound.'

On shallowness in attitudes to persons see also, more recently, Raimond Gaita, *A Common Humanity* (London: Routledge, 1998), pp. 26–27: 'Our sense of the preciousness of other people is concerned with their power to affect us in ways we cannot fathom and in ways against which we can protect ourselves only at the cost of becoming shallow.'

naturally thought of as a receptacle *for utility*, or something not significantly different from the classic conceptions of utility as pleasure, happiness, or preference-satisfactions. And so it is no surprise that adherents of the receptacle view of the person are nearly always consequentialists—or something so close to consequentialists as makes no real difference.

Let me show some evidence for this claim. First point: from the very best to the very worst in consequentialist normative ethics, it is considered entirely unproblematic to describe individual persons' lives as 'worth living', 'not worth living', 'barely worth living', 'nearly worth living', etc. (It is for example impossible even to state most of Parfit's arguments in Part Four of *Reasons and Persons* without using descriptions of these sorts.) So far as I can see, the consequentialist deployment of these terms rests typically on the thought that the value (or disvalue) of the existence of any particular person is completely determined by the value (or disvalue) of that person's utility (or disutility). To think this way is automatically to exclude the possibility that the person *himself*, and not his utility, might be an object of value.[24] And this, of course, is precisely the content of the receptacle view.

[24] Of course, a consequentialist could also say that the existence of any particular person has *some* value in itself, but that this value can sometimes be outweighed by the disvalue of that person's disutility. One question for the consequentialist who says this is: What is meant by this talk of *outweighing*? Another question is: What actions (or omissions) are supposed to be justified by this alleged outweighing? Even if someone's life *is* 'not worth living', it is not obvious—especially not if the values of pleasure/ pain and of human life are incommensurable—that there is any good sense in which he *ought* to

I shall take a longer look at a second piece of evidence for the claim that consequentialists and adherents of the receptacle view are more or less coextensive groups. This second piece of evidence—it is, of course, not entirely unrelated to the first—can be found by considering some of the commonest recent answers to that rather important question of applied ethics, 'What's wrong with killing?'. Here are three of these answers:

> The wrongness of killing us is understood in terms of what killing does to us. Killing us imposes on us the misfortune of premature death. That misfortune underlies the wrongness... The misfortune of premature death consists in the loss to us of the future goods of consciousness... What makes my future valuable to me are those aspects of my future that I will (or would) value when I will (or would) experience them... What makes killing us wrong, in general, is that it deprives us of a future of value. Thus, killing someone is wrong, in general, when it deprives her of a future like ours. (Don Marquis, 'An argument that abortion is wrong', in Hugh LaFollette, *Ethics in Practice,* First Edition (Oxford: Blackwell, 1997), pp. 95–96)

> [The wrongness of killing a person is] the wrongness of permanently depriving her of whatever it is that makes it possible for her to value her own life. (John Harris, *The Value of Life* (London: Routledge, 1986), p. 17)

> What is fundamentally wrong about killing, when it is wrong, is that it frustrates the victim's time-relative

be dead. Still less that we ought to procure his death. Cp. my paper 'Why euthanasia is in no one's interest', *Philosophy Now* 40 (March 2003), pp. 10–12.

interest[25] in continuing to live. (Jeff McMahan, *The Ethics of Killing* (Oxford: OUP, 2002), p. 195)

These answers treat the wrong of killing as a wrong of deprivation. Killing is wrong because it is *taking something away from* someone. But this view of the wrong of killing seems unnatural and superficial. It is usually true, of course, that to kill someone is to deprive them of good things. But that deprivation is not the main thing wrong in killing, even when it is part of what is wrong. In killing, the main point is not that something is taken away from someone, but that *the someone* is taken away. The central wrong in killing is not the wrong of *depriving* the individual person (not even: the wrong of depriving her of everything). It is the wrong of *destroying* the individual person.

This seems to me the obvious way of explaining the wrongness of killing. The primary reason why killing persons is wrong is that it is wrong deliberately and directly[26] to destroy things that are themselves intrinsic goods; and particular persons are intrinsic goods. It is a testimony to the power of the receptacle view in contemporary philosophy that so few other philosophers apparently find this obvious.[27] At any rate, all

[25] McMahan p. 80 makes the distinction between an interest and a timerelative interest like this: 'One's interests are concerned with what would be better for one considered as a temporally extended being... One's present time-relative interests are what one has egoistic reason to care about *now*'.

[26] The usual qualifications apply about (1) involuntariness, (2) omission and (3) intention. On (2) and (3) see my 'Two Distinctions that Do Make a Difference', *Philosophy* 2002.

[27] Jeff McMahan's view of the wrongness of killing, the 'Intrinsic Worth Account', might seem an exception to this generalisation (McMahan,

three of the accounts just quoted clearly pre-suppose the receptacle view of the person, and fail even to consider the possibility that I am trying to make space for—that the wrongness of killing is the wrongness of destroying intrinsic goods. Perhaps this is why all three accounts are apt to leave the reader haunted by an inarticulate sense that something crucial has been left out. We may add that all three accounts share an obvious and fatal flaw: they cannot explain what is wrong with killing someone who is not going to have a future life of value *anyway*, e.g. because if you don't kill him at 3.58.59, he will be struck by a freak thunderbolt at 3.59.00. (Or does the wrongness of killing him diminish, the closer you get to the time when he will die whatever happens?)

Some other consequentialist accounts of the wrongness of killing go wrong in other ways than by being overtly

The Ethics of Killing, p. 242): 'While the *badness of death* is correlative with the value of the victim's possible future life, the *wrongness of killing* is correlative with the value or worth of the victim himself... a person, a being of incalculable worth, demands the highest respect. To kill a person, in contravention of that person's own will, is an egregious failure of respect for the person and his worth... because killing inflicts the ultimate loss—the obliteration of the person himself—and is both irreversible and incompensable, it is no exaggeration to say that it constitutes the ultimate violation of the requirement of respect.' In fact McMahan is not an exception, because what he means by a 'person' is a 'being with psychological capacities of sufficient complexity and sophistication' (quoted from personal communication, 1/2/03). In other words, McMahan straight-forwardly accepts a Receptacle View: he thinks that the human substance has no value in itself, and only becomes valuable when certain favoured properties (the psychological capacities) are instantiated in that substance.

dependent on a receptacle view of the person. So, for instance, Peter Singer explicitly denies that he holds a receptacle view about what he counts as persons[28], and bases the wrongness of killing on the wrongness of thwarting preferences (Singer, *Practical Ethics* (Cambridge: CUP, 1993), p. 94):

> [Preference-]utilitarianism judges actions. . . by the extent to which they accord with the preferences of any beings affected by the action or its consequences. . . According to preference utilitarianism, an action contrary to the preference of any being is, unless this preference is outweighed by contrary preferences, wrong. Killing a person who prefers to continue living is therefore wrong, other things being equal.

As I said above, there could be a form of the receptacle view that saw the person as valuable because the person is the place where preferences get satisfied (preference-satisfaction being what matters). But this is not Singer's view; Singer is not—so far as I can tell—saying that killing a person is bad because it deprives them of the opportunity to be the locus of further preference-satisfactions. Rather, Singer means simply that killing people is bad because preferences are sovereign, and most people prefer *not* to be killed.

So the problem here is Singer's doctrine that preferences are sovereign; i.e., his equation of preferences with

[28] Singer, *Practical Ethics* p. 126: 'Rational, self-conscious beings are individuals, leading lives of their own, and cannot in any sense be regarded merely as receptacles for containing a certain quantity of happiness. . . In contrast, beings who are conscious, but not self-conscious, more nearly approximate the picture of receptacles for pleasure and pain.'

interests. Singer never argues for this equation. He just announces it (Singer, p. 94): we should take 'a person's interests to be what, on balance and after reflection on all the relevant facts, a person prefers'. Singer tells us that this equation is 'plausible', but it is not easy to agree. (Familiarly, 'balance' and 'reflection' will leave a resolute and clear-headed Nazi quite unmoved. He will just end up with a *considered* preference for murdering Jews.)[29]

So what are interests, if they are not simply preferences? There is space here to say only this. Interests, properly understood, are always interests in well-being. So what a person's interests are depends on what well-being is for a person. But again, what well-being is for anything depends on what that thing is. So what a *person's* interests are depends on what a person is.[30] By this route too we are led back to the central and fundamental question for ethics that I identified on p. 4: the general metaphysical question 'What is a person?'.

That question returns at this point anyway, because I want to consider a third way in which consequentialist accounts of the wrongness of killing often fail. As I have pointed out, some of these accounts take killing to be wrong because it is a deprivation of future utility. For the receptacle view of the person, this is the obvious way to explain the wrongness of killing; and as I have pointed out, the implausibility and superficiality of this explanation seems to be a

[29] And don't say that no Nazi *could* be resolute and clear-headed. Self-evidently, lots of Nazis were both.

[30] On this too cp. my 'Why euthanasia is in no one's interest', *Philosophy Now* 40 (March 2003).

serious argument against the receptacle view. However, as I shall now argue, it is also possible to take killing to be wrong because it destroys a person, where the person is understood to be an object of intrinsic value, and *still* be fatally, though perhaps covertly, reliant on the receptacle view of the person: not in your account of why killing persons is wrong, but in your account of what a person is.

The Psychological Account of Personhood, the clearest and best-known version of which is developed by Parfit in *Reasons and Persons* (Oxford: OUP, 1984), Part III, provides an example of what I have in mind. As Jeff McMahan puts it in his recent critique of the Psychological Account (*The Ethics of Killing*, p. 43):

> According to the Psychological Account of Identity, the criterion of personal identity is nonbranching psychological continuity. To determine when a person ceases to exist, we track his life forward in time by following the relation of psychological continuity until it ceases to hold. When it ceases to hold, the person ceases to exist.[31]

McMahan's explanation of 'psychological continuity' is this (p. 43):

> Psychological continuity (as understood by the Psychological Account) consists of overlapping chains of strong psychological connectedness... there is strong psychological connectedness when the number of direct psychological connections from day to day is at least half

[31] Cp. Parfit, *Reasons and Persons* pp. 204–209.

the number that hold over each day in the life of a normal person.

For the Psychological Account, all persons are psychologies. Not all psychologies are persons, because psychologies that fail to display 'strong psychological connectedness' do not qualify as persons. For Parfit and other proponents of the Psychological Account, you do not count as a person unless you are a being that has a psychology in which there appear sufficiently many 'R-relations'[32] between the past and the present.

Here we could ask what counts as sufficiently many, and why. Or we could request an explanation of how R-relations are to be counted, or of how many R-relations between today and yesterday a normal person experiences. Parfit, perhaps, will not be too discomfited by such questions, since his project is, in the end, to undermine the notion of a person, by showing that it has vague edges. A simpler and more important question for the Psychological Account is this: How we are supposed to individuate or reidentify the psychological items standing on the ends of the R-relations in the first place?[33]

The Psychological Account assumes that the notion of continuity of psychology can be logically prior to the notion of continuity of person. It assumes that we can coherently say, for instance, that some memory X is a memory of some particular experience Y, whilst leaving it entirely open whether X

[32] Parfit's term: see, e.g., *Reasons and Persons* p. 262.

[33] The argument of the next two paragraphs is developed further in my 'Persons in time', in Heather Dyke, (ed.), *Time and Ethics* (Amsterdam: Kluwer 2003).

and Y are experiences had by the same person. As Wittgenstein, Ryle, Sir Peter Strawson, Elizabeth Anscombe, and other writers have repeatedly pointed out, this way of thinking is a complete mistake.[34] It makes it sound as if we could build up a world of persons on the metaphysical basis of a world of experiences. But the whole point about the world of persons is that it is a public world, and the whole point of the notion of an experience is that experiences are private. So we cannot treat experiences as the building-blocks of persons, any more than we can treat sentences as the building-blocks of houses. They're simply the wrong kind of thing to play that role.

Moreover, in Strawson's words (*Individuals* p. 102), 'States of consciousness could not be ascribed at all, unless they were ascribed to persons'. It's not just that experiences are categorically different from persons, and so cannot be seen as in some way ingredients of persons. It's also that the existence and identity of any experience is logically dependent upon the existence and identity of some person. So not only does the Psychological Account of persons talk about the wrong sort of thing, namely experiences. It also undermines itself by talking about experiences. Such talk is only available to the Psychological Account in the first place, because a different account of personhood is true.

[34] Wittgenstein, *Philosophical Investigations* (Oxford: Blackwell, 1951); Ryle, *The Concept of Mind* (London: Fontana, 1950); Strawson, *Individuals* (London: Methuen, 1959); Anscombe, 'The First Person', in Rosenthal, (ed.), *The Nature of Mind* (Oxford: OUP, 1991).

Briefly, what this argument proves is that the Psychological Account has to be wrong because a psychology is not and cannot be a person: it is a property of a person. (Usually a very complex property; but that does not alter my basic point.)

This conclusion that a psychology is not a person but a property of a person brings us back to the receptacle view. It shows that the Psychological Account's proposal that the persons who have intrinsic worth are psychologies is really a proposal to accord intrinsic worth to the properties of the person, and not to the person herself. It therefore turns out to be a disguised version of the receptacle view of the person. The Psychological Account crucially mislocates the person in the person's psychological properties. Human beings that only *could* have those psychological properties, and do not actually have them, are for the Psychological Account mere empty vessels waiting to be filled, or (using my other metaphor) bank accounts with nothing in them yet. Since they do not actually have the relevant properties, their value is as yet no more than zero.[35]

[35] Parfit's Psychological Account is not the only theory whose account of persons in this way ends up as a version of the receptacle view. *Mutatis mutandis,* my comments on Parfit apply also to Singer (again), *Practical Ethics* pp. 86–87: 'I propose to use "person", in the sense of a rational and self-conscious being, to capture those elements of the popular sense of "human being" that are not covered by "member of the species Homo sapiens".' And to John Harris, *The Value of Life* pp. 16–17: 'persons are beings capable of valuing their own lives.' And to Michael Tooley, 'Abortion and Infanticide' [1972], in Singer, (ed.), *Applied Ethics* (Oxford: OUP, 1987), p. 82: 'An organism possesses a

This makes the Psychological Account flatly incompatible with any serious attempt to value people in general not merely for their properties, but for themselves. It has to be incompatible with that attempt, because it draws the boundary between the properties and the person herself in the wrong place. The Psychological Account's explanation of the worth of human life is, in the end, no less superficial, and no less pathological, than the other versions of the receptacle account that I have rejected here.

And so, for the fourth and last time, we are face to face with the crucial question where exactly we *should* draw that line: "What is a person?" I have not tried to answer that question in this paper. I have only tried to get certain importantly wrong answers out of the way; to argue that persons—whatever they may be—are particulars of absolute value; and to show that the reason why we should resist the attraction of certain sorts of *im*personal absolute, is precisely

serious right to life only if it possesses the concept of a self as a continuing subject of experiences and other mental states, and believes that it is itself such an entity.' And to Mary Anne Warren ('On the Moral and Legal Status of Abortion', in H. Lafollette, (ed.), *Ethics in Practice* (Oxford: Blackwell, 1997), pp. 83–84): 'What characteristics entitle an entity to be considered a person? This is not the place to attempt a complete analysis of the concept of person-hood... All we need is an approximate list of the most basic criteria of personhood... I suggest that among the characteristics which are central to the concept of personhood are the following: (1) sentience... (2) emotionality... (3) reason... (4) the capacity to communicate... (5) self-awareness... (6) moral agency.' Mary Anne Warren's more recent 'multi-criterial theory of moral status' (see her book *Moral Status*) is also, in its application to persons, a version of the receptacle view.

because those absolute values make it impossible (whether logically or psychologically or both) for us to give particular persons the place in our ethical thinking that they deserve. As to the still unanswered question of what the person is, perhaps I should simply let Miss Anscombe herself have the last word:[36] '"The person" is a living human body'.[37]

[36] Anscombe, 'The First Person', p. 79.

[37] Afterthought: The suggestion that persons are 'living human bodies' is often countered by the Martians Question (first clearly put, perhaps, by Warren as cited in Note 34): 'There might be persons of other species—intelligent aliens. These persons would not be living *human* bodies.' Correct. The right response is to widen the definition of persons: 'persons are living human (or intelligent alien) bodies'. But, the Martians Question continues, 'So how do we *recognise* persons? The intelligent aliens show that persons are not recognized by their being living bodies, but by their displaying a particular type of psychology. So a person can't be simply a living human (or intelligent alien) body. A person must be at least a living body of some kind *that possesses a particular psychology.*'

This is a *non sequitur.* The criteria whereby we *first diagnose* a natural kind—water, say—may include e.g. wetness. It does not follow that water is essentially wet, still less that water *is* wetness. Similarly, the criteria whereby we first diagnose personhood need not be even *part* of the essence of persons. Still less need personhood be identified with the sum of those criteria. (See Kripke, *Naming and Necessity* (Oxford: Blackwell, 1973), pp. 116ff.) Further, the normal use of this line of argument—which, as in Warren, is to exclude e.g. very old and very young humans from personhood—depends upon unstated presuppositions about what counts as *possessing* a particular psychology or other characteristic. It is assumed that, because the infant does not actually perform any reasoning, we cannot describe it as a rational being. Yet we also describe the infant as a biped, even though the infant does not actually walk on two legs, and as a mammal, even though the infant does not actually breast-feed anyone (and will never even be able to, if it is male).

On the So-called Logic of Practical Inference

A. W. PRICE

Different questions generate different forms of practical reasoning. A contextually unrestricted 'What shall I do?' is too open to focus reflection. More determinately, an agent may ask, 'Shall I do X, or Y?' To answer that, he may need to weigh things up—as fits the derivation of 'deliberation' from *libra* (Latin for 'scales'). Ubiquitous and indispensable though this is, I mention it only to salute it in passing.[1] Or he may ask how to achieve a proposed end: if his end is to do X, he may ask 'How shall I do X?' Or he may ask how to apply a universal rule or particular maxim.[2] Aristotle supplies examples in *De Motu Animalium* (7.701a7 ff.), whose wording I freely adapt to my own purposes:

[1] Here I follow Aristotle's bad example: he notes that the etymology of 'choice' (*prohairesis*) indicates that its object is 'selected in preference to other things' (*pro heterôn haireton; Nicomachean Ethics*, 3.2.1112a16–17), but then focuses his attention, almost exclusively (though note 3.3.1112b16–17), upon means to ends.

[2] I set aside such reasoning as 'I promised to do X; so I will do X.' At least as it stands, no one could suppose that this is logically valid. It presents a reason for which the speaker intends to do X.

A1 reasons to a necessary means to achieving an end:

I will make a cloak.
To make a cloak I must do A.
So, I will do A.

A2 reasons to a sufficient means to achieving an end:

I will make something good.
A house is something good.
So, I will make a house.

B1 applies a universal rule:

Every man must walk.
I am man.
So, I must walk.

B2 applies a conditional that speaks of a particular agent at a certain time:

I will now make a cloak if I need one.
I need a cloak.
So, I will now make a cloak.

A paraphrase of 'Every man must walk' may bring out the affinity of B1 with B2: 'For all *x*, if *x* is a man, *x* must walk.' Both, therefore, involve reasoning from a hypothetical intention or requirement to a categorical one.

I wish to contrast two strategies for explaining such practical inferences. One builds informally upon Anselm Müiller's thesis that practical reasoning is characterized by an inherent teleology: it is thinking of a kind to help achieve a given goal, or fulfil a given requirement. It is in the nature of such thinking that, as Müller puts it, 'To reason practically is to consider which actions can promote one's end, *with a view to* realizing this end *by means of these* actions', in such a way that the content of the thoughts fits *them* to be already at the service of the end.[3] The thinking is *itself* of a kind to be for the sake of some practicable end, both under the general description 'deliberating about how to do X' (say), and in the specific form that it turns out to take.[4] If all goes well, *forming* new

[3] 'How Theoretical is Practical Reason?', in C. Diamond and J. Teichman (eds) *Intention and Intentionality: Essays in Honour of G. E. M. Anscombe* (Brighton: Harvester Press, 1979), 91–108; 98–9; cf. 'Der dreifache Ziel-Bezug des praktischen Denkens', in J.-E. Pleines (ed.), *Teleologie: ein philosophisches Problem in Geschichte und Gegenwart* (Würzburg: Königshausen & Neumann, 1994), 163–82; 169. In one respect, the second piece may be more judicious than the first: we may agree that the thinking must hope to succeed *on the ground of its content,* without being persuaded that the teleology of a practical thought is 'internal to its own content', so that 'the distinction between the content and the employment of a thought is of limited validity only'; 'How Theoretical is Practical Reason?', 99.

[4] Yet in its specific form the deliberation can only instance what Müller analyses as 'unreasoned purposiveness'. For it would be incoherent to reason as follows about what form the deliberation should take: 'I will do X; a (or the) way to find out how to do this is to reflect that my intention to do X will be best realized by doing Y; so let me reflect that my intention to do X will be best realized by doing Y.' As Müller comments, 'This is a problem when the first order reflection is represented *by a conception of its very content*'; 'Mental Teleology', *Proceedings of the Aristotelian Society* 92 (1991/2), 161–83; 166. Still peculiar would be this inference: 'I will do X; a (or the) way to do this is to form an intention to do Y; so, I will form an intention to do Y.' Intentions are transparent to their objects, and this is only readable as a distortion of the familiar 'I will do X; a (or the) way to do this is to do Y; so, I will do Y.'

intentions will help *towards* doing X, and *fulfilling* them will be a way or means *of* doing X; parallel structures of intention and intentional action will relate to the same practical purpose. In G. E. M. Anscombe's example of a sequence of act-descriptions, (a) moving one's arm up and down, (b) pumping, (c) replenishing the house's water-supply, and (d) poisoning the residents,[5] we can trace—*if* the intentions were formed by practical inference—two parallel series of acts and intentions: the man who deliberately does (a) in order to do (b), in order to do (c), in order to do (d) will then already have reasoned conversely 'I want to do (d); so, I will do (c); so, I will do (b); so, I will do (a).' Here each of (a), (b), and (c) comes first to be *intended*, and next to be *enacted*, for the sake of (d).

The germ of the idea is present in Aristotle: 'Thought itself moves nothing, but that which is for the sake of something and practical' (*Nicomachean Ethics*, 6.2.1139a35–6; cf. *De Anima*, 3.10.433a13–15). Distinctive of practical thought is that any stretch of it has the function of subserving the very end—varying from occasion to occasion—to which it is attempting to identify effective and practicable means. As Müller conceives it, such thinking is essentially first-person. Yet our intuitions about it may well be paralleled by intuitions about the applicability, which is equally third-person, of such phrases as 'had better', or indeed 'ought to'. We need not debate any relative priority between first-person practical reasoning leading to 'I will . . .', and third-person reasoning concluding 'He had

[5] *Intention*, 2nd edn (Oxford: Basil Blackwell, 1963), §23.

better . . .'. Against any reduction of the first to the second would be the conceivability of a community of agents who reasoned practically on their own behalf, but lacked the language-game of assessing their own and others' options by applying such concepts as 'had better'.

How does this relate to *inference*? Simon Blackburn offers a wide gloss on the term: 'The process of moving from (possibly provisional) acceptance of some propositions to acceptance of others.'[6] Here this may require extending beyond the acceptance of *propositions* (true or false); but otherwise its imprecision suits us well, and unqualified uses of 'inference' within this paper will carry no stronger connotation. A more restricted notion is *deduction,* which Blackburn glosses as follows: 'A process of reasoning in which a conclusion is drawn from a set of premises. Usually confined to cases in which the conclusion is supposed to follow from the premises, i.e. the inference is logically valid.'[7] Of course, theoretical thinking that has point is not content simply to trace entailment-relations. Good theoretical thinking—thinking that succeeds in making relevant inferences, or achieving useful generalizations, or providing explanations, or prompting discoveries—is not distinguished by rules of logical validity. Our question is whether there are any rules of valid inference that are special to practical inference, and provide *a* (if not *the*) criterion of its success.

For a different strategy may try to supplement Müller's teleological reflections by defining distinctive rules

[6] *The Oxford Dictionary of Philosophy* (Oxford & New York: Oxford University Press, 1994), ad 'inference'.

[7] Ibid., ad 'deduction'.

of inference that lead from premises containing at least one inherently practical premise to a conclusion directive of action. This, too, goes back to Aristotle (*NE* 7.3.1147a24–31):

> The one opinion is universal, while the other concerns particulars . . . Whenever a single opinion results from them, the conclusion must in the one case be asserted by the soul, but in practical cases immediately enacted; e.g., if everything sweet should be tasted, and this is sweet (which is one of the particular premises), the man who is able and not prevented must at the same time also enact this.

In our own time, one thinks of R. M. Hare, P. T. Geach, and Anthony Kenny. They have hoped to identify a practical logic, of imperatives or 'fiat's, parallel to, or contrastive with, the familiar alethic logic that takes us from propositions to propositions in ways that preserve truth. Practical rationality becomes a form of logical rationality with its own rules of inference.

We may call the first strategy *pragmatic*, the second *logicist*. I shall be arguing for the first over the second.

Connected with a choice between the pragmatic and logicist strategies is a choice between different ways of construing expressions of intention. English permits a distinction between 'I will do X', expressing an intention, and 'I shall do X', making a prediction.[8] One contrast is in onus of match: as Anscombe put it, if there is a mismatch between

[8] However, the distinction between 'shall' and 'will' is inverted in questions (so that 'I will do Y' answers 'How shall I do X?'), in the second and third persons (so that 'You shall do X' is a command or expression of intention, 'You will do X' usually a prediction), and in American English. So it is only a tendency, not a rule.

what I say and what happens which constitutes a mistake, then in the one case it is the prediction that is mistaken, while in the other it is the action.[9] This may suggest that expressions of intention rank rather with commands fulfilled or unfulfilled than with statements true or false. Kenny has proposed a genus of *fiats* of which commands and expressions of intention are species. Commands belong with requests within the species of *directives*: 'A directive is a fiat uttered to an agent: it gives the agent to understand that he is to realize the fiat.'[10] Expressions of intention might be construed as directives to oneself; or else they may form a distinct species, as do optatives (expressing wishes). Common to all fiats remains a distinguishing onus of match.

Alternatively, Anscombe's observation (which is about where to locate *mistakes)* may leave open that even expressions of intention are assertions *of a kind*, and are falsified if action fails to follow. One indication of this is translation into ratio obliqua. If someone tells me 'I will do X', I may report him as saying *that he will do X*, which records an assertion without specifying whether it was a prediction or an expression of intention. Can we explain this? J. David Velleman has this proposal: 'My choice makes it true that I'm going to act, by representing it as true that I'm going to act. It therefore has the same direction of fit as belief.' He distinguishes the *direction of fit*, which expressions of intention share with assertions, from the *direction of*

[9] *Intention*, 56.

[10] *Will, Freedom and Power* (Oxford, Basil Blackwell, 1975),

guidance, which they share with expressions of desire: 'An attitude's direction of guidance consists in whether the attitude causes or is caused by what it represents'; the mistake is then to suppose 'that a cognitive direction of fit entails a passive direction of guidance; and, conversely, that only states with a conative direction of fit can be active or practical'; rather, 'The decision to do something . . . has the cognitive direction of fit and the associated aim of being true, despite having a practical direction of guidance.'[11] He proposes that intentions are predictions *of a kind* to cause their own fulfilment.

We may call Kenny's view of expressions of intention *conative*, Velleman's *constative.* On the constative construal, A1, viewed as a piece of logical inference, is straightforwardly deductive; for all its constituent propositions are capable of truth and falsity, and logically its premises cannot be true but its conclusion false. Might this suit the logicist strategy? Actually, not. A1 then becomes an instance of the following deductive schema (call it C1):

I am going to do X.
Whoever does X also (in fact) does Y.
So, I am going to do Y.

Take this instance (call it C2):

I am going to get drunk.
Whoever gets drunk has a hangover.
So, I am going to have a hangover.

[11] *The Possibility of Practical Reason* (Oxford: Clarendon Press, 2000),

Then consider the equivalent 'mixed' inference, with both first premise and conclusion replaced by expressions of intention (call it C3):

I will get drunk.
Whoever gets drunk has a hangover.
So, I will have a hangover.

This is wholly unintuitive as a *practical* inference: in a practical inference from an end, the conclusion relates to means, not to consequences. The example illustrates that a prediction that *p* may entail a prediction that *q*, and both *p* and *q* be possible objects of intention; and yet an expression of intention that *p* may not entail any expression of intention that *q*. For predicted side-effects of realizing one's intentions are not thereby intended, even if they are welcome.[12]

Hence, if the logicist hopes to capture the practicality that A1 possesses (as Aristotle intended it) and C3 lacks, he needs to read A1 as an instance not of C1, but rather of the following schema:

Da. I will do X.
Db. A necessary means to doing X is doing Y.
Dc. So, I will do Y.

Conativists must hold that Da entails Dc only *via* Db, whereas, if we construe them constatively, Da entails Dc

[12] The point is well made, and in this connection, by Candace Vogler, 'Anscombe on Practical Inference', in E. Millgram (ed.), *Varieties of Practical Reasoning* (Cambridge Mass.: MIT Press, 2001), 437–64; 460.

via not only Db, but also the more general 'A necessary condition of doing X is doing Y' (call this Db*).

I have illustrated the difference between Db and Db* by an example where doing Y is an inevitable corollary of doing X, and not a means towards it. Other examples are of necessary preconditions. A. N. Prior drew attention to this case: that the F.B.I. chief wants to (bring it about that he) catch a Communist does not entail that he wants to bring it about that there is a Communist (which he is rather taking to be true already); for to bring about that *p* is not to bring about all that *p* entails.[13] On the constative reading, the following deduction is valid:

I will catch a Communist.
I will only catch a Communist if there is a Communist.
So, there is a Communist.

Here, however one reads the first premise, it is impossible to read the conclusion as an expression of intention. Hence this cannot be a practical inference.

Prior's example is salutary, and his point can be extended. On the face of it, it is plausible to suppose that, if I intend to do X, and am aware that doing Y is *integral* to doing X, then I already intend to do Y. But suppose that doing X is dying nobly, and doing Y is dying. I can intend to die nobly without intending to die—for death is not intendable by those for whom it is plainly inevitable. (Perhaps Christ is the only person who ever intended to die.)

[13] *Objects of Thought* (Oxford: Clarendon Press, 1971), 138.

A man who intends to do X, to which doing Y is integral, may also intend to do Y; but whether that is so will vary according to content and context.

II

Let us now start to assess the prospects of the rival strategies by returning to A1 and A2. Given (say) that an agent intends to do X, he may ask himself, 'How shall I do X?' Thus Aristotle writes of those who deliberate (e.g., doctor, orator, statesman), 'Having set the end, they consider how and by what means it is to be attained' (*NE* 3.3.1112b 15–16). And Hare remarks similarly, 'Whenever we are told to do anything, or whenever we ourselves form the intention of doing something, the question arises of how to do this, unless (as in the case of very simple commands or intentions) the answer is so obvious that the question does not need to be asked.'[14]

The least problematic, but not always practicable, form of reasoning to an answer has this form, which combines A1 and A2 in reasoning to a means both necessary and sufficient:

I will do X.
The means to (or way of) doing X is to do Y.
So, I will do Y.[15]

[14] 'Practical Inferences', in his *Practical Inferences* (London: Macmillan, 1971), 59–73; 59.

[15] Practical inferences that share the form of B2 seem equally secure: given that *p*, to do X if *p* is to do X. It may, of course, turn out wiser to recoil from the conclusion than to abide by the first premise. Suppose that this ran, 'We will destroy your cities if you try to destroy ours.'

However, it is often the case that the agent is only ready or able to reason to a necessary condition of doing X (which might lie behind A1), or that doing Y is only one among several possible ways of doing X (as within A2). It is then unclear how to apply the maxim that to will the end is to will the means. Two alternative logics have been proposed, of *satisfaction*, and of *satisfactoriness*. The contrasting principles of these are clearly set out, in application to inferences with a single premise, in some pages in Hare that I shall now adapt to fiats.[16] Since to any fiat there corresponds an assertion to the effect that the fiat will be satisfied, one can reason in accordance with ordinary constative logic from a premise to the effect that a certain fiat will be satisfied to the conclusion that a certain other fiat will be satisfied. (It is taken to be irrelevant to logic whether either fiat is actually entertained or expressed.) For example, from the premise that 'Fiat (I do X and Y)' will be satisfied we can infer the conclusion that 'Fiat (I do X)' will be satisfied, since this inference merely puts in another form the inference from 'I am going to do X and Y' to 'I am going to do X.' Equally, which may seem more paradoxical, one may reason from 'Fiat (I do X)' to 'Fiat (I do X or Y).'[17] In this logic, 'satisfaction' is a value which is preserved in the same way as truth is in ordinary constative inferences. So much for the *logic of satisfaction*.

[16] 'Practical Inferences', 62–4. Very similar, about fiats, is Kenny, *Will, Freedom and Power*, 81–2.

[17] Note that the form of words 'I do X or Y' describes the performance not of a disjunctive act (there is no such thing), but of one of a pair of acts.

By contrast, in the *logic of satisfactoriness* the preserved value (the analogue of truth in ordinary logic) is satisfactoriness relative to a given set of values or purposes. This logic has determinate rules that are the mirror-image of the rule of ordinary constative logic (and thus, also, of the logic of satisfaction). For example, since there is a valid inference from 'You are going to do X and Y' to 'You are going to do X', there is a valid inference in the logic of satisfactoriness from 'Fiat (I do X)' to 'Fiat (I do X and Y)'—though this seems paradoxical.

It is unclear how either logic is to be applied to inferences with multiple premises, perhaps in mixed moods.[18] And we have already seen that there we cannot permit practical inferences that simply reflect or reverse indicative ones. How, for example, is the logic of satisfaction to escape licensing an inference from 'Fiat (there is a communist and I catch him)' to 'Fiat (there is a communist)'? For the corresponding indicative inference is certainly valid. It is therefore already an objection to both logics that their role has to be strictly circumscribed. Yet we can compare them as proposing alternative models for inferring one fiat from another *given* the statement of a means either necessary or sufficient for its satisfaction. Thus an inference from 'Fiat (I do X)' to 'Fiat (I do Y)' is licensed by the logic of satisfaction within the scope of a supposition 'Doing Y is a necessary means to doing X', but by the logic of satisfactoriness within the scope of a supposition 'Doing Y is a sufficient means to doing X.'

[18] See Alfred F. MacKay, 'Inferential Validity and Imperative Inference Rules', *Analysis* 29 (1969), 145–56.

Initially, I shall not discuss either logic directly. Instead, I shall consider problems that arise in any case, first with practical reasoning to a *necessary* means, then with practical reasoning to a *sufficient* means.

Suppose that you tell me 'Do X and Y': have you thereby also told me to do X? When it is not already given that I am going to do X, *part* of what you tell me to do, in telling me to do X and Y, is indeed to do X. To tell me 'Do X and Y—but don't do X' would be to contradict yourself. And I can reason that I cannot obey your command without doing X. Yet in order to assess the bearing of this on the teleology of practical inference, we have to move into the first person: is it always apt to move from 'I will do X and Y' to 'I will do X', when both express intention, by practical reasoning? It may not be at all, for the reason that doing X may be an unintendable aspect of intentionally doing X and Y. (Doing X and Y might be causing myself a hangover by getting drunk.) Yet, if doing X and doing Y are equally focal within my intention to do X and Y, then *part* of what I intend, when I intend to X and Y, is indeed to do X. And, at least on the constative construal, there can be no objection to an inference from 'I will do X and Y' to 'I will do X' that merely unpacks, or unpicks, the content of my intention (which is itself neither an intention, nor intrinsically the content of an intention). But it need not follow that proceeding from 'I will do X and Y' to 'I will do X' has point *as a piece of practical inference.* No doubt, having practical point comes in degrees. If doing X is something that it is possible for me to do in order to do X and Y, then I may *intelligibly* advance, for the sake of doing X and Y, from 'I will do X and

Y' to 'I will do X'; yet a question of *advisability* may remain. Will my forming an intention to do X make it more likely that I actually do X and Y? What if doing X without doing Y is a *very* bad idea (far worse than doing Y without doing X), and doing X will make it *less* certain that I do Y? (Suppose that, while I should be able to do Y as well, doing X will use up most of my time and energy.) If so, that doing X is necessary to doing X and Y looks like being immediately either the content of an idle thought, or the father of a rash intention. I may more safely advance to an intention specifically to do X *after* I have made sure of doing Y; for, given the probabilities in this case, it would not be wise for me to pursue my purpose of doing X and Y by immediately proceeding, non-idly, to an intention to do X.[19]

Now consider reasoning to a sufficient means. One objection to it can, I think, be disarmed; another observation shows that it is hardly logical inference. It has to be

[19] However, the inference may be at once non-idle and innocuous if it serves to initiate deliberation about how to do X—*if* such is needed—that will not be put into effect until it is certain that the agent will do Y. Another example has a different structure which does not invite that qualification. Suppose I decide, 'I will go to Paris by train.' This entails 'I will go to Paris'; but how acceptable *as a piece of practical reasoning* is 'I will go to Paris by train; so, I will go to Paris'? Suppose that I can only go to Paris by train or plane; then that, and 'I will go to Paris', together entail 'I will go to Paris by train or plane.' So we have this inferential sequence: 'I will go to Paris by train; therefore, I will go to Paris; therefore, I will go to Paris by train or plane.' But 'I will go to Paris by train; so, I will go to Paris by train or plane' could only with great ingenuity be presented as a piece of *practical* inference.

conceded that doing Y may be a sufficient means to doing X, which is rational, and yet itself be unacceptable or irrational. This may be because doing Y is forbidden (as when doing X is acquiring £50 in cash, and doing Y is robbing the till), or because it is excessive (suppose that doing X is the same, and doing Y is withdrawing £500 from one's bank account). In reply, Kenny proposes that we restrict the means by extending 'the goal-fiat from which the practical reasoning starts'.[20] Yet he may be wiser when he later rejects any such attempt to preclude defeasibility (the defeating of a piece of reasoning, itself satisfactory, by the addition of further premises): 'The notion of a premiss which is complete enough to prevent defeasibility while specific enough to entail a practical conclusion is surely chimerical.'[21] Deliberation requires an initial target to aim at, which means a target consciously defined or definable; but a target that aimed to encompass all relevant considerations would exceed the imagination and defeat the understanding. Sarah Broadie makes the point that deliberation is in part calculation (cf. Aristotle, *NE* 6.2.1139a12–13), and so demands a goal present to consciousness. She offers a nice analogy: 'It may be wise to acknowledge that our identified target is no more than the tip of some iceberg, but it does not follow that the entire iceberg is our target, or that we can approach a submerged whole otherwise than by setting our sights on what we can see of it.'[22]

[20] *Will, Freedom and Power*, 91. [21] Ibid., 94.

[22] *Ethics in Aristotle* (New York: Oxford University Press, 1991), 236.

Yet there is a better way out, which does not address all sources of defeasibility, but can block inferences to the unacceptable. In practical deliberation, the initial end is supplemented by what Müller has called 'quasi-ends' or 'limiting ends': these are background or standing considerations, not necessarily moral, which do not set deliberation in train themselves, but tell for or against certain ways of behaving, and so, with varying stringency, constrain or influence the choice of means.[23] Pertinent considerations include these: each quasi-end is too general, leaving too many options open, to form the target of a piece of deliberation about what to do; decisions are made against the background of an indefinite set of quasi-ends (which constitute much of a man's character); ends are adapted to quasi-ends, not quasi-ends to ends (unless over a period of time); an end may be adopted intentionally, whereas quasi-ends come to bear spontaneously. Action would often be impossible if one could not select an end for the occasion; but one is not content to respect one quasi-end and disregard the rest. Thus there are any number of possible ways of acquiring £50 that do not come up for consideration because they are obviously improper or disproportionate. So an

[23] For 'quasi-Ziele', see Müller, 'Der dreifache Ziel-Bezug praktischen Denkens', 164; for 'einschränkende Ziele', see his 'Wie notwendig ist das Gute? Zur Struktur des sittlichen Urteils', in L. Honnefeider (ed.), *Sittliche Lebensform und praktische Vernunft* (Paderborn: Ferdinand Schöningh, 1992), 27–57; 44. To quasi-ends that are both negative and stringent one may apply the term 'side-constraint'; see Robert Nozick, *Anarchy, State, and Utopia* (Oxford: Basil Blackwell, 1974), 28–35.

unacceptable inference from 'I will do X' to 'I will do Y' can be excluded by extending the implicit background, and yet without expanding the explicit starting-point.[24]

So practical reasoning to a sufficient means may be *generally* defendable, to a necessary means *often* defendable. However, despite the title that they share, it must be emphasized that the 'logics' of satisfaction and satisfactoriness carry quite different aspirations. The logic of satisfaction hopes to identify what the speaker is committing himself to; and this is identified with what he cannot reject without contradicting himself. The logic of satisfactoriness imports a weaker notion of successful reasoning. This reasoning is defeasible, since the addition of premises may cancel a previous implication; and it hopes to identify conclusions that the speaker has no good reason to reject, but not conclusions that he cannot reject consistently.[25] For better or worse, the logic of satisfaction is more of a *logic* than that of satisfactoriness.

My conclusion so far is this: inference from an end to a means that is necessary but not sufficient may be logical and yet not practical, whereas inference from an end to a means that is sufficient yet not necessary may be practical but is not logical.

[24] Verbally, the agent may simply add to his judgement that doing Y is sufficient for doing X the protecting clause 'And there is nothing that excludes my doing Y.'

[25] The point is made by Hare (with acknowledgement to R. F. Stalley); 'Practical Inferences', 65–6.

III

I now turn to practical reasoning that shares the form of B1 (when its conclusion expresses an intention):

Every man must walk.
I am man.
So, I must walk.

Here Kenny makes a concession to Hare that brings them briefly together, but unites them in confusing a distinction.

Hare and Kenny wish or are willing to subsume deliberation from a rule under deliberation about necessary conditions. While generally privileging practical reasoning to sufficient conditions, Kenny allows a role to practical reasoning to necessary conditions in the case of following rules: 'We reason to necessary conditions in practical contexts, for example, when we are seeking to obey a negative prohibition.'[26] Hare had adapted an example from Aristotle (*DMA* 7.701a13): 'Given that I am a man, my marching is a necessary condition for fulfilling the requirement that all men are to march. It is not a sufficient condition, because *my* marching will not fulfil that requirement unless everybody else does.'[27] Thus any single act of compliance becomes a necessary but not sufficient condition of universal compliance. A single act can seldom count as a *means* towards that;

[26] *Will, Freedom and Power*, 89.

[27] 'Practical Inferences', 60–61. Strictly, however, there are no circumstances in which *I* can count as fulfilling the requirement.

yet, without subsuming rule-case reasoning within means-end reasoning, the proposal assimilates them to an extent.

Yet there is reason to deny that the requirement (a) 'No man is ever to tell a lie' is equivalent to the desideratum (b) 'Let it be the case that no man ever tells a lie.' This is not essentially a matter of stringency: some rules (e.g. of etiquette) are readily overridable, and some desiderata are imperative. The distinction is rather this: on any occasion when I refrain from lying, I am fulfilling a necessary condition of the satisfaction of (b), but *observing* (a). It could be that the satisfaction of (b) needs to be all or nothing; but (a) does not proscribe lying for the sake of the satisfaction of (b); nor does it permit, what (b) leaves open, that, in some predicaments, one might tell a lie oneself as a way of reducing the incidence of lying by oneself or others. Thus it is consistent to add to (b), but seldom to (a), the further desideratum (c) 'But let it also be the case that no one refrains from lying unless everyone does so.' For (c) supplements (b), but conflicts with (a) in every world in which not everyone complies with (a).

How might the distinction be registered within the language of fiats? Perhaps by a difference of scope. Thus (a), 'No man is ever to tell a lie', might be represented by

(a*) $(\forall x)$ $(\forall t)$ (x is a man $\supset$ Fiat (x does not lie at t)),

where the placing of 'Fiat' mirrors the placing of 'is to' in (a) within its grammatical predicate, but (b), 'Let it be the case that no man ever tells a lie', by

(b*) Fiat (($\forall x$) ($\forall t$) (x is a man $\supset$ x does not lie at t)).

However, this would not be welcomed by Kenny, who wishes to keep all tropics or signs of mood, including 'Fiat', outside the phrastic or sentence radical.[28] He writes, 'The main positive reason for keeping tropics out of phrastics is the enormous gain in simplicity.'[29] But we may wonder whether it is intelligible to quantify across a sign of mood.

A securer way of marking a difference is to make distinctions of scope with respect to the modals 'must' and 'ought'. Geach has insisted that 'ought' is an operator that attaches to predicates, and not to propositions.[30] The distinction may not apply to theoretical 'ought's conveying a factual probability, such as 'It ought to stop raining soon'; but Geach seems right about practical 'ought's applying normative considerations, even when the subject of the 'ought' is implicit or indeterminate.[31] By contrast, it would seem that practical 'must's may attach either to predicates or to propositions. So 'He must do X' may be equivalent either to (i) 'It is necessary that he do X', or to (ii) 'It is necessary for him to do X' (which is unambiguously captured by 'He needs to do X'). (i) can answer the question 'Who must do X?', (ii) the question 'Who needs to do X?' (ii) presents the

[28] *Will, Freedom and Power*, 74–9. [29] Ibid., 78.

[30] 'Whatever Happened to Deontic Logic?', in Geach (ed.), *Logic and Ethics* (Dordrecht: Kluwer, 1991), 33–48.

[31] A degenerate exception is 'It ought never to have happened' (loosely derivative from 'It ought never to have been allowed to happen'). Yet I detect no ambiguity of scope within 'We ought to do X.' When I speak of practical or theoretical 'ought's or 'must's, I do not mean that the terms themselves are ambiguous.

necessity as one that *he* lies under, while (i) leaves it to the context to determine on whom the necessity lies (which will not always be on him). Thus, though *walking out with* is a symmetric relation, yet, if Jack has promised to walk out with Jill, then, in that regard, it is necessary *for him to* walk out with her, but *not for her to* walk out with him. 'It is Jack who ought to walk out with Jill' may emphasize either that is Jack who should walk out with Jill (and not John, say), or that the obligation is not reciprocal. Thus we may paraphrase (a) and (b) above as follows: 'No man is ever to tell a lie' can be rendered unambiguously by 'No man ought ever to tell a lie', whereas the rather artificial 'Let it be the case that no man ever tells a lie' can be rendered by 'No man must ever tell a lie' on *one* reading—not the most natural one—of that sentence.

That there is no logical inference from 'No man ought ever to tell a lie' to 'I will not now tell a lie' is evident from another general difference between 'ought' and 'must'. In the context of selecting means to ends, 'must' always excludes alternatives, whereas 'ought' often permits alternatives, though it indicates that, if there are any, they are counter-indicated. Thus, if I must do Y in order to do X, doing Y is required for doing X; *if* there are any ways of doing X without doing Y, they are excluded. If I ought to do Y in order to do X, then there may be alternative ways of doing X; yet, if there are, they are counter-indicated. Within the context of a reasoning relative to an end, I must do Y if that is *necessary* for my end, if only in the light of my quasi-ends; I ought to do Y if, given my quasi-ends, I cannot otherwise achieve my end in a way that is *appropriate* or *befitting* to my role and situation. This shows that no 'ought'-judgement is the kind of thing to be satisfied or fulfilled. Within the dichotomy of 'Est' and 'Fiat', 'ought' falls within 'Est'. This is less clear of 'must', whence a temptation to distinguish the practical 'must' from the theoretical by supposing that the former attaches to imperatives, as the latter to indicatives. Yet it tells against this that 'If no man must ever tell a lie . . .' is permissible as 'If let no man ever tell a lie . . .' is not. And practical necessities can only arise from the *being in force* (or otherwise *operative*) of rules or requirements, whatever that comes to, and not (which would be syntactic nonsense) from any imperatives themselves. Broadly, a judgement 'I ought to do X' indicates that there are good, a judgement 'I must do X' that there are compelling, grounds for doing X. Hence the latter more often expresses an intention.

IV

Can there *be* a logic or imperatives, or of fiats? If not, the logicist strategy was anyway built on sand. I shall largely focus upon imperatives (which are the only uncontested fiats that stand in clear relations of consistency and inconsistency); some of what I shall say should be adaptable to fiats in general.

First, a few intuitive remarks, mostly about directives. There is a special difficulty (as David Wiggins has put to me) about *who* is to perform an imperative inference. Take commands in the specific sense (directives that carry institutional authority). Should the inference be performed by the speaker who initially issues the imperative? This is problematic. If I command you to do X by saying 'Do X', I intend (or—to cover deviant cases—purport to intend) to be trying to make you do X *by that very utterance.* But if I first explicitly infer 'Do X' from (say) 'Do X and Y', it becomes irresoluble whether it is not rather by saying 'Do X and Y' that I intend to be trying to make you do X.[32] So is it rather the recipient who needs to make the inference? Some inferences he may very well need to make, but not from a reiteration of the command, which he has no authority to impose upon himself. (If he had the authority to command himself, he would also have the authority to disobey himself.)

Commands are just one species of directive. Aurel Kolnai noted the oddity of accompanying a command by a justification for it. It is as if the commander said, 'For these reasons you would be well advised to decide upon and follow such and such a course of action; but anyhow you have to do so.'[33] By contrast, there is nothing odd about issuing the instruction 'Don't walk on the ice—it is thin.' And requests and pieces of advice are commonly

[32] The same point arises with *telling that.* I can tell you that *p*, or that it is the case that *p* because *q*. But within the context '*q*; so *p*' I cannot both be telling you that *q*, and that *p*. If I tell you that *p* by saying '*p*', I standardly intend to cause you to believe that *p* just through my saying '*p*'; this does not hold if I present *p* as an inference from '*q*; so *p*.'

[33] 'The Justification of Commands', *British Journal of Educational Studies* 16 (1968), 258–70; 260. I owe the reference to Wiggins.

accompanied by the giving of grounds. (Indeed, advising someone to do something relates closely to telling him that he ought, or has reason, to do it.) However, we must not equate citing a *reason* or *ground,* constituted by some fact, with supplying a *premise.*[34] If I request or advise you to do Y, I may also request or advise you to do Y *for some reason.* But a piece of advice, say, to do Y is not happily *grounded* upon a prior piece of advice to do X, even if doing Y is a means to doing X. What is rather needed is a reason for doing X, which will then be also a reason for doing Y. If I tell you to do Y, and, when asked for a justification, tell you to do X, to which doing Y is a means, and, when asked for a justification for *that*, tell you to W, to which doing X is a means, I can go on indefinitely without giving you a single reason for doing Y.

It is also plausible that logical premises must purport to state facts. Suppose I infer logically, '*p*; so, *q*.' Here 'so' marks that *q* follows, *given p*, and 'given *p*' means 'given *that p*', where *p* must be a proposition, true or false. This is also arguable from the relation, which is surely close, between the inference '*p*; so *q*', and the hypothetical 'If *p*, *q*.' It would be surprising if an imperative or other Fiat, which is not a proposition, could occur among the premises of a logical inference, though not within the antecedent of a conditional.

[34] To insist that a reason or ground must be a fact is not to settle the interesting question, which is what *makes* a certain fact a reason or ground, for *an* or *any* agent, for him or her to act in a certain way.

Now for a more protracted argument. What might intuitively ground the notion of imperative inference? It is not enough to note that we certainly have a concept of *implicitly telling someone to do something*; for that equally applies, for instance, to Henry II's asking 'Who will rid me of this turbulent priest?', which only intimated an imperative.[35] Yet we might hope to be able to make sense of a narrower notion of *telling someone to do something by implication*. According to Trinity anecdote, Housman might well have said to Hardy, 'Do write another novel—but don't write another *Jude*.' If he had, would he not have been telling him, by implication, to write a new novel not like *Jude?* But the notion of 'telling to by implication' needs more scrutiny. A problem, as I see it, is that there are alternative ways of lending it precision, and no one of them is sufficiently privileged to underwrite a logic.

One conception of it is this:

> (1) I tell you to do X by implication in saying what I say if you will be disobeying me if you do not do X.[36]

Another conception is narrower:

> (2) I tell you to do X by implication in saying what I say if you will be disobeying me, if you do not do X, *in not doing X*.

[35] I owe point and example to Wiggins.

[36] Note that talk of disobedience implies—what needs to be understood—that it is up to you whether you do X or not. To tell someone to die nobly is not to tell him by implication to die.

(2) may support an inference from (a) 'Do X and Y' to (b) 'Do X' (when both doing X and doing Y are properly commandable). For, if I say (a), you disobey that *in not doing X,* if you do not do X, since doing X is *part* of doing X and Y. (1) may additionally support an inference to (b) from (c) 'Do X if you do Y' and (d) 'Do Y.' For, if I utter (c) and (d), you are bound to be disobeying me if you do not do X, though this may be *either* in not doing X, supposing that you do Y, *or* in not doing Y (which is to disobey a premise, and not a conclusion). Arguably (1) is too coarse-grained. For if (c) and (d) together really *entailed* (b), then surely not to do X would be straightforwardly to disobey them *in not doing X*—which it is not, since, if I do not do Y, it is *in not doing Y* that I am disobedient.

There is further objection to inferring (b) from (c) and (d) in accordance with (1). Set out the inferential possibilities as follows:

(A) Do X if you do Y.
(B) You are going to do Y.
(B*) Do Y.
(C) So, do X.

Should we suppose that it is adding (B), or (B*), that yields (C) out of (A)? Parallel indicative inferences (and our initial B2) surely suggest that it is (B). Uttering (B*) may well exclude asserting the negation of (B), viz. 'You are not going to do Y', since imperative utterances, if they are at least to purport to be attempts to cause compliance, presuppose that compliance is open; yet they need not imply that compliance will follow. So if we take a case where the addressee may fail or refuse to do Y, and (A) has told him to do X if he does Y, but perhaps not otherwise (it is consistent to add 'And do X *only* if you do Y'), it is implausible to suppose that adding (B*) to (A) commits the speaker by implication to (C). Consider an example: suppose that I advise you to take a holiday abroad, and to take out travellers' cheques if, but only if, you are going to do so; have I thereby *already* advised you by implication to take out travellers' cheques?

And yet there is further uncertainty within (2) itself. If you ask me, after I have said 'Do X and Y', 'Am I to do X?', the answer cannot be 'No'—though it might be 'Yes—and Y.' I may not intend an implicit 'Do X' to cause you to do X *independently of the other conjunct*. If I tell you '*p* and *q*', I authorize you to walk away with an unconditional belief that *p*—there can be nothing wrong in your doing that, though I may prefer you also to come to believe that *q*. If I tell you to do X and Y, I do not authorize you to walk away with an intention to do X, especially if, unless you make a point of doing Y, you are more likely, if (or even if) you do X, *not* to do Y than to do Y.[37] There may be a background rule, 'Don't do X without doing Y'; indeed, if there is one, telling you to do X *and Y*

[37] Michael Martin puts the point to me as follows: 'Assume that the assertibility of imperatives is tied to the desirability of what is requested; then it is easy to set up a circumstance in which "X and Y" is highly desirable but "X" is not, because "X and not-Y" is very undesirable, and is a much more likely outcome among X-situations than "X and Y".'

may well be an allusion to it. If we try to identify the utterances that give you (as I am putting it) the right to walk away with a simple intention to do X, the answer can only be 'Do X' itself, or any command logically equivalent to it. And then there is no significant telling by implication.

Consider two examples of conjunctive instruction: 'Dilige et quod vis fac' ('Love, and do what you like'), and 'Light the fuse and step back three paces.'[38] To the extent that it may be difficult to love, and easy to linger by a lighted firework, any inferences to 'Quod vis fac' and 'Light the fuse' are—what shall I say?—*inhibited*. Certainly to set about fulfilling this conjunct without first giving thought to the other, or in despair of fulfilling both, is neither licensed by the instruction, nor commendable as partial compliance. (It is no extenuation to say, 'Well, I did light the fuse.') Now this may invite a reply: 'Consider the sentence, "The butler took possession of some of the princess's effects with the Queen's permission"; this certainly entails "The butler took possession of some of the princess's effects"—and yet the police had better not believe *this* without also believing *that*.' (I am sure that Hare would have responded so.) However, it plausibly makes a difference that imperatives have a practical function that is essential to the kind, even if not invariable within its instances: that of *telling* people to do things as a way of *getting* or *inducing* or *leading* them to do them (the

[38] I owe the first of these to Wiggins (Augustine, *In epistulam Iohannis ad Parthos tractatus*, 7.8), the second to Bob Hale.

last even holding of advice).[39] I can add 'Take it or leave it' after telling you that *p*, but not after telling you to do X. Hence extracting 'Do X' from 'Do X and Y' is *inherently* dangerous in a way that extracting *p* from '*p* & *q*' is not. The second looks much more like an unimpugnable inference than the first.

The logicist may respond by distinguishing, in his turn, between logic and pragmatics: just as—I have conceded—(i) 'I will do X and Y' entails (ii) 'I will do X' (if both are read constatively), although proceeding to (ii) after (i) can be inadvisable (or worse) as a piece of practical inference, so—he may urge—(iii) 'Do X and Y' may entail (iv) 'Do X', although proceeding to (iv) after (iii) can be in practice inadvisable (or worse). The trouble remains that the pragmatics of imperatives are part of their essence. Even if I can infer (ii) from (i) without thereby forming any new intention, I cannot advance to a serious utterance of 'Do X' without thereby telling an addressee to do X.

[39] Thus Anscombe, *Intention*, 3: 'An imperative will be a description of some future action, addressed to the prospective agent, and cast in a form whose point in the language is to make the person do what is described. I say that this is its point in the language, rather than that it is the purpose of the speaker, partly because the speaker might of course given an order with some purpose quite other than that it should be executed (e.g. so that it should *not* be executed).' In this way, a conventional device such the imperative mood has a function analogous to that ascribed to living things by unquantifiable 'Aristotelian categoricals' such as 'Rabbits are herbivores', which is true of *the rabbit*, but maybe not of *every rabbit*; Philippa Foot, *Natural Goodness* (Oxford: Clarendon Press, 2001), 27–9, takes both phrase and example from Michael Thompson.

I conclude that the notion of 'telling' someone to do something 'by implication' is too indeterminate to define rules of imperative logic. What do we have instead? Surely any number of informal modes of inference. If you tell me to do something, there may be point in my reasoning about how I am to avoid *any* failure to comply, or *some particular* failure. Imperatives indeed have a content (to be *told* to do something is to be told to do *something*), and so invite not just a reflex of compliance, but reflection about *how* to comply. But the starting-point will be something like, 'I am told to do such-and-such'—and not the imperative itself.

V

If we decline to regiment practical inference by the logics of satisfaction and satisfactoriness, and indeed reject the very idea of a logic of imperatives and fiats, we are taken starkly back, without the illusion of logical scaffolding, to the teleology of practical thinking.

Let us reconsider the paradoxes. Hare, in defending a logic of satisfaction, found himself defending an inference from 'I will do X' to 'I will do X or Y' on the ground that doing X or Y is indeed a logically *necessary* condition of doing X, whereas Kenny, in advancing a logic of satisfactoriness, found himself defending an inference from 'I will do X' to 'I will do X and Y' on the ground that doing X and Y is indeed a logically *sufficient* condition of doing X. We may rather seek a ground for refusing to countenance *as practical* any of the following inferences : from 'I will do X' to 'I will do X or Y', from 'I will do X' to 'I will do X and Y', and from

'I will get drunk' to 'I will have a hangover.' Happily, the insight that we need is not one that we have to achieve ourselves, for it is already present in Anscombe's paper 'Practical Inference'.[40] We must keep in mind that practical inference from 'I will do X' is governed by the question 'How shall I do X?' Much the same objection then applies to all three inferences: having a hangover is not a means to getting drunk, just as—certainly in most cases—neither doing X or Y, nor doing X and Y, is means to doing X. No doubt there are exceptions, but they prove the rule. As Anscombe writes, 'Effecting two things may indeed often be *a way of* effecting one of them; but the admission of arbitrary conjuncts is one of those forced and empty requirements of a view which shew that here is something wrong with it.'[41]

We can still accommodate cases of overkill. Anscombe gives a notorious example of doing a lot in order to achieve less: 'The British ... wanted to destroy some German soldiers on a Dutch island in the second world war, and chose to accomplish this by bombing the dykes

[40] Though written long before, this is most accessibly printed in R. Hursthouse, G. Lawrence, and W. Quinn (eds) *Virtues and Reasons: Philippa Foot and Moral Theory* (Oxford: Clarendon Press, 1995), 1–34; the relevant pages there are 12–13, and 20–21.

[41] 'Practical Inference', 13. Kenny came to agree: 'Her point shows that the logic of satisfactoriness concerns merely the relations between states of affairs qua want-satisfactions: in order to be applied to the *bringing about* of states of affairs—and thus to become a genuinely practical logic, rather than a wish-fulfilment logic ensnaring Midases and useful only to fairy godmothers—it needs supplementing with a logic of the description of action'; *Will, Freedom and Power*, 84 n. 11.

and drowning everybody. (The Dutch were their allies.)'[42] In this case, a single action, bombing the dykes, was a way of drowning everybody on the island, and hence of drowning everybody on the island who was German. As she later adds, 'What is in question here is something outside the logic that we are considering, namely whether there is "one action" which is a way of effecting (p & q) and therefore a way of effecting p.'[43] Some partly similar cases might well be described otherwise: an action may have the intended result that p, and the predicted side-effect that q. On some moral views, this difference is more than notional: according to the doctrine of double effect, one is not to do good through intentionally doing evil, but may cause evil incidentally (so long as it is not disproportionate) through doing good. If so, this had better not be a distinction that is manipulable by *choosing* how to think about an action; yet its application is complicated by the fact that an end that is genuinely embraced may yet be optional and occasional.

What we cannot permit as pieces of practical reasoning are inferences from 'I will do X' either to 'I will do X or Y' or to 'I will do X and Y', where 'or Y' adds an arbitrary disjunct and 'and Y' an arbitrary conjunct. The objections to such inferences are two, one indicated by Anscombe, one by Müller. Where 'or Y' is an arbitrary disjunct and 'and Y' an arbitrary conjunct, 'doing X and/or Y' denotes neither a single act, nor a pair of acts, that constitutes a means to doing X. This is a point about action.

[42] 'Practical Inference', 13. [43] Ibid., 21.

And proceeding from 'I will do X' either to 'I will do X or Y' or to 'I will do X and Y' can get the agent no closer to doing X; so the inference cannot be for the sake of doing X. This is a point about the teleology of deliberation. The two points connect: practical inference is itself at the service of the end to which it seeks to select a means.

One way of putting my conclusion is in terms of a variety of 'so's. Instantiations of the schema 'I will do X; so, I will do Y' may be conveying any one of the following relations: that my doing X *entails* my doing Y; that my being about to do X is a *reason* for my doing Y; or that my intending to do X makes more or less *intelligible* my forming an intention to do Y. The first relation has nothing specially to do with practical inference. The second relation is perhaps *the* topic of ethics, but not my concern here. The third relation is distinct from both. Thus suppose an agent reasons: 'I will drink paint; this is paint; so, I will drink this.' This is not logical inference (for there may be other paints going); nor does it give a reason for drinking this (which rather inherits the irrationality of drinking paint). Yet the initial intention to drink paint still prepares the way for the final intention to drink this, which is then not *brutely* unintelligible. In less peculiar cases, the agent has a reason for doing X that carries over to doing Y, and then the inference itself has more point. Indeed, within practical inference rationality is typically transmitted from one intention to another.

Thus sequences of intentions can be assessed as making sense, or having point, in the same informal way as sequences of acts: from intending to do X I derive an intention to do Y, just as I shall do Y in order to do (or be doing) X. The intelligibility of practical reasoning derives from the intelligibility of action for a purpose, and not vice versa; one might say that thinking of this kind is a mental rehearsal of intentional action.[44] There are sensible and less sensible ways of proceeding in thought as in deed; and assessment must attend to the contingencies of the case, and not aspire to apply a special logic.[45]

[44] This should hardly surprise: purposive action is not a prerogative of homo sapiens.

[45] For help in revising this paper substantially after the lecture I am indebted to Dorothy Edgington, Stephen Everson, Michael Martin, Anselm Müller, Tom Pink, Joseph Raz, Ian Rumfitt, and David Wiggins.

Absolute Prohibitions without Divine Promises

SABINA LOVIBOND

Thermopylae

Honour to those whoever in their lives
Have set the bounds and guard Thermopylae.
Never moving from the line of duty;
Righteous and fair in all their actions,
With sympathy as well and with compassion;
If they are rich, generous, and if again
They are poor, generous in little things,
Still helping others as much as they can;
Always speaking the truth,
Yet without bitterness against the liars.

And again greater honour becomes them
When they foresee (and many do foresee)
That Ephialtes will be there in the end,
And that the Medes, at last, they will get through.

C. P. Cavafy (1863–1933)[1]

1. Elizabeth Anscombe's 'Modern Moral Philosophy'[2] is read and remembered principally as a critique of the state of ethical *theory* at the time when she was writing—an account of certain faulty assumptions underlying that theory in its different variants, and rendering trivial the points on which they ostensibly disagree. Not unreasonably, the essay serves as a starting point for the recent Oxford Readings collection on 'virtue ethics', and as an authoritative text on the failings of other approaches with which philosophy students have to acquaint themselves. Yet what really commands attention on rereading it is Anscombe's denunciation of the impotence of current moral philosophy to generate resistance to certain quite specific forms of wrongdoing. The question that provides a kind of gold standard here, recurring several times in the course of the discussion, is that of the killing (or judicial execution or other 'punishment') of the innocent in order to avoid some putatively greater evil, or to bring about some sufficiently great good.

Punishment of the innocent appears early on in the essay[3] as a species of the genus 'injustice', and Anscombe notes that 'in present-day philosophy an explanation is required how an unjust man is a bad man, or an unjust action a bad one'; whereas, in her own (much-quoted) view,

[2] G. E. M. Anscombe, 'Modern Moral Philosophy' (hereafter 'MMP'), in her *Ethics, Religion and Politics: Collected Philosophical Papers, Volume III* (Oxford: Basil Blackwell, 1981), to which page numbers here refer; also in Roger Crisp and Michael Slote (eds) *Virtue Ethics* (Oxford University Press, 1997).

[3] MMP, p. 29.

it would be a 'great improvement' if generic terms such as 'untruthful', 'unchaste', 'unjust' were treated as bedrock for the purpose of guiding action: 'We should no longer ask whether doing something was "wrong", passing directly from some description of an action to this notion; we should ask whether, e.g., it was unjust; and the answer would sometimes be clear at once.'[4] But with the turn towards consequentialism in Moore and his successors, a situation develops in which 'every one of the best known English academic moral philosophers [with some qualification in regard to R. M. Hare] has put out a philosophy according to which, e.g., it is not possible to hold that it cannot be right to kill the innocent as a means to any end whatsoever and that someone who thinks otherwise is in error'.[5] Anscombe draws the conclusion that 'all these philosophies are quite incompatible with the Hebrew-Christian ethic. For it has been characteristic of that ethic to teach that there are certain things forbidden whatever *consequences* threaten'—and she supplies a longish list which is headed by 'choosing to kill the innocent for any purpose, however good'.[6]

In the closing pages of the essay,[7] where Anscombe undertakes to describe the advantages of abandoning the portentous 'moral ought' and replacing it with terms such as 'unjust', the example chosen is again the abusive treatment of the innocent—here, the act of '[getting] a man judicially punished for something which it can be clearly seen he has not done'.[8] This (type of) act, she argues, is

[4] Ibid., p. 33. [5] Ibid. [6] Ibid., p. 34. [7] Ibid., pp. 38–42.
[8] Ibid., p. 38.

intrinsically unjust, in contrast to some others which are unjust in normal circumstances (e.g. 'to deprive people of their ostensible property without legal procedure, not to pay debts, not to keep contracts, and a host of other things of the kind').[9] In exceptional circumstances, some actions which are normally (though not intrinsically) unjust may become permissible, and the expected consequences of a proposed action may be relevant here—'as, e.g., if you could use a machine [belonging to someone else] to produce an explosion in which it would be destroyed, but by means of which you could divert a flood or make a gap which a fire could not jump' (ibid.) And this feature will introduce a measure of unavoidable imprecision into moral thinking, since the attempt to draw explicit boundaries around the class of genuinely exceptional cases must soon give way to a general (quasi-Aristotelian) sense of 'what's reasonable', resting not on a canon of judgment but on familiarity with a range of examples. Problems about whether or not a proposed course of action would constitute (e.g.) injustice, Anscombe has already told us,[10] call into play the method of casuistry. But she says of this method that 'while it may lead you to stretch a point on the circumference [of ethics], it will not permit you to destroy the centre'; for the centre consists of instances in which, given a certain description of a proposed action (e.g. 'judicially punishing a man for what he is clearly understood not to have done'),[11] no argument is possible as to whether the action is unjust.

[9] Ibid., p. 39. [10] Ibid., p. 36. [11] Ibid., p. 39.

To repeat, then: in some instances there will be room for disagreement about the description of an action as unjust, but in others there will not, regardless of any expected consequences; and this, in Anscombe's view, is an advantage of the kind of moral thinking that substitutes terms like 'injustice' (as a source of moral guidance) for the special, 'moral', sense of 'ought', 'right', 'wrong', 'obligation', etc. We should not be embarrassed if we cannot produce an explanation of *why* an action such as procuring the judicial execution of the innocent should be absolutely excluded from consideration; it is more reasonable to think of the person who regards this ('in advance') as open to question as being the one with the problem: such a person 'shows a corrupt mind'.[12] Yet it is the teaching of 'all the well-known English ethicists since Sidgwick'[13] that such a course of action is not automatically ruled out as impossible for a morally conscientious person, or (to put it another way) that someone could adopt a 'moral' principle, legitimately so called, to the effect that 'in such-and-such circumstances

[12] Ibid., p. 40. Brad Hooker quotes these words in *Ideal Code, Real World* (Oxford: Clarendon Press, 2000, p. 130) and comments in a footnote: 'Anscombe's quip, while perhaps amusing, is a paradigm case of arguing by begging the question at hand.' I must confess that the 'quip' is lost on me. What phrasing should Anscombe have chosen in order to make her point simply and sincerely? Also, if we expand the quotation by a few words, we find that she says of the kind of thinker she is envisaging: '*I do not want to argue with him;* he shows a corrupt mind' (emphasis added). What more could she have done to indicate that she is not arguing but *declining to argue*?

[13] Ibid., p. 42.

one ought to procure the judicial condemnation of the innocent'.[14] This is the disgrace of 'modern moral philosophy'.

2. Why is it necessary to insist so fiercely on the contrast between those ethical theories that do, and those that do not, regard it as possible in principle for a decent person (a 'virtuous character') to entertain such a course of action? Isn't this possibility somewhat academic?

In fact, Anscombe reveals in a paper of about the same date ('War and Murder', published in 1961)[15] that she thinks it is nothing of the sort. Although 'it is one of the most vehement and repeated teachings of the Judaeo-Christian tradition that the shedding of innocent blood is forbidden by the divine law',[16] this teaching is now in eclipse: 'with the fading of Christianity from the mind of the West, [it] once more stands out as a demand which strikes pride- and fear-ridden people as too intransigent' (ibid.), and 'even the [traditional] arguments about double effect—which at least show that a man is not willing openly to justify the killing of the innocent—are now beginning to look old-fashioned'.[17] Actuated by a 'terrible fear of communism', some Catholics 'are not scrupling to say that *anything* is justified in defence of the continued liberty and existence of the Church in the West'.[18]

[14] Ibid.

[15] G. E. M. Anscombe, 'War and Murder' (hereafter 'WM'), in her *Ethics, Religion and Politics.*

[16] WM, p. 57. [17] Ibid., p. 60.

[18] Ibid. This 'anything goes' attitude did not die out with the end of the anti-communist cold war. Thus Polly Toynbee writes on the U.S. bombing of Afghanistan: 'Seeing only distant puffs of smoke, a queasy

The deeper reason for alarm about 'modern moral philosophy', then, is that by virtue of the predominance it gives to consequentialist thinking it has entered into complicity with the kind of developments in international politics, and especially in attitudes to warfare, which (in Anscombe's view) the 'fading of Christianity' has made possible. As politicians have grown accustomed to contemplating the obliteration bombing of cities, so, it would seem, academic moral theorists have licensed them to make 'decisions of principle' relative to which such actions could on occasion be judged legitimate.[19]

The religious narrative that frames this accusation is by no means the only possible setting for it. Writing in 1994,[20] the historian Eric Hobsbawm argues that 'barbarism has been on the increase for most of the twentieth century',[21] and among the grounds for this claim he specifically notes

public is left to imagine the worst—civilian bloodshed and a military stalemate. Air war is always a public relations disaster . . .' However, she continues, 'It is a kind of decadence to forget that *only one thing matters—the right side must win*' (*The Guardian*, 7th November 2001; emphasis added).

19 MMP, p. 42.

20 'Barbarism: A User's Guide' (hereafter 'Barbarism'), in his *On History* (Abacus, 1998), to which the page numbers here refer; also in *New Left Review* 206 (July/August 1994). This essay was originally a contribution to the 1994 series of Oxford Amnesty Lectures. For another succinct review of the 'totalization' of warfare over the past century, see Michael Howard, 'Can War be Controlled?', in Jean Bethke Elshtain (ed.) *Just War Theory* (Blackwell, 1992), pp. 28–31. Also falling within the scope of Hobsbawm's discussion is the practice of torture by governments ('Barbarism', pp. 342–348).

21 'Barbarism', p. 335.

that 'the very concept of a war of total national mobilization [such as the First World War] shattered the central pillar of civilized warfare, the distinction between combatants and non-combatants'.[22] But what constitutes 'barbarism', for Hobsbawm, over and above the general trend towards moral and social breakdown and the accompanying process by which 'we have got used to killing',[23] is 'the reversal of what we may call the project of the eighteenth-century Enlightenment, namely the establishment of a *universal* system of . . . rules and standards of moral behaviour, embodied in the institutions of states dedicated to the rational progress of humanity'[24]—a project he sees, even now, as 'one of the few things that [stand] between us and an accelerated descent into darkness'.[25]

I imagine there will be many who are persuaded, as I am, by the historical thesis to be found both in Anscombe and, more concretely, in Hobsbawm—the thesis that a certain central rule of 'morality' or of 'civilization', the prohibition on killing the innocent, has come to be perceived in recent times as too idealistic or 'intransigent'; who share, as I do, Anscombe's conviction that philosophy ought not to indulge this view; but who do not subscribe to the religion that fuels her protest, or indeed, perhaps, to any religion (disregarding for present purposes the Nietzschean view that unless you get rid of morality, you cannot plausibly claim to have got rid of God). For someone in this position, the question arises: could we, by way of descriptive devices for identifying an action as prohibited ('untruthful, 'unchaste', 'unjust' . . .), and without the

[22] Ibid., p. 339. [23] Ibid. [24] Ibid., p. 335. [25] Ibid., p. 336.

aid of the specious 'moral ought', provide ourselves with a secular but nevertheless secure basis for resistance to the compromises condemned by Anscombe? And would the resulting form of moral rigorism be a doctrine by which we could live?

3. As we have seen, Anscombe proposes a standard of practical morality that would turn on recognizing a particular course of action e.g. as 'unjust', and on moving from this description to the thought that one has (at least) *a* reason not to do it, and perhaps (depending on whether the act is intrinsically unjust, or whether its status in this respect is capable of being affected by circumstances) that it is absolutely excluded from consideration. But she does not want us to picture that move as dependent on the presence of any generically 'action-guiding' factor such as the Humean tradition would look for here, nor (if this is different) on any special force or atmosphere attributable to the word 'moral'. And if we dispense with the idea of a special, 'moral' sense of 'should' and 'ought' and make do with these words in their normal (unemphatic) role (athletes should keep in training, pregnant women watch their weight, etc.)[26], then the question can perfectly well arise—as Anscombe reminds us[27]—whether committing injustice might not sometimes be *the best thing to do,* i.e. the thing one should do or ought to do.

'And the answers will be various': one possible answer, suggested by the moral philosophy of Plato and Aristotle, is

[26] See G. E. M. Anscombe, *Intention,* 2nd edn (Oxford: Basii Blackwell, 1963), p. 64.

[27] MMP, p. 41.

that since injustice is a vice it follows that despite any apparent benefits to be gained from unjust conduct, one's life will still be 'spoiled in essentials' by engaging in it; in other words, it is an *a priori* truth that the unjust person cannot flourish.

But in drawing attention to the possibility of this answer, Anscombe takes herself to be indicating a problem rather than a solution. For (she says) 'philosophically there is a large gap, at present unfillable as far as we are concerned, which needs to be filled by an account of human nature, human action, the type of characteristic a virtue is, and above all of human flourishing. And it is the last concept that appears the most doubtful'.[28] Anyone who takes seriously the idea of a non-accidental connection between flourishing and avoiding wrong-doing, or between wrong-doing and the spoiling (in essentials) of one's own life, has to adopt some attitude or other towards the abundant evidence—or, anyway, ostensible evidence—that honesty is not always the best policy. Plato and Aristotle have their own respective genres of commentary on this evidence; religious believers of various descriptions may be able to treat it as an article of faith that it will profit them to abstain from injustice, without insisting on an explanation of how (this being something they are content to '[leave] it to God to determine').[29] Alternatively, of course, one may simply refuse to entertain a conception of 'flourishing' that would make the link between a virtuous life and a flourishing life anything *but* accidental, in which case one will sometimes

[28] Ibid. [29] Ibid., p. 42.

consider an admittedly unjust action to be necessary on grounds of expediency. But at least it does not occur to the holders of any of these views to *traduce* 'morality' by making out that acts of intrinsic injustice might in suitable circumstances be deemed to be consistent with it.

Now, presumably the reason Anscombe names an account of human 'flourishing' as one of the main desiderata of a possible new approach to moral philosophy is that she does not intend the interest of that approach to be limited to believers in the 'special [divine] promises' mentioned in the concluding pages both of 'Modern Moral Philosophy' and of 'War and Murder'—promises which she sees as shielding those who do believe in them from the thought that it might ever be *necessary,* for example, to 'wage a war with Russia involving the deliberate massacre of cities'.[30] She must think it is at any rate worth exploring the possibility of bypassing Christian belief and retrieving directly from its classical sources the idea that one needs to avoid injustice because one's life will be 'spoiled in essentials' by committing it.

We had better pause here to remind ourselves of the element of anti-naturalism in this view—I mean, of the violence it offers to what might be described, in an admittedly 'unphilosophical' vein, as 'human nature'. To say *fiat iustitia, ruat caelum* is to give hostages to fortune: if there is even so much as one moral requirement that we are seriously going to treat as *absolute,* i.e. as a requirement that is never to be called into question, then this policy is liable

[30] WM, p. 61.

sooner or later to produce consequences which, by any normal human standards, will count as disastrous. In referring here to 'normal' human standards, I mean to express agreement with the view of Rosalind Hursthouse[31] that although initiation, through upbringing, into the outlook of the virtuous—or even the morally 'good enough'—person undoubtedly leads one to apply terms like 'happiness', 'profit', 'loss', 'harm', 'disaster', and so forth in a somewhat different way from the uninitiated, there is no absolute rupture between the respective ways in which these terms are understood by the two groups, just as there is no absolute discontinuity between the groups themselves. Certain occurrences are to be acknowledged as harmful by any rational human standard—a point that seems, in fact, to be tacitly conceded by Anscombe, since she deplores the practice of stipulating for the purposes of argument or thought-experiment that the *only* way to escape some putative disaster is to do an intrinsically unjust thing (whereas if such 'natural' disasters as death, mutilation, bereavement, etc. were of no essential importance from the point of view of human flourishing, one might have thought we could face them with equanimity).

In short: if we agree that between the virtuous person's conception of gain and loss and that of the immoral (or amoral) person there is no absolute opposition, but only a relative one mediated by our gradual initiation into the 'moral point of view', then we must expect to encounter

[31] Rosalind Hursthouse, *On Virtue Ethics* (Oxford University Press, 1999), ch. 8; see esp. pp. 179–185.

cases in which refusing to do something intrinsically unjust (or otherwise forbidden) will lead to disastrous results for the person concerned—'disastrous', that is, in a sense accessible alike from earlier and later stages in the process of initiation; and we must maintain this expectation even if, as Hursthouse thinks, the cultivation of virtue is *in general* a rational life-strategy, a policy with good statistical prospects of ensuring happiness, just as a sensible diet (etc.) has a good statistical likelihood of preserving health.[32] For statistics, however encouraging, offer no guarantees. What, then, can overcome our natural resistance to the possible sacrifice of life or liberty—that of others, as well as our own—to a determination to keep certain commandments 'whatever consequences threaten'?

4. Those without religion cannot, by definition, believe themselves to be in possession of any divine promises; so they cannot have the kind of grounds to which Anscombe appeals in 'War and Murder' for the thought that, appearances notwithstanding, there are some things it can never be necessary to do (and hence that we always have the option of refusing to do them—as we must, if the idea of an *absolute* prohibition is to make sense). Can they, then, find some other, secular grounding for this thought?

Let us return to the idea of the Enlightenment project as one of establishing a '*universal* system . . . of rules

[32] This is intended as a possible reply to the moral sceptic, not as an account of our actual incentives to co-operate with the process of moral upbringing when we ourselves are subjected to it.

and standards of moral behaviour', a system that could regulate human relationships both within and between (what would traditionally be regarded as) distinct 'societies'. In terms of this project, the closest functional equivalent of what we are supposed to get from Anscombe's divine promises would seem to be a conviction that there are some things it can never be necessary to do in the name of, or with a view to bringing about, a dispensation of universal respect for enlightened values. If we believed in a historical determinism whereby this dispensation was guaranteed, with suitable help from self-conscious political agents, to come about in reality, then we could think of ourselves as being in possession of a promise that at some future date, after the successful accomplishment of the historical *telos,* our own time-bound decisions—and specifically our treatment of some courses of action as being absolutely excluded from consideration— could be ratified by a 'judgment of history': 'Look, we got here somehow without (e.g.) Lovibond pressing the button.'

But perhaps hardly anyone nowadays does still hold this theory.[33] Perhaps all it takes to qualify as an optimist, among contemporary adherents of Enlightenment,[34] is the

[33] On the influence of 'obstetric imagery' in the Marxist tradition (implying that political agency only facilitates what is destined to happen anyway), and on the intellectual consequences of renouncing this imagery, see G. A. Cohen, *If You're an Egalitarian, How Come You're So Rich?* (Harvard University Press, 2000).

[34] I mean among those who regard Enlightenment values, with Hobsbawm, as 'the only foundation for all the aspirations to build societies fit for *all* human beings to live in anywhere on this earth, and

more modest belief that a successful exit from our present historical-cum-ecological predicament is *possible*. An optimist, then, in this context, will be someone whose political thinking is accessible to hope—an attitude which, as Philippa Foot reminds us, deserves to be counted among the virtues, 'in part because we are often tempted to think that all is lost when *we cannot really know that it is so*'.[35] And this suggests a possible secular interpretation of the words Anscombe puts into the mouths of her nuclear-warmongering co-religionists when they have to answer for themselves on the day of judgment: 'We could not obey your commandments, for we did not believe your promises'.[36] The equivalent declaration in a non-religious setting would be: 'We could not take seriously the idea of an absolute prohibition, because we did not believe things could possibly turn out all right unless we helped them along by practising torture, procuring the judicial execution of the innocent, bombing civilian targets, etc.' It is plausible to hold that someone who said this would be at fault, in that even if we can no longer think of history as working towards an immanent *telos* of its own, still a person of good character will *resist* the belief that 'all will be lost' unless they perform such and such an action which, as it happens, is intrinsically unjust. They will, characteristically, gravitate towards the contrary belief, namely

for the assertion and defence of their human rights as persons' ('Barbarism', p. 336).

35 Philippa Foot, *Natural Goodness* (Oxford University Press, 2001), p. 74n.

36 WM, p. 61.

that there must be some not completely disastrous alternative to doing this morally unacceptable thing.

5. But isn't it sometimes obvious that unless you overcome your scruples you will be reduced to the position of an impotent spectator of disaster? Anscombe has two things to say about this in 'Modern Moral Philosophy'. The first is that 'the point of considering hypothetical situations, perhaps very improbable ones, *seems* to be to elicit from yourself or someone else a hypothetical decision to do something of a bad kind',[37] and here she comments that this must tend to create a climate of tolerance towards the relevant kind of bad action in much more humdrum circumstances—i.e. it must be morally damaging. This is persuasive so far as it goes, but it hardly seems to address the objection: 'Yes, but what if we *actually* find ourselves in one of those extreme situations?' And in fact this objection evidently arose at the original reading of Anscombe's paper, for she reports in a footnote[38]—and this is the second passage I have in mind—that someone asked in discussion what she thought should be done if 'a government [were] required to have an innocent man tried, sentenced and executed under threat of a "hydrogen bomb war"'. Her reply to this struck me at one time as rather childish, but it no longer does so. She argues, first, that people who made such a demand could not be expected to behave predictably whatever one did; but, more important, this kind of thought-experiment assumes that 'only two courses are open: here, compliance and open

[37] MMP, p. 37. [38] Ibid., p. 40, n. 6.

defiance'—whereas in reality '[n]o one can say in advance of such a situation what the possibilities are going to be—e.g. that there is none of stalling by a feigned willingness to comply, accompanied by a skilfully arranged "escape" of the victim'.

I take it that the key words here are 'in advance'. We might say that Anscombe seeks to distance herself from her opponent with regard to the relationship between *thinking in advance* and *thinking in the heat of the situation.* At an abstract level, both parties agree that it is desirable to bring these two operations into line, so that one can be spared the retrospective knowledge that one has acted against one's principles. But they envisage different ways of doing this. Anscombe endorses the traditional view that on one hand we have the well-known requirements of morality (or—to use her preferred idiom—of justice, truthfulness, chastity and so forth), while on the other hand we have the obscurity of lived experience, which subjects us to temptation and leads us on occasion to entertain possibilities we normally (and rightly) rule out. The specific, unforeseeable character of our real-life moments of decision is a source of moral danger, on this view; but at the same time, we need not picture ourselves as helpless in the face of such danger, because a person of good character—which, let us assume, includes a measure of practical intelligence—will often be able to invent escape routes, i.e. to devise courses of action that are neither morally nor consequentially intolerable. So we are told both that there are some demands of virtue, or rather some prohibitions, which are absolute—'you are not to be tempted by fear or hope of consequences'—but also that we have to trust in our own ability to find a way of respecting these prohibitions, in any concrete circumstances that may arise, without incurring disaster (in Hursthouse's more-or-less-natural sense) as a result. Of course, this ability is limited, so it is not ruled out that we may incur disaster by respecting the prohibitions, or alternatively find ourselves violating the prohibitions when the threat of disaster becomes more pressing than we can bear—this is the behaviour of a 'normally tempted human being', as Anscombe remarks.[39] But the point is that one should not try to deal with all this in advance, otherwise than by cultivating the necessary qualities of character. A religious person might perhaps say that it is a matter of faith (one has to believe that God will guide and support one in difficulties). Alternatively, and without reference to religion, it might be said that we have to trust that escape routes will suggest themselves when needed—though there is no way of ensuring that they will.

The 'modern moral philosopher' also seeks to align thinking-in-advance with thinking-under-fire. But he does so in a way that grants an undeserved cognitive status to the opportunistic, or just plain desperate, state of mind of (what Anscombe would call) the 'normally tempted' person. His idea is that since such courses of action as killing the innocent can suggest themselves to a morally normal (not vicious) person under the pressure of circumstances (if the circumstances are sufficiently grim—or sufficiently rich in

[39] Ibid.

possibility), we ought to have a moral theory that acknowledges this fact and that allows us—in advance—to entertain the kind of actions we may find ourselves contemplating *in mediis rebus,* i.e. to treat these as not absolutely ruled out, however questionable they may seem. This, however, is the style of thought of which Anscombe says that it 'shows a corrupt mind'. She thinks we must recognize that a person of basically good character, though with normal human imperfections, will regard some actions in principle as being absolutely prohibited, yet may still perform one of these actions in a concrete situation through inability to see a tolerable alternative: this abstract recognition of our own moral fallibility is not a sign of corruption on the part of the philosopher. But you do have to be corrupt to embrace in advance the idea of your own performance of a *specific* intrinsically unjust act.

6. We might hesitate here over the suggestion that any case in which we seem to have reason to act against one of Anscombe's absolute prohibitions must fall under the heading of *temptation.* In order to maintain this view, we have to be ready to insist that not only disreputable (e.g. selfish) motives, but also *pro tanto* worthy (e.g. benevolent) ones, can tempt one to violate the demands of morality. For example, since the Hebrew-Christian ethic prohibits 'choosing to kill the innocent for any purpose, however good', it rules out the acceptance by Bernard Williams's 'Jim'[40]

[40] See Bernard Williams, 'Consequentialism and Integrity', in Samuel Scheffler (ed.), *Consequentialism and its Critics* (Oxford University Press, 1988), p. 34. (This text was originally published in J. J. C. Smart

(that faithful friend of undergraduate essayists) of the famous ultimatum: either kill this one 'Indian', or if you refuse, stand by while he and 19 others are killed. In Williams's story, the 20 villagers and their relatives understand the situation and are begging Jim to comply, so he can hardly overlook the case in favour. Yet since he can comply only by choosing to kill an innocent person, the pleas of the relatives, and his own benevolent impulse to save as many lives as he can, constitute (on the absolutist view) a 'temptation' for Jim, an incentive to commit an intrinsically unjust act. What he must do *(pace* Williams, who concludes without enthusiasm that 'the utilitarian is probably right' about Jim's dilemma)[41] is to refuse the ultimatum, and what his friends must say to him afterwards, to help him overcome his understandable horror and sense of complicity in the resulting deaths, is: 'No, you are no murderer, if you did not will those deaths, and if you had to act in the way that led to them or else do something absolutely forbidden.'[42]

and Bernard Williams, *Utilitarianism: For and Against* (Cambridge University Press, 1973), pp. 82–118.)

41 Ibid., p. 50. (It would be misleading, though, to cite this discussion as a clear instance of the kind of moral philosophy Anscombe has in her sights, since the weight of Williams's argument in it falls mainly on the anti-consequentialist side.)

42 The quoted words are based on a passage in WM (p. 58), explaining the 'doctrine of double effect'. It is, of course, a purely accidental feature of the present example that the threatened harm is to fall on others rather than on Jim himself (as would have been the case if the ultimatum had taken the form: 'Kill this one (innocent) person, or *we* will kill *you*'). The absolutist, as we read elsewhere, maintains that '[w]e may not commit any sin, however small, for the sake of any good, however

This reference to the *direction of Jim's will* reminds us that Anscombe's proposed way out of the predicament of 'modern moral philosophy' can be understood as involving a renewed insistence on the need for the human will to be, in various respects, well disposed, if the subject of that will is to qualify as a good example of the natural species 'human being'. (This idea also forms the basis of Philippa Foot's project in *Natural Goodness.*) Accordingly, we now have to ask ourselves: do we agree with the substance of what Anscombe is saying, explicitly or otherwise, in 'Modern Moral Philosophy' about the way in which a person's attitude to hypothetical moral dilemmas reflects on the quality of their will?

Suppose we feel certain that Jim would act wrongly in accepting the captain's ultimatum, and that he should be able to find all the moral support he needs in the judgment of the absolutist ('No, you are no murderer . . .'). In that case, we are in a position to agree with Anscombe that if he does accept it he can be correctly described as *succumbing to temptation*—though we may of course take a lenient view and say that his action is one of those envisaged by Aristotle as deserving, not praise indeed, but pardon, given the

great, and if the choice lies between our total destruction and the commission of sin, then we must choose to be destroyed' ('The Justice of the Present War Examined', in Anscombe, *Ethics, Religion and Politics,* p. 79). He or she will regard Williams's scenario simply as one in which the principle contained in the first conjunct of the sentence just quoted is particularly likely to be occluded by the presence of benevolence as a motive.

limitations of human nature;[43] that Jim's benevolent motives reveal him as, at worst, a '*normally* tempted human being'. But then, Anscombe does not make it her business to supply the relevant certainty, but only to point to the intellectual consequences of its presence or absence; the certainty itself constitutes, in a way, the dark heart of her reasoning. To recall a passage we have already noticed: '[C]an't it reasonably be asked whether one might ever need to commit injustice, or whether it won't be the best thing to do? Of course it can', she writes; '[a]nd the answers will be various'.[44] We have to draw our own conclusions about the merits of these answers. But then again, in working our way towards those conclusions we may be led to question the 'intellectual virtue' of the attitude that motivates Anscombe's final, scornful dismissal of 'modern moral philosophy' in the closing paragraph of her essay—I mean that of refusing, hypothetically or 'in advance', to regard acceptance of the ultimatum put to Jim even as a possible option for a conscientious person in his position. We may ask: isn't this attitude also at fault in so far as it inflicts (hypothetically—and perhaps by extension, *actually*) a kind of moral ostracism on people who may be no worse than ourselves, but who have fared worse in the matter of 'circumstantial luck'? Is it obvious that the likely effects of imaginative identification with Jim—which might of course include saying 'Yes, in refusing the ultimatum one *would* be bound to feel like a

[43] Aristotle, *Nicomachean Ethics* 1110a23–26; cf. *Eudemian Ethics* 1225a25–27.

[44] MMP, p. 41.

murderer'—are worse than those of setting one's face against such identification from the start?

But while Jim (and the kind of case he stands for) may show the ethical absolutist in a somewhat unattractive light, we should resist the conclusion—encouraged here, no doubt, by a 'one-sided diet of examples'—that an attachment to absolute prohibitions must stem either from religious dogmatism or from a 'decadent' refusal to engage with political reality. An analogy may help to bring this out. The question is sometimes raised in moral philosophy: which type of person is more admirable, the one who does the right thing frictionlessly and without internal conflict, or the one who overcomes their own wayward impulses and does the right thing by force of will? (The first view is traditionally associated with Aristotle, the second—though much more controversially—with Kant.) Now it may be that while there is some educational value in thinking about the rival claims of these candidates, the original question is still in a way a bad one, since there is *something* (though a different thing) to admire in the moral constitution of each of them—in one the successful integration of character, in the other the successful containment of elements that resist integration—and that we can learn more by simply keeping the relevant values in clear view than by insisting on an order of rank between them.[45] Likewise, perhaps, with the attitudes manifested in ethical absolutism and, on other hand, in the recognition of cases in which someone's

[45] I owe this point to some remarks made by Oswald Hanfling in a seminar discussion.

decision to violate a putatively absolute moral requirement is not rightly described as *succumbing to temptation*, but rather as a (possible) conscientious response to extreme circumstances. Anscombe's contention, admittedly issuing from the standpoint of the 'Hebrew-Christian ethic', is that the latter attitude—along with the kind of ethical theory that seeks to underwrite or rationalize it—is essentially corrupt (or corrupting). And this doctrine may seem to rely to an objectionable degree on traditional authority in presuming to block the move (e.g.) from the particular feelings of sympathy we are likely to have for Jim, if he accepts the ultimatum, to a more general questioning of the idea that there could be any kind of conduct at all that was literally to be excluded from consideration '*whatever* consequences threaten'.

Yet the absolutist position has merits of its own, which are removable from any overtly 'Hebrew-Christian' framework.[46] At any rate, it deserves a measure of loyalty from anyone—religious or otherwise—who wants to reserve the option of saying that a certain course of action is excluded from consideration because it would be (for

[46] Perhaps moral thinking calls into play, from time to time, different intellectual qualities which are not capable of perfectly harmonious coexistence. Singlemindedness, steadfastness and resolution are indeed virtues, but so is imaginative versatility or 'largeness'. It is interesting to note that if Anscombe is, in effect, exalting the former above the latter, she is following in the footsteps of Plato (with his suspicion of *poikilia* or 'variegatedness': see especially *Republic*, Book III) as well as in the Judaeo-Christian tradition of 'keeping commandments'.

example) intrinsically unjust. And this is something that may well need to be said from time to time by those who see themselves as heirs to the Enlightenment project, with its constitutive values and constraints. For them too, the perception of a certain course of action as morally impossible (the term 'moral' drawing attention, now, to one kind of reason among others rather than to a special atmosphere, 'mesmeric force' or the like) will be one that they can express in terms of non-negotiable requirements imposed by their own tradition on anyone adhering to it: by saying e.g. that it would violate a universal standard of human behaviour or would show contempt for human rights. And for them too, such requirements can be decisive in practice: that is, one can quite intelligibly refuse to be 'tempted by fear or hope of consequences' into thinking that it is *necessary* to do something which one can do only by violating them, e.g. to use certain sorts of weapon as means to a military objective.

Such people would seem to be in the position envisaged by Anscombe when she imagines someone saying, in response to the loss of belief in a divine legislator: 'I have to frame my own rules, and these are the best I can frame, and I shall go by them until I know something better'—'as a man might say "I shall go by the customs of my ancestors"', she comments.[47] In effect, they are going by the 'customs'—or rather by the habits of thought and sensibility— of a bunch of honorary ancestors, namely the sponsors of that 'progress of civility' which took place between the eighteenth and the

[47] MMP, p. 37.

early twentieth century.[48] And there is nothing to be ashamed of in this, since as Anscombe also observes, 'Whether [it] leads to good or evil will depend on the *content* of the rules or customs of one's ancestors. If one is lucky it will lead to good.' In the absence of divine legislation, and assuming for present purposes (with Anscombe and, at a further remove, with Wittgenstein) that the idea of 'legislating for oneself' is untenable, the policy of adherence to a set of rules or customs which are 'the best that we can frame' from the resources made available by our upbringing and education does not seem particularly pitiful. 'If one is lucky it will lead to good': although here we have to accept some degree of responsibility for making our own luck, since it is up to us to be aware, also, of another kind of moral hazard, namely that our upbringing and education, and the scheme of values we have constructed out of them, may not be as satisfactory in their content as we hope—and think—they are. Our attitude is, or should be, the one Anscombe grudgingly describes as 'hopeful in this at any rate: it seems to have in it some Socratic doubt where, from having to fall back on such expedients, it should be clear that Socratic doubt is good'[49]

The customs of our ethical 'ancestors', interpreted as best we can from our own historical standpoint and held up to scrutiny against the background of a constant awareness of our own limitations: whether or not we identify ourselves, with Hobsbawm, as heirs of the Enlightenment,

[48] Cf. Hobsbawm, 'Barbarism', p. 336. [49] MMP, p. 37.

these seem to be the available sources for a code of human conduct within which some actions would be excluded from consideration, though not because a supreme being had given orders to that effect. But now, what about the question of sanctions? Once again: 'Can't it reasonably be asked whether one might ever need to commit injustice, or whether it won't be the best thing to do?' The residual force of this question can be brought out by asking: is it possible for an atheist, and moreover for one who takes the Aristotelian course of rejecting unduly denatured or moralistic conceptions of benefit and loss, to make sense of the claim that their life—or in the case of state action, the life of those represented by the relevant government—might be *spoilt in essentials* by resorting to injustice? For the religious believer, Anscombe has suggested, 'the way it will profit him to abstain from injustice [can be] something that he leaves it to God to determine, himself only saying "It can't do me any good to go against his law"'—but then the believer can fall back on 'special promises'.[50] Are we any nearer to providing the non-believer with something to say on this point?

I referred earlier to Nietzsche's gibe about self-styled atheists who are not the genuine article because they are no less committed to 'morality' than they would have been as conventional Christians. What I think is true in this last claim—the one about equal commitment—is that an atheist who is not a moral sceptic, i.e. one who does not consider

[50] MMP, p. 42.

morality to be a mere ideological construct, will want to think of him- or herself as intellectually equipped to be *no worse* than a theist. (Perhaps this wish is isomorphic with that of Kant to show that religion 'within the limits of reason alone' could supply everything that was worth preserving in revealed religion.) In this spirit, it is worth considering the possibility that the atheist, here too, can continue to think on the lines that Anscombe describes. 'In general, I believe (since I do not disown the special, ethically informed conceptions of gain and loss instilled in me by my upbringing) that if I commit an act of intrinsic injustice I shall be damaged—even damaged "in essentials"—by that act. Sometimes terrible situations arise and it looks as though the only alternative to committing such an act is to die, or suffer severe injury, or stand by while these things happen to other innocent people. My duty is to cultivate the strongest possible mental defences against believing at any given moment that I am in such a situation, and to hope that if this belief ever seems to be forcing itself upon me, I will be fortunate and/or clever enough to find an escape route. But although I can see in the abstract that things might easily turn out as I hope they will not, it can't do me any good to advance mentally to meet the moment when my respect for some absolute requirement might be compromised.'

To talk like this is of course to persist in looking on one's ethical future in, precisely, a hopeful (as opposed to a despairing) perspective—the perspective that eludes those Catholic cold-warriors who, in Anscombe's account, 'must be prepared to say to God: ... "We could not obey your commandments, for we did not believe your promises.'"[51] Yet this still does not seem to be the whole story, for some people, like the ones celebrated by Cavafy, manage to remain at their posts—to keep the 'commandments' of the morality they acknowledge—even without hope: at any rate without the hope that things will turn out all right *for them*, and the ending of the poem strongly suggests that Cavafy means something more than this. How do they do it; what is their incentive? Perhaps it is simply that they have become accustomed, or even attached, to the post in question and lack the desire to make alternative arrangements. If so, they deserve not condescension but honour, as the poet says.[52]

[51] WM, p. 61.

[52] I am grateful to Jeffrey Seidman for detailed comments on an earlier draft of this lecture, as well as to all those members of the audience who took part in discussion on the occasion of its delivery.

Moral Obligation

THOMAS PINK

1. The problem of moral obligation[1]

Moral philosophy characteristically sees moral standards as reasons. That an action would be kind or just or in some way morally admirable is supposed to give us a reason for performing it. And surely there is something right about the thought that moral standards imply reasons for conforming to them. For we offer the morality of an action as a relevant consideration in practical argument—a consideration to support that action's performance. You should provide the help, because it would be kind, or just, and so forth. And an argument, surely, is in the business of offering reasons for what the argument supports.

Now reasons and the arguments which convey them apply not only to our actions but to our psychological attitudes as well. We can have reasons for actions; but equally we can have reasons for nonactions such as our general beliefs and desires. And the force of all these reasons and the arguments which provide them seems to be this—it would be sensible or advisable to perform this action, to form this belief or desire. Of course, there may be conflicting

[1] My thanks in particular to Joseph Raz for discussion of this paper.

reasons—there may be reasons for believing one thing or for doing one thing, but opposing reasons for believing or doing quite another. And here the reasons in favour of one belief or action may defeat the opposing reasons for believing and acting otherwise. In which case the sensible person will be moved by the victorious or defeating reasons to believe or act as they support; it would be foolish or less than sensible for him to be moved by reasons which have been defeated. For just as the force of reason is to leave what it supports advisable, so it also leaves what it opposes inadvisable. To disregard the force of reason and argument is to be like someone who ignores good advice. It is to be less than sensible, or even to be downright foolish.

But are moral standards simply standards of reason just like any others? Is the force of moral standards the ordinary force of reason—this force which it is sensible to attend to and foolish to disregard? One feature of morality makes this question pressing.

This is the fact that morality appears to provide us not merely with reasons, but also obligations or duties. Certain actions are obligatory, so that it is right to perform them. Other actions count as breaches of obligation, so that it is wrong to perform them. And talk of obligation, of standards of right and wrong, seems very different from talk of ordinary reason and reasons.

For with obligation, something distinctive and different seems to be going on. Suppose someone breaches a moral obligation. The criticism which they meet is rather different from that which meets mere disregard of reason. Unless they have some excuse, such as ignorance, compulsion and the like, people who breach obligations are blamed for what they have done. And to blame someone is not so much to criticize them as foolish or as less than sensible, but rather to hold them responsible for having done wrong. Ordinary reason is recommendatory—it is something which it is inadvisable or foolish to disregard. But obligation is different. Obligation or duty is something that we are blamed as wrongdoers for breaching. Moral obligations are standards that do not merely advise or recommend our conformity, but demand it.

But there is something eise distinctive both about moral obligation and the notions of responsibility and blame which go with it. It seems essential to the very nature of moral obligation that it exist as a Standard on agency—on action or omission. We can only be under a moral obligation to do or omit doing things. We simply cannot be under a moral obligation for things to happen independently of our own action. And that is because our moral responsibility, our responsibility for meeting moral obligations, is entirely and essentially for how we ourselves act or fail to. We cannot be morally responsible or to blame for what happens independently of our own action or omission. Or so it is very natural to suppose.

Reason and reasons, and with them rational criticism, considered quite generally, can be for non-agency as well as for agency—for ordinary beliefs and wants as well as for actions and omissions. But moral obligation and blame, it seems, are for action or omission alone.

Moral obligation does look very much like a sort of reason. For we do refer to an action's moral obligatoriness in argument, when we are trying to persuade someone to act in the way that we are making out to be obligatory. 'You must help your mother; it would be quite wrong not to', we might say. But if moral obligations are reasons, they are of a very special kind. For while non-agency as well as agency can count as sensible or advisable, it seems, as we have seen, that only agency can be obligatory. And, as I have said, obligatoriness seems a matter of demand and not mere recommendation.

Moral obligation, then, seems to be a kind of agency-specific demand—a demand specifically directive of how we act. But obligation also seems to be a form taken by reason. The question we face then is how reason can provide us with agency-specific demands. And there are two radically different answers to this question—two answers which I now intend to explore.

2. Positivising models

There is one feature of moral obligation which has, in the history of philosophy, proved of fundamental importance. In obligation the language of morality approaches that of the positive law. By *positive law* I mean the laws imposed on specific communities by legislation valid for those communities in particular, whether it be the legislation of custom or the legislation of formal statute and decree. For notions of obligation, of right and wrong, of being responsible and to blame or of having an excuse—all these are also expressed in the language of those who impose and enforce requirements under positive law. 'You are under an obligation to do it' could be spoken by a moralist—or by a judge or official enforcing the law of the land. And the senses in which the term 'obligation' is being used in the two cases seem, at the very least, closely related.

The parallels between moral obligations and obligations under positive law—*legal* obligations, as we naturally term them—seem considerable. In both cases we have the same idea, not of mere recommendation, but of demand. And we also have a connexion with the direction of action. For in the positive legal case too, obligation seems something centrally directive of how we act.

For in so far as positive law is about actually getting us to comply—about getting us actually to meet our obligations—it is very natural to see it as concerned with the direction of agency. To be more exact, it is natural to see it as concerned with the direction of things that people can affect voluntarily, through voluntary action or omission. By affecting things voluntarily or through voluntary action I mean bringing things about or preventing them, on the basis of a will, a decision or intention, so to bring them about or prevent them. Action that is voluntary, I shall say, is what we do motivated by a will or pro attitude towards doing it, such as a decision or intention to do it.

The first point to make about legal obligatoriness, is the way it induces obedience to the law. When they move us to comply, legal obligations do so as legislatively created features of outcomes or states of affairs—features that move us to decide to produce those obligatory States of affairs.

The law might prohibit cars from speeding above thirty miles per hour in a certain area, for example. People learn of the prohibition. They see that driving below thirty is now required by law—it is legally obligatory. And, if they are law-abiding, their immediate response is accordingly to decide to drive within the new speed limit—a decision which they will generally carry out, driving within the limit being something that most people at least have the capacity to do should they so decide.

Legal obligatoriness in such a case is a legislatively created feature of an outcome—a feature which we see as helping justify our production of that outcome, as giving us a reason to produce it. If the law-abiding are asked why they are now driving below thirty, they will give as their immediate reason that that is the new speed limit; that is now what the law requires. The law-abiding will treat the existence of the legal obligation as part of the reason or justification which they have for doing what is legally obligatory.[2] People respond to this justification and obey the law, when they do, by noting the existence of the legal obligation,

[2] Are people right to treat the fact of its legal obligatoriness as a reason for doing what is legally obligatory? And if at least sometimes they are, how more precisely is this reason generated: through sanctions connected with the law; or through the fact that doing what is legally obligatory facilitates coordination or the support of mutually advantageous institutions; or in some other way? These are questions for another time. In this discussion my interest is primarily in moral obligation, not legal. I mean merely to take legal obligatoriness as being, for the sake of argument, what, rightly or wrongly, many people treat it as being—a feature that can help give us reason to perform the actions and produce the outcomes that possess it. It is the correctness of conceiving of moral obligatoriness in a similar way that is my main concern here.

deciding to produce the outcome that it makes obligatory and justifies—and by then producing this outcome on the basis of that decision.

In so far as legal obligatoriness does move us to comply in this way, then, it does so as a reason-giving feature of the *voluntary*—of what we have the capacity to do on the basis of deciding to do it. Of course, there is nothing to stop things being made legally obligatory that people in general cannot bring about voluntarily or at will, on the basis of deciding to do so. But then even if people are genuinely willing and anxious to comply—even if they do decide to do or try to do what the law requires—such laws will not actually succeed in getting many people to meet their obligations and obey the law.

We may or may not always have a capacity to obey the law. But when we do have it, this capacity is a capacity to do the obligatory thing voluntarily, on the basis of a decision to meet our obligations and comply with the law. And that establishes a connexion between legal obligatoriness and the direction of action. For to do something voluntarily, on the basis of a decision to do it is, surely, intentionally to perform an action. What one does on the basis of deciding to do it is done intentionally or deliberately, as one's action. Legal obligations then move us to comply as voluntary agents—agents who decide to do what the law requires, and then obey the law in and through what they voluntarily do.

In the case of legal obligations, then, we can explain how they are directive of action. They are directive of action in that they are legislatively created features of the voluntary—features which, in a range of cases at least, we treat as generating reasons for producing, through voluntary action, this outcome rather than that, reasons that we can respond to on the basis of deciding to produce those outcomes which possess this very feature of legal obligatoriness.

And if legal obligations are not merely recommendatory but demanding, it seems this too can be explained. They are not ordinary reasons because they arise through the commandments or decrees of a legislative authority, the state—an authority which, moreover, has the right and, in general, the willingness and the power, to use coercive force and punishment to enforce conformity. This is an authority which demands conformity of us, and does not merely advise it.[3]

Why not view moral obligatoriness in similar terms? Positive legal obligations are imposed on particular communities by positive legislation valid only for those communities. Moral obligations work in just the same way, but as things commanded or required of every-one, and imposed by a moral legislator, such as God—a legislator whose authority is quite general, and whose decrees are somehow available to everyone's reason. Of course, no doubt unlike many positive laws these moral requirements will be ideally fair, in that we always have the capacity to meet them voluntarily, if we so decide or will—unless perhaps that capacity is lost or lacking through our own fault. And in the same way that we have reason to comply with the

[3] In fact, this account of the demandingness of obligation is one that the remainder of this paper will put into question.

decrees of positive legislators, so we have even more reason to comply with the decrees of this moral legislator.

Elizabeth Anscombe thought in fact that this was the only way to make sense of a distinctively moral obligation. Moral obligations would have to be imposed on us through the legislative decrees of a divine law-giver. Give up belief in God, do moral theory in entirely secular terms, and there is no longer any room for the idea of a distinctive standard of obligation within morality. The term 'moral obligation', she claimed, will now be empty, without any further literal application.[4] For a virtuous action not only to be virtuous, but actually to be morally obligatory, in Anscombe's view, just is for that action to be commanded of us by a moral law-giver.

So we have one view of how moral obligation can provide a form of direction specific to action. This view is

[4] For Anscombe, absent continued belief in God as divine lawgiver, all we are left with is a metaphorical use of the term 'obligation'; we must give up belief in moral obligatoriness itself. Moral obligatoriness can no more exist without what would constitute it—the feature of being divinely commanded—than can criminality without the institution of criminal law:

> 'But if a [divine command] conception is dominant for many centuries, and then is given up, it is a natural result that the concepts of 'obligation' , of being bound or required as by a law, should remain though they had lost their root... it is as if the notion 'criminal' were to remain when criminal courts had been abolished and forgotten... 'Elizabeth Anscombe 'Modern moral philosophy', *Virtue Ethics,* Roger Crisp and Michael Slote (eds.) p. 31 (Oxford University Press 1997).

essentially positivising. It takes moral obligatoriness to be a feature of voluntary actions and outcomes as legal obligatoriness can be a feature of voluntary actions and outcomes; and it takes moral obligatoriness to be reason-giving in broadly the same way. And, if this is felt to be necessary, the association of obligatoriness with demand can similarly be modelled in positivising fashion—by appeal to an actual threat of, or at least the legitimacy of, reinforcing coercion and punishment.

But should we assimilate moral obligatoriness to legal obligatoriness—moral law to a form or analogue of positive law?

There is in the English language tradition one important sceptic about this positivising conception of moral obligatoriness. For David Hume, moral standards, including standards of moral obligation, are fundamentally different from positive laws—even positive laws that are ideally fair. Moral obligations are indeed standards that we are blameworthy for breaching. But as such they certainly do not apply solely to what we can do or omit doing voluntarily, on the basis of deciding so to do. Hume put the point in an important passage:

> Philosophers, or rather divines under that disguise, treating all morals as on a like footing with civil law, guarded by sanctions of reward and punishment, were necessarily led to render this circumstance, of voluntary or involuntary, the foundation of their whole theory... but this, in mean time, must be allowed, that *sentiments* are every day experienced of blame and praise, which have objects beyond the dominion of the will or choice,

> and of which it behoves us, if not as moralists, as speculative philosophers at least, to give some satisfactory theory and explication. Hume *Enquiry Concerning the Principles of Morals*, appendix 4, 'Of some verbal disputes'.

Whatever else in this passage of Hume one might disagree with, one thing does seem true. Blame, the response to breach of a moral obligation, need not be for some voluntary action or omission or outcome of such. It can perfectly well be for motivations that are entirely non-voluntary—that we cannot in general form or abandon at will, and just in order to comply with some command or decree that we should either hold those motivations or give them up.

We blame people not just for the voluntary actions which their selfishness motivates, but for that very selfish motivation itself. We blame people simply for being selfish—for their lack of any concern for others; for their lack of any willingness and intention to respect and further the interests of others as well as their own. The wrong for which these people are being blamed, the breach of obligation, is quite clearly located in their motivations. We tell them that it is quite wrong of them to be so selfish; that it is quite wrong of them to be so lacking in concern for others.[5] But a benevolent or altruistic motivation of will seems not to be voluntary. We cannot adopt a concern for others at will,

[5] Hence Hume supposes, rightly, that there are moral obligations or duties to benevolence, and to concern for one's children—see *Treatise of Human Nature,* Book 3, Part 2, Section 1, 'Justice, whether a natural or artificial virtue?'

just on the basis of deciding to care about them. We cannot become unselfish just because someone has told us to become unselfish, and even threatened to punish us if we remain selfish. Indeed the threat of punishment seems more apt to engage our self-concern than lessen or remove it. A concern for others and a genuine intention for their good—this seems a motivation that we form, if we form it at all, non-voluntarily and in response to what we understand of the nature of other people and their needs, and not at will, on the basis of a decision to form it, and simply in order to obey some selflessness-mandating directive or decree.

The scope of moral obligation and blame goes deeper, then, than mere regulation of the voluntary. Moral obligation and blame are directly concerned with motivations that are generally non-voluntary—that people cannot in general adopt or abandon at will.

Again, the positivising account of moral obligation's demanding-ness seems false too. To begin with, it is surely a real moral problem whether and which moral obligations should be coercively enforced, and which cases of wrongdoing or breach of obligation should be met with actual punishment—as for example the New Testament story of Jesus and the woman taken in adultery might remind us, where the idea of an action's being wrong is importantly detached from the idea that we ought to be punishing it.[6] Since the issue is a proper matter for moral debate, we should surely not, therefore, write the legitimacy of

[6] See St John's gospel, chapter 8.

enforcing punishment and coercion into our very definition of what moral obligatoriness is.

Nor can obligation's demandingness be explained by the legitimacy even of the lighter form of pressure that consists simply in expressing blame for its breach. For blame is a kind of criticism— and a criticism which may sometimes be better not delivered even if wrong has been done. And the content of the criticism—that the person blamed has not been merely foolish, but is responsible for having done wrong, involves the very demandingness that we are trying to explain. So it would be circular to explain what obligatoriness is by appeal to the legitimacy of delivering this criticism.

In any case, the demandingness of moral obligation is surely not to do with the actual likelihood of people responding to its breach with blame or punishment, or with any reason that might exist for them so to respond. It surely has to do with something quite different—namely, the kind of reason we have for meeting the obligation in the first place. If we are under a moral obligation to help, that is not because there is reason for people to force us to help or to berate and punish us if we fail to help; and it is not because such responses are actually likely. It is surely because there is a specially demanding kind of reason for us to help—a reason which has to do with the kind of call made on us by the needs which the help would meet, and not with any kind of chastisement for not helping. These needs do not merely recommend our help but demand it. And this brings us to our second model of moral obligatoriness—our second theory of how reason can take the form of a demand specifically on how we act. And this theory will give quite a different account, both of the scope of moral obligation—its connexion with directing action— and of its demandingness.

3. Anscombe on obligation and divine command

Go back to Anscombe's view of what a distinctively moral Obligation would be. Her view is that the moral obligatoriness of a virtuous action could only consist in that action's being decreed or commanded by a divine legislator. That is just what moral obligatoriness is, what it consists in—the feature of being decreed or commanded by such a moral superior. Which is why disbelief in the existence of such a moral law-giver and his decrees, in her view, deprives talk of a specifically moral obligation of its content.

Anscombe is clearly putting forward a version of a divine command theory of moral Obligation. Now by a divine command theory I shall mean simply this: any theory which regards all moral obligations as having their source or origin in acts of divine will or command. But it is important that even if we were to maintain such a theory of moral Obligation, and regard all moral obligations as arising out of divine commands, we need not do what Anscombe also does—and identify obligatoriness with the feature of being divinely commanded. And, if we reflect, it is very clear why we should not.

It may turn out to be true that many voluntary actions which are genuinely obligatory are commanded by a superior—perhaps it may even turn out to be true, as many people who believe in God suppose, that all of them are. But that being commanded is surely a feature of the action which generates a justification for performing it—it is not itself the action's obligatoriness, which is surely something fundamentally different, namely the force with which that feature of being commanded justifies the action. The force of the justification provided is this: not so much that not performing the action would be inadvisable or foolish, but that not performing the action would be blameworthy as wrong. And the features which justify an action are one thing; the force with which those features justify it is quite another. It is a category mistake to confuse the two.

This is true even where we are using the language of obligation in the context of positive law. As I have already noted, we certainly talk of actions being 'legally obligatory' or obligatory under positive law. And in this case obligatoriness does look like another justifying or reason-giving feature of an action, analogous to being commanded. For what else is an action's 'legal obligatoriness' or its being obligatory under positive law but what I have so far described it as being: a legislatively-created feature of the action—the feature of being decreed by a government—a feature which can then serve to justify the action's performance?

On the other hand, on more careful reflection, even here it seems absurd to locate obligatoriness as no more than a reason-giving feature. For if we do that we have lost the idea of demandedness essential to obligation, which seems, as I have observed, to be not a reason-giving feature of an action, but the peculiar force with which some other features of an action justify its performance. Take an action such as paying one's taxes. It is not as if, besides its other features, this action has a further, additional feature—the feature of being obligatory—which simply recommends or makes it the more advisable to perform it. Rather, given the other features that the action has, including being decreed by the state, and supporting the state's welfare services and the like, we *must* perform it: to fail to would be to do wrong. And the action's obligatoriness is the force of that justificatory *must* or demand—a force generated by the feature of the action's being decreed by the state, and so not that feature itself. And this sense of a demanding force arises even in relation to positive legality, as something generated by the decrees of positive law—certainly for those who accept that positive law's claim to impose obligations is genuine.

This is a point about obligatoriness which any divine command ethics can perfectly well respect. Suppose it is claimed that all actions which are morally obligatory are so only because they are the subject of the will or command of a superior such as God. Just to make that claim need not be to say anything about what moral obligatoriness itself consists in. It is simply to say that all moral obligatoriness must have a very specific source—in the command of a superior. So in making this claim we may be doing no more than making a necessary link—between the justificatory force of obligatoriness or demand, and the reason-giving or justification-generating feature of being commanded. And simply to make that link is not to say anything more about what the force of moral Obligation comes to, let alone to reduce moral obligatoriness to nothing more than the feature which generates it.

But if we do state a divine command ethics in these terms—moral obligatoriness does not consist in being divinely commanded, but is a justificatory force which has to be generated by divine commands—we can no longer follow Anscombe. Those who oppose divine command theory, who make moral obligatoriness independent of divine commands, can no longer be reproved in the terms that Anscombe reproves them—for depriving the term 'moral obligatoriness' of all meaning. For we ourselves are no longer using divine command theory to explain what moral obligatoriness is. We are merely using divine command theory to put a metaphysical condition on moral obligatoriness's generation—a metaphysical condition that is surely fully open to debate.

We can distinguish then between those theories of moral obligation which operate with what I shall call a *Feature model* of obligatoriness—identifying moral obligatoriness as some distinctive reason-giving feature of action; and those which operate with what I shall call a *Force model* of obligatoriness, identifying moral obligatoriness, not with any reason-giving feature of action, but with a distinctive and agency-specific justificatory force—a justificatory force which other features of an action besides its obligatoriness generate, and a force not of mere recommendation or advice, but of demand. And I think divine command theories of moral obligation could perfectly well be developed within the framework of either model, as in fact could theories of moral obligation which oppose appeal to divine commands. Rather more fundamental to making sense of moral obligation than any debate about divine command theory, in my view, is understanding the Force model and what might depend on or follow from its truth.

So let me say now a little more about what a Force model of moral obligatoriness involves. The Force model is deeply intuitive, I think. But it has been largely absent from English language philosophy since the early modern period—a development which, with the very notion of there being such a thing as a Force model, has gone largely unremarked by the English-language philosophical tradition. But it is not mere inattention that has left the Force model without clear modern support. No matter how intuitive it may initially seem, the model is deeply inconsistent with a number of assumptions fundamental to current English language philosophy— both in the theory of normativity and in the theory of action.

4. The Force model

We have seen that moral obligations are cited in argument—when we are offering reasons or justifications for doing one thing rather than another. So let us look, in very general terms, then, at the structure of practical justification or reason, and at what elements it involves. Take again actions that are *voluntary*—by which word 'voluntary' meaning, as before, actions that we perform, when we do, on the basis of some motivating pro attitude towards performing the action, such as a decision or intention to perform it.

Deliberation or reasoning about how to act, practical deliberation, is principally and centrally about which such voluntary actions to perform—about whether to cross the road say, or make someone a gift of money, and the like. In deliberating we consider the various features which these possible voluntary actions have. We consider the actions both as possible ends in themselves, things possibly worth doing for their own sake, and as possible means to attaining further ends. Certain features of the voluntary then generate reasons or justifications for performing this voluntary action rather than that—reasons having a certain kind of force. And we immediately respond to the force of this justification, when we do, by deciding or forming an intention to perform the action concerned.

What kind of force might a justification possess? That is something which we shall be discussing, but one thing seems clear. The nature of the force is clearly linked to the kind of criticism that someone is liable to if they disregard the justification provided. For when one is criticized for ignoring a justification, it is in the nature of that criticism that it will assert the very kind of justificatory force which has been ignored.

What kinds of justificatory force are there? One kind of justificatory force, certainly, is what I shall call the force of Recommendation. With this force reasons recommend the actions which they support, or make the performance of those actions advisable. In so doing they may defeat rival reasons for alternative actions—and thereby leave the action justified more advisable or sensible than those alternatives. To ignore the force of Recommendation is to be liable for criticism as foolish or less than sensible.

The force of Recommendation is a force of reason—it is a force which reasons or justifications can certainly have. Indeed, I would go further, and conjecture that anything which counts as a reason will have some amount of this force. For to offer a reason for doing something is always, at the very least, to offer some recommendation for doing that thing, or to give some advice in its favour.

But there is another kind of force which I think that reasons can have—the very force which we have just been discussing, and which I call the force of Demand. This does appear to be a quite distinct kind of force. And that is because it is accompanied by a quite distinct and distinctive kind of criticism. To disregard the force of Demand is not obviously to be foolish or less than sensible. Instead it is to go in for wrong-doing—wrong-doing for which, if one lacks excuse, one is blameworthy. The criticism that meets unexcused wrongdoers is blame—the message of which is that one is fully responsible for having done wrong. And as we have already observed, that criticism does seem rather different from the criticism that one has been foolish, or less than sensible.

And our thinking about moral obligatoriness seems to treat it, not as a reason-giving or justification-generating feature, but as a special and quite distinct justificatory force—this force of Demand. Providing help to someone in grave need can be morally obligatory. But if so, this is not because, in addition to its relieving need the action has a further feature, being morally obligatory, which means that it is all the more advisable to perform the action. Rather, the action's moral obligatoriness consists in this—the fact that the action would relieve grave need does not merely recommend, but demands that we perform it. And the force of this demand, which is generated by the fact that the action would relieve need, and which is what the action's moral obligatoriness consists in, is that if we failed to help, and if we lacked any excuse for our failure, we would be blameworthy. We would be responsible for doing wrong. And for something to be morally obligatory just is for it to be justified with this force of Demand.

Suppose we adopt a Force model of moral obligatoriness, and not a Feature model of it. This has one immediate effect. We avoid the question of trying to work out how moral obligatoriness might give us reason to act.[7] That question becomes a pseudo-question. Moral obligatoriness

[7] The assumption that obligatoriness or rightness is a reason-giving feature, and wrongness correspondingly a feature that gives a reason against, is fundamental to Scanlon's contractualism. Scanlon thinks that a theory of right and wrong must show 'how an act's being wrong' provides 'a reason not to do it' (*What We Owe to Each Other* (Harvard, 1998) p. 153). For Scanion, this reason-giving character is explained by identifying wrongness with an action's being excluded by any reasonable social con-tract:

> 'Contractualism offers such an account [of wrongness]. It holds that an act is wrong, if its performance under the circumstances would be disallowed by any set of principles for the general regulation of behaviour that no one could reasonably reject as a basis for informed, unforced general agreement.' Ibid p. 153.

This paper is therefore directed at an essential foundation of Scanlon's contractualist theory of right and wrong. The consequences for moral theory of abandoning this foundation are considerable and ramifying. I explore these consequences and compare my views against Scanlon's at greater length in my forthcoming *The Ethics of Action*, volume 2 *Action and Normativity*.

no longer moves us as a reason-giving feature—as something which itself gives us reason to act. It instead moves us as the force with which other things give us reason to act. And so we need no longer try to find some favoured reason- or justification-generating feature with which to identify moral obligatoriness. We need no longer worry whether an action's moral obligatoriness consists in its being commanded by God, as Anscombe thinks; or in its being the kind of action which would form part of any reasonable social contract, as contractualists such as Scanion think; or in its maximizing happiness, as many utilitarians including Bentham have thought.[8] Moral obligatoriness is not itself

[8] Thus in his *An Introduction to the Principles of Morals and Legislation,* Bentham writes:

> '6. An action then may be said to be conformable to the principle of utility, or, for shortness sake, to utility, (meaning with respect to the community at large) when the tendency it has to augment the happiness of the community is greater than any it has to diminish it...
> '10. Of an action that is conformable to the principle of utility, one may always say either that it is one that ought to be done, or at least that it is not one which ought not to be done. One may also say, that it is right that it should be done; or at least that it is not wrong it should be done: that it is a right action; at least that it is not a wrong action. When thus interpreted, the words *ought,* and *right* and *wrong,* and others of that stamp, have a meaning; when otherwise, they have none.' Pp. 12-13 J. H. Burns and H. L. A. Hart (eds.) (London, 1970).

See also the consequentialist G. E. Moore:

> 'Our "duty", therefore, can only be defined as that action, which will cause more good to exist in the Universe than any possible alternative. And what is "right" or "morally permissible" only differs

any of these features; its relation to any of these features is at best that of being a justificatory force which such a feature might generate.

So, instead, the question to ask now is—since moral obligatoriness is a justificatory force, what features do actually generate it? And this question is not easy to answer in simple terms. But nor is it any harder to answer, I think, than the question, what generates the force of Recommendation? I very much doubt whether there is a single property that all and only recommendable voluntary actions have and which makes them sensible or recommendable things to do. At best one can only gesture at the full range of very different considerations we ordinarily appeal to when we advise or recommend some particular action as a good idea. Similarly I see no reason to suppose that there is a single property that all and only morally obligatory actions have and which is what makes them all obligatory. Some actions are obligatory because to do otherwise would be unjust. Others because to do otherwise would be cruel. And so on. But certainly, even if there were one single property that made all actions with it obligatory, as we have seen, specifying that property would not be to specify the thing which moral obligatoriness is. A hope of specifying what moral obligatoriness is should not, therefore, tempt us into the unpromising hunt for that single property.

from this, as what will not cause less good than any possible alternative.' *Principia Ethica*, p. 148 (Cambridge 1903).

5. Moral obligatoriness as a demanding force of reason

On this new Force model of moral obligation, we have identified moral obligatoriness with a further kind of justificatory force—a force not of Recommendation, but Demand. And blame is a form of rational criticism—but of a very specific kind. It is criticism for disregarding this force of Demand. We have within practical reason then two kinds of justificatory force—the forces of Recommendation and Demand. These are both forces of practical reason. That is, they are both justificatory forces, forces which attach to reasons or justifications. But the two forces are nevertheless distinct. It therefore becomes a serious and I think still a largely open question what the relation is between them. Suppose I act wrongly and am fairly blamed for so doing. Must I also have been foolish or less than sensible to act as I did?

If blameworthy wrong-doing were ipso facto less than sensible, then the following would be true. The recommendatory force of any reasons which we might have had for doing wrong—such as any reason deriving from the fact that our own self-interest would be furthered—this recommendatory force would always have to be defeated by the demanding reasons we had for doing right. Only that way would the wrong action which we are being blamed for be less than sensible too. But perhaps, on the other hand, reasons equipped with the force of Demand need not work in this way. Perhaps their demands can still bind us even if there are opposing recommendations which stand undefeated. In which case to be moved by these opposing recommendations will still be wrong and blameworthy—but it will not be foolish.

So is blameworthy wrongdoing always less than sensible? I simply do not know the answer to this question. Nor I think does anyone else. Indeed, it seems to me to be a matter which ethical common sense leaves quite open. Common intuition never ordinarily suggests that if someone has been blameworthy for doing wrong, they must ipso facto have been foolish or less than sensible— that if they had any justifications, based say in their own self-interest, which recommended doing what they did, these must have been defeated by the rival reasons, based for example in the interests of others, which recommended, indeed demanded that they act otherwise. Common sense is, I think, remarkably silent on this point. The foolishness of doing what is wrong is not usually raised as an issue. What is raised as an issue is its wrongness—and this is expressed in that quite different criticism of the wrongdoer that we call blame. It is the wrongness of doing what is wrong that ordinarily matters—not some hypothesis about how wrongdoing is less than sensible. It is philosophers, not ordinary people, who have wanted somehow to show that by its very nature wrongdoing is not only blameworthy, but foolish.

So the force of moral obligation is a force disregard for which is wrong. On the other hand, disregard for it may not necessarily be foolish. We do not, I think, yet know the truth on that point. But then we face an obvious problem. What is left of the thought that the force of moral obligation is a force of reason, if it is not necessarily against reason in the sense of foolish or less than sensible to disregard it?

Some philosophers have wanted, in the tradition of Hume, to defend a reason-scepticism about moral obligation. They have wanted to deny that an action's moral obligatoriness implies the existence of a reason for performing that action. And they have correspondingly wanted to deny that blame is a form of rational criticism. And if it is an open question whether blameworthy wrongdoing is foolish or less than sensible, their view becomes perfectly intelligible. For elsewhere rational criticism, criticism for disregarding the force of reason, does ordinarily involve the charge of folly or at least of being less than sensible. To criticize someone for disregard of reason in ordinary belief is exactly to criticize them for forming beliefs that are not sensible. If blame does not work in this way, then the suspicion arises that perhaps blame is not, after all, a form of rational criticism at all. To breach a moral obligation may not be to disregard the force of a reason.

But at the same time I think it might still be an error simply to detach moral obligation from reason. For the force of obligation could still be rational—a force of reason—in this sense: it could still attach to reasons as reasons. It might still attach to considerations that, as any reason-giving features must, also have some recommendatory force—that can also make the obligatory at least a sensible thing to do. And obligations might still bind us only on condition that this recommendatory force has not been defeated. That is what may yet make moral obligatoriness a force of reason. It may be a force which binds us only on condition that it attaches to undefeated reasons.

The common understanding of moral obligation, its ordinary use in ethical argument, seems to respect this condition. We never hold someone to anobligation, or blame them for doing something wrong in breach of it, while at the same time admitting that they would have had to have been a fool to meet the obligation. Consider an all-powerful tyrant whom we blame for wronging some of his weaker and less popular subjects by despoiling them for his own gain—something which he does with complete impunity. Though we blame the tyrant, we may not be confident of showing that he is being foolish or less than sensible to act as he does. Indeed I think that ordinarily we need not be interested even in trying to assert the tyrant's folly, let alone show it. But insofar as we do blame and condemn the tyrant for having done wrong, nor are we ever willing to admit either that he would have to have been a fool to refrain from the wrongdoing. If we really did think that he would have to have been a fool not to do what he did, we would hardly regard him as blameworthy for doing it. And that seems basic to our ordinary understanding of blame.

Moral obligatoriness then is a distinctive justificatory force—a force which is distinct from that of ordinary recommendation, and which it is wrong for us to disregard; but which, at least for all we know, it may not be foolish or less than sensible for us to disregard. On the other hand, as we ordinarily conceive it, it still seems to be a force of reason, attaching to reasons or justifications—to considerations which must have sufficient force undefeatedly to recommend the obligatory action in question, and leave performing it a perfectly sensible thing to do. We do not blame people for doing what they do, if we think they would have to have been fools not to do it.

6. Moral obligatoriness as an agency-specific justificatory force

I have so far been assuming that moral obligatoriness and blame are something agency-specific—that we are under moral obligations and to blame for what we ourselves do or omit doing, and not for what happens independently of our own action. But David Hume thought that this was not so—that we can properly be directly blamed for motivations that are *passive* in the sense of being nonactions, being psychological attitudes which are not our own doing, which precede and explain our actions without being actions themselves. And he thought that this followed from the fact that, as he clearly saw, we can be directly to blame, not simply for voluntary actions which harm others, but for the motivations which precede and explain such voluntary actions. Not only can we be blamed for harming and neglecting others. We can be blamed purely and simply for our selfishness.

For like many, perhaps most philosophers in the modern English-language tradition, down to Donald Davidson and his many followers in our own day, Hume identified action with voluntariness—with what we do on the basis of a prior will or motivation to do it, such as an intention to do it. Hume, like many other philosophers, deploys what I call a *voluntariness-based* model of action. For Hume, that is just what action is—a voluntary effect of a prior pro-attitude towards its performance, such as a will, a decision or intention to perform it. So any kind of moral Standard that was agency-specific would have to be a standard solely on the voluntary, on what we do on the basis of having decided or intended to do it—and Hume saw, quite rightly, that moral obligatoriness is not such a standard.

Legal obligatoriness, obligatoriness under positive law, on the other hand, looks rather different. At least as something to which we can respond and which we can obey, legal obligatoriness seems as we have seen to be a reason-giving feature of the voluntary. It is a feature that we respond to by detecting that a particular outcome has it, and then, motivated by a concern to meet our legal obligations, deciding to produce that particular outcome. At least on an idealizing picture of it then, legal obligatoriness attaches to outcomes that we can produce through voluntary action, on the basis of a decision to do so. Legal obligatoriness does look far more like a standard on the voluntary—and so far more like a standard on action as Hume conceived action.

Which led Hume to think that the idea of moral obligation as a standard specific to agency was just an error, and a particular kind of error—a positivising confusion of moral obligation with some version, perhaps idealized, of legal Obligation. It was simply the result of a false assimilation of moral obligation to legal obligation's regulation of the voluntary, through (as he put it) 'philosophers, or rather divines under that disguise, treating all morals as on a like footing with civil laws, guarded by sanctions of reward and punishment.'

In this Hume was I am sure mistaken. I think it is ethical common sense, and not just philosophy, which naturally restricts moral obligation and blame to agency and its consequences. But I think that common sense does not do this in a positivising way. Common sense does not treat moral obligation as directive of action by modelling moral obligation on some idealizing picture of legal obligation. I shall now argue that the tendency to model moral obligation on legal obligation is in fact very much peculiar to philosophy—and, especially, that it is rather characteristic of much English-language philosophy since Hobbes. Modern English-language philosophy has been forced into such positivising strategies as the best or at least one of the most obvious ways left open to it of making sense of moral obligation's intuitive status as a demand on action—a status which really has quite another basis.

I have said that practical reasons or justifications involve features of voluntary actions generating justifications for their performance—justifications which have a given force. But to what must this force apply? Clearly, to the voluntary action justified. But not there alone. To move us any justificatory force must also address and apply to our prior motivation—to our will. A justification for performing a voluntary action A must equally apply, with the same force, to justify a prior motivation to do A—such as a decision or intention to do A:

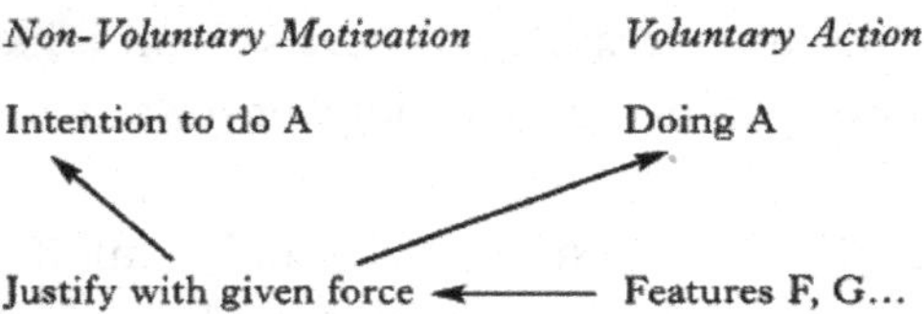

It is important that the force of a practical reason or justification must be able to apply to our motivation as well as to the voluntary action motivated. For that is how justifications for voluntary actions such as giving help to the needy and the like move us to perform the actions which they justify—by providing the same justification for, and so justifying with precisely the same force, the motivation, the decision and intention, which deliberate performance of the voluntary action would require. A justification which could never address the will with the same force with which it supports the voluntary action justified simply could not move us into action. We would, as rational, justification-sensitive beings, note the justification for giving the help—yet we would be unmoved by it, since we lacked the same justification for being correspondingly motivated to help. But it would be quite absurd for a practical justification to bypass the will in this way. For then we would have supposed justifications for action which, however, were incapable of moving even rational, justification-sensitive agents to act. And no genuine justification for action can so lack the force to move us to do what it justifies.

As for the force of Recommendation, so too for the force of Demand—a force of reason which moves us, as I have observed, not because it is foolish or less than sensible to disregard it, which I think common sense treats as very debatable, but because it is wrong and blameworthy to disregard it. This force of Demand must be able to apply to the will itself and not just to the voluntary actions willed. And with the force of Demand, the force which it is blameworthy to disregard, comes obligation. Not only are we under a moral obligation actually to help our neighbour, but if the force of that obligation is to move us, we must also be obliged to will or intend that our neighbour be helped. Not only can the interests of our neighbour oblige us to perform voluntary actions that are likely to protect those interests—whatever our real motive for performing those actions might be. Our neighbour's interests can also oblige us to a specific motivation—to have the protection of our neighbour's interests, and not merely the furtherance of our own, as our intended end.

That is just what we ordinarily suppose—insofar as we do regard people as under some obligation to have concern for others, and blame people for their very selfishness, their failure to have as their intended end the interests of others as well as their own; insofar as we regard selfishness itself as wrong, and not just the harmful or neglectful voluntary actions which this selfishness motivates.

But consider now what else the Force model implies. There is a special kind of justificatory force—a force which is generated by certain features of the voluntary. As a force of practical reason it must in particular apply to the motivation on the basis of which voluntary actions and outcomes are produced. It must be a force that can move us, and apply to the will—to our capacity for decision and intention. But this force, the force of Demand, must also be agency-specific—as agency-specific as the moral obligatoriness which it communicates. Since whatever it applies to is morally obligatory, whatever it applies to must be a capacity for agency. And since the force is agency-specific, since it applies to and directs our capacity for action and our capacity for action alone, the will to which it perforce applies must in particular be a capacity for deliberate and intentional action—and the will must count so, not by happy coincidence, but *because* it is the kind of capacity which a force of practical reason such as Demand addresses.

The will then must be not just a cause and motivator of actions, of the voluntary actions willed, but a locus of action itself. That I decide or form an intention to help you rather than hinder you, that I decide and form an intention to further your interests and not just my own—this must be as much my own deliberate doing and something that I can determine for myself, as is whether eventually I actually help you or hinder you. But so I think we ordinarily suppose. We do hold people responsible for what ends or goals they adopt or fail to—for what ends or goals they decide on and intend. And that is because we think that the taking of a specific decision, the forming of a specific intention—which after all is the adoption by the agent of a particular end or goal—can be something which the agent himself deliberately and intentionally does. Our decisions are not things which passively come over us, like a surge of desire, or the dawning of a realization. What we decide is directly up to us as our own deliberate doing.

These at any rate are the very terms in which many philosophers once understood action and its relation to moral obligation. Moral obligatoriness does not attach to actions as a reason-giving feature of the voluntary. It is instead a special kind of justificatory force— a force which is agency-specific, and which as a justificatory force extends beyond the voluntary, beyond the actions willed, to their cause in the will itself, and which directs the will as a locus of agency in its own right. We can I think uncover just this model of the relation between action and moral obligation in the natural law theory of medieval and early modern scholasticism.

In this natural law tradition, action was not restricted to what we do voluntarily, on the basis of a prior will or decision or intention to do it. Action was generally understood in quite different terms—terms which I call *practical reason-based* rather than voluntariness-based.[9] Action was conceived not as any kind of voluntary effect,

[9] For further historical discussion, see my, 'Suarez, Hobbes and the scholastic tradition in action theory' in *The Will and Human Action: from Antiquity to the Present Day,* Thomas Pink and Martin Stone (eds.) (Routledge, 2004), and especially my 'Action, will and law in late scholasticism', in *Moral Philosophy at the Threshold of Modernity*, Jill Kraye and Risto Saarinen (eds.) (Kluwer, Dordrecht: Synthese Historical Library, 2004).

A systematic philosophical discussion of both the practical reasonbased and the voluntariness-based models, together with a defence of the practical reason-based model, is to be found in my forthcoming *The Ethics of Action,* volume 1, *Action and Self-Determination* (Oxford University Press, forthcoming). A popular account of the debate and its relation to the free will problem is to be found in my forthcoming *Free Will: A Very Short Introduction* (Oxford University Press, 2004).

but as something quite different. Action was conceived as the exercise of a capacity to respond to practical justifications—the capacity to respond to practical justifications being one which, as we have just seen, is exercised at the point of motivation and will itself, at the point at which we take decisions to act, and not just at the point of the voluntary actions willed or decided upon. And action so understood was supposed to be governed not only by a justificatory force of Recommendation, by standards of sense and folly, but also by a quite distinct and agency-specific force of Demand. The force of Recommendation was communicated by advisory *consilia* or counsels; that of Demand by mandatory *praecepta* or precepts. And moral obligation, the voice of natural as opposed to positive law, extended exactly where the justificatory force of precept or Demand extended—to the will, which was seen as being as much bound by moral obligations as any voluntary action willed, and precisely because obligatoriness was understood as a justificatory force of reason. As Francisco Suarez put it, very forcefully, though taking the matter as generally understood and quite uncontroversial:

> So teaches Saint Thomas and on this point everyone. And the point is established because the law of nature is placed in reason, and immediately directs and governs the will. So it is on the will first and foremost that as it were by its very nature the obligation of the law is imposed. So the law is not kept unless through the exercise of the will. Francisco Suarez, *De Legibus*, Book 2, chapter 10.

It is in Hobbes, in the seventeenth century, that we find within the English language tradition a major assault on this practical reason-based conception of action—an assault which then undermines the Force model of moral obligatoriness which entirely depends on it. For Hobbes, action is no longer viewed as the exercise of a capacity to respond to practical reasons or justifications. And the will is no longer taken to be a capacity for action. Action is instead restricted to what we do voluntarily, on the basis of a prior motivation or will to do it, such as a decision or intention to do it. Action now occurs only as a voluntary effect of prior motivations of the will—motivations of the will which as non-voluntary antecedents of action in terms of which action is being defined, must themselves be passive.

But if action is thus restricted to occurring as a voluntary effect of motivation which is passive, that knocks out the Force model and its idea of obligatoriness as an agency-specific justificatory force. The motivation which leads us to perform this voluntary action or that—this is something which, as we have seen, the force of any practical justification which is to guide us must perforce address. But this motivation is now a passive antecedent of action. It is no longer a case of action in its own right. So there can be no agency-specific justificatory force—no justificatory force which applies to and directs our capacity for action, and that capacity alone. From now on, the application of the force of any practical justification must evenhandedly straddle the active-passive divide—the divide between action and non-action.

Once we restrict agency to what we do voluntarily then, if we are to preserve the restriction of moral obligation to governing action, moral obligatoriness must be restricted to what we do voluntarily too. Moral obligatoriness must not directly apply to our non-volun-tary motivations as well. The most obvious option is to relocate moral obligatoriness from being a justificatory force into being a reason-giving feature of the voluntary—a feature rather like a voluntary action's being commanded or made legally obligatory. We may even follow Anscombe as well as many others both before and after her, down to Robert Merrihew Adams at the present time,[10] and simply identify moral obligatoriness with the feature of being decreed or commanded by a moral legislator such as God. Obviously such a feature can still give us reason to become motivated to perform the voluntary actions which have it. It had better do so if the feature is to move us to comply. But in so doing the feature need not itself apply to our motivations as well. I can perfectly well command you to perform a voluntary action, such as raising your hand, without ipso facto also commanding you to will or intend to raise your hand. The justificatory force generated by my command that you raise your hand must, like any such force, actually extend to the will; when my command to raise your hand gives you reason to raise your hand, it must also give you the same reason to intend to raise your hand. But my command to you to raise your hand need not likewise extend to the will. All I have commanded

[10] For a sophisticated and very interesting recent defence of a divine command theory of moral obligation in Feature model terms, see Robert Merrihew Adams's *Finite and Infinite Goods* (Oxford University Press, 1999).

you to do is raise your hand—not intend to raise it. For you to fail to intend to raise your hand might involve contempt of my authority. But it would not itself constitute actual disobedience or actual breach of a command. As for commands so for legal obligations—and so, now, as reason-giving features of the voluntary, for moral obligations as well.

And since the justificatory force associated with moral obligation can no longer be a force which is agency-specific, that force can no longer lie in the blameworthiness of remaining unmoved by it—not if motivation is now to be passive, but blame is to remain tied to being for how we act. The justificatory force must instead lie in something else—and what else but in disregard for it being foolish or less than sensible? The agency-specific force of Demand makes way for the non-agency-specific force of Recommendation.

And so the idea of an agency-specific force of Demand disappears. The force of practical reason becomes wholly the force of Recommendation—the force that it is sensible to be moved by, foolish or less than sensible to disregard; and this therefore will be the only justificatory force with which moral obligatoriness is now to be associated. But of course it really is very difficult to assimilate moral obligatoriness to some kind of Recommendation-generating feature. Not only is it not clear what in general the feature could be—a rich source of irresoluble speculation. We are also thinking about moral obligatoriness in terms of quite the wrong force. The justificatory force inherent in obligatoriness cannot be adequately cashed out in terms of the supposed inadvisability of disregarding it—in terms of the thought that to remain unmoved would always be less than sensible or even very foolish. For, first, that thought is not obviously true—perhaps wrong-doing need not be foolish at all. And anyway, even if it were true, there is another difficulty. Since the morally obligatory now comes only with the justificatory force of advice, how do we distinguish it from the merely highly advisable? For both now seem *merely highly advisable.* How, without a justificatory force of Demand, to reintroduce the idea of demandedness? There is one very obvious way, of course—by bringing in, as something essential to obligatoriness, the likelihood or at least the legitimacy of the enforcement of obligations through social pressure, coercion or punishment. As Mill put it:

> It is part of the notion of Duty in every one of its forms, that a person may be rightfully compelled to fulfil it. Mill *Utilitarianism,* chapter 5.

And we so arrive at the positivising view's final element—the highly debatable and dubious appeal to enforcing sanctions and punishments to characterize what moral obligatoriness is.[11]

[11] Of course, if not merely the legitimacy, but the actual likelihood of punishment for its breach is made constitutive of moral obligation's very nature, the claim that it is always foolish to breach moral obligations becomes very much more plausible—but at the cost of greatly increased doubt about whether much of what we ordinarily suppose to be morally obligatory really is so.

By now we can see that the conception of moral obligatoriness which Anscombe thought was the only possible one—the Feature model-assuming conception of it as consisting in an action's being commanded by God—is not the only possible one, and certainly not obviously our original one. Indeed, I rather suspect that Anscombe's conception of moral obligatoriness as being divinely commanded may in fact be a very local and rather modern English-language phenomenon.

It is true that the earlier medieval natural law tradition did contain many supporters of a divine command theory of moral obligation. But equally, a fact of which Anscombe seems to have been unaware, it also contained many opponents of divine command theory too. Though that fact should not by now be too surprising. For this tradition, theists and Christians though its members were, certainly did not see itself as having to rely on appeal to divine commands to determine what moral obligatoriness is. Whether they were for divine command theory or against, there seems to have been wide support for a Force model of moral obligatoriness, as opposed to a Feature model. Take Francisco Suarez—one natural law theorist who did support the divine command theory. Suarez certainly agreed that all moral obligations had to have their ultimate source in divine commands. But he certainly did not identify moral obligatoriness with or reduce it to the feature of being divinely commanded. Far from claiming to explain in other terms what obligatoriness is, Suarez happily used the notion in his specification of the content of the very legislative volition by which God imposed obligations. The content of the legislative volition is, not that a given action be performed, but that a given action be obligatory.[12] For Suarez, as for other members of his tradition, moral obligatoriness was a primitively understood justificatory force distinct from that of counsel or Recommendation—a force which the feature of being divinely commanded might generate, but which was not that feature itself. Far then from being something which modern moral philosophy has naughtily abandoned, Anscombe's particular conception of what moral obligatoriness is may very much be modern moral philosophy's creature and creation.[13]

[12] According to Suarez, for law and obligation is required

> '. . .aliquem actum efficacis voluntatis. . . haec autem voluntas non oportet, ut sit de ipsa observatione seu executione legis. . . Per se requiritur ut sit de obligatione subditorum, id est, ut sit voluntas obligandi subditos, quia sine tali voluntate non obligabit illos. . .' *De Legibus ac Deo Legislatore,* Book 1, cap 4 in Volume 5 of Suarez's *Opera,* Vives (ed.) 1856, p. 15.

[13] In his commentary on Judith Jarvis Thomson's *Goodness and Advice,* (Princeton, 2001) (see pages 128–9), Schneewind notes the distinction within the 'modern' or seventeenth century natural law tradition between demand and mere advice. But that distinction is not in itself remarkable. It is common property to any who wish to distinguish between moral obligations and ordinary reasons. What Schneewind does not do is distinguish between Force and Feature models of moral obligation—nor does he note the shift over time from medieval and renaissance natural law theory's reliance on a Force model to modern philosophy's characteristic reliance on a Feature model. Notice also that Schneewind sees the seventeenth century natural law tradition as tying the idea of demand to divine commands. That, especially if we

Whether in the end as philosophers we endorse or abandon it, the tie of moral obligation to the direction of action need have nothing in common with positive law's direction of the voluntary. If the tie prove genuine, it need not be defended by any analogy with positive law. Nor, if the tie prove an illusion, need we follow Hume and view it as an illusion generated by the example of positive law. The intuitive tie of moral obligation to the direction of action may in fact be best explained on quite a different basis: in terms of the idea of a special kind of agency-specific justificatory force, a force which directly addresses a capacity which we have for exercising reason practically and so in the form of action—a capacity exercised in the will, in our decision making and intention-formation, as much as in action that is voluntary.

Of course, to defend the reality of moral obligation as conceived by the Force model would require far more work. Not least, it would require a new theory of action as something that can occur, not just as voluntariness, but in

include late scholastic thinkers, it did not exceptionlessly do—and anyway certainly not in the way that Anscombe does.

For a major late scholastic account of law and obligation which opposes any divine command theory, see the immensely important commentary on the *Pritna Secundae* of Aquinas's *Summa Theologiae* by Suarez's contemporary and intellectual opponent in the sixteenth century Jesuit order, Gabriel Vasquez, which I discuss in detail in 'Action, will and law in late scholasticism'. For an invaluable contemporary synopsis of the views of Suarez, Vasquez and many others in the scholastic tradition, see Poncius's supplement to the 1639 Lyon edition of Scotus's *Quaestiones in Librum Tertium Sententiarum,* Distinctio 37, Scotus, *Opera Omnia*, Wadding (ed.), vol. 7, pp. 857–77

pre- or non-voluntary form, as the exercise of a capacity to apply reason practically, at the point of decision making and will. But perhaps such a theory of action may yet turn out to be just what our ordinary conception of moral obligatoriness requires.[14]

[14] See again my forthcoming *The Ethics of Action*. While volume 1, *Action and Self-Determination* defends just such a practical reason-based theory of action, volume 2, *Action and Normativity*, provides a general theory of moral normativity in line with the argument of this paper.

The Lesser Evil

AVISHAI MARGALIT

1. The Problem

'The Russian Revolution and the National Socialist ascendancy in Germany are the two most important sources of evidence of moral philosophy in our time, as the French Revolution was for Hegel and Marx, and later to Tocqueville and for Mill. Although both revolutions produced, both in intention and in effect, a triumph on a gigantic scale, there are often remarked differences between the evil effects planned and achieved.' This is an observation made by Stuart Hampshire, a keen philosophical connoisseur of the 20th century.[1]

It is embarrassingly banal to say that these two historical events shook the world. But it is less banal, although true, to say that these two events created a change in the world order which had in turn grave moral consequences. Both paved the way to unparalleled murderous regimes (especially if we view Mao's regime as connected, even if indirectly, to the October Revolution).

It is injustice, not justice, which brings us into normative politics; despotism, not freedom. Moral political

[1] Stuart Hampshire, *Innocence & Experience* (London: Jonathan Cape, 1999).

theory should start with negative politics: the politics that informs us on how to tackle evil before it tells us how to pursue the good. Stalin's Communism and Hitler's Nazism are perhaps the most glaringly dark examples, if I may be allowed the oxymoron, of evil. Thus negative moral politics should be informed by these two examples, and it should be able to provide us with the moral vocabulary adequate for coping with them. Indeed the way we judge these two examples, and especially the way we compare them, is a test case as to how adequate our moral account is. This in any case is the way I understand Stuart Hampshire's opening statement.

Morality, like wine tasting, calls for constant comparative judgments. It may even be the case, as Gilbert Ryle perhaps thought, that like in the case of wine tasting there is not much theory involved in morality: there are merely subtle variations of comparative judgments. If a theory is to emerge from the efforts to make such comparative judgments cohere it is a little theory and not a grand one.

One crucial comparative judgment that tests such a moral theory and gives a taste for it is the moral comparison of the lesser evil between Stalin's Communism and Hitler's Nazism. Note that I do not submit for comparison generic communism and generic fascism. I do not in my comparison tip, say, Pol Pot as against, say, Generalissimo Franco. Already the moral comparison between the regimes of Hitler and Stalin is burdened with the fact that Hitler ruled for 12 years whereas Stalin ruled for double that time-span. What does the double span mean? Should we compare what Stalin actually did to what Hitler would have done had he spent in power the time Stalin did, or should we compare Stalin doings only to what Hitler actually did? I shall compare facts to facts and not facts to counterfactuals. So I shall compare the actual ruling of Stalin to the actual ruling of Hitler even though we can easily imagine the moral havoc Hitler would have inflicted had he ruled for double the time he actually did.

Be it as it may, one thing is clear: the comparison between Stalin's regime and Hitler's regime is more focused and more confined and defined in space and time than the general comparison between generic communism and generic fascism.

2. Churchill's Judgment

On June 21 1941, at a dinner in Chequers, Churchill made the statement that Hitler in planning to attack Russia and that he, Hitler, counts on Right Wing sympathy in Britain and the USA not to let their governments intervene. But Hitler is wrong, Churchill stated, and Britain will help Russia. After dinner the issue of helping Russia came up again. Mr. Colville, Churchill's private secretary, asked him how come he, Churchill, the arch anti-Communist, was going to support Russia. Doesn't this support for Russia, he asked, amount to 'bowing down in the House of Rimmon' (meaning, compromising his principles)?

There are two senses of compromising one principles: a rotten compromise, when one loses one's integrity as in doing something for money, and compromising out coercive necessity. Churchill's secretary alluded to the

Aramaic military commander Na'aman who, after being cured from leprosy by the prophet Elijiah, promised to worship God alone. But then, as an afterthought, Na'aman asked the prophet to be excused in those cases when he had to follow his master, the earthly king, and bow down to the Aramaic idol Rimmon. The prophet granted this request. Hence the biblical sense of bowing down in the House of Rimmon is the necessity sense of compromise, not the rotten one. This in any case is how I understand the question that Churchill was asked. Churchill's reply is a vintage Churchill: 'Not at all. I have only one purpose; the destruction of Hitler, and my life is much simplified thereby. If Hitler invaded Hell I would make at least a favourable reference to the Devil in the House of Commons'. (*The Grand Alliance*, p. 370).

The day after Churchill went on the air. In his speech he compared the two regimes. 'The Nazi regime is indistinguishable from the worst features of Communism. It is devoid of all theme and principle except appetite and racial domination. It excels all forms of human aggression. No one has been a more consistent opponent of Communism than I have for the last twenty-five years. I will unsay no word that I have spoken about it. But all this fades away before the spectacle which is now unfolding. The past with its crimes, its follies and its tragedies flashes away.' And then he went on to make some favourable remarks on behalf of the devil Stalin. I believe that Churchill made the right moral choice in siding with Stalin against Hitler. This I maintain is true even according to our retrospective knowledge of Stalin's crimes, the extent of which presumably was not available to Churchill.

There is no question that Stalin's worst crimes were committed in the years before the War. There is no question that Hitler's worst crimes were committed during the War. When Churchill made his judgment Stalin had already committed his worst, whereas Hitler was far from doing his worst yet. And yet I believe Churchill was right not because Stalin's worst is not up to Hitler's worse-than-worst, but because Hitler's evil was radical evil, undermining morality itself. Stalin's evil monstrosity was different, and Churchill correctly sensed the difference when he said that Hitler stands for one thing and that is 'racial domination'. This is what I shall argue.

One may wonder if my understanding of Churchill's choice is not an exercise in misguided moralism. This line sees Churchill as having made a political judgment, not a moral one: he deemed Hitler more dangerous to Britain and to the British Empire than Stalin.

I do not think so. Churchill obviously was concerned with the interests of Britain, as he understood them. And it is true that he judged Stalin as less dangerous than Hitler, not just because Stalin in foreign affairs was the devil he knew whereas Hitler was the new devil. But Stalin's crimes were all inwardly directed, toward Russians, whereas Hitler's crimes were outwardly directed, to the enemies outside. Hitler was more dangerous to Britain than Stalin, who was rather prudent in his foreign policy.

This is all true. But I believe that on top of Churchill's political judgment there was a moral judgment. This is I how I understand his reference to Hell and the Devil in his reply to his secretary. He invoked hell and the devil because he believed that there is a moral choice that he had to take, not just a political choice. My task here, however, is not to assess Churchill's sincerity, but the soundness of his moral judgment.

Churchill made his judgment well into the war. But one of the first Gallup polls conducted in the US was taken in January 1939, before the Second World War broke out. Americans were asked a rather poignant question: in case a war breaks out between the Soviet Union and Germany, whom do they prefer to win the war. 83 per cent favoured a Soviet victory as against 17 per cent for Germany. (Eric Hobsbaum, *The Age of Extremes* p. 143). The Americans, like Churchill, were no friends of communism, and yet in comparing the two they clearly opted for Russia as the lesser evil. I believe that, naïve and unworldly as those Americans were, they correctly sensed that in Hitler's racism there was something more sinister than in Stalin's awfulness. There is no question that by the time the Gallup poll was conducted millions of people had been murdered under Stalin, just the political famine of 1932–33 brought about the destruction of some six million people. But even if we compare the 'purges' that Stalin instituted in the Communist party to Hitler's in the National Socialist party, Hitler by then had very little to show for Stalin's liquidation of 700,000 people in the Great Purge of 1937–38.

3. The Devil's Accountant

There are languages that have curious arithmetic. They count one, two, three, and then they say many; above three matters blur. Having been born in a relatively hot country I believed that every temperature below zero Celsius is more or less the same—that it is just very cold. Only after experiencing some cold winters abroad I realized that −10C feels very different than −20C. When it comes to numbers of the killed we believe that above a certain threshold it all blurs. The number of the dead passes as 'many'. But morally, numbers should count. Murdering two million people is twice as bad as murdering one million.

This does not mean that sheer numbers affect the impression the killing makes on us. In a curious way, the converse is almost true. The Romans crucified thousands upon thousands but only one crucifixion—and even that was only for three days—made such a momentous impression on humanity. More was made of the death of Anna Frank than of the other million and a half Jewish children who were murdered in the Holocaust. Numbers play almost an inverse role in our ability to identify with the victims. Numbers numb, individual stories make for vivid impressions. But then, moral arithmetic is not about impressions.

'A murder is a murder' is a deep tautology. Morally we should count all the murdered as equal. If so, all there is to the comparison between Stalin's regime and Hitler's regime is the to compare the number of people that each regime murdered. Of course there are other evil deeds that the two regimes inflicted, but they surely pale in comparison with their mass murders. So let us stick to the numbers of the dead, if we agree that they were indeed murdered, not just killed.

On the principle that the life of every human counts for one, no less and no more, the cardinal evil of mass murder should be measured by cardinal numbers and by cardinal numbers alone. It is an additive function once it is determined that it is murder. On this view we should not pay attention to other considerations and to other numbers; they all dim our moral judgment. We should not for example toy with ratios, such as the ratio of those murdered to the total population or with counting children or women or the elderly. The relevant population is humanity at large and nothing else. Thus the ratio of the victims to the total population in Cambodia of Pol Pot (one fourth of the population), which is much higher than the ratio of the victims in Mao's China (about one 12th of the population), does still not put Pol Pot in the league of Mao. Mao's regime is responsible for 65 million murders, as compared to the meagre two millions of Pol Pot's regime.

A serial killer gets in court—in some courts—a string of life sentences according to the number of his or her victims. This is a symbolic token of the principle that murder is murder and the value of life of every victim counts the same, all on an individual basis. Any other principle of evaluating the degree of evil in mass murder above and beyond the number of people killed is wrong. Genocide on this view is not more evil, *qua* murder, than murdering a comparable number of people who are not identified by religion or ethnic affiliation. Murdering, say, the Budapest quartet is not more evil *qua* murder than murdering four people taken at random. The genocide of the Jews, and with it the destruction of their culture, should not count as more evil than the murdering of the kulaks just because the kulaks do not belong to a cultural group but merely to a bureaucratic category, already imposed from above by Stolypin (1906). Genocide usually involves further consequences that are evil and that may be lacking in an anonymous mass murder, such as the destruction of valuable forms of life, or—in the case of the Budapest quartet—a terrible loss to music. But these further evils should not be compounded with the evil of murder.

Jonathan Glover is undoubtedly right is writing: 'The numbers of people murdered by Stalin's tyranny far surpass those killed in the Nazi camps'[2]. But this comparison is far from telling us the whole moral story between the two. A great deal depends on whom we consider responsible for the victims in Europe of World War II. I count them as resting with Hitler.

Does this mean that the 700,000 or so Germans civilians who were killed by the Allied bombing of Germans cities should be billed on Hitler's count? Is not Churchill himself accountable for killing those German civilians? Should Russian soldiers fighting in a battlefield be counted as people who were murdered?

The moral counting of the dead in the Second World War is indeed not a straightforward matter, as the example of the German civilians killed by the Allies shows. Moreover, it sounds to me quite absurd to regard all of the German soldiers, many of whom were great enthusiasts of the Nazi regime, as victims of that regime—as some German conservatives represent them today. Still, tricky as billing the

[2] Jonathan Glover, *Humanity* (London: The Penguin Press, 1989), p. 317.

account of the deaths of WWII may be, and allowing for discount in all cases of doubt, I believe that Hitler's hellish bill is such that it tops all of Stalin's victims in the years of terror.

To wit: the moral accountability for the dead is not a simple mechanical counting of corpses. Corpses of Russian children are not corpses of Red Army soldiers, to be lumped together as victims. Soldiers can fight, children cannot; hence the two cannot be lumped together as victims. Yet there is something right in the mechanical criterion of measuring degrees of evil by the number of victims. And my claim is that if we add to the responsibility of the Nazi regime all the victims of WWII, not just those who were murdered in the camps, Stalin's regime, hideous as it was, comes out as the lesser evil.

4. The nature of the victims

As a first approximation, Stalin's regime murdered its own people, whereas Hitler's regime murdered other people. One could be a loyal Nazi and feel secure in Hitler's Germany. No one except Stalin could ever feel secure under Stalin's rule. In fact, due to Stalin's downright paranoia, even Stalin did not feel secure, as the affair of the Jewish doctors plot indicates.

Stalin's reign of terror was the reign of random terror. There was a quota of victims to be filled, irrespective of any wrong done. Innocent people were routinely rounded up, many of whom were party loyalists. Indeed Stalin's terror was directed toward party members as much, if not more, than toward outsiders. This created the curious perception (that has a great deal of reality to it) that many of the perpetrators in Stalin's system were also victims. So it was not as simple as what Akhmatova described as the two Russias, one sending the other to the camps. Stalin even executed heads of the NKVD like Yezhov and Yagoda, Stalin's relentless executioners in the worst of times in the thirties. They too, beside Bukharin, Rykov, Kresinsky and for that matter Trotsky, fall into the ambiguous category of perpetrators-victims.

There was nothing like it in Nazi Germany. Apart from the Rohm purge there was very little that Hitler did against party loyalists or any other kind of loyalists. The Gestapo terror was directed toward true political rivals such as the communists, or toward minorities such as the Jews.

Hitler's rule was to a large extent a prime-mover's rule, the rule of an unmoved mover. Aristotle's example of an unmoved mover is of a loved one who is unaware of being loved and yet causes others to act and to try hard to second-guess her wishes and to fulfil them. What took place in Nazi Germany was not an outcome of Hitler's explicit intentions. Nor was it an outcome of an impersonal political structure.

It was Hitler's role as the prime mover, who was sometimes an unmoved mover, that made the Nazi system work. I believe that Ian Kershaw's account of Hitler is close to the prime-mover model, and is all the better for that.

The point however is that Hitler's rule over the Germans, except for a short period during his ascendancy to power, was not based on a great deal of terror. The emphasis of course is on the rule over the Germans, not over the nations he conquered during the war. In the conquered countries he reigned by terror and nothing but terror. Stalin's rule, in contrast, was based essentially on terror. It was so either because this was the only way to make his cruel command economy work, or as a way to move an immovable bureaucracy, or because of his despotic tendencies—or because of all these three reasons together.

Stalin's terror was not just rule by fear. It also served as a source of legitimacy in the eyes of the party members and sympathizers. Many of them believed that it was not only they who were terrified of him, but the enemies of the revolution too. They wanted the enemies of the revolution to be scared. The loyalists believed that his brutality served as a justified means to defend the revolution. It was the old idea of Ivan the Terrible, that fear and trembling are the sources of legitimacy and not substitutes for it.

The triumphant Stalin, especially after the WWII, like Ivan the Terrible after the victory over the Tartars and the Teutonic Knights, ruled not just by fear and trembling but also by fear and admiration. But what does this account, if true, have to do with our moral comparison between the two regimes?

For one thing it calls for a distinction between comparing Stalin and Hitler on the one hand, and comparing the regimes of Stalin and Hitler on the other. We tend to conflate the two and to refer to the regimes by the synecdoche 'Hitler' or 'Stalin' much as we refer to the two individuals. But even if we maintain that the individuals Hitler and Stalin were equally evil or that Stalin was more evil than Hitler, the regime in terms of the people involved should be assessed differently. In one regime its own people were terrorized, and this is partly why they did their evil deeds. In the other regime they did it willingly. Hitler's people did what they did willingly, whereas many of Stalin's people did what they did because they were coerced by a stupefying fear. One should not buy Khrushchev's picture, delineated in his famous secret speech to the 20th party conference, according to which it was Stalin and Stalin alone who was responsible for the terror, while the rest were all his victims. Or, as he expressed it to Djilas: 'If Stalin tells you to dance, you just dance.' Many, not Stalin alone, created the monstrosity of the rule of terror, and Khrushchev himself had a great deal to do with it. And yet there is something right about his account. It is the ambiguity of victims-perpetrators that makes the case of Stalinism more morally ambiguous than the univocal case of Hitlerism.

5. The moral status of the fellow travellers

The moral comparison between Stalinism and Hitlerism involves the moral comparison between the sympathizers of the two regimes. What serves as an excuse for those who lived under terror does not serve the sympathizers who were not subjected the Stalinist terror. They supported Stalin's regime rapturously. So what makes Drieu La Rochelle, a Nazi sympathizer of his own will, a moral anathema and why is there a soft spot for Louis Aragon, the Stalinist enthusiast? After all it was Aragon who wrote the despicable poem 'Prelude to the Cherry Season' (1931) with its recurrent mantra 'long live the GPU'. There is no question that we would have treated him very differently were he to write, 'Long live the Gestapo'. But the GPU, known better by its later acronym the NKVD, was an instrument of oppression far more ubiquitous than the Gestapo. Until the war there were about 8000 Gestapo tormentors, as compared to the 350,000 in the GPU.

It is this kind of question about the moral equivalence of say Aragon and Drieu that gives the feeling that there nothing more to the moral comparison between Hitlerism and Stalinism than settling scores with former communists and their fellow travellers. But exposing the hypocrisy of the left is not much of a serious moral question to test our moral theories against. There may very well be such a motivation among those who raise the issue of the lesser evil between Communism and Nazism. Still, this does not mean that we should not be troubled by the question of why among our best friends there are former Stalinists but not former Hitlerists, and why we make allowances to them that we would never dare make to Hitlerists. 'Speak for yourself,' you may retort. But I don't think that I am speaking only for myself in raising this semi-biographical question.

There is no question that in the thirties there were people who sensed that there was something wrong about Stalin's Russia but believed that they were facing in an acute form of the question of the lesser evil. The only force, they reasoned, which is both able and committed to stop Nazism is Communism. Given that the real moral choice was Communism or Nazism, they opted for Communism on the lesser-evil argument.

What made it easier to pose the problem in such terms were agitprop agents with a real flair for propaganda, like Willi Munzenberg. Such skillful propagandists were clever enough in changing the terms of the choice by creating 'popular fronts' that posed the question as either Fascism or Anti-Fascism. Siding with Russia was simply the only efficient way of combating Fascism. After the war many of those who made such a choice of the lesser evil in the thirties were grateful for the heroism of the Red Army and of the Russian people's sacrifices in the war that brought Hitler down. They remained loyal to Russia and its wartime leader as an act of gratitude. These sympathizers had to cope with the embarrassing episode of the pact between Hitler and Stalin, but the heroism of Stalingrad later on more than made up for it.

Of course, not all Stalin's sympathizers were of the lesser-evil type; most were communists who viewed his communism as a positive good rather than a lesser evil.

And many of those had embraced communism because they were morally motivated, whereas no one embraced Nazism for moral reasons. This is a significant fact. Communism offered a moral vision; not so Nazism. And many were attracted to the moral vision of a non-exploitative classless society. But I would like to address the different kind of supporters, those who were clear-headed enough to see that there is something deeply disturbing about Stalinism and yet were convinced that Stalinism is the lesser evil. Were these people justified?

In asking this question I do not ask whether they were right in believing that the situation is one of dichotomous choice, either Communism or Nazism. But rather, given that they so believed, were they allowed to side morally with Stalin at the time? Well they were entitled like Churchill to believe in the lesser evil argument. True, Churchill also believed that the choice is not either Communism or Fascism but that there is a much better third alternative: *he himself.* But in the appeasement atmosphere of the time it is hard to blame those who believed in the either-Fascism-or-Communism view of the world.

My claim then is not that those popular front people can be excused for their factual assessment of the world but rather that they are very much entitled to their moral assessment of the lesser evil, just as Churchill was right is preferring the devil to Hitler. I still believe, however, that they were all wrong at the time about the lesser evil argument, since, judging by conventional standards of decency and justice, Stalin's regime in the thirties was by no means the lesser evil of the two. And yet these people sensed something right and important, namely, that Hitler introduced an altogether new and different kind of evil.

6. The Attack on Morality itself

Here is an important distinction between Communism and Nazism. Nazism is an attack on the very idea of morality, whereas Communism, perverse as it was under Stalinism, does not amount to such an attack. The idea is that the main presupposition of morality is shared humanity. Nazi racism both in doctrine and in practice was a conscious attack on the idea of shared humanity, and hence on the very possibility of morality itself. Stalinism was a terrible doctrine, not just an awful practice, but the doctrine did not amount to the very denial of morality. Or so I shall argue.

I borrow from Kant the expression 'radical evil,' though I do not borrow his content. On my account radical evil is any attack on morality itself. By attack I do not mean just a doctrinal nihilistic assault of the idea of morality but an assault by a combination of doctrine and practice. Nazism, in this sense, is radically evil.

Stuart Hampshire too regards Nazism as an attack on morality and not just as a gross violation of morality. But Hampshire puts the stress on Nazism's attack on the idea of justice. Understanding justice as the constraints we humans impose on the two human urges— one for domination and the other for a greater share of the rewards for ourselves— then Nazism, in Hampshire's view, is all about unrestricted domination.

I put the stress on what I regard as the presupposition of morality, namely the idea that all human beings should be subjected to moral treatment solely in virtue of being human. Setting aside 'soft' racism in the sense of trivial racial prejudices, the hard racism of the Nazi variety, namely that which calls for eradicating inferior races such as the Jews and the Gypsies and for enslaving the Slavs, is a flagrant negation of the idea of shared humanity. Acting on such negation of shared humanity, as the Nazi regime clearly did, is promoting radical evil. It undermines morality itself.

A distinction should be introduced between external evil and internal evil. External evil is radical evil that amounts to a denial of the moral point of view. Internal evil comprises gross violations of morality without denying the idea on which moral judgments are based. The question to be asked in terms of this distinction is, should we exempt Stalinism from the charge of radical evil?

7. Was Stalinism radically evil?

Stalinism professed to be Marxist. Let us take this claim at face value. The problem of denying morality seems already to be a problem for Marxism.

Marxism is an ambivalent doctrine about morality. It is motivated by the moral idea of the evil of exploitation. Yet it views morality as an ideology, namely as a set of values and ideas that emerge in particular historical circumstances and function to consolidate the economic and social order of that historical stage. Ideology is most effective in its role of maintaining the status quo when it presents itself as the natural order of things, that is, as something that cannot be changed by human action. Both bourgeois economics and bourgeois morality are based on a 'natural' assumption of scarcity: we human beings face, in all societies and in all circumstances, competing demands on scarce resources. The well-known paradox of the diamonds poses this question. Why is the price of diamonds so much higher than the price of water, even though we need water to sustain our life and we can easily do without diamonds? The answer that Adam Smith gave is scarcity. In comparison to diamonds there is water is in abundance and this explains why water is cheaper than diamonds.

Aristotelians such as Maimonides thought that scarcity is a fact about the world of matter but not about the world of the spirit. Hence the right way to live is the contemplative life of the spirit. This is exactly the move that Marxist thinking tries to block. Contemplative life is according to Marxism not the only form of life worth living, nor even the preferable one, and it is not the only way to escape scarcity. If paradise is the dream of humanity, as life without scarcity, the Marxists believe that there is no need for such daydreaming. Properly understood, scarcity is an outcome of historical conditions, not of natural conditions. The obstacle of scarcity can be removed in historical times. It can be removed on the one hand by technological innovations that would increase immeasurably what the material world can offer us. And on the other hand it can be removed by creating a classless society with no competing claims on the available resources. This will be done by radically changing people's desires, and hence their patterns of consumption, so much so that the latter will not be governed by scarcity.

With scarcity gone, economics and morality whither away. In a world without scarcity there is no need for morality any more than there was need for Adam and Eve in paradise to eat from the tree of knowledge so as to know good from evil. Abundance undermines the need for the distinction between good and evil.

We may very well think that this communist utopia of overcoming scarcity is no more realistic than trying to secure a place in the biblical paradise. But the question is whether the idea of overcoming scarcity, and hence undercutting morality, falls under the heading of undermining morality itself and thus counting as a radical evil. My answer: not in the least. After all, in religions that entertain the idea of paradise there are movements that view paradise in antinomian terms. Paradise is a place free from religious laws. This does not mean that those movements do not take the religious laws seriously in this world. The mere fact that Communism aspires to overcome morality by creating such conditions that there is no need for it does not undermine morality any more than the aspiration to create a situation of perfect health undermines medicine.

But this is of course is far from being the whole story about the relation between Communism and ethics, not to say Communism in its Leninist form. Attached to the idea of bringing about a classless world with no need for morality is the idea that there should be no moral constraints on the project of bringing about such a world. So the situation we are facing is not that of morality now, paradise later. Instead, it is hell now for paradise later: such a great end surely justifies all means. The cliché 'the end justifies the means' is meant to tell this story of ignoring morality in the name of a future without scarcity. So there is no morality at the end, but also no morality on the way. If this is no negation of morality, what is?

Sidney Morgenbesser once questioned the cliché by asking jokingly what else should justify the means if not the end. Well, there should be something else on the road to bringing about the end: there should be what Nozick calls 'side constraints'. Stalinism is a glaring case of disregard of any moral side constraints in bringing about the desired end. But then the claim is that the way to understand Stalinism morally is not by deontic side constraints but as a huge exercise in Pascal's wager. A socialist world without scarcity in the future has an infinite utility. The overwhelming expected utility of the future world justifies, on utilitarian grounds, any amount of suffering today. The infinite future bliss dwarfs the suffering of today on an expected utility ground. This Pascalian wager, namely betting on future history, is a bad argument, since if you pump infinite utility into future socialism or into kingdom come then anything goes. Every state of affairs has a tiny probability of bringing about the blissful future: multiply it by the infinite utility of the future and you get an infinite expected utility that justifies that particular state of affairs. In short, the Stalinist use of Pascal's wager can justify fascism as it can justify communism. It can justify everything and hence it justifies nothing.

But with all this moral sophistry about the blissful future, there are of course questions about the road, whether it leads at all to the Promised Land. Or, to switch to a more familiar metaphor, the question is whether besides breaking eggs Stalinism can produce an omelette. Put literally, were the means taken by Stalinism instrumentally adequate to bringing about the end?

If the end is a world without scarcity then the answer should be a resounding no. But if the end was to create an industrial society that could stand up to enemies such as Nazi Germany, then the answer is yes. Awful as these means were, the outcome of WWII shows that they were indeed adequate for that goal. But this gambit of shifting the goal, at least temporarily, from socialism to industrialization is, morally speaking, a red herring. It was used by Stalinist apologetics to justify Stalin's choice of the right method to overcome Nazism. As if Communism was born to combat Nazism, and as if there was no pact between Stalin and Hitler, a pact that Stalin was determined to keep. It is a case of shooting first and drawing the bull's eye later.

8. In the name of future humanity

The practice of Stalinism was hellish but its ideals were moral. With Hitlerism both the practice and the ideals were fiendish. So much worse, you might say, for Stalinism. It is much worse to act immorally in the name of moral ideals, just as it is worse to be a hypocrite and act immorally than to act immorally without being hypocritical about it. The Nazis at least did not pretend to behave morally.

I disagree. The cliché that hypocrisy is the homage paid by vice to virtue has, I believe, a profound meaning. Hypocrisy, irritating as it is, at least recognizes morality; and Communism, even in its wretched Stalinist form, is not nihilism. Nazism, unlike Communism in general and Stalinism in particular, is a denial of shared humanity. This is my claim. But is it true?

In a chapter entitled 'The Attack on Humanity' Jonathan Glover rightly points out that Nazi practices carried dehumanization to relentless extremes. But my point is that not only the practice but also the doctrine was one of denying what Raimond Gaita calls 'common humanity', and I call shared humanity. But then the question is, is it true that the Nazi ideology, confused and confusing as it was, denied the idea of shared humanity? After all, Glover uses as a motto for one of his chapters Hitler's saying, 'Those who see in National Socialism nothing more than a political movement, know scarcely anything of it. It is more even than a religion: it is the will to create mankind anew.' One may cogently argue that this idea would not be alien to Stalin, let alone to Mao. They all talked and acted in the name of a future humanity that they were going to create; none of them was committed to a shared concrete humanity. So why does it matter if you are excluded from future humanity for being a parasitic bourgeois, as in Stalinism, or for being a parasitic Jew, as in Nazism? After all, both categories of human beings, bourgeois and Jews, were perceived in equally inhuman terms—'parasites'.

The idea of future humanity and the idea of shaping 'a new man' are the fantasy of many ideologies. Moreover, the idea that there is a class of people that anticipate the future man and the future humanity, be these people 'the workers,' 'the bureaucrats,' or 'the students,' is also an idea shared by many radical ideologies. With it also goes the idea that the humanity of today is, in biblical terms, a 'desert generation' bound to perish on the way to the Promised Land. Stalinism, I maintain, is an extreme case of this dangerous fantasy of callousness towards concrete people in the name of abstract future humanity.

But Hitlerism is something very different. It is the dismembering of humanity into races. It thereby excludes, as a matter of doctrine groups of people from being deserving of moral consideration of whatever sort. If the Slavs are destined in Hitler's 'future humanity' to be slaves, the ontological and moral status of the Slavs is no better than that of domestic animals.

When it comes to Nazism there is no room for morality. At most we can find in Nazism perverse hygiene, run by the category of filth. Filth is regarded as a degenerative disease and thereby the degeneration of the master race. Future humanity in Hitler's fantasy is no humanity. It is the master race that replaces the idea of humanity. This is radical evil if anything is. So on my account Churchill was right in preferring the devil to Hitler.

The Ethics of Co-operation in Wrongdoing

DAVID S. ODERBERG

1. Introduction

There are a number of ways in which a person can share the guilt of another's wrongdoing. He might advise it, command it or consent to it. He might provoke it, praise it, flatter the wrongdoer, or conceal the wrong. He might stay silent when there is a clear duty to denounce the wrong or its perpetrator; or he might positively defend the wrong done. Finally, he might actively participate or co-operate in the wrongdoing. These various activities, apart from cooperation, typically occur before or after the commission of the wrong itself, only provocation being essentially before the fact. As such they fall into the categories of seduction or comfort, seduction being essentially pre-commission and comfort post-commission.[1] In seduction *(mutatis mutandis* for comfort), the seducer typically leads another into doing wrong who has not definitely made up his mind. He does not assist in the commission, but he leads to its occurring. If the principal (as I will call the one who commits the wrong) has made up his mind, actions which might otherwise

[1] Even if they occur during the commission, they occur with a view to that part of the wrong which either has been done or is yet to be done.

amount to seduction are best characterized as amounting to scandal, since they do not lead to wrong but reinforce the principal in his wrongful intent or provide to third parties a bad example since they connote approval of the principal's action.[2] Closely related to the concept of seduction is that of solicitation, though perhaps these are best thought of as two aspects of the same kind of activity. Seduction can be thought of as a strong form of inducement to wrong, typified by command, counsel (where the seducer knows the advice is likely to be relied upon) and enticement through praise or provocation. Solicitation is a softer form of inducement typically involving requests, appeals, and invitations. Whereas the seducer or solicitor leads another into wrong but does not assist in its commission, the co-operator does not lead the principal into wrong but assists in its commission.

The concern of this paper is with co-operation itself, or active participation in the wrongdoing of another. In mainstream modern moral philosophy the ethics of co-operation has received scant attention, let alone any sort of elaboration. Attention is given almost exclusively to the principal act and its moral evaluation. Yet the truth is that co-operation is pervasive throughout the world of action and that its evaluation is a specialized area of ethics. Moreover, whatever the reason for its neglect in contemporary ethics—whether carelessness, forgetfulness, or an underestimation of its importance as a moral issue—the ethical

[2] Though the scandalous actions might also lead to future wrongs by the principal.

evaluation of acts of co-operation cannot be read off in any sort of mechanical way from the evaluation of principal acts. If this unstated assumption does not lie behind the neglect, perhaps there is another assumption to the effect that the evaluation of principal acts is difficult enough without having to contend with a whole other area of enquiry whose comprehension obviously does depend on how principal acts are to be assessed. If so, one can sympathize with the thought whilst refusing to neglect such a vital aspect of moral theorizing. If ethics is about knowing what one must, may, or cannot do, then co-operation simply cannot be ignored, pregnant as it is with a plethora of concrete cases for judgment, real moral dilemmas that directly affect the everyday transactions of all of us. Such is the stuff of casuistry in its truest and most noble sense, which is what gives ethics its point. Fortunately one can, to a large degree, abstract from the particular kinds of principal act with whose co-operation the moral theorist should be concerned. This paper will in the main stick to cases of principal acts on whose morality most people of good will can agree; but if there be disagreement, it should not be difficult to substitute relevantly similar examples which illustrate the same principles of evaluation as applied to co-operation.

The investigation of the ethics of co-operation is important not only for its concrete applicability and its intrinsic conceptual interest, but also because we can draw from it larger lessons about normative moral theory. These will be brought out in the course of the discussion but since our main concern will be with the principles of co-operation themselves they will only be mentioned briefly. Further, although there is a developed positive law of complicity, it is not my purpose to outline that law or compare and contrast it with the moral principles guiding co-operation. For one thing, the law of complicity has broader scope, covering such actions as counselling and inciting another to criminal behaviour. For another, the law of complicity does not apply to many kinds of action that are clearly subject to ethical evaluation. In addition, whilst a study of the positive law can provide valuable assistance in ethical evaluation, it is the ethical principles themselves which need to be grasped first and the positive law which must be evaluated in light of them. Such an investigation, important as it is, is not my purpose here; having said that, occasional reference to the law of complicity will be made. Finally, since the discussion of co-operation involves numerous distinctions and controverted questions it will sometimes only be possible to indicate where a problem lies and suggest possible approaches for further investigation. With these restrictions in place we will still be able to survey the terrain in a way that brings out how unjustly neglected a topic the ethics of co-operation in wrongdoing evidently is.

2. Kinds of co-operation

Co-operation can be defined as material assistance afforded to another, whom one has not seduced, to carry out his purpose of doing wrong. As such, the co-operator should be distinguished from a co-ordinate agent or equal principal in the commission of a wrong. Co-ordinate agents have the same wrongful intent, such as when two people agree to burgle a house, one taking the goods and the other driving the getaway vehicle, or when several people agree jointly to assault a third party. The co-ordinate agent is always guilty but the co-operator may be guiltless.[3]

Co-operation may be characterized in a variety of ways, and so we need a number of distinctions to mark these. The distinctions fall into the three categories of kind of act, degree of influence, and level of responsibility. As to kinds of act, co-operation may be formal or material. The formal co-operator intends the wrong committed by the principal. Example: Alan gives Bill on request information as to how to enter a locked building he has no right to enter. Material co-operation does not involve such an intent. Example: Fred, held at gunpoint, does not resist while burglars search his employer's office. What is crucial here is not that the formal co-operator intend to commit any wrong, but that he intend that the principal should commit the wrong with which he assists. Again, the formal co-operator need not believe that the principal act is wrong; he should simply intend that it occur. In addition, formal co-operation can be explicit or implicit. It is explicit when the co-operator's end is precisely the wrong of the principal, such as joining a terrorist organization while agreeing with its

[3] In the common law of complicity, the driver of a getaway car would probably be guilty as an accomplice by having 'aided and abetted' the burglary. As an aider and abettor he would still be guilty of the principal offence of burglary, but since his action would not be thought of as coming within the legal definition of the offence he would be treated has having assisted rather than committed it.

aims. It is implicit when the co-operator does not intend to associate himself with the wrong of the principal but nevertheless intends for some other reason that the principal should do what he is set upon doing (or consents to its being done); for example, joining a terrorist organization not because one subscribes to its aims but for the sake of some social or financial advantage. This would be different from, say, an intelligence agent's joining such a group where the sole purpose is to infiltrate and expose it. In the former case the co-operator is presumed to be prepared to do whatever the others do, as long as he gets his advantage—and he can be so prepared without necessarily subscribing to the organization's aims. In the latter case, the spy would not be prepared to carry out terrorist acts—in which case he is a material, not a formal co-operator. The point is that implicit formal co-operation occurs when by the nature or circumstances of the case (including the co-operator's behaviour) the co-operator's end includes the guilt of the principal.[4]

[4] In the common law, an intent to co-operate may be inferred from proof that the accused realized that his conduct would, or would very probably, assist or encourage the principal: *National Coal Board v Gamble* [1959] 1 QB 11, [1958] All ER 203; *Clarkson* [1971] 3 All ER 344, [1971] 1 WLR 1402. According to Devil J in *Gamble,* if a man sells a gun to another which he knows will be used for murder, he cannot escape from guilt as an abettor merely because he sold the gun only for the money and not in order that the victim be killed. Even if the co-operator does not desire the commission of the principal offence, both morality and the common law recognize that intent to assist may be implied by the circumstances. But whether, in a given case, assistance is best characterized as implicitly formal or only material (though still unlawful) depends largely on difficult questions surrounding the

Also as to kind of act, co-operation can be positive or negative according as the co-operator does something to assist the principal or does nothing to hinder him. So in the previous examples Alan is a positive and Fred a negative co-operator. Again, positive co-operation can be moral or physical—moral when it primarily involves words and gestures providing assistance, physical when the help primarily involves bodily action. Voting for an unjust law, for instance, has the nature of moral rather than physical co-operation. Little will be said about negative co-operation, other than that its existence presupposes a voluntary abstention and its guilt an Obligation to act. Robert is not a negative co-operator if he is bound and gagged while his employer's office is robbed; Sandra does not negatively co-operate in the destruction of the Amazonian rainforest by sitting in front of her television.

As to degree of influence, co-operation can be immediate or mediate, depending on how near to the principal act it is. This is one of the most difficult distinctions to grapple with, and we will return to it, but suffice it to say for the moment that sharing in the principal act is immediate co-operation and sharing in some act that precedes or follows it is mediate. Helping a thief to remove property from another's premises is immediate; but giving him the keys to the house or driving the getaway car (assuming there was no joint plan) would be mediate. Another distinction that needs later examination is between co-operation which

distinction between knowledge and intent which have long dogged the philosophy of mind and action.

is indispensable and that which is not. If the principal agent depends on your co-operation it is indispensable, such as when someone supplies drugs to another who cannot get them elsewhere. If the supplier is one of many available, then the co-operation of any one of them would be dispensable, or not causally necessary for the principal act. Furthermore, mediate co-operation can be proximate or remote, and this by reason of causal nearness or of definiteness. As to the former, the proximity depends on how close the act of co-operation is to the principal wrong. Giving a ladder to a burglar is more remote than holding the ladder while the burglar ascends.

Note immediately that whilst it is not inappropriate to speak in particular cases as though an act were absolutely remote or proximate, this is never literally the case. Holding the ladder is more proximate that giving it; but less proximate than assisting the burglar with a push up the remaining few rungs. Proximity is therefore a matter of degree, and this because it is relative to the circumstances of the case, in particular to what alternative acts it might be compared with. The same goes for proximity as to definiteness, which depends on how clearly the co-operation points to the primary act. Here we may speak of a 'moral connection' with the latter. Example: selling a gun to a robber is proximate because it points definitely to the planned wrong; but selling some scrap iron to a robber who happens to be an expert gunsmith is remote. Selling a burglar a crowbar, torch and set of lock-picking equipment is proximate; selling him a balaclava is remote, as he may want it only to keep warm rather than to prevent identification. Again, proximity is a relative matter and a matter of degree. Of course the robber might only want the gun so he can shoot tin cans, and the burglar might specifically ask for the balaclava in the middle of summer. Here we can draw the first general lesson about moral theorizing: that it is one thing for relativity to enter into it, and another for relativism to do so. There is nothing relativistic about saying that a co-operative act was relatively proximate. The circumstances and nature of the case are fixed, including the range of choices and actions open to the participants. Given these, we can reach wholly objective evaluations of their behaviour.

Another general lesson immediately suggests itself: namely that these sorts of sliding scale militate against, not in favour of, a mathematical approach.[5] We can say that Charlie's co-operation was more remote than Donald's assuming the cases are sufficiently similar for a comparison to be made. We can even say that Charlie's act was in itself proximate on any reasonable interpretation of his case in isolation; but we will only be able to fall back on similarly non-mathematical terms like 'definitely', 'clearly', 'unmistakably', 'to any rational person', and so on. There can be no mathematical Standard of proximity any more than an absolute one when circumstances are considered; both points were made long ago by Aristotle in respect of moral judgment in general, and we do well to heed them.

[5] For an egregious example of the idea that there can be such a thing as 'moral mathematics', see D. Parfit, *Reasons and Persons* (Oxford: Oxford University Press, 1984).

The third lesson concerns the multi-factorial and multi-dimensional nature of moral evaluation. Suppose George co-operates remotely with Harry's embezzlement inasmuch as he supplies him with a computer to produce various fraudulent documents. A computer as such points only very vaguely to a nefarious intent and remoteness as such lessens the guilt attached to the co-operation. But if George *shares* the purpose for which Harry requires the computer, the mitigating effect of the vagueness will be cancelled as George becomes a *formal* co-operator. Similarly, supplying a revolver to a robber is a very determinate form of co-operation but the potential guilt on that score is cancelled if the supplier does not share the guilty purpose and is otherwise a lawful co-operator. And these are only simple abstract cases; in reality there are many variables that have to be considered and the moral judge has to perform the delicate act of holding one variable fixed while determining the effect of another. The evaluation is multi-dimensional since the variables move along different axes; for instance one may have to combine evaluations of knowledge, intent, circumstance, vagueness, causal nearness, dispensability, and so on. The significance of one may be mitigated or exacerbated by that of another. Whilst we should expect our moral evaluations to converge on definite answers, this does not mean we should expect the relevant Information in a given case to accumulate mono-dimensionally, as though all that were required, for example, were the amassing of units of utility whether these be measured in terms of preference satisfaction, desire fulfilment, increase of pleasure or whatever other unit of calculation might be the consequentialist flavour of the month. Morality just is not like that.

Finally, as to level of responsibility, co-operation can be unjust or merely unlawful. It is unjust if it involves an injury to a third party, and this would then entail a duty of restitution or reparation, such as when someone receives stolen goods. If the co-operation is only unlawful there is no duty of restitution but there will be still be a number of other duties, as with any immoral act: satisfaction where possible, acts of repentance evincing a sincere desire not to perform the wrong again, the duty to make amends for any scandal, and submission to any penalty imposed. An example of unlawful (but not unjust) co-operation would be supplying drugs: the recipient carries out the primary wrong and the supplier co-operates with it, but no third party is involved. Although the principles under examination here apply to both kinds of co-operation, our concern will not be cooperation *qua* act of injustice but only co-operation in general (*qua* wrong against charity, where the duty of charity involves the desire to promote and be the agent of virtue in others rather than vice).

3. Lawfulness of co-operation

Formal co-operation is always wrong. If performing an act is wrong, then so is conspiring to do it, attempting to do it, tolerating it, and *a fortiori* assisting someone to do it. Formal co-operation involves approval of the wrong and willing participation in its guilt, hence it is opposed to charity, to the virtue or duty violated by the principal, and also to the virtue or duty violated by the co-operator when the act of co-operation has its own malice, e.g. perjury.

Evaluating material co-operation, on the other hand, is a more difficult matter. In itself it would seem to be unlawful, for the simple reason that charity requires you to strive to prevent another from doing wrong, whereas in material co-operation you *help* him to do it. The duty of charity, however, has its limits. There is in morality no general duty to prevent the doing of evil at any cost, any more than there is a general duty to bring about the doing of good. The first principle of morality is indeed to do good and avoid evil, but this must be correctly interpreted. Every person must not intentionally do evil himself, and so he is equally prohibited from intentionally, that is formally, assisting another to do evil. But he cannot be obliged to avoid any and every bringing about of evil at his own hands, even if unintended, for the simple reason that there is very little people do in the ordinary course of their lives which does *not* involve their bringing about evil effects, even as a consequence of wholly good actions. Hence if morality is not to reduce people to virtual inaction, it has to permit the bringing about of evil effects in some circumstances, as long as those effects are not intended but only tolerated or permitted as side effects of intended actions not in themselves objectionable. Providing assistance to another in the commission of a wrong, so long as that wrong is not intended by the provider, can then be seen as just a special case of a general principle. The evil committed by the wrongdoer may causally depend to *some* degree—though never wholly, since the exercise of free will prevents one person's intended actions being causally determined by another's—on the acts of the assistant, but so long as the assistant only tolerates or permits that evil, responsibility need not be sheeted home to him as well. To put it another way, although there may be a causal dependency, the sort of causation is only *instrumental:* the co-operator, as long as he does not intentionally do anything which is itself forbidden, acts lawfully in a way that he knows the co-operator will abuse and exploit in order to commit a wrong.

But under *what* circumstances is material co-operation lawful? The duty of charity, as was said, has its limits, and one of those is relatively serious inconvenience to oneself. For instance, if on your way to pick up your child from school you walk past a beggar on the street and have no money on you, you are under no obligation to go to your nearest bank and make a withdrawal so you can give some to him, however admirable it may be if you did so. Would the inconvenience really be serious? It would, *relatively so,* inasmuch as it would be disproportionately inconvenient for you to go to your bank just so you could hand over a few pence. Hence the need for a grasp of *proportionality* in evaluating such cases. Another way of putting the same point is that you are entitled to permit a lesser evil in order to prevent a greater one: you are allowed, in the example just mentioned, to permit the beggar to go without a cup of coffee to spare yourself having to go to the bank. That it is allowable to permit a lesser evil in order to prevent a greater evil is one thing, and it is hard to see how one could object to it. But to say that one is allowed to *choose to do* a lesser evil in order to prevent a greater one is another thing altogether, and belongs not to genuine moral theory but to the sophistry of consequentialism, the sort of ends-justifies-the-means modern moral philosophy derided by Elizabeth Anscombe as corrupt.[6] (Whether one is ever allowed to *advise* the doing of a lesser evil is a more complex matter, however.[7])

Applying these thoughts to material co-operation, it can be seen that one may co-operate materially with another's wrongdoing in order to prevent a greater evil than the evil one permits to occur by co-operating (and this by means of permitting the principal to exploit the co-operator's lawful behaviour). What is the greater evil? It is the evil that would result from the potential co-operator's *refusing* to co-operate, which will involve either or both of evil suffered by the potential co-operator himself and evil caused to others. It should by now be becoming clear that the conditions and provisos that have been stated above in respect of material co-operation amount to just those conditions and provisos that together constitute one of the

[6] See G. E. M. Anscombe, 'Modern Moral Philosophy' in her *Ethics, Religion and Politics: Philosophical Papers, vol. Ill* (Oxford: Blackwell, 1981), 26–42.

[7] The most probable answer is that one generally may not advise the commission of a lesser evil for the general reasons stated above; but that if the lesser evil were already a virtual part of the greater, one could advise that the other person commit it instead. Example: Anna intends to steal £100 from Bertha; Christina, to prevent the theft, advises Anna to steal £50 instead. Here the act of stealing £50 is a virtual part of the act of stealing £100; Anna has already made up her mind to steal from Bertha, so Christina is not acting at all as a cause of theft (or seducer into theft), *a fortiori* not as a cause of the theft of £50 (or seducer); and Anna thereby prevents the greater evil, namely the theft of £100.

indispensable planks of any moral system worthy of serious consideration: the Principle of Double Effect (PDE). It turns out that the ethics of co-operation just is a special case or application of PDE, and this indicates another general lesson: the case of co-operation provides good grounds for the explanatory necessity of PDE for morality. Defenders of PDE usually argue for it directly, and this is of course important; but it is an equally necessary and potentially fruitful exercise for supporters of PDE to argue for it indirectly by examining ways in which other, disparate parts of morality ultimately depend on it as the best explanation of their own theoretical plausibility.

4. Application of PDE to the ethics of co-operation

It is not the intention of this paper to expound and directly defend the Principle of Double Effect: this can be found elsewhere.[8] Rather, it is to apply the principle to the specific case of cooperation; this will, one hopes, have the threefold outcome of explaining the ethics of co-operation, as well as illustrating PDE in action, and defending it indirectly by showing its explanatory value for the particular subject under examination.

The first plank in the explanation is the fact that material cooperation involves two effects: the evil effect of

[8] See D. S. Oderberg, *Moral Theory* (Oxford: Blackwell, 2000), ch. 3. See also T. D. J. Chappell, 'Two Distinctions that Do Make a Difference', *Philosophy* 77 (2002), 211–33.

the wrong commit-ted by the principal and the good effect of avoiding a loss and/or retaining or procuring a good on the part of the co-operator. Next, since PDE prohibits the use of a bad means to obtain a good end, the co-operator may not use the principal's wrong to secure some good: that would be formal co-operation. Hence Martha may not help Nicole to defraud her employer in order that Nicole obtain money to donate to her local charity. *A fortiori,* the co-operator may not intend the evil effect whether or not she uses it as a means to a good end.

What it is crucial to consider at length, then, are the requirements (a) that the act of the co-operator must be good or at least morally indifferent, and (b) that he have a sufficiently weighty reason for permitting the wrong of the principal. The first requirement is simply the obligation never intentionally to do wrong, and so one may not do it even as part of a larger context involving co-operation with another and the potential securing of some good for oneself or others. But how do we assess whether the co-operative act is good, evil or indifferent? We have to look at the nature and circumstances of the case. As to nature, we can say for example that assisting in a rape, say by holding down the victim, is intrinsically wrong, as would be assisting in the enslavement of another, say by providing a venue for slave auctions. Such cases are clear. But it is also the case that assisting in the distribution of harmful drugs is intrinsically wrong, as is assisting in the production of pornography.[9]

[9] If you think the latter is permissible, you can change the example to child pornography.

A central question to be asked in these cases is whether the co-operative act (or the material involved in it) has any potentially innocent or good use in the actual context: if not, it is by nature bad. On the other hand, where the act has potential good and bad uses, it is in itself indifferent, for example assisting in the manufacture of firearms or poisons. To say that the act is by nature bad should not be seen as gliding over the distinction between acts that are bad of themselves—the strict sense of 'by nature bad'—and those that are bad because in the context there is no way any good could reasonably be thought to come from them—what might be called 'bad by nature, all things considered'. Holding down a rape victim is strictly bad by nature; distributing poison in circumstances where there is no reasonable expectation of a good use for this (e.g., there are no pests that need destroying, no medicinal use for the poison, etc.) is bad in itself, given the relevant considerations. We can see that the distinction between the latter sort of wrong act and acts that are wrong in the circumstances is a fine one; but some such distinction should be drawn.

In the case of circumstantial wrong, the act is not of its nature bad but may in the circumstances signify approval of evil, give scandal, endanger the virtue of the co-operator, and so on. Hence it is not in itself wrong to pick up a hitch-hiker, but it is wrong in the circumstances to pick up a hitch-hiker who asks to be taken to a place where he can carry out a robbery.[10] Nevertheless, co-operation is not necessarily evil

[10] Note: if you do not know the hitch-hiker's purpose until after the event you are an unwitting, and hence not even *material* co-operator.

in virtue of one's certain knowledge of the wrongful purposes of the principal, or that the principal will be strengthened in his evil designs by one's assistance. In this regard two points needs to be made. First, circumstances which appear at first glance to point to scandal or danger might be such that these are not really present on examination. For instance, if you are forced at gunpoint into handing over the details of your business partner's bank account so another can steal from it, have you acted wrongly in the circumstances? Of course if you were forced at gunpoint into robbing your partner yourself you would be an accomplice to theft, i.e. a co-principal, and as the Socratic maxim goes it is better to suffer evil than to do it: the theft is an intrinsic wrong. On the other hand, giving over someone's bank account details is not of itself wrong. Also, since you do not share the thief's intent you are not a formal co-operator; presumably your will is set directly against that of the thief. And the circumstance of your being held at gunpoint manifestly vitiates any potential for scandal.[11] Even if it does not, however, the second point is that scandal, like any evil effect, may be permitted for a sufficient reason, and in this case the threat to your life would surely count as just such a reason. (As we will see, the threat to life allows not

[11] Should you worry that some people will be scandalized by your behaviour in virtue of not having been informed that you were held at gunpoint? No, since there is no obligation to suffer a great loss (e.g. your own life) just to avoid the scandal of those who rush to judgment (what is sometimes called Pharisaic scandal). The right answer to such people is: 'If you are scandalized, that's your problem.'

just the permission of scandal but of the evil resulting from the theft itself.)

Contrast the above with the case of the hitch-hiker, where the driver is under no compulsion, has full knowledge of what his passenger intends, and although he does not share that intention he is indifferent to it because he freely assists (for whatever purpose, say because he might receive some money at the end of it or because it's 'no skin off his nose' since he is travelling in the desired direction anyway). The thought that he might drive along to the place of robbery while muttering under his breath, 'I don't like this one little bit', hardly commends itself to right-thinking people as absolving him of wrongful co-operation: such behaviour is scandalous and a danger to the virtue of both parties. One might distinguish the hitch-hiker case from the theft case by applying the plausible pre-sumption[12] that a person intends the freely chosen (i.e. duress-free) natural and probable consequences of his acts: this would make the driver an implicit formal co-operator. Better, however, to rest it simply on the principle that morality requires one to avoid evil as far as one reasonably can, and that as far as PDE goes, the good effect achieved by the driver (getting his passenger to his desired destination) is not a sufficient reason for scandalously allowing the passenger to exploit the driver's hospitality by committing a serious wrong.

Another case is where the co-operator *knows* that his assistance will give scandal, either to the principal or to

[12] Present with qualifications in the common law until its abolition by statute in 1967.

third parties. (In the bank case the assistant knows precisely the opposite because of the public fact of his being held at gunpoint. In the hitch-hiker case the driver, let us suppose, does not know his behaviour is scandalous because his state of mind is one of indifference; scandalous, though, his behaviour really is.) For instance, is it permissible for an employee of a funeral director to assist in the burial of a known terrorist when he knows he will be sacked if he refuses but that if he participates he will give great scandal, perhaps signifying (wrongly) approval of the terrorist's behaviour? There is nothing in the nature of the act that makes assistance at a funeral wrong, but circumstances indicate otherwise. Nevertheless, there may be good reasons for permitting the evil of scandal (in most cases), and losing one's livelihood would appear to be one of them. In other words, the circumstance of scandal does not render the act wrong considered in abstraction from its effects and from other circumstances. But PDE also requires that one take steps to minimize the evil effects that one permits, and in this case the employee should, if possible, make well known his disapproval of the terrorist's behaviour.

As we have anticipated, the evaluative brunt of cases of material co-operation falls on the requirement of PDE that there be a sufficiently weighty reason for permitting the evil that results from it. The conditions that make up this requirement apply to all double effect cases, and their application to co-operation is especially illuminating. Here again we enter a realm of sliding scales, multi-factorial and multi-dimensional evaluations that do not pretend to mathematical precision and that require sensitivity to circumstance, the sort of sensitivity that only the truly practically wise person can demonstrate in its fullness. Absent such wisdom we are all never-the less bound to aspire to it and to make the best judgments we can on the facts of any case that come before us. But whatever our ability to judge, the principles themselves that will be outlined com-mend themselves for their adherence to common sense. In fact, as I have said elsewhere,[13] the Principle of Double Effect just is the codification of ethical common sense, not the arcane, logic-chop-ping invention of philosophers it has so often been portrayed as.

First, the graver the wrong of the principal, the graver the reason must be for co-operation. Thus you need a greater reason for co-operating in an assault than for co-operating in theft. Secondly, the nearer in the causal chain the co-operation would be to the principal wrong, the greater the reason. Thus a greater reason is needed for proof-reading a terrorist-training manual than for selling paper to its printer. Thirdly, the greater the dependence of the wrong on the co-operation, the greater the reason. Hence you need a greater reason for selling heroin to an addict if he cannot get the drug elsewhere than if he can easily do so. Nonetheless, the easy availability of co-operation from another does not of itself entitle you to sell the drugs, if the other conditions are not fulfilled, for instance if there is no loss on your part if you do not sell them. Fourthly, the more certain the wrong, the greater the

[13] See note 8.

reason. If Ellen has made up her mind definitely to burgle a house, you need greater reason to assist her than to assist Fiona who has decided to do it only if a number of other uncertain conditions are fulfilled (e.g. as long as she can find a suitable house and muster enough boldness). Again, the mere fact that the wrong is not certain to be carried out is not enough reason of itself to permit co-operation; it is just another factor to be taken into consideration. Fifthly, the greater the obligation to avoid the co-operation or prevent the wrong, the greater the reason. A much greater reason is needed on the part of those who are duty-bound *ex officio* to prevent a wrong—such as a policeman, parent or teacher—than on the part of those who are not. Again, this is common sense: a policeman who defends his assistance of a criminal by claiming that he was held at gunpoint rightly receives less sympathy than an innocent bystander precisely because it is part of the policeman's job to take on risks to life and limb in preventing crime.

So far we have spoken of the gravity of the principal wrong and of scaling reasons for co-operation against such factors as proximity, dependence and certainty. But how should we calibrate the scale of seriousness of principal wrongs and reasons for co-operation themselves? To reiterate, the calibration cannot be mathematical; it must incorporate other factors that are themselves susceptible only of judgments of degree and of relative importance that are responsive to circumstance. In general, we can say that reasons for cooperation correspond in gravity with the importance of the goods and evils involved. The greater the good lost or evil incurred if cooperation is refused, the greater the reason that obtains. But what constitutes a great good as opposed to a small good? Circumstances will be crucial: for instance, we can plausibly say that a day's wages is a great good for an average worker, and the loss of them a great evil; but it would be only a small good for a rich person. The question has to be what effect the good has in that person's life, taking into account her work, her family commitments, her broader communal obligations, her life-style, and so on. There is simply no way of saying that such-and-such an amount of money or property is or is not a great good in the abstract; the loss of a day's wages by a poor third world farmer might be catastrophic and hence count as a very serious evil indeed rather than just a great one. Similarly with an evil such as pain. The threat of physical pain levelled at a brave and highly disciplined soldier if he refuses to co-operate in some infraction of the rules of war will not give him as serious a reason for offering assistance than it would a woman, a child or a sensitive, bed-ridden Romantic poet. What about the anger of an employer, or a reaction from others that puts one to shame, or the stirring up of feelings of disgust or great sadness? Again, on the whole, and speaking quite generally, such things can plausibly be counted as great evils, things that one would naturally go a fairly long way to avoid. But in the context of a particular case, taking into account all relevant circumstances, we will have to modify our judgment of just how serious the good or evil is in that person's life. Which is *not* to say that anything goes; that the judgment is subjective or 'all relative' in the worst, viz. philosopher's, sense; that it is a matter purely of convention or stipulation; worse, that it is arbitrary, or that it is not susceptible to rational discussion and solution. Fortunately morality provides us with principles for even the worst dilemmas, for instance that if one is in doubt one should take the safer course, which would be for instance to preserve one's moral integrity at the cost of a material loss; or that if, as between two courses of action, it is impossible on all the available evidence to decide which one to take, then one may take either.

Having settled rationally upon a base level of seriousness for goods and evils in a particular context, however, it is then much easier to calibrate our scale with that context kept relatively stable. For instance, having determined that the loss of a day's wages is a serious evil in such-and-such a context, we can then confidently assert that the loss of a large proportion of one's material goods would constitute a very great evil and hence provide a very grave reason for co-operation. So would severe, protracted pain, unemployment, or great shame or indignity. Even worse would be such things as complete loss of one's position in life, incurable disease, perpetual loss of liberty, and so on. And we can say that the most serious reasons for co-operation are provided by the most serious evils, such as public safety, national security, loss of life, impoverishment, the utter ruin of one's reputation, and so on.

Armed with a scale of goods and evils we can proportion these to the scale of seriousness of wrongful actions co-operation with which is to be evaluated. We can start with a grave wrong by the principal and move upwards, and this will indicate how to approach wrongs that are less than grave. Where the principal wrong is grave but does not involve an injustice to a third party, the reason for cooperation need not be as serious as when the wrong is grave and unjust. To take the former case first, we need to factor in both the dispensability or otherwise of the co-operation and its proximity. Immediate and indispensable co-operation is most closely connected morally with the main wrong and so can only be justified by a grave loss to self (or another, which is implicit in what follows). Fred may co-operate in this way with his employer's minor deception of a client by, for instance, supplying information to which only he is privy, if he risks a public dressing-down by the employer if he refuses. Needless to say, the refusal to co-operate would be admirable, but it would not be strictly obligatory. It should be noted again that no material co-operation, not even of the immediate kind, is the same as complicity. The accomplices share wrongful intent (unless one of them is labouring under fear or ignorance, which can proportionally decrease responsibility for the act). The immediate material co-operator has no wrongful intent; further, an act that would be wrong in one context, such as intentionally carrying stolen goods to a waiting car, is indifferent or even good in another. After all, it is plausible to argue that a starving man may indeed take food from the owner without her consent, because her will would be unreasonable if she refused. Similarly, from the viewpoint of the victim of harm due partly to material co-operation, one can say that it would be unreasonable not to allow the co-operator to act for a sufficiently serious reason.

Co-operation which is immediate but dispensable or mediate but indispensable would be lawful to avoid a moderate loss since neither is quite so close to the principal wrong as immediate and indispensable assistance. Example: giving drink to an alcoholic in a crowded bar, in order to avoid a scuffle (a moderate loss), would be immediate but dispensable, and hence permissible. Giving the drunk the address of his favourite off-licence, assuming that only the co-operator knows or is in a position to give it (the drunk being too ill to remember), would be mediate but indispensable, and the same rule would apply. Note that one can (as in most of these cases) argue about how the relative seriousness is assessed: is a public dressing-down by one's boss worse than a scuffle in a bar? Again, circumstances need examining, but in the abstract one can say that a loss to others is not always worse than a loss to oneself. Indeed, all things being equal, natural charity obliges one to attend to one's own goods before the comparable goods of others, and hence to regard their loss as more serious for the agent that a comparable loss to a third party. Finally, mediate and dispensable co-operation is permissible even to avoid a slight loss. Example: a butcher may sell meat to a cook who will serve it to an irresolute but serious vegetarian (say, one who has taken a vow not to eat meat) if the cook can easily get the meat from another source and some profit will be lost if the butcher refuses to sell it.

When the wrong by the principal agent is grave *and* an injustice to a third party, the reason for co-operation needs to be proportionately greater than where no injustice is involved, but if the third party is a private person the reason need not be as great as when the injustice is against the public good: wrongs against the public good are worse than against private parties. If the co-operation is immediate and indispensable, one may co-operate to avoid a loss to self that would be worse than the loss to the third party. How do we tell if it is worse? One way would be if the harm to self were more certain than the harm to the third party, e.g. a certain serious loss of property as against a merely probable loss of property. Another would be a loss of a higher kind than that suffered by the third party, e.g. loss of health as opposed to loss of property. Yet another would be a greater loss of the same kind, such as loss of a lot of money as against loss of a small amount. Example: George is threatened with death if he does not hand over his employer's private papers to a burglar. The basic principle is that it would be unreasonable of the third party to expect someone to suffer a greater loss so as to spare him: again, it might be heroic, but it is not obligatory. What if the loss to the co-operator and to the third party are the same? Here the duty of charity would again oblige one in the ordinary course of morality (i.e., leaving aside heroic behaviour) to attend to one's own goods first.

Perhaps there is room for debate over the last point, but what is more clear is that if the co-operation is immediate and dispensable or mediate and indispensable it would be allowed in order to avoid an equal loss to self. For instance, suppose George is not threatened with death if he refuses to hand over the papers, but the burglar, who is able after a protracted search to find the papers himself, threatens to steal equally valuable papers from George if he is put to such trouble. George's co-operation would be immediate and dispensable, but allowable in order to avoid the comparable loss to himself. Another example: Bill intends to rob a house but cannot get there without Charles's driving him: the co-operation is mediate but indispensable. If Charles refuses, Bill will arrange for his henchmen to rob Charles's own house, stealing items of comparable value. Here Charles may co-operate; but if he knows that his house does not contain anything as valuable as what Bill proposes to steal from the third party's house, his loss will not be equal and so he cannot co-operate even if he knows his own property will be violated. Could we speak of a greater loss of a lower kind justifying Charles's co-operation? It is doubtful that such a term is meaningful: difference of kind makes comparisons of quantity all but impossible, unless the losses compared are measured in purely subjective terms. If we take purely physical pain to be of a lower kind than purely mental (even such a distinction is doubtful), perhaps we can say that a co-operator might suffer more physical pain by refusing than the third party would suffer mental torment: and this might justify cooperation.

Finally, if co-operation is neither immediate nor indispensable, it is justified by the avoidance of a loss to oneself less than the loss to the injured third party but at least comparable to it. For example, if several third parties stand to lose a lot of money by your co-operating, you may still co-operate to avoid, say, the loss of a lot of money yourself, but not to avoid a minor ticking-off for refusing to help.

If the wrong by the principal agent is against a public good but not against public safety, even greater reasons are necessary for co-operating than those already given. If the co-operation is immediate and indispensable it is permitted in order to avoid a greater public evil (in quantity or kind), or an equal public evil plus a grave loss to self. The basic principle is that certain evils may be tolerated for the sake of the public good, e.g. if not co-operating with their production would lead to even worse public disturbance. So for instance, suppose a large company planned to introduce a defective (but not dangerous) product into the marketplace, and an employee responsible for quality control who wanted to blow the whistle was told that if he denounced the plan publicly the Company would take its production overseas with the loss of thousands of jobs (including perhaps his own). In this case the employee would be permitted negatively to co-operate by not blowing the whistle.

If the co-operation is immediate and dispensable or mediate and indispensable, it is permitted when necessary to avoid an equal public evil or a very serious personal evil proportionate to the public harm done. In the example just mentioned, suppose the product were moderately below standard and the company could still get its product into the market and issue a press Statement mitigating the effect of a denunciation; then the employee could co-operate if the alternative meant that he lost his job or the company delayed plans for further expansion. Or suppose the employee's knowledge if disseminated were an ineliminable obstacle to the company's plan, but he could only inform the public by passing on sensitive information that would eventually lead to a denunciation by someone else, say a consumer Organization: the same principle would apply.

Finally, if the co-operation is mediate and dispensable, it is permitted in order to avoid a grave loss to self which cannot be prevented except by co-operating. The 'cannot' is the cannot of moral not physical necessity. The employee might be able to prevent the loss of wages, say, by resigning and taking on a less satisfying job elsewhere (and then blowing the whistle on his former employer), but it is doubtful whether he would be obliged to suffer that sort of inconvenience if the public evil he could prevent did not amount to a real threat to public safety.

Suppose, even more seriously, that the wrong by the principal agent is against the public safety—then one may not co-operate but should resist. The reason is that there is no greater good to justify the co-operation, and *a fortiori* it cannot be justified by appeal to a private good. It might be argued that, as in the previous categories, cooperation that is immediate and indispensable might be justified by appeal to a greater danger to public safety, which would have to be one of degree rather than one of kind; that co-operation which is immediate and dispensable or mediate and indispensable is justified by appeal to an equal threat to public safety; and maybe even that mediate and dispensable co-operation is permitted to avoid a very serious loss to the co-operator or at least a very serious public evil falling short of a threat to common safety. This is arguable, but I would submit that there is a strong moral intuition to the effect that when it comes to a real threat to public safety, such as war, terrorism, mass outbreak of illness, mass environmental damage, and so on, one ought not to co-operate in any way but resist, because the cost is too great. If this intuition is not as commonly held as might be thought, then one can simply argue as just suggested but make a distinction between public safety in general and a supreme threat to public safety of the kind that amounts to the worst a society can suffer, such as massive loss of life and threats to future generations, the sort of threat that full-scale war, for instance, can generate. In such a case at least, the intuition is strong that one ought never to co-operate: the principle behind it that the individual has a fundamental civic duty to suffer any loss, including death itself, to save the state and its major institutions.

A further point, implicit in what I have already sketched but worth stating explicitly, is that loss to others as well as to oneself can justify co-operation. So for instance, one may co-operate to save the principal himself from loss, for example giving unadulterated heroin to an addict who would otherwise die by taking an impure dose. One can co-operate to avoid a worse loss to the victim of the principal, e. g. by assisting in (but not oneself perpetrating) an assault to avoid a murder. Co-operation is also possible to prevent greater injury to the common good as long as one is co-operating only in indifferent matters (i.e., not intrinsically evil). For anyone in politics who manages to retain some principles this is of course a highly current and sensitive issue. One may compromise with political opponents whose policies are in general objectionable in order to secure the passing of good laws, assuming the good to be secured sufficiently outweighs the likely harm done by the compromise. What about voting for unjust laws in order to prevent the passing of even worse ones? There are at least two possible ways of looking at such cases, though one needs to know the detail before being able to apply the principles with any confidence. One is to say that voting as such is indifferent and hence that the politician may seek to prevent one public evil by voting for a lesser one.

On the other hand, one might argue that voting for an unjust law is not morally indifferent—it is not simply putting one's name down on paper, or lifting a finger or saying 'yes'. Rather, it is both making a statement and directly enabling legislation with practical effects to be passed, even if a person's vote is only one of many elements that have to be in place for the bill ultimately to reach the statute books. Further, there is the question of whether the vote will cause a harm beyond that of mere scandal: it is common to be put in the position of having to decide whether to vote for a law which the politician knows will not in the end be passed, but which is part of a process that may stymie the passing of a worse law. As was noted earlier, scandal may be permitted for a good reason, but again the act that causes the scandal must not itself be intrinsically wrong. One question to ask is: what reasonable interpretations of the act are open to impartial observers? In the case mentioned above of attending the funeral of a terrorist, it is quite reasonable to assume that the employee of the funeral parlour is simply doing his job and no more; but it is not reasonable to assume that he approves of terrorism if he is well known for his opposition to it. In private cases such as that, nevertheless, his views are unlikely to be well known, and reasonable people could well take him to be showing solidarity with the terrorist: hence the need to try to minimize potential scandal by declaring his opposition wherever possible.

Yet politics is a very public matter, and a parliamentarian who is well known for his opposition to certain things may be thought to be permitted at least to allow the scandal of voting for a law unlikely to be passed, because his act could not reasonably be interpreted as a declaration of support for what is unjust. Nevertheless, there is something disquieting in the idea that one can, as it were, hide behind a reasonable interpretation of one's external acts in order to avoid the guilt that attaches to what, considered in itself, is an intrinsic wrong. Circumstances are part of the determinant of the morality of an act but they are not the whole story, and the Principle of Double Effect should not be taken to imply—as it has so often been caricatured as implying—that if the motive is pure and the circumstances not necessarily incriminating, one can escape the responsibility that attaches naturally to one's deliberate acts. Can a mad scientist really avoid the charge of murder simply by declaring: 'I didn't intend to kill him by chopping his head off, only to test my theory that decapitated people can actually survive the loss of their heads.' (Maybe he has been reading some strange papers on personal identity and concluded that the head is not the most important part of the body for survival.) Of course one will almost certainly say that no such interpretation could reasonably be put on his behaviour, and so he *must* have intended murder. Well and good, but not every context would allow such a conclusion, and yet in no context would we wish to exculpate the decapitator from murder short of a world where, say, heads really could be reattached to their bodies without loss of life.

The point is that although it is ultimately the private intention of the agent that determines responsibility, and although reasonable interpretations in the circumstances can verify that intention, the natural description of an external act can conflict with both, and all we can say is that in the private or internal forum the agent may be innocent, but as far as public morality is concerned he must be treated as having acted wrongfully. Hence whatever one's private intent, and whatever the circumstance, voting for an unjust law just is an act that constitutes support for injustice, and so, I would submit, it could not be permitted even if doing so prevented a worse injustice, and scandal were minimal, and even if the law voted for were certain never to come into effect. The act would amount to the explicit doing of wrong at worst, implicit formal co-operation in the doing of wrong at best. As to whether the politician could *advocate* the law even if he had no intention of voting for it himself, apart from the potential charges of scandal and hypocrisy we need to apply the principles mentioned earlier regarding the advocacy of a lesser evil.[14] I would argue that the legislator could only do so if he were advocating what was already an implicit part of the unjust law already on the table, e.g., if his fellow lawmakers planned to vote for a law confiscating millions of pounds from innocent people, he could advocate that they vote for the confiscation of thousands of pounds

[14] See note 7.

instead. But he could not advocate that they vote for a different wrong altogether, such as the imprisonment of the innocent people from whom they wished to steal. In any case he should broadcast his disapproval of their plan to the widest possible audience.

5. Some further problems and cases of co-operation.

In this section I want to look at some miscellaneous matters and further cases to help sharpen our understanding of how to apply the ethical principles of co-operation. First, as to the sale and manufacture of potentially harmful items, the general rule is that the greater the wrong that will be committed by the principal, the greater the reason needed for making, repairing or selling the item. The most serious wrongs require the most serious reasons for co-operation. Hence, one may not sell poison or drugs to someone contemplating suicide or murder, except at the peril of death to oneself or another. The less certain the principal's intent, the less serious the reason, but since the evil contemplated is of the gravest kind, lack of certainty can only go so far in excusing co-operation. One could plausibly say that if the plan (e.g. for murder) were highly likely to be frustrated anyway, one need not be under threat of death oneself to be allowed co-operate, but there must still be a threat of serious loss. The more closely connected an item is with wrongful use, the graver must be the reason for participating in its sale, manufacture or repair. Can a corporation sell devices which are easily converted to use for torture to a country with a bad human rights record? Since there is potential injustice to third parties, a high likelihood of abuse of the items, and the sale may well be indispensable (e.g. if the devices are specialized), the corporation could not simply plead loss of profits as an excuse, or even potential bankruptcy, since these are not proportionate to the injustice constituted by torture (assuming we are talking about innocent victims). But suppose the devices are ordinary items with a multitude of uses, one of which could be for torture if they were converted. Then they would be more remotely connected with the probable injustice and a lesser reason would suffice, such as loss of profit. Proximity is not just about where in the causal chain the co-operator's act is located, but whether the act in some way provides a probable instrument of wrongful use. For instance, the inventor of a device that is easily converted to use for torture needs a greater reason for going ahead with his invention that the seller of prison clothing to a regime notorious for human rights abuses. Generally speaking, one can say that it is seriously wrong to make or sell articles whose ordinary use is seriously wrongful, bearing in mind that if the article can only be used wrongfully (again, with the moral use of 'can', i.e. the only reasonable Interpretation of how the object will be used in the circumstances is to do wrong) the co-operation might well be implicitly formal.

The more a customer depends on a particular manufacturer or merchant for an item of potentially wrongful use, the more serious the reason for making or selling it. In the real world co-operation will rarely be absolutely indispensable, in that there are nearly always ways of getting around someone's refusal to assist, so all we can say is that indispensable co-operation is such that refusal would at least seriously hinder the carrying out of the wrongful purpose. Further, if the seller, for instance, has knowledge that *some* of his customers have wrongful purposes but does not know *who*, then he can sell for the usual reasons, such as the avoidance of loss of profit. The reason here is that he should not (without further knowledge) presume evil on the part of any particular person, and so the complete lack of certainty of identity lessens the reason required to co-operate. So if, for example, a seller of firearms knows that some-one will probably use one of the guns to commit a robbery, the lack of knowledge of identity means he can sell his wares for the usual reasons.[15] Needless to say, if the law of the land requires him to carry out checks as to who may or may not buy the weapons, he must do so; but if there is no such law, morality does not require that he make special enquiries unless he has reason to suspect particular individuals. To say that he must check routinely who might or might not carry out a robbery with the guns he sells would be unduly burdensome. Again, suppose he sells crowbars: is he bound

[15] What about knowledge by the seller that *some* wrongful act will be committed, but ignorance as to *which?* The same considerations would apply to lack of knowledge of the identity of the offence as to lack of knowledge of the identity of the offender. Needless to say, *formal* co-operation in both cases is impermissible. In common law, intentional co-operation involving lack of knowledge of the identity of the offence is sufficient for liability: *DPP for Northern Ireland v Maxwell* [1978] All ER 1140; it is difficult to know whether the same would apply to lack of knowledge of the offender.

to enquire willy nilly which customers might use a crowbar bought from him to carry out an assault? Having said that, if the items he sells are *typically* used to do wrong, rather than merely *frequently,* he should make enquiries unless he is morally certain his customers' intentions are not bad. For example, he cannot sell poison to a total stranger merely on the customer's say-so that it is for medical use.

Another consideration concerns whether the co-operation would be with an act violating natural law or merely positive law. You need a more serious reason to co-operate with the former than with the latter where the two are of a comparable nature, since natural morality is of a higher order that merely man-made law. Of course insofar as a particular human law simply reflects and enforces natural law, violating it takes on the character of a violation of natural law as well as a violation of positive law. For example, co-operating with a principal's theft requires a more serious reason than assisting her to evade tax; co-operating with someone's adultery requires a greater reason than assisting him to conceal financial Information from a spouse contrary to court order, assuming the disclosure is not itself a moral requirement as well. In addition, a less serious reason would be needed for co-operating with the violation of a positive law whose breach is more easily excused than the violation of some other positive law. For example, if Michael shows Norman a useful illegal parking spot, the justification for doing so is less than were he to show him a good place illegally to dump toxic waste, since the former is more easily excused than the latter. (What if Norman has no excuse for parking illegally, and Michael knows this? Then the ordinary reason for co-operation, such as grave loss to self, would suffice: the comparison between parking and dumping is no more than that, viz. a comparison; establishing intrinsic grounds for co-operation is a separate matter.)

As far as the co-operation of employees and subordinates is concerned, we can also make a few observations. Merely keeping records, for instance, is morally indifferent, but helping to cover up fraud would normally make the employee a formal co-operator, explicit if the employee shares the principal's fraudulent intent, implicit if he is motivated by, say, pity or loyalty. If the co-operation is remote and dispensable, the mere fact that one is employed by the principal will excuse, because employees are not expected to go about questioning their employer as to the reason for every instruction. Employees are not responsible for their employer's intentions but merely for the performance of what is assigned to them. If, however, co-operation is proximate, the mere fact that one is employed is not sufficient excuse: there must be some other reason justifying the assistance and proportionate to the wrong planned. For instance, an employee could justifiably drive his employer to a place in which he will carry out a fraudulent transaction if he is under threat to life and limb. Nevertheless, the easier it is to refuse, the less excusable it is to co-operate: e.g., it might be easier for a pupil to refuse a teacher's request for help in concealing bad behaviour at the school than for a tradesman employed by the school. On the other hand, in some circumstances co-operation might be more excusable on the part of a natural subordinate than an employee, since the former might find it harder to escape the authority figure's influence: for instance, a child might be dependent upon a tyrannical parent and so unable to avoid co-operating because incapable of, say, running away from home if the parent asks for co-operation in a serious wrong.

6. Conclusion

We have seen that the ethics of co-operation is a complex and subtle area of moral theory. I have merely sketched the principles and their application, but many questions require exploration that there has been no room to undertake here. In particular, I would single out three issues. The first concerns the identification of principal wrongs. The ethics of co-operation is in a sense independent of what one takes to be the sort of action with which assistance is morally questionable. One might go so far as to say that it is wholly topic-neutral, and so should be employed by all moral theorists who at least recognize that some actions are wrong, including those who reject the idea of intrinsic wrongness or evil broadly construed. On the other hand, the ethics of co-operation is obviously parasitic upon an adequate grasp of right and wrong: that is to say, if we want to apply the principles correctly in order to reach true judgments about how to act, we have to identify what is genuinely right and wrong. Here moral theorists are in notorious—dare one say scandalous— disagreement, and so it must be asserted that the correct ethics of cooperation depends crucially on an adequate theory of the good.

Secondly, the ethics of co-operation depends on a correct theory of intention and action. Without the conceptual resources to individuate these—which in turn depends on the metaphysics of mind—the ethics of co-operation breaks down in its early phases, as does the Principle of Double Effect on which it depends. Specifically, if we are to be able to single out initial acts of co-operators for the purpose of characterizing them as good, bad, or indifferent, we must be able to give a convincing account of how this singling out is done. Here it is difficult to see how anything other than a strongly realist theory of intention can suffice.[16]

Thirdly, further work needs to be done on concepts such as proximity and dispensability of co-operation in order to see how precise they can be made without falling into spurious characterizations that illegitimately partake of mathematical or quasi-mathematical approaches. As I have claimed, such concepts and the distinctions built on them are not reducible to mathematical formulae, and do commend themselves to our intuitions as to how actions receive their moral flavour. They are generally workable as they stand, but there is no doubt that hard cases Stretch them to the limit in the absence of further precision. Like the Principle of Double Effect itself, such notions are, I claim, non-negotiable; but our understanding of them may only grow incrementally, and this will depend at least in part on the sort of prudent and sensitive judgment of which modern moral philosophy, unfortunately, is in such great need.

[16] For a defence of realism about intention, see *Moral Theory*, pp. 110–26.

Authority

ROGER TEICHMANN

I

As children, we are often told both what to do and what to think. For a child to learn at all, it must in the first instance simply trust those, such as parents, who teach it things; and this goes for practical as well as theoretical learning. Doubting is necessarily something that comes later, for to be able to doubt one must have *some* beliefs already, e.g. concerning what sort of reasons count as good reasons, and what count as bad. But in growing up, a person does, or should, develop the capacity for rational doubt, and also the capacity for rational resistance to being told what to do. The first capacity constitutes a critical faculty, and the second is an essential constituent of practical autonomy.

A proponent of the value and importance of these two capacities may claim the following: firstly, that a grown-up person should only believe something if they have satisfied themselves that there are good reasons for believing it; secondly, that a grown-up person should only do something if they have satisfied themselves that there are good reasons for doing it. The second part of this claim clearly needs restricting, since one can do things just for the fun of it, such as hopping over a puddle, or absent-mindedly, such as tapping one's fingers, without thereby appearing less than fully rational. But if we are considering the case where someone is telling you, or asking you, to do something, mightn't it be true that autonomy requires you to obey, or accede to the request, only if you are satisfied that there is good reason to do so?

Let us allow that a rational person ought in principle to be able to give a good reason why they have fulfilled some order or request; the question now is, if a person gives as a reason 'Because X told me to', can that ever count as a good reason? Or does giving such a reason show that one is not fully autonomous, where that is a species of failing?

In considering these questions, it is helpful to compare the case of doing something because you were told to with that of thinking something because you were told it by someone. In each case, we may speak of someone having authority—practical authority in the first case, intellectual authority in the second. The questions about autonomy which I just mentioned have analogues in the intellectual domain, namely: If a person gives as a reason for thinking something, 'Because X told me so', can that ever count as a good reason? Or does giving it show that one has an insufficiently developed critical faculty—that one can't 'think for oneself'?

I shall argue that the reasons 'X told me to' and 'X told me so' must, on occasion, be good and sufficient reasons. In seeing how they *can* be good reasons, we shall see what limitations need to be placed on practical and intellectual self-sufficiency.

II

Here are four cases concerning belief.

Case 1. I ask you: 'Why do you think President Bush is planning a war against Iraq?' You reply: 'Because he wants to finish off business left unfinished by his father'. Let's say I think this over and it strikes me as plausible. In that case, if I give reasons for believing the hypothesis, they won't include that you told me so, but will rather advert to such things as: President Bush's character, as manifested in things he's said and done, the implausibility of other hypotheses as to why he's planning a war, and so on and so on. It was mulling such matters over that will most likely have led me to accept your hypothesis. My reason for asking you your opinion will have been, typically, that I thought you the sort of person capable of seeing what is likely to be true (on this topic), and that your pointing some such things out to me would enable *me* to see them as likely to be true. This is not a case of what I will call 'intellectual authority', since it is not a case of my taking your word for something.

Case 2. I know you are an expert on insects, and I ask you: 'What is that beetle on your shoe?' You reply: 'It's a Colorado beetle.' I take your word for it. And if asked my reasons for thinking it was a Colorado beetle, I could say: 'X told me, and I happen to know X is an expert on insects, so what he said is likely to be true'. This is a case of intellectual authority.

Case 3. I am attending a lecture on the history of Cuba as part of my continuing education, and you, the lecturer, tell the class that Fidel Castro was born in 1927. Once again, I believe you. If asked my reasons for thinking Castro was born in 1927, I would probably say: 'I learnt it in a history lecture'. I do not, let's imagine, know anything about your qualifications as a lecturer or your expertise—rather, I take these things for granted, as we say. It's true that I might say something like, 'A place like that wouldn't employ ignoramuses as lecturers'; but I might not really have any positive evidence for such a claim. Again, I may just 'take these things for granted'. This, too, is a case of intellectual authority.

Case 4. On my way to the train station, I ask you, a passer-by, what the time is. You look at your watch and say 'Three thirty'. I believe you. Never having met you before, I know nothing of your truthfulness, sanity, ability to tell the time or competence with English, and hence could mention none of these things, or similar, when giving my reasons for thinking it's three thirty. Much as in the last case, I might just say, 'People don't tell pointless falsehoods in such contexts'. I take it for granted that you're honest and the rest of it. This case, however, is not a case of intellectual authority.

Case 1 and case 2 are alike in that I am able to give good reasons, in the sense of good evidence, for my belief: in the first case, evidence having to do with President Bush, in the second case, evidence having to do with your expertise and character. In cases 3 and 4, such positive evidence is, I am claiming, unavailable; though there is still the question whether I don't have a good *reason* to believe something, namely the reason, 'I was told by such and such a person'.

Cases 2, 3 and 4 are alike in that each one is characterized by a certain placing of the onus of proof, as I shall call it. Specifically, the onus of proof is with me if I am minded to reject what you say. You, an expert, say that it's a Colorado beetle; if I, a non-expert, reject your opinion, I will need to give some reason for doing so if I am not to appear perverse or silly. Similarly for the history lecture. If I don't take the lecturer's word for Castro's date of birth, I will surely need to have some good reason for not doing so—it is not in general down to the lecturer to back up such a claim, if questioned, even if he can back it up. Once again, the onus of proof is with the doubter. Finally, if, asking you the time, I reject your reply, this will be perverse, silly, even insulting, unless I can give some reason— such as that it's obviously night-time.

Cases 2 and 3 are alike, as I have said, in being cases where a particular person may be said to have intellectual authority.

III

We have, then, various criss-crossing similarities and dissimilarities among these four kinds of case. Let us return to the first feature I talked about, that of my having evidence for a belief. As I imagined earlier on, someone may require of rational grown-ups that they always have good reasons for what they believe; and may, further, deny that you give a good reason just by saying, 'I was told so by such and such a person', unless, that is, 'such and such a person' means 'someone I know to be an expert'. Could this rather

Cartesian figure make a case for the rationality of a student at a lecture, or of an inquirer after the time o'clock?

To do so, he or she would probably need to propose some sort of inductive backing for the beliefs in question. 'In the past, I have never, or rarely, been deceived by such a person, so. . .etc. etc.'. The first problem with this manoeuvre is that one may not, in fact, have adequate memories of all the relevant previous occasions, on which to base the putative inductive hypothesis. A second, and deeper, problem is that one's confidence that one has not been deceived in the past rests very largely on one's not having had reason to reject what one was told in the past; it does not rest on one's having always, or usually, been given adequate evidence for the things one was told. (That the various things one was taught all 'hang together' will be a rather weak sort of evidence for their truth.) If I say to you, 'But how do you know those who taught you history and so on *weren't* deceiving you?', what could you possibly reply?

In the face of such questions, the age-old temptation has been to follow the path of scepticism. If we are to resist that temptation, we need to give due weight to the notion of 'onus of proof'—the feature of cases 2, 3 and 4 which I mentioned above. Essentially, the sceptic's demand is unreasonable when it misplaces the onus of proof on the person asserting something, rather than on the person doubting it.

How exactly does this work?

It's fairly easy to see how the onus of proof gets determined in the case of known expertise. If I *know* that you know a lot about insects, and that you're a normally truthful sort of person, I would be clearly less than rational not to accept your opinion about the beetle without good reason.

The fourth sort of case, in which I automatically believe the word of a stranger, is quite different, and involves the sort of general background conditions to human life to which Wittgenstein so often draws our attention. Human society and human language would break down in all sorts of ways if we didn't: agree in judgment a lot of the time; tell one another the truth a lot of the time; co-operate with one another a lot of the time. But human society and human language do, in fact, get along all right, tick over and survive.

A transcendental argument is even available here. Language-use is only possible if people are inclined to speak truly, at least in certain delineable areas of human life—we are, here and now, successfully speaking a language—so people are in fact by and large inclined to speak truly, at least in certain delineable areas of human life. One can add to this sort of argument the observation that for many types of linguistic intercourse, someone's word will need to be taken on trust: if this is not possible, neither will those types of linguistic intercourse be. One such type of linguistic intercourse is 'finding things out from strangers'.

Now a reflective person *could* see the benefits of these latter types of linguistic intercourse, and so *could* see a reason to participate properly in them—by supplying truthful answers and by taking people's words for certain things. Here would be a *practical* reason for taking someone's word for something: 'I took his word for it, because the custom of taking people's word for such things is essential for a vast amount of information-sharing, and information-sharing is a good thing'.

This explanation would be in terms of what has been called an 'Aristotelian necessity'[1]. But of course many people are not so reflective as to be able to come up with such an explanation; they have simply been trained in a certain way, have developed the habit of taking people's words for certain things, and (presumably) have not very often experienced problems as a result.

Perhaps it could be said of such people that their critical faculties are not as developed as they might be, but it couldn't, without further ado, be said that this fact amounted to a failing or a defect on the part of those people. As I've said, taking someone's word for something cannot, by itself, be criticized—to think that it can is to systematically misplace onus of proof. Nor can a lack of philosophical reflectiveness on its own be deemed a failing. If there is a possible failing in this area, it will be that of gullibility; but this means taking people's words for things when as a matter of fact you shouldn't. A good critical faculty will enable a person to have a nose for deceit, hypocrisy, balderdash, and so on; and it will often have to be a 'nose' for these things, insofar as it cannot always be a matter of applying a method. To reject something you're told because it is inconsistent with other things which you know would indeed be to apply a 'method' of sorts; but in those areas where you are minded to ask people for information, you very often don't have a relevant background of better-known truths. Hence the need to rely on your 'nose'. (We shall return to this.)

[1] Cf. G. E. M. Anscombe, 'On Promising and its Justice', *Collected Philosophical Papers, Vol III* (Blackwell, 1981), 15.

There is another possible failing to be mentioned also: excessive scepticism, i.e. not taking people's word for things when you should. Instinct or common sense should prevent this also. Gullibility and scepticism can thus be seen as excess and defect of trust, with the right epistemic attitude being an Aristotelian mean.

I turn now to the third case, that of the history lecturer. The onus of proof is on me, if I am minded to reject what the lecturer says. Why? Is it because the lecturer is an expert? Well, what if he is not, but is in fact a bad appointment, impossible to sack, whose reputation has not yet reached the ears of the students in my class, including me? It is still the case that I need good reason to reject what he says. If I discovered his inexpertise, or knew better than him on some topic, then I would have such reason; but in my present state, rejecting his statements would manifest the vice of excessive scepticism, or of perversity, or silliness. Unless, that is, I just have a good nose for unreliable types, or for unlikely-sounding stories; in this case, I could justifiably withhold my assent, though it is arguable that to express my dissent publicly, given my inability to provide articulate reasons, would be going too far.

Anscombe wrote that

> The right that a fallible teacher has, in that he has authority. . .is the right that those he has to teach should be generally prepared to believe their teachers. At all frequent disbelief when what he says is true will be, then, an injury done to the authority of the teacher—as well as

> having about it whatever badness attaches to being wrong without excuse.[2]

Elsewhere she said that 'the ground of authority is most often a task', going on:

> Authority arises from the necessity of a task whose performance requires a certain sort and extent of obedience on the part of those for whom the task is supposed to be done.[3]

Here, as the reference to 'obedience' makes clear, she was speaking of practical, not intellectual, authority. But the point about a necessary task applies equally to the intellectual case. Education is necessary for us. But the task of educating is only possible where those learning are generally prepared to accept the word of those teaching them. The task of teaching would be hindered terribly if it was always up to the teacher to satisfy his pupils, either of his own expertise, or of the evidence for each of his statements. Hence the onus of proof, as I have been calling it, must lie with the pupils.

The institution of educating people requires that, by and large, those appointed to teach will know more than their pupils in the relevant area, and will want to discharge their duties properly. What is required, in fact, is the truth of empirical generalizations about human beings analogous to those general facts about human beings which we take for

[2] G. E. M. Anscombe, 'Authority in Morals', ibid., 45.

[3] G. E. M. Anscombe, 'On the Source of the Authority of the State', ibid., 134.

granted when, e.g., asking strangers for information. This analogy between cases 3 and 4 is connected with the fact that in both cases one takes someone's word for something, without need of positive evidence. But case 3 involves the idea of a task to be performed, and a consequent right to be believed, and these things help to account for why we speak of the authority of the teacher, when we do not speak of the authority of the stranger. To reject what the stranger tells you for no apparent reason would, indeed, very often be insulting, inviting the complaint: 'Why did you ask me if you weren't going to believe me?'. But the complaint of the lecturer would be different in kind: 'Rejecting what I say makes my job of teaching you much more difficult'.

IV

So much for intellectual authority. What about practical authority?

Something that needs to be noticed straight away, before we go very deeply into the question, is that doing something on the word of another (as we might put it) comes in many varieties. You can be ordered, requested, advised, wheedled, encouraged. . .; and there are, in English and other languages, various linguistic forms corresponding in a rather unsystematic way to these and other speech acts. We will need to be aware of this variety of practical cases if we are not to fall into the trap of simplifying.

It might be thought that 'practical authority', properly speaking, applied only to the case of ordering. I am not sure whether this is true of ordinary usage or not; but in any case, there are, as we shall see, analogous points to be made about doing as were made earlier about thinking, when I was discussing intellectual authority.

Now if there is a practical analogue for 'thinking what is true', it would seem to be 'doing what is right', or 'doing the right thing'. 'The right thing' is not here intended as equivalent to 'the morally right thing', whatever that means: the right thing to do if you want to get to York by midnight would be an example of a 'right thing to do'. And with both thinking what's true and doing the right thing, there is a *prima facie* possibility of having or lacking *reasons*.

We can, in fact, construct cases analogous to the four kinds of case discussed above. With cases analogous to the first two, however, it can be a bit unclear whether it is a practical or an intellectual matter. Take a case analogous to Case 1: if I ask you what you think I should say in my letter to the newspaper in order to guarantee that it gets published, is your opinion 'action-guiding' or is it something merely true or false, correct or incorrect? Or is it both? You could clearly use any of a large number of linguistic forms: 'If I were you, I'd say X'; 'Why don't you say X?'; 'Say X'; 'You should say X'; 'You could say X'; and so on. And it would be difficult to pick out certain of these forms as on their own determining whether what you say is a mere statement or something more practical. Similar remarks go for certain cases analogous to Case 2, such as when I ask you how I might best please your mother on her birthday.

The right response to such puzzles may well just be: 'Say what you like, according to the minutiae of the case'. After all, the terms 'practical', 'intellectual', 'action-guiding', 'statement', and so on, are themselves pretty nebulous. Nevertheless, something can be said here: namely, that there may be more or less of an expectation that I should act upon what you say. If you suggest that I write to the newspaper that my MP is an arrogant and corrupt scoundrel of limited intelligence, and I decide instead to write simply that he is not all that an MP should be, that's probably no big deal, even if you feel like saying, 'Why did you ask me, then?'. Since there is no expectation, simply arising from the nature of our interaction, that I will follow your advice, we could as easily call that advice 'an expression of your opinion about what is most likely to get the letter published' as call it 'a suggestion what to write in order to get the letter published'. The word 'advice' often conveys just this sort of indifference as to whether we have a theoretical or a practical utterance.

But here is another scenario. A doctor advises you to cut out cucumbers from your diet, to which she believes you are obviously allergic. Here there does seem to be some sort of expectation that you will follow the doctor's advice. The nature of that expectation will depend to some extent upon the role and status of doctors in one's society. Thus, it makes a difference whether you are paying a doctor. An extremist might say that a paid doctor provides a service which entails *no* expectations as to your behaviour beyond the expectation that you do in fact pay. But this looks too strong: how *can* the doctor really provide the service in question unless you cooperate? The service, I am assuming, is the traditional one associated with doctoring, whose aim is to cure or prevent disease or physical suffering in the patient. Another service is imaginable where no expectations are engendered as to the customer's behaviour—namely, the providing of medical information. But this is not the same as doctoring, for which there must exist such expectations.

With doctoring, there is, in Anscombe's phrase, a 'task to be performed', analogous to the task of education. The onus is on the patient who is minded to reject or not act upon her doctor's advice that she give or have good reasons for behaving thus. The picture is complicated by the fact that what is at stake for a patient can often be grave, not only as regards illness, but as regards treatment. You generally won't suffer much if you accidentally accept a falsehood from your teacher, but you may suffer quite a lot if you accept treatment from a doctor that accidentally poisons you. The idiosyncracies of personal biology make this eventuality quite possible; those idiosyncracies also mean that it can on occasion be questionable whether a doctor is more likely than her patient to know what's best for her patient. A doctor may have expertise in medicine without having expertise about *this person's* body chemistry. But since her present task really concerns *this person*, her case is (once again) not like that of the teacher, who is meant to have expertise merely with respect to the subject being taught, not with respect to the psyches of her students—at any rate if the 'teaching' is essentially an imparting of information.[4] You can teach in classes.

[4] This qualification is an important one, and applies to much of what I say about teaching in this article. A teacher of *philosophy* should be more interested in the psyches of his or her students than in the

All in all, then, it is perhaps easier for a person to have good reasons for not following doctor's orders than it is to have good reasons for not accepting what one's teacher says, at any rate in our society. This is quite compatible with there being that onus on the patient of which I spoke. For doctoring to be possible, people must be generally prepared to follow the advice of a doctor without the doctor having to demonstrate her expertise, or having to give evidence for the efficacy of medicines, etc. Naturally, a good doctor has to be able to talk and answer questions—but then, so does a good teacher.

Here, then, is a species of 'practical authority'. A doctor does not, however, command obedience, for the reason that she has no sanctions to wield against the unco-operative patient, beyond deciding not to be that person's doctor any more. There are, of course, good reasons for this arrangement. An army officer, by contrast, may wield sanctions against unco-operative corporals—and here we do speak of 'disobedience'. There seem likewise to be good reasons for *that* arrangement: roughly, that for an army to function effectively in battle, soldiers (a) must be prepared to obey orders without question (given always that those orders are not clearly *ultra vires),* and (b) should not be at liberty to decide to stop soldiering whenever they want to. *If* we are to have armies, *then* there will be these requirements.

This brings us to a crucial difference between the practical case and the intellectual case. Here is Anscombe:

imparting of information, and to that extent cannot enjoy the same sort of authority as a history teacher.

> . . .the one with authority over what you do, can decide, within limits, what you shall do; his decision is what makes it right for you to do what he says—if the reproach against you, when you disobey him, is only that of disobedience. But someone with authority over what you think is not at liberty, within limits, to decide what you shall think among the range of possible thoughts on a given matter; what makes it right for you to think what you think, given that it is your business to form a judgment at all, is simply that it is true, and no decision can make something a true thing for you to think, as the decision of someone in authority can make something a good thing for you to do.[5]

A certain practical task, deemed to be necessary, may require a setup where some people are generally prepared to obey others. The orders given them will in the paradigm case have as their end 'that the right thing be done'; but disobedience may merit sanctions not only on account of the possible fact that the right thing didn't get done, but also simply on account of the order's not having been obeyed.[6] Moreover,

[5] 'Authority in Morals', ibid., 44.

[6] *Pace* Joseph Raz. In *The Morality of Freedom* (58–9), Raz argues that where there is already a reason for people (or for a person) to do so-and-so, there cannot be any *extra* reason to do it in virtue of there being a (legitimate) directive to do it. Raz says that this would be 'counting twice'; and prefers to speak of a reason to obey or comply as 'pre-empting' or 'replacing' the original reason to do so-and-so.

But there are as many reasons for doing so-and-so as there are possible grounds for complaint if one omits to do it: i.e.(here) two—the reasons being (a) that the ends in question would be best served by doing so-and-so, and (b) that one should not be disobedient

as Anscombe puts it, the thing ordered can *be* the right thing to do simply because it was ordered—always assuming that the basic conditions are met for its counting as a proper order.

But isn't all this terribly authoritarian? Doesn't it attempt to justify the response 'Because I say so!', a response which must surely strike any rational-minded, autonomous person as utterly inadequate to the dispassionate query which prompts it?

Consider by way of analogy the institution of property. To use one of Anscombe's examples, if I ask you not to go into my study, all that makes it right for you not to go into my study is that I asked you not to. The having of property is only possible if people can get others to do things, or more often to refrain from doing things, to what is theirs, just by asking. The point of the institution is not really well-described by saying that those with the 'authority' are to issue orders or requests aiming at some independently-determined good results; rather the good or goods at stake just relate to people being free to dispose of what they have in the way they want. But this does mean that the response 'Because I say so' may be an adequate response. Whether it is also an adequate response in a case like that of

(undermine X's authority, etc.). The reasons for having a set-up requiring obedience may indeed refer to the ends mentioned in (a)—those reasons won't, by the way, include (a) itself; but it's quite compatible with this that the force of (b) be additional to, because different in kind from, the force of (a).

army discipline depends on whether the appeal to the point of the military set-up supports the requirement of this kind of obedience—as the appeal to the point of the institution of property supports an analogous requirement.

If the giving of an order suffices in some context to make fulfilling the order 'the right thing to do', does this presuppose that the set-up or institution can be justified? Assuming slavery to be a wicked institution, shouldn't we say of a slave-owner's orders to his slaves not to leave the farm, that the giving of those orders does *not* make staying on the farm the right thing to do? I think we do need to speak this way; but it need not follow that a slave-owner has no authority to require things of his slaves. For a 'right to be obeyed' can be a matter of custom or law, connected with rules that get expressed by means of modals, thus: 'A slave must not leave the farm without permission'. A rule can *apply* somewhere, though lacking *force:* for the rule to have force is for the set-up requiring it to be conducive to, or constitutive of, human good.

If the distinction between a rule's applying and its having force can be made sense of in this way, and if we connect rules and rights in the way Anscombe suggests we do, then there is room for speaking of the right to be obeyed, and hence of authority, in a way neutral as to justification. Anscombe herself does not seem to have followed this line. To some extent the two approaches differ only terminologically; but this is a matter I won't go into any further at this point, beyond saying that as a matter of English usage, 'authority' does often carry no connotations of justification—as where 'those in authority' amounts pretty much to 'those in power'.[7]

V

The intellectual vices of gullibility and scepticism have their practical analogues. One can be too much in awe of authority, too prone to obeying people; and on the other hand, one can be too prone to disobeying, or too inclined not to recognize authority at all. There isn't a 'method' here, any more than there is a 'method' when it comes to believing things that you're told, and for similar reasons: what is often needed is that a person should do things because others tell them to, *without* having applied any such method (without having satisfied themselves that so-and-so was the right thing to do). You need instinct and common sense, and a certain amount of reflectiveness, to help you determine whether a given person does have a right to be obeyed, or a justifiable expectation that you act on what they say. The onus, very often, will lie with the person who does not comply, co-operate, accede to requests, or obey orders—I mean the onus of showing reasons why they won't do these things.

But now there is a difficulty. For the idea of an onus of proof seems actually to clash with the idea that one must rely on instinct and common sense—and this goes for both

[7] For more on the distinction between a rule's applying and its having force, see R. Teichmann, 'Explaining the Rules', *Philosophy*, October 2002.

the intellectual and practical domains. If in certain contexts there is an expectation that I should believe what I'm told, or do what I'm told, unless I can give reasons why not, then when I *do* give such reasons and thus carry the onus of proof, I cannot be relying on instinct alone: I must have got as far as garnering some reasons, some sort of argument, in favour of my disbelief or my non-compliance. And if having good reasons is necessary for disbelief and non-compliance, shouldn't it also be necessary for belief and compliance? Which brings us back to the picture of the rational and autonomous person as always requiring good reasons.

Why were instinct and common sense brought in in the first place? Let us recap: certain necessary tasks can only be performed if those performing them are not generally required to give reasons for what they say, or for the genuineness of their authority; but this means that those under their authority will very often have to lack independent reasons for believing or acting on what they say, or for trusting their authority—for typically they will not have access to such reasons; this in turn means that unless people are to do or think whatever they're told in these contexts, they need to be sensitive to indicators of falsehood, or of folly, or of fraudulence—for if they lack access to reasons that would support the authority of others, by the same token they lack access to reasons that would throw doubt on it. So a sensitivity to indicators is what is required.

Of course, what is being assumed is that it would be a bad thing if people did or thought whatever they were told, even in set-ups whose *general* justification was clear (as with lecturing, doctoring, policing, etc.). It would be a bad thing because of certain empirical facts of human nature, e.g. to do with the corrupting influence of power. So instinct and common sense are needed in particular for the case where you withhold belief or compliance. But you may therefore often be unable to give articulate reasons for such withholding, at least then and there: then and there, although the onus of proof is on you, you cannot bear the onus. Since you will, as Anscombe says, be doing an injury to the person in authority if you are in fact *wrong*, then you should, as it were, think twice about withholding assent or compliance. But not being able to give articulate reasons may not be a dire thing, even if you are *right*; you may receive some opprobrium or even punishment, and may be unable to say (then and there) why you shouldn't receive these, but if you are right, that itself is your justification. Those frowning upon or punishing you should, and probably will, know that they are in the wrong. And of course a rational person will often want to find out whether there *are* reasons in support of what he or she had originally felt instinctively; will want, in short, to take up the onus of proof. The onus certainly doesn't have the absurd property of being *impossible* to carry.

Hence there is after all no clash between the idea of an onus of proof and that of a reliance on instinct and common sense.

VI

A few final words about authority in morals. Is there such a thing? it may be asked. It does seem that a moral teacher, if such a creature exists, cannot be a mere imparter of information, nor yet of rules for living, at any rate if such imparting would involve the pupil's 'taking the teacher's word' for things. There are two related reasons for saying this. Firstly, a large part of moral wisdom surely consists, as Aristotle thought, in a capacity for intuitive judgement concerning the particulars of a case, a capacity which is not adequately expressed or captured by any list of facts nor set of rules. Secondly, the application of what one has been told of an ethical or practical nature involves, as Anscombe pointed out, an *interpretation.* In her words:

> '. . .the reckoning what to do or abstain from in particular circumstances will constantly include a reference, implicit or explicit, to generalities. . .Such generalities or principles are: to do good and avoid doing harm; not to do what will get you disrepute; not to do what will make you poorer; not to take other people's property. . . .Now there is indeed a sense in which only the individual can make his own decisions as to what to do, even if his decision is to abide by someone else's orders or advice. For it is he who acts and therefore makes the final application of whatever is said to him. . .[D]oing what one is told is an interpretation and so with doing, however obedient one is, one can hardly escape being one's own pilot.'[8]

Nevertheless, it seems perfectly possible that one person should have more 'expertise' than another about life, people, the consequences of actions, and so forth—and these

[8] 'Authority in Morals', ibid., 48.

certainly are, or can be, moral matters. Such expertise comes with experience, also with reading and learning. And now there does seem to be room for something like 'taking a person's word for it'; for it may be clear that someone *does* know more than you do, e.g. about what things traumatize small children. The case would be analogous to our Case 2.

A case analogous to Case 3 would be one in which there was a task to be performed. If the task in question is that of moral education as such, it belongs, it might be said, to the task of being a parent. For adults in a society such as ours it is harder to conceive of such a task—for if the task is 'teaching people how to live well', there is a question why anyone would want to enrol on the course. You might want to find out how to live well, or do the right thing, in some domain of life into which you were soon to enter—marriage, for example, or teaching—and you might seek advice or guidance on these matters, matters which are of ethical import. But seeking guidance on how to live well quite generally would be rather peculiar.

Even where people seek advice about how to conduct themselves in various domains of life, they do not thereby make it true that there is some overall 'task to be performed', of a kind that supplies us with the notion of a moral authority. To say that there is a task to be performed, in this context, is to say that people need to be told how to live well, or do the right thing, in various walks of life, and that this need can be met by a set-up involving experts (in a broad sense of 'experts'). But, for a society of any complexity, this is surely a case of many tasks, not of one; and whether there *is* in fact a 'need' must depend on particular facts about the particular walk of life. Perhaps there is some such specific need, and a set-up involving experts would meet it: still, the experts involved would not be 'moral experts'. They would be experts on childcare, or on marital matters, or on the customs of a country to be visited, or on how to give up drinking, and so on and so on.

There is one further problem with the idea of a quite general moral authority. I said earlier that if you are in the position of thinking or doing things because an authority tells you to, then you need to have a measure of instinctive judgment or common sense, a faculty that enables you to detect folly, falsehood, or fraudulence. But a person who has, through experience of life, acquired such a faculty to any significant degree may very well have acquired a more general knowledge of what makes people tick. This more general knowledge will make you something of a moral expert already. Of course there may well be people with more life-experience and more moral expertise than you; but your capacity to recognize them for what they are will to some extent be a case of 'Takes one to know one'. And moral dialogue will in that case tend to resemble the dialogue we had in our original Case 1 rather more than that in Case 2. Advice, rather than instruction, would be what was aimed at. There is at least this much, I think, to the Kantian ideal of moral autonomy.

The Force of Numbers

JOSEPH RAZ[1]

A view as widely endorsed as it is disputed says, formulating it in my own words: *The only thing we have reason to do is promote value.*[2] This I will call **The promotion of value** thesis (or principle).

Variants of the promotion of value principle are widespread. They emerged as a generalization of an aspect of Utilitarianism, sometimes taken to be the plausible part of Utilitarianism. The promotion of value thesis is not committed to the Utilitarian account of value, namely that pleasure, the avoidance of pain or the satisfaction of preferences are the only things of value. It does, however, share with Utilitarianism an understanding of reasons for action.

In recent times something like the promotion of value thesis was regarded by many as obviously true. Even those who rejected it often acknowledged its power and

[1] I owe much to comments on earlier drafts by Jonathan Adler, Anthony Price, Andrei Marmor, John Broome, Dan Priel, Mike Martin, Ian Rumfitt, Leif Wenar, G. A. Cohen and especially Tom Pink.

[2] I take the natural reading of this to say more than that one should do only what is good, but rather that one should do what is most good, or something like that, as will be explained below.

appeal.[3] Opposition to the thesis triggered some influential developments in the writings on practical reason over the last 30 years or so. Contemporary Contractualism[4], for example, arose as a way of rebutting it.

In this paper I will argue against the thesis, suggesting that, first, an account of practical rationality has to include an account of reasons for action. Second, that while it is a principle of rationality that we should act for the better reason(s) that principle has nothing to do with maximization, or the promotion of value. Third, that no version of the promotion of value principle that I can think of is consistent with various reasons for action whose existence is known to us. There are many different versions of maximizing, consequentialist accounts of practical rationality. I will consider only two of them. Naturally the arguments advanced here apply only to the versions I consider, though I believe that they can be easily adapted to yield objections to other versions.

[3] See Scanlon, 'Utilitarianism and Contractualism' *Utilitarianism: For and Against*, B. Williams and J. J. C. Smart (eds.) (Cambridge: Cambridge University Press, 1973). One of its most determined and influential opponents, Elizabeth Anscombe, appears never to have felt this appeal. She rejected anything like the promotion of value thesis silently, not feeling the need to analyse its underlying mistakes, or to dispel its magic power. The nearest she came to an argued rejection is in the brilliant and enigmatic page and a half comment on a paper by Mrs P. Foot, published in the *Oxford Review* 1967.

[4] In the hands of both Rawls (*A Theory of Justice* (Cambridge: Harvard University Press, 1971)) and Scanlon (*What We Owe to Each Other* (Cambridge: Harvard University Press, 1998)).

1. A sympathetic background

My doubts about the thesis arise in spite of the fact that I will accept the view about the relationship between values and reasons which it presupposes, namely:

> **The reason/value nexus:** *A reason for action is valid only if and because it is a reason for an action which is good (has value) or which, directly or indirectly, secures, or can reasonably be thought to secure, something of value.* Alternatively, and more narrowly, some maintain that the value of an action or of its consequences, and only they, are reasons for it.

This means that any criticism of the promotion of value thesis in this paper will emerge from a position which is, in important ways, sympathetic to the thesis. Moreover, I will assume that even promoters of value allow for a distance between values and reasons arising in two ways:

First, while the desirability of an action is determined by its value relative to that of its feasible alternatives, its desirability need not determine the reasons for its performance. These depend, according to this line of thought, not on the desirability of the action, but on the desirability that it is reasonable to think it has, taking account, among much else, of the likelihood of successfully performing it (and its alternatives), and the likelihood of various outcomes of its performance.

Second, even though the reasons for an action relate to its desirability, i.e. its relative value, they need not be its relative value. In some circumstances, those trying to

> perform actions because they think that they are desirable, or that it is reasonable to believe that they are desirable, succeed less than those who are guided by other considerations.

'Success' here means bringing about the most desirable actions, i.e. those with the highest relative value. Where lack of success is not accidental, but is due to some features likely to cause it whenever they recur, then there are additional reasons, namely those considerations which would lead, were one to attempt to be guided by them, to the greatest degree of success.[5] I will not comment directly on these

[5] On some views these 'indirect reasons' will not be additional reasons; rather they are the only reasons. I think that this view is mistaken. It may be motivated by the thought (mentioned in the text below) that it is a necessary condition for anything being a reason that one can, in principle, be guided by it. But this thought does not require us to accept that 'the indirect reasons' are the only reasons. We can be motivated to perform the action by the original reasons, and the case for recognizing indirect reasons requires nothing more than that one would be more likely to conform to those reasons if one is not guided by them, but by some alternative considerations. In such cases it is natural to take the alternative consideration to be a special kind of instrumental reason enabling one to conform to the source reason, rather than replacing it. My analysis of the way rules issued by legitimate authority function (see *The Morality of Freedom* (Oxford: Oxford University Press, 1984) Ch. 3) is an example. If I am right then this is an additional objection to the view which says (stated very roughly) that valid reasons are those facts which, if people take to be valid reasons, and try to follow them, would lead to the most desirable actions being performed. However, the complications of the indirect interpretations of the promotion of value thesis are too many to encompass here.

observations. I will assume that the promotion of value principle can be accommodated to allow for them, and in my formulation of the reason/value nexus and of the maximization theses (below) some such accommodation is made.

I should, however, remark in general terms about the assumptions underlying these claimed gaps between value and reasons, as they will be much relied upon later in my argument. Special cases apart, one satisfies what reason requires of one by conforming with it, that is, if I have a reason for a particular action on a particular occasion I conform with that reason, and do all that reason requires of me, if I perform that action on that occasion, no matter what my reason is for doing so. I need not act for that particular reason, nor even be aware of it.[6] However, it is a condition of something being a reason for action that it is possible, conceptually possible, for the people for whom it is a reason to take it as a reason, and to act for that reason.

The underlying thought behind the promotion of value thesis is that the value of actions makes them worthwhile. Perhaps we should pitch it higher than that: their value marks, other things being equal, failure to perform them as a fault (and in certain circumstances makes such failure a wrong). For many of those who reject the promotion of value thesis, in any shape or form, the main culprit is the value/reason nexus, leading them to its complete

[6] Indeed, sometimes it may be better if one conforms to the reason without being guided by it (as when it is better to avoid raping people without ever contemplating whether to do so).

rejection.[7] This underlying thought is, however, insufficient to vindicate the promotion of value thesis. It can lead to the promotion of value thesis only if various additional conditions are met. For example, it must be the case that when we act to promote value we succeed in doing so better than if we acted on the basis of any other considerations. Promoting value, we could say, is what justifies actions, and because of that, when the additional conditions are met, it is also the reason for the actions. The two gaps I pointed to allow that the condition just mentioned is not always met, and allow for consequential modifications to the theses.

An additional condition is that the value of an action can be a reason for it only if it can in principle be taken as a reason by the agent, who can, again in principle, guide his action by that reason. This additional condition will be the focus of the discussion which follows. But first let me introduce an additional implication of the promotion of value thesis, which I will call **The maximization thesis:** *A reason for action is undefeated only if and because, in the circumstances, the action for which it is a reason is the action which, of all feasible alternatives, will, or can be reasonably believed to, best promote value, where that is measured by a*

[7] Or to its modulation either through the introduction of some reasons which do not derive from the value of the actions for which they are reasons, or by relativizing values or reasons to agents in the way introduced by T. Nagel in *The Possibility of Altruism* (Oxford: Oxford University Press, 1969), given these names by D. Parfit (*Reasons and Persons* (Oxford: Oxford University Press, 1984) p. 143), and developed and applied to values as well as to reasons by A. Sen in 'Rights and Agency' (*Philosophy and Public Affairs*, 1982).

balance of value gained or likely to be gained by it against the value lost or likely to be lost because of it.

The views commonly identified as upholding maximization can be, and often are, expressed in different terms. Indeed in the course of the paper I will explore alternative ways of understanding maximization. There are others. I claim nothing more than that the theses here discussed are sometimes endorsed, and are plausible enough to merit consideration.

Some objections to maximization are due to the fact that often both those who uphold it and whose who object to it exaggerate its power. They sometimes assume that it entails, or at least has the result, that among any possible set of conflicting reasons, or at least among any reasons which in fact do or will conflict, one only prevails, defeating all the others. Some people assume that any set of rational principles guiding decision and choice is either incomplete or invalid if it does not yield one correct choice in any practical conflict. This view is indefensible, and its rejection means that if conflicts regularly remain unresolved, in the sense that the reasons for more than one of the incompatible but available options are undefeated it is often less natural, often merely a technical matter to describe actions which conform to reason as maximizing.

In previous writings[8] I emphasized the prevalence of unresolved conflicts, and of choices not determined by reasons. In particular I tried to show how most ordinary

[8] See in particular *The Morality of Freedom* Ch. 13, and *Engaging Reason* (Oxford: Oxford University Press, 2000), Chapters 3 and 4.

decisions are taken in the face of incommensurable reasons. My discussion this time will not rely on these factors. I will question the validity of the maximizing principle itself, rather than challenge its scope and force.

2. Maximization and reasons

It is a basic principle, embedded in our concept of reasons, that one should in one's actions conform to the better reason. That is

PR1: It is irrational knowingly to act or try to act so that one's action (if successful) conforms to a less good reason, being aware of one's ability to act so as to conform to a better one.

Related is the principle saying:

PR2: When facing a conflict of reasons Reason requires that action which conforms to the better reason.

These principles have nothing to do with the promotion or maximization of value. They do not even presuppose any relationship between value and reasons. Yet they may appear to compel maximization in a few easy steps. For example it may be thought that the following are derivable if one adds a few indisputable premises:

First, when there are several reasons for the same action their combined weight is a positive function of their individual weights.

Second, the stringency of any reason for any action is proportionate to the value which the feature the presence of which constitutes the reason confers on the action for which it is a reason.

Conclusion: Promoting value is the general nature of reasons for action.

Assuming the value/reason nexus, and subject to the two gaps between values and reasons mentioned above, it is plausible to accept the second premise. But the first premise, which means that the combined weight of two reasons for the same action is greater than the weight of either of them, is false and those who accept the promotion of value thesis are almost always careful to reject it. It is worth spending a few minutes considering some of the reasons for its rejection. They show that the better reason principle is neither itself a principle of aggregation, nor does it entail aggregation, at least not if the entailment relies on the first premise. Had the premise been true maximization would have been not a moral or evaluative belief, but a requirement of reason, a condition of rationality. The rejection of the first premise denies maximizers one argument for that conclusion.

Imagine that I have reason to go to Paddington station to catch a train to Birmingham where I am due to lecture later today, and that I also have another reason to go to Paddington, to catch a train to Oxford where a friend is arriving from abroad for the day. However, I cannot both meet my friend and get to Birmingham for my lecture.[9] I have conflicting reasons, and the two reasons to go to

[9] And the trains will depart shortly so no further information can become available in time to affect the case.

Paddington derive from two conflicting reasons. Hence the force (strength, stringency, weight, etc.) of my overall reason to go to Paddington is no greater than the force of the weightier of the two reasons to go there. It appears, therefore, that the first premise applies only to reasons which do not derive from conflicting reasons.[10] But does it apply to them without further restriction?

Imagine that I have a headache and I have reason to go to the pharmacy, buy aspirin and take it. I also have reason to take an Advil tablet, and therefore I have another reason to go to the pharmacy, i.e. to get Advil. The reason to take Advil and the reason to take aspirin do not conflict: I can take both. But I have no reason to do so. I will assume that taking one of them will yield all the benefits that can be expected. Therefore there is no advantage in taking both. The situation is typical of cases where there are various ways, not necessarily equally satisfactory, of conforming to a reason. We then have reason to adopt each one of them, though some of them may be better than the others. Once we successfully conform, one way or another, with the root reason the reasons to pursue it in other ways lapse. The various reasons to pursue the means for satisfying the root reason are dependent reasons. Conforming to one makes the others lapse. Dependent reasons provide another exception to the first premise. For our purposes we can take one reason to be dependent on another if conformity with the second cancels the first. If one has several reasons for taking the same

[10] I ignore the impact of the possibility, where it exists, that due to change in circumstances the conflict may disappear.

action then the overall force of one's reasons to take that action is a positive function of them only if they are independent reasons, which do not derive from conflicting reasons.

The interesting lesson from these examples is that, since whether or not reasons are independent of each other, in the sense explained, depends on moral or other evaluative considerations, the first premise cannot be amended to yield a formal principle with universal application. Here is an example which illustrates the point. Think of a small community, say a family, and of reasons applying only to its members. Both of us are members. I have reason to help you and also a conflicting reason to buy myself a CD. Are they independent? They appear to be. But suppose that given that I have a conflicting reason to buy a CD, which is a reason of a kind that I am known within the community to have, if I buy myself a CD someone else will help you, and because this is so, once I buy the CD I no longer have a reason to help you. Does that undermine their independence? Does my reason to help you depend on my reason for buying a CD because if I buy myself a CD I no longer have a reason to help?

Of course, the characterization of dependence among reasons that I gave is too vague and needs tightening. We can make it more precise so that the two reasons in the example will turn out to be dependent if and only if the fact that given that I have a reason to buy a CD, someone else will help you if I do not is sufficient to establish that I am not at fault for not helping you myself. Otherwise they are independent. If the reasons in the example are dependent, the first premise does not apply to them, and the principle of maximization does not apply.

Once the characterization of dependence is made precise the resulting revised first premise may turn out to be a principle of practical rationality. But it will not be a principle which applies to all reasons for action. It turns out to apply only to some such reasons, and whether it applies to any pair of reasons is a matter of substantive moral or evaluative judgment. Possibly regarding reasons to which the principle applies maximization reigns (I will question that later), but whether any kinds of reasons are subject to maximization is a moral or evaluative question.[11]

In fact, even when revised as suggested, the first premise is subject to additional exceptions. I will give but one example: We have reasons not to kill people, and not to rape them, deriving, I will assume, from a duty of respect for people, which is rooted in the fact that people are valuable in themselves.[12] We also have reasons not to kill and not to rape deriving from the fact that the law of our countries, and I will assume it to be a legitimate, morally binding law, forbids murder and rape (as well as an additional reason deriving from the penalties specified for murder and for rape). But the existence of legal reasons against murder or against rape does not make my reason not to murder or not to rape more stringent than it would have been without it.

[11] It is possible, of course, to give a relatively formal characterization of 'dependent reasons', but thus understood the first premise, and therefore maximization, is false, unless subjected to additional exceptions, themselves based on substantive evaluative claims.

[12] See my account of duties of respect in chapter four of *Value, Respect and Attachment*.

The same applies to some promises. If I promise not to murder or not to rape someone I have no greater reason not to do so than I had before. To make the case more vivid imagine a country where the law permits killing or raping retirees. When I visit that country (and am not subject to the law of my country) I have as much reason to refrain from either killing and raping retirees as I have when at home. The absence of a legal reason not to kill retirees makes no difference to the overall stringency of the reasons not to kill and not to rape. Yet the law (in the country imagined) and the promise do constitute reasons.[13]

Note that I am not claiming that the law or promises, when morally binding, do not make a normative difference, or that they never affect the stringency. On the contrary, it is a condition of the adequacy of explanations of the nature of law or of promises that they show how they do, and when they do, when binding, affect the stringency of the action applying to us. The point I am making is that we rely on substantive accounts of the nature of various values and reasons in reaching conclusions about their interaction, and not on a formal principle of maximization.[14] That, if valid at all, applies only when the substantive considerations indicate that it does.[15]

[13] This is the assumption, i.e. that the law generally is morally acceptable.

[14] The examples rely on the fact that we have duties not to rape and not to murder, independently of the law and of the promises.

[15] Some people think that what is special about murder and rape is that the reasons to refrain from them are maximally strong, and therefore cannot be enhanced by the law or by promises. This is a supposition that cannot be accepted without other theoretical claims. Otherwise, it will turn out to assume not only that the reasons against rape and

3. Is 'promoting value' an intelligible principle of practical reason?

All this is well understood by maximizers who do not rely on the first premise.[16] I spent some time explaining why, to show that an apparently quick route from the fact that we ought to act for the better reason to the promotion of value is a dead end.

The picture of practical reasons I have been implicitly relying on has it that various facts endow actions with value, or disvalue. They are reasons for or against an action. Reasoning from them we establish what we may or must do. It is perhaps easier to see the case for maximization if one looks at the relations between values and conclusive reasons directly, without the mediation of so-called *prima facie* reasons for action. After all while we can readily understand claims that we ought to maximize value, claims that we ought to maximize reason are meaningless, and the claim that we ought to maximize reason satisfaction is a neologism whose artificiality makes it vulnerable.

Putting the promotion of value in the world centre stage, maximizers can say that *a conclusive reason for an*

murder are of equal stringency, but also that that the reason to avoid killing one person is as strong as the reasons not to kill a million. These conclusions or the additional assumptions needed to avoid them may well be true, but are unlikely to give any support to the promotion of value thesis.

16 Some maximizers analyse practical reasons in terms of expected utility, and, of course, the expected utility of the combined occurrence of two events is not the sum of the expected utility of each of them occurring.

action consists in the fact that the state which will result from our taking the action is (or is likely to be) of greater value than any feasible alternative state.

They have no need for presumptively sufficient reasons. Once formulated in this way all the exceptions discussed above are taken care of, and need not be separately identified and individually excluded. One obvious doubt about this elucidation of conclusive reasons arises out of its reference to the value of states. I have no objection to the idea that some states are good or bad, or that they are better or worse than others. But this explanation of conclusive reasons assumes that there is something like the overall value of a state, which is presumably a function of the good-making and bad-making properties which it has. In other words, this explanation of conclusive reasons assumes that value aggregates, and that the value of a state is a function of its evaluative properties, that we can say not only that a state is good in some ways, and bad in others, but also how good or bad it is overall. In short, the explanation begs one question about the promotion of value, which is whether value aggregates, whether we can talk of the cumulative value of states in that way.

I will, however, leave this matter on one side to raise another familiar doubt: given the above understanding of conclusive reasons, is the promotion of value principle an intelligible principle of practical rationality? The principle is about what reasons for action we have. It says that the only reason is to promote value, that is to perform that action that will (or is likely to) promote value more than any of the available alternatives. As I explained above, many actions are without fault even though they were not taken for the right reason. Yet I also assumed that only what can be followed in action as a reason, only what can be taken to be a reason for action can be a reason for action. Could any faultless action be taken to promote value?

Most of the time when people discuss their reasons the promotion of value is not one of them. Advancing education, expanding job opportunities, designing ways to relieve the tedium of boring tasks at home or at work, are among the reasons we have for various activities. Maximizing value is hardly ever a reason we consider and follow. But can we do so in all cases where we have a good reason for action? If we can then perhaps the reasons which we normally follow can be seen as instances of that reason, as specific ways of promoting value on this occasion. We would then be able to argue, for example, that when we take an action because it advances job opportunities our reason is really (though implicitly) that opening up new job opportunities is, in the circumstances, the way to promote value. Given that promotion of value is, on this view, the only reason there is, it is not surprising that it remains implicit, in the background, and that in thought and argument we concentrate on the ways it is instantiated on the various occasions for action.

A common objection has it that some reasons of importance cannot be seen as instances of the promotion of value, even when they are conclusive. For example, I sit at home with nothing special to do, and a friend calls and offers to come over for conversation and a glass of wine. In the circumstances, there was nothing wrong with my being at home with nothing special to do. I like my friend and will enjoy spending the evening chatting with him. Moreover, he will be somewhat disappointed if I decline his offer. It seems to me that I have an undefeated reason to invite him over. Is it my way of maximizing value in the circumstances? My reason is the pleasure of my friend's company, and the appropriateness of inviting him (the inappropriateness of declining in the absence of a sufficient reason) given our friendship. It is not the case that I regard these reasons as a way of promoting value in the world. If I do I fail, for example, to act in friendship.[17] And if I am generally a maximizer I have no friends, unless they are deceived about my reasons.

How successful is the objection? It is easy to underestimate it. One familiar reply, for example, has it that it is successful against those who take friendships to be instrumentally valuable, that it shows that one cannot be a friend without taking friendship to be intrinsically valuable. But, the thought is, acknowledging that friendship is intrinsically valuable is compatible with the promotion of value thesis, for the value of a successful friendship is a constituent part of the goodness of the state in which the friendship features. The promotion of value thesis tells us to choose the action which would result in a state most likely to be better than the available alternatives, and in assessing value we take account

[17] When acting in (or out of) friendship the friendship is a (part of the) reason for the action, but the reason is not necessarily for the sake of the friendship, understood as aiming to protect it from erosion, or other dangers.

of the value of constituent states which are intrinsically good, as well as of instrumentally good states.

In itself this reply will not save the promotion of value from the objection. It leaves untouched the objection that the promoter of value cannot act out of friendship. That is so whether he acts 'out of friendship' because doing so will cause valuable consequences or because acting out of friendship is a way of promoting value, of increasing the amount of value in the world by performing an act which is itself valuable. Even in the second case one does not act out of friendship at all, for one's true goal is increasing the amount of value in the world and the friendship or the act one is currently performing are ways of doing so.

In assessing this objection we should be careful not to confuse it with others. It does not rely on the claim that to act out of friendship one's deliberations must refer to the friendship, or to any other specific reason, nor on a claim that for the action to be consistent with the promotion of value principle one must take it in light of that goal. The objection presupposes that for the principle to be valid *it must be possible* to take the action both out of friendship and (simultaneously) in order to promote value, seeing acting out of friendship as a way of doing so. The objection would not have been good had it been necessarily the case that acting out of friendship is promoting value. The objection rests on the fact that acting out of friendship is only contingently related to promoting value. If on balance acting out of friendship will not promote value (because there is another action which will produce more value) then, so far as the promotion of value principle goes, we have no reason to act out of friendship.

In other words, the promotion of value principle can acknowledge only that acting out of friendship can be a conditional reason. We have reason to do so if it promotes value. We need not deny that when acting out of friendship will not promote value we should not so act, that in those circumstances we should take the action which will promote value, to allow that the reason to act out of friendship is not merely a conditional reason (any more than the reason to keep a promise is conditional because sometimes it is, all things considered, right to break a promise). It follows that if we have reasons to act out of friendship pure and simple, rather than out of friendship as a way of doing something else, then the promotion of value principle is mistaken, for there is at least one reason, or really one kind of reason besides promoting value.

To have any chance of being true the promotion of value principle has to be modified to be not a thesis about what reasons there are, not even about conclusive reasons, but about when action is justified, that is without fault, whether undertaken for good reasons or bad.

There can, however, be another response to the objection above. One can jettison the promotion of value principle, but hang on to the *maximization* thesis. To remind you, the *promotion* of value is a principle about what reasons we have. The maximization principle, on the other hand, says nothing about what reasons we have. It is a principle of conflict resolution directing that when there are conflicting reasons the better reasons are those conformity with which will lead to a state of the world likely to have in it more value than the alternative. If the promotion of value principle is mistaken, while the maximization principle is true, people are able to act out of friendship and nothing more, but when the reasons for acting out of friendship conflict with reasons for another, incompatible act, that reason is the better one which will lead to higher expected value.

The difficulty with this line of thought, upholding maximization while rejecting the promotion of value, is that it leaves it unexplained why conflicts are to be resolved in accord with the maximization thesis. If promoting value is not what we are after why in conflict between reasons is the better reason the one conformity with which leads to more value? I see no way of answering this question, and therefore will continue on the basis that maximization presupposes the promotion of value, but that the promotion of value cannot, because of the objection we considered, be a principle about what reasons we have.

4. Can 'the promotion of value' be the ultimate principle of action?

The reinterpreted principle of the promotion of value says nothing directly about what reasons there are. Rather, it is a principle about the justifiability of actions, whatever reasons there are for them, and whatever the reasons for which they were taken (when they were taken): *an action is justified (i.e. faultless) only if and because it is the most desirable action of those available to the agent at the time.* If maximization is a requirement of rationality it is so not because of the nature of reasons but because of the nature of values, in terms of which actions (or whatever else is subject to justification) are to be justified. But is it? First, note that even if the promotion of value is interpreted along the lines suggested, the problems raised above do not disappear. Any account of practical rationality has to do more than characterize a test under which action is defensible or justified. It has also to explain the relation between reasons and the principle of justifiability of actions. It is a condition of the validity of both the revised promotion of value principle and of the doctrine of reasons for action that they mesh, that is that valid reasons are such that acting for them would lead one to comply with the promotion of value principle, or at least to do so better than would acting for any alternative considerations.

This point will return to haunt us, but let it be put on one side for the moment. I will avoid the complex question of whether we should maximize instrumental value. There are difficult questions there, though one thing is clear: by definition an object's instrumental value is due to the value of its likely effects, or the effects it can be used to achieve, or creates opportunities to achieve, etc. In the last resort instrumental value depends on, and derives from non-instrumental value (and that is so even if there are agents who must pursue, or maximize what is of instrumental value and ignore other kinds of value). Therefore, if the promotion of value and maximization principles do not apply to all intrinsic values they cannot without reservation apply to all instrumental values.

So finally we face the central question about the promotion of value: what is to be promoted or maximized?

What does it mean to maximize (non-instrumental) value, given that value is a property of objects, events, actions, institutions, people, and much else? An answer which no one believes to be correct, is that we should maximize the number of valuable things. But why not? The reply is that different things of value vary in how valuable they are. Therefore, a small selection of well chosen things may, taken as a totality, be more valuable than a larger number of individually less valuable things. We should, the maximizers will remind us, promote not things of value, but value.

This explanation leaves intact the suggestion that other things being equal we promote value by adding another valuable object to the world. But should we amass as many good paintings as possible? That is not what promoting value means to maximizers, and for good reason. There is little point in a storehouse full of paintings which no one will ever see, however beautiful they are. We are not considering the value of the activity of creating them. That activity is consistent with destroying them once created. What is at issue now is the value there is in maximizing the number of good paintings in existence as a way of maximizing the value of the totality of the paintings in existence. Why does promoting value not entail maximizing the number of good paintings in order to maximize value in the world, other things being equal? I suspect that there is a temptation to say that good paintings are only instrumentally good. What is good non-instrumentally is painting them, looking at them, or contemplating them, or living with them, or being inspired by them, and so on, or doing all that with understanding, or with pleasure, and so on.

Succumbing to it yields the result that beauty, and all other aesthetic values, are only instrumentally valuable.

It is best to resist the temptation. Yielding to it leads to the conclusion that having the experience of listening to Schubert or of looking at a painting by Cézanne is as good as actually doing so.[18] I will take for granted what you may call a reality principle, which while not denying that illusory experiences may be instrumentally valuable (e.g., in calming one down, or taking one's mind off undesirable thoughts), says that they are not intrinsically valuable (except as ways of realizing certain special kinds of valuable ends, like experimenting with illusions). However, it is possible to try to explain in a more plausible way, consistently with the promotion of value principle, why it is pointless to maximize the number of good paintings. Good paintings, and other intrinsically good objects, do not matter in themselves. They are constituents of complex states of making them, appreciating them, or whatever, that are intrinsically good not merely as constituents of more complex intrinsic goods. Only such goods, that is those which are of value not merely as a constituent of other valuable objects, activities or states, are the object of the promotion of value principle. It does not apply to good paintings, novels, etc., which are intrinsically good merely as constituents of good activities, objects and states.

There is nothing here which should be taken as an objection to the normal usage of 'intrinsic value', according

[18] See, e.g. Nozick's famous experience machine in *Anarchy, State and Utopia* (NY: Basic Books, 1974).

to which good works of art are intrinsically valuable, as well as, often, valuable instrumentally, e.g. having a market value. It merely means that we should limit the kind of intrinsic value to which the promotion of value principle applies to those which are not valuable only as constituent components of valuable objects, activities, experiences, etc.

5. Types of values and their promotion

How convincing is this narrowed promotion of value principle? To answer we need to consider different kinds of values, and since it is not possible here to go into an elaborate classification, I will confine my comments to two kinds, which will be identified only broadly, and imprecisely. **One** consists of experiences and activities of people and other creatures or objects which 'count in themselves'.[19] To simplify I will refer only to people. **The other** consists in many moral values, especially those relating to social institutions and to conduct among people in the absence of personal relations among them, e.g. fairness, justice, tolerance, respect. I will call the second kind 'enabling values', and the first 'meaning of life values'. The reason is that while striving to rectify injustice, improve tolerance, etc. can give meaning to the life of those who so do, just living in a society which is just and not suffering from intolerance, unfairness etc. does not give meaning to the life of those who do so. Friendships, and valuable social activities (dances, parties,

[19] See my discussion of things which are valuable in themselves in *Value, Respect and Attachment* (Cambridge University Press, 2001) Chapter 4.

food, sex, conversation, and the rest), sporting activities, leisure pursuits and hobbies, an interest in literature and the arts, and such like can give life a meaning.

Enabling values come closest to conformity with the promotion of value principle. The realization of these values is a matter of degree, in as much as a society or people can be more or less just, more or less tolerant, and so on. It is best to achieve the highest possible degree, but in practice this is commonly impossible. In fact quite often people and governments face choices between options each favouring some of those values at the expense of the others. We thus engage in trade-offs which, when the options are not incommensurable, may be subject to the maximization principle. I will say little about them except by way of gesture. Some enabling values are what I call satiable values, that is they can, in principle, be satisfied to a maximal degree. This is particularly so with values such as fairness and toleration whose satisfaction means that the corresponding vice is avoided. We are fair when we are not acting unfairly. We are tolerant when we do not manifest intolerance. Since it is possible, in principle, to avoid the offensive conduct it is possible, in principle, to be in a situation where fairness is maximally realized, and nothing can be done to make the world more fair or more tolerant. Such values are good candidates for maximization. Other enabling values are not like that. They allow for indefinite improvement. Generosity and mercy are examples of those. One can always be more generous and merciful than one is. I believe that the promotion of values does not apply to those values, for reasons similar to those which make it inapplicable to meaning of life values. But I will say no more about this and turn to those meaning of life values. Are they to be promoted?

There are two obvious objections. The first addresses the applicability of the promotion of value principle. The second addresses directly the maximization principle. First, suppose that I can listen many times to the Schubert Octet with attention and appreciation. Even if I do so twice a day for many months I still get a lot out of doing so. Will doing so increase value in the world? Will the world be a better place, other things being equal, if I listen to the Octet twice daily? I have to admit that I find no meaning in the supposition that doing so will, other things being equal, increase value in the world. I suspect that those who are inclined to affirm that this will increase value do so because they think that (a) given that I will appreciate and enjoy the Octet I have reason to do so. (Suppose that I do not: It would follow that if I do listen to the Octet one more time I am acting against reason, which is absurd.) (b) Unless I have a reason which is either incommensurate or no worse than the reason to listen to the Octet the reason to listen is the better reason. They are fortified by the belief that whenever the situation is as in the example one would have other reasons which will not be defeated by the reason to listen to the Octet, and the absurdity of supposing that one must on pain of irrationality listen to it all the time will not arise in practice. I agree with this judgment. But see no comfort in it for the promoter of value. The argument rests on the relations between reasons. Namely, on taking reasons to be presumptively sufficient, and as entailing that knowingly and voluntarily failing to conform with a reason which is better than all conflicting reasons is irrational. This argument, whatever we think of its merits, does not rely on the thought that we ought to maximize or promote value, a thought which remains without content when applied to cases of this kind.

We can return to friendship to illustrate the second objection, the one applying directly to the maximization thesis as a thesis about trade-offs in conflict. If the maximization principle reigns supreme then it would seem that, other things being equal, when I move to a new town and am looking to forge new friendships I should, other things being equal, make friends with a person whose neighbours will benefit from this new friendship rather than with someone who has no such neighbours. Assume that the benefit to the neighbours of the first person is real and visible, but that forgoing the benefit will not condemn them to great misery. It is incompatible with relations between friends that one chooses who to be friends with not because of a liking for the friend, concern for him and for oneself, but out of concern for his neighbours. If maximization dictates that our choice is wrong when we do not choose the person whose neighbours would benefit, then maximization cannot be co-ordinated with a correct theory of reasons, and is to be rejected.[20]

[20] Notice that having reinterpreted maximization as well as the promotion of value as principles justifying actions, without being principles about what reason we have, I am not claiming that they are right only if we can act in order to conform with them. The objection is based on the weaker assumption, namely that the principles which justify actions must be co-ordinated with the doctrine of reasons for

There seems to be an obvious reply to these objections. Listening to Schubert, or making friends, is good only in context. Listening to Schubert is not, for example, good if it is the only thing that person does. It is good only if it makes his or her day good, and that depends on listening to Schubert having a proper place within that day, alongside food, work, and much else. But then, why care about how good the day is? What makes a day a more worthy unit than an hour? Nothing, I think, is the right answer. Pointing to the day is just a step to what is, ultimately, the relevant context, namely the life of that person as a whole. So finally we arrive where some of you may well have wanted to start: what counts is the well-being of people (and of other beings that count).

6. Promoting well-being

Some maximizers take well-being to be the only intrinsic value (other than values which are mere constituent components of value), and therefore well-being is what we ought to promote and maximize. For the purposes of the present discussion we need not endorse this view. We can allow that enabling values are intrinsically valuable in their own right. The question we need to examine is whether when options open to us affect meaning of life values, and let us confine ourselves to cases in which they affect no other values, that

action, i.e. that acting for sufficient reasons will not turn out to be unjustified, and that whether or not it is justified will not be a matter of chance.

action is justified which best or most promotes the well-being of people.

The question now arising is whether the promotion of well-being is consistent with the reason/value nexus, which claims that the value of an action is a reason for it. For example, I have a reason to paint if I can paint reasonably well, creating reasonably attractive paintings. I do not mean that I must do so. Only that I have reason to do so, and if I choose to paint then, other things being equal, my action will not be against reason. Similarly with listening to Schubert's Octet; I have reason to do so, and if I do then, other things being equal, my action would be justified, for I conformed to an undefeated reason. But my well-being is not promoted by listening to the Octet for the umpteenth time. There are endless examples of this kind. Susan has many friends. Friendship is important for her well-being. But will her well-being improve if she strikes up another friendship? It will make no difference to the overall quality of her life, or to her happiness or well-being. Does it follow that if she does strike up another friendship her action will be unjustified? Surely not.

The argument is not that she is entitled to prefer spending time with her friends over working to help the poor, or supporting her declining father, or fighting to correct some injustice she can help to correct. I am not claiming that such moral considerations, or the interests of other people, may not conflict with and defeat the reason that she has for the new friendship, or for listening again to the Octet, or for painting a new picture. My claim is that she has reason to engage in all these activities, and that other things being equal, her doing so would be justified, regardless of whether or not it contributes to her well-being.

I take this to be a refutation of the promotion of value thesis. Each such example is sufficient to refute the thesis. Here is another. In some twenty five minutes I have to go somewhere. There is nothing much of importance to my life or the world that I can do in the intervening time, so there is no reason which defeats the reason for watching some moderately amusing TV program. That is all I need to satisfy myself to do so. I need not establish, and it is not true, that my life, or anybody else's, will be better for doing so. There are any number of such refuting examples. They relate to the reasons people have to go to the cinema, to have a glass of wine, to spend an evening talking to a friend, to have a pleasant afternoon walking the hills, and so on and so forth. In normal circumstances none of these reasons does or can affect the well-being of anyone, yet they often go undefeated, and hence justify the actions they are reasons for. Following them is both intelligible and defensible. Their status as reasons and as justifications of actions does not depend on their contribution to the maximization of well-being, or of anything else.

I remarked earlier that maximizers owe themselves an account of reasons for action which squares with the promotion of value being the only justification of action. That is what they cannot do.

7. Conclusion—should we ever maximize?

In this paper I was concerned to dispute the theses of the promotion of value and of maximization, as (a) principles of reason; (b) sole determinants of reasons for action; (c) sole principles justifying actions. I did not examine substantive evaluative theses, such that the promotion of well-being is a concern which defeats all others when they clash. Nor did I examine the practical implications of the rejection of principles of maximization. These implications are particularly far reaching once one recognizes, as I and others have argued[21], that agents pursuing their own concerns in friendships, careers, or any interest they pursue, not because of a general duty to all mankind, do not, and by and large cannot, regard their own well-being as the underlying reason for their actions. This leaves a vast domain of actions outside the reach of the promotion of value thesis, even if, which is not to be taken for granted, it applies to our moral duties towards others.

Does it mean that numbers do not count? Far from it, but I have gone on too long to explain how and when they do. Briefly put numbers have the force to affect reasons for action in two main ways:

First, given any number of independent reasons N, one conforms better to reason if one conforms with N reasons than with N-1.

Second, there are special limited, but possibly quite numerous, domains where there are special duties to maximize. For example, it may be reasonable for the law to require company directors to maximize profits (subject to some

[21] *The Morality of Freedom*, Ch. 12, *Engaging Reason*, Chs. 12 and 13, Scanlon, *What We Owe to Each Other*, Ch. 3.

> limits), or it may be reasonable to think that it is one of the tasks (that is that it is a *prima facie* duty) of governments in today's world to minimize wasting natural resources in their country.

The understanding both of practical reason and of practical politics will be greatly advanced if we can put to rest the ghost of general principles of maximization or promotion of value, and turn our attention to the justification and limits of such special duties.

Reason, Intention, and Choice[1]
An Essay in Practical Philosophy

GAVIN LAWRENCE

It is the famous first thesis of Anscombe's 'Modern Moral Philosophy' that we should lay aside moral philosophy—indeed '*banish ethics totally* from our minds'! (p. 38, paragraph 36)—'until we have an adequate philosophy of psychology'.[2] By a 'philosophy of psychology' I understand Anscombe to mean grammatical investigations into various psychological concepts that hold the key to ethics. Anscombe herself instances 'action', 'intention', 'pleasure', 'wanting' ('more will probably turn up if we start with these'). Without such an understanding, she thinks we will simply go astray.

In *Intention* she addresses herself to this task, at least as regards 'intention', 'action' and 'wanting'. Indeed of the

[1] I should like to thank Philippa Foot, Pamela Hieronymi, Anselm Müller, Seana Shiffrin, and Julie Tannenbaum for their helpful comments, and the Royal Institute of Philosophy and Professor O'Hear for inviting me to contribute to this series of lectures in honour of Professor Elizabeth Anscombe.

References to *Intention* (Oxford: Basil Blackwell, 1957) are to the second edition (1963), and are by section number, and then paragraph number (e.g. '17.2'). References to Anscombe's papers are to the *Collected Papers*, (Oxford: Basil Blackwell, 1981), Vol. I–III.

[2] Compare also 'Modern Moral Philosophy' op. cit. Vol. III, p. 29, para 14; *Intention* 39.1–2, 41.1; *Collected Papers* Vol. Ill, introduction p. viii.

four concepts mentioned in 'Modern Moral Philosophy', it is only the concept 'pleasure' that is left

> 'in its obscurity; it needs a whole enquiry to itself' (*Intention* 40.4, p. 77).

In this paper I *explore* the question whether Anscombe's desire to keep ethics out of the 'logical features of practical reasoning' (38.1, p. 72) doesn't lead her to cut those features down too far; whether, that is, there is not more to human action and practical rationality at the *grammatical* level than she seems inclined to concede. And I wish to connect this with her suspicion and criticism of Aristotle's concept of preferential choice (*prohairesis*).

Part 1

In *Intention* section 5 Anscombe asks:

> 'What distinguishes actions which are intentional from those which are not? The answer that I shall suggest is that they are the actions to which a certain sense of the question 'Why?' is given application; the sense is of course that in which the answer, if positive, gives *a reason for acting*. But this is not a sufficient statement, because the question "What is the relevant sense of the question 'Why?'?" and "What is meant by 'reason for acting'?" are one and the same.' (5.1, p. 9).

Anscombe then sets out to characterize this sense of 'Why?'—to show where it has application and where it does not (cf. 6.1).

Here Anscombe takes as non-controversial the closeness between an action's being intentional and its being done for a reason. Indeed one might suppose that, in the above quotation, Anscombe is equating that sense of 'Why?' she seeks to elucidate with that of there being a reason for acting: that you are acting intentionally if, and only if, you have a reason for acting. That would be a misinterpretation. She is claiming that an action is intentional where a certain sense of 'Why?' *is granted application*, that sense being one where the answer *if positive* gives a reason for acting. The answer may *not* be positive—and *yet* not be a rejection of the question.[3] Thus the answer may be 'I just did, for no particular reason' (18.1; 20.6; 21.2; 38.3;), or 'I just am, that's all' (20.1; 20.5) or 'I just thought I would' (17.2; 18.1; cf. 44 case (a)).[4]

[3] 'The answers to the question 'Why?' which give it an application are, then, more extensive in range than the answers which give reasons for acting.' *Intention* 18.6; cf. 17.2.

[4] Differently tensed versions of the same answer, yet apparently not to be aligned simply with past, present and future. For example, while 'No reason—I just thought I would' can be an answer to a future action—'Why are you going to Brazil next year?'—it can also occur in answer to 'Why are you φ-ing' or 'Why did you φ?'. (It is to be distinguished from such locutions as the following: 'why are you standing in line?' 'I just thought *I would like* to go to next week's concert.' This gives the intention with which the action is done.)

There are other non-positive answers, such as 'it was an impulse' or 'it was an idle action—I was just doodling' (17.2). Again the response 'I don't know why I did it' can, I think, be used in much the same way as 'for no particular reason, I just did', i.e. with the implication that there wasn't much, if anything, by way of reason (cf. also 'I don't know why; I just did')—but where perhaps there is usually a reason and so a positive answer was expected (17.3).

What of replies like 'because I (just/really) feel/felt like it', or 'because I (just/really) want/wanted to'? These can express a variety of things (cf. 51). They can be used rather like 'I just did': doesn't one sometimes say

So, firstly, Anscombe wants to allow that an action may be intentional yet done for no reason. But, secondly, although there are such 'non-positive' answers, they could not, she argues, be the *only* ones; on the contrary

> 'the occurrence of other answers to the question "Why?" besides ones like "I just did", is essential to the existence of the concept of an intention or voluntary action' (*Intention* 20.9; cf. 21.2).

In particular there must be such things as (a) expressions of intention for the future, where you cite a future goal ('I am going to φ'), and (b) further intentions in acting—as when you say you are φ'ing *with the intention of*, or *for the sake of*, or *in order to*, ψ, revealing the rational order or structure of your actions (actual or projected). If so, the concept of intention has the kind of unity that Anscombe claims for it in the first paragraph of *Intention*.[5]

'for no reason—I just felt like it' (although see 51.2–3)? But they can also be used to put one's action in the light, or context, of an urge, or a whim or a taste ('Why on earth are you eating a *Marmite* sandwich?'. 'I really felt like one' (*pace* perhaps Anscombe 51.2)). There are cases where such replies may be positive answers to 'Why?' and so offer reasons for action (cf. 35.3—5). This area is very complex, with its differently nuanced locutions (cf. the difference between 'just' and 'really').

[5] See *Intention* 1.1. Without these other uses (a) and (b), Anscombe feels (much of) the point of the concept would be lost. The argument of *Intention* 20 tries to make good on this claim and deserves more consideration than Anscombe's opponents allow (e.g. J. D. Velleman, *Practical Reflection* (Princeton: Princeton University Press, 1989), 112–113). That we talk *of* intention in these various contexts is no accident, and to concentrate on just one such context may lead us into falsity. (*In abstracto* the question whether we are dealing with one or more

As regards the first point above, one can worry, as Scott MacDonald does,[6] whether replies like 'for no reason' don't really mean 'for no *good* reason' or 'for nothing much of a reason' (or perhaps 'for no further reason')—and that all intentional actions are, as indeed the etymology might suggest, end-bent (or end-directed): that is, done for the reason of—in the intent of—the end to which they are aimed.

Scott MacDonald may be correct about many occurrences of those expressions. Yet there seem also cases where prima facie the agent acts intentionally but for no reason. There are, for example, the kind of actions done in or out of emotions that Rosalind Hursthouse investigates in her paper 'Arational Actions'.[7] One might, I suppose, object that many of these are not 'really' actions at all, but 'just' expressions of some emotion. Yet why can't an emotion be vented in an *action*, such as throwing plates, or ruffling someone's hair,

concepts lacks sense; we need to know what game of 'individuating concepts' we are playing).

I take it that expressions of intention for the future and intentions-with-which are fairly obviously closely connected. When asked why I am standing in line, I say 'I'm going to see Verdi's Macbeth': this is the expression of a future goal or end I have set myself; but clearly it is close to the reply 'in order to see Verdi's Macbeth'. Of course this is not always the case. One can express intentions for the future—one's goals—without having yet set about doing anything to secure them or having much, or indeed any, idea of what steps one is going to take in order to realize them.

[6] S. MacDonald, 'Ultimate Ends in Practical Reasoning', *Philosophical Review*, C, No. 1 (1991), 39.

[7] R. Hursthouse, 'Arational Actions', *Journal of Philosophy*, LXXXVIII, No. 2 (1991), 57–68.

or an exasperated slamming of a door?[8] (To reply, 'Look either these are to no end, and so not intentional actions, or they are to some end, even if only that of the expression of the emotion', would just reveal the grip of the commitment[9]). Or, to take a rather different kind of example from those considered by Hursthouse, consider a case of advanced fiddling: while talking to you I arrange some matchsticks in the form of a house. If asked why, I reply 'Oh, no reason, I just did'.[10] (Interestingly, here I may give positive answers to 'Why?' asked about the 'constitutive parts' of this—e.g. if asked why I put that match there, I might reply 'to represent a window').

But either way a more or less tight conceptual connection is kept between Anscombe's 'Why?' and 'reason for

8 Cf. *Intention* 20.4, p. 32. Perhaps Anscombe would regard some of these cases as involving backward looking motives rather than intentions, or motives in general: cf. 13 passim. The area here is very complex, and, as Anscombe says, needs a fuller investigation of motive. (For example, does acting *out of* E—where E is some emotion—always signify a motive? And what contrasts are there between this form of expression and doing something 'in E' or 'E-ly'?).

9 And it offers no reason to accept it. (Of course one could take it as an instruction about linguistic use—a stipulation to the effect that one is not to count, or that the speaker doesn't count, an action as 'intentional' unless it is end-bent. But then such instruction is not *a propos*).

10 I call this a case of advanced fiddling because it is not, I think, a case of the sort of fiddling that Anscombe would regard as voluntary rather than intentional—a mere physical movement (e.g. twiddling one's thumbs or strumming with one's fingers): see *Intention* 49, p. 89. Clearly I was arranging the matches in the form of a house with door and windows etc.

action': for where positive, the answer will give a reason for action, and the above quarrel is over whether all answers are really in effect 'positive' ones.

However my current worry about the closeness Anscombe sees between an action's being intentional and its being done for a reason is not over this sort of case, but rather over ones where there is clearly a positive answer to Anscombe's 'Why?'.[11]

So, here I am, fat and fifty, most concerned to lose weight and stay around to discharge my parental responsibilities for some years to come, yet suddenly really wanting—in the sense of *craving*—a chocolate ice cream, forbidden item. To get one, I would have to ask one of our hosts where to find an ATM machine to get some cash. So now weakly I decide to ask someone where, say, Professor O'Hear is. They ask why I am looking for him. And—making them regret they ever asked—I truthfully reply: 'I want to find him *in order to* ask him where I can find an ATM machine *in order to* get some cash *in order to* zoom off to the shops *in order to* buy a chocolate ice cream *in order to* wolf it down.' We have here a seemingly rational pattern, or order, of action—of one act being done with the intention of, or for the sake of, another—centred on a goal whose attainment I have decided on. The answer surely gives my reason (or reasons) for looking for Professor O'Hear.

Or does it? Is this really a *reason* to look for him? I shouldn't— and shouldn't by my own lights—be *taking steps* to secure an ice cream to eat. I think it not good—or not

[11] As is also true of Scott MacDonald, op. cit. note 6.

good in my current circumstances—to eat an ice cream. My 'reason' is no reason at all! Yet I am acting intentionally—foolishly, but intentionally: my doctor will censor me, my wife will censor me, even I will censor me—and all the more because I acted intentionally, and quite deliberately—it wasn't a thoughtless impulse, as in a group meal one finds oneself unguardedly eating something one suddenly realizes—putting two bits of life, say sausage and doctor, finally together—is of course one of the things on the doctor's 'no-no' list. But given my situation—my values and beliefs—do I really have a reason to look for Professor O'Hear? I am *not* thinking here of a case of self-deception—where, my judgment temporarily clouded or whatever, I falsely suppose eating the ice cream *the thing to do*! But then if I am not thinking that way, *how* am I thinking of myself, my reasons, and my actions? Do even *I* suppose I have *reason* to seek out Professor O'Hear on such a score? Or do I think: 'no, I am flying in the face of Reason and its pronouncements—the reasons it shows me there are; I have no doubt about what I should do, about what *reasons* there are for me; but I'm going to act against the lot—I'll regret it in the morning, but there it is.'?

There are competing intuitions here. On what I shall call the *Low Road of Reason*, of course I have a reason *why* I am looking for Professor O'Hear, or a reason *to* look for him—not a good reason perhaps, not a reason I am very proud of, but a reason nonetheless— and what it is will appear if you ask me Anscombe's question 'Why?': a question which, after all, I may even answer by saying '*My reason* for looking for Professor O'Hear is. . .'. On the other road—the

High Road of Reason—I do *not*, although (wretch that I am) I decide to go for the ice cream, and to look for Professor O'Hear. Yet given my circumstances and my values, I have no *reason* to pursue this end nor to take any steps to achieve it —not even the step of calculating the steps to achieve it: only reason to resist it, abjure it, abandon it, to put it utterly from me. There *is no* reason to pursue *that* pleasure at *that price,* and *I agree.*[12] Perhaps in a better world—where I am thin and thirty—I would have reason to pursue this end and satisfy this

[12] One retort that it is natural to make here is:

(i) surely your desire gives you *some* reason; or the fact that you would enjoy—or at least that you think you would enjoy—eating the ice-cream gives you *some* reason to pursue it;
(ii) it is simply that, on consideration, you think this outweighed by other reasons;
(iii) but akratically you go along with the defeated reason,
    (a) whether, a la Davidson, on an irrationally drawn 'unconditional best judgment' to the effect that so acting is best;
    (b) or simply on a judgment that this is *a* good, or that there is at least *something* good about so acting.

But, in my case, I think that the fact that I would enjoy eating the ice-cream is no reason at all to pursue that end *in my current circumstances.* Perhaps I even think that the fact that I would, or might, enjoy it in *these* circumstances is even worse! Wouldn't it show a degree of selfishness, and indifference to the welfare of others? etc. (Perhaps I can already predict that the enjoyment will in the event be spoilt by such awareness). I am ashamed even to be thinking of pursuing this course of action, and ashamed to be pursuing it.

Another retort would be to concede that the presence of a desire for the ice-cream doesn't per se give me any reason; but to suppose instead that it is my akratic decision to pursue that end that gives me reason to

craving, and enjoy it. But I am not in that world, and I know it. And in this vein I say: 'Well, there's no reason really for me to be looking for Professor O'Hear. Indeed I shouldn't be: all the reasons are against it. But where is he?'.

We might ask: does this decision and way of acting reveal me as a *rational agent*? Well, aren't there inclinations to say both 'yes' and 'no'? A mere brute, we may think, surely couldn't act like this, setting itself an end at such a distance, plotted and calculated towards—brought by reasoning, or deliberation, within the compass of attainment[13]. Yet this isn't acting on reason!—for isn't that supposed to end you up (or to tend, or to aim, to end you up) with something that you at least *suppose* is good? Surely I don't have reason—any reason—to pursue something I believe rightly to be *bad*, or bad that I pursue. Aren't we inclined to say, in Platonic spirit, that reason's own purpose has been derailed, and its calculative abilities have here been hijacked in the service of appetite?! That we have here a rational agent acting irrationally—as only a rational agent can do?

Now we may suspect that the tension we feel here is fake—a product of some misunderstanding or muddle.

look for Professor O'Hear. After all, if having so decided, I then fail, say, through laziness or incompetent scheduling, to do this, it seems I am open to further criticism. ('Gavin is so hopeless—he can't even be akratic effectively!'). But if I think I don't have reason to decide that way in the first place, is it so obvious that I then have *reason* to take the appropriate means to effect that decision?

[13] Cf. P. Foot, *Natural Goodness* (Oxford: Clarendon Press, 2001), 54 (and the references there to Aquinas).

Perhaps there are simply different uses of 'having a reason'—different conversations that employ it, which have different interests or emphases (say, wider description and justification), and different conditions on there being a reason for an agent to φ. Perhaps we are simply confusing a notion of 'acting on *a* reason' (or having *a* reason to act) with 'acting *on reason*' (or 'acting rationally')—that is, acting on Reason considered as a faculty, i.e. acting in accordance with the standards set by the proper operation of that faculty (the standards of rational agency). However I want to try and preserve the tension for the moment.

Of course matters are further complicated by controversies over how we should conceive of practical rationality and over practical reasonhood—over the conditions for something's being a practical reason for someone to do something.

Here I am only concerned with what can in some general way be regarded as good-centred, or *sub specie boni*, conceptions.

One version of this, which I dub the *Traditional Conception* of practical reasonhood since I think of it as held by Plato, Aristotle, and Aquinas, goes roughly as follows.[14]

Practical reasoners, as such, aim at calculating and then doing what is the best thing open to them to do—they aim at what they *should,* as rational agents, do. That is, they aim at that, doing which, they would be acting, or living,

[14] See further my 'The Rationality of Morality', *Virtues and Reasons,* R. Hursthouse, G. Lawrence and W. Quinn (eds.) (Oxford: Clarendon Press, 1995), passim, but especially 119–47.

well—and this unqualifiedly (*hap-los*) and completely generally (*holos*), and not merely in some partial respect *(kata meros*), such as acting or living healthily.[15] Our actions as practically rational agents are thus *sub specie boni*—in the sense of 'under the aspect or formal description of being *the* good thing to do, or as what would be our acting well unqualifiedly'. In effect this is to say: the formal aim (or function or job) of a Rational Doer is Rational Doing (or a life composed of Rational Doings)—and so their material task is to work out what specifically constitutes Rational Doing—or acting well—so as to Do it. We could equally say: practical reasoners, as such, aim ever to be living and acting *wisely*—to make all their actions wise ones—for such wisdom is success in practical rationality. And best is wisest: for it is irrational to go for a less good action when a better is available. Thus it is a constitutive principle of practical rationality, so conceived, ever to go for what is best to do. Now, on the Traditional Conception, their judgments about what it is wise to do, about what they *should* do in order to be acting well—their *practical evaluations*—are doubly assessable.[16] For their conception of what *ends* are worth pursuing in life, or in this situation, may be erroneous, as also may be what means (constitutive or instrumental) they judge best. Thus if I judge: 'The Xs need cheering up: (so) I should visit them', I may judge falsely because the end I am pursuing (cheering them up) is not a good one (whether in

[15] Cf. Aristotle, *Nicomachean Ethics,* 6.5.1140a25–31

[16] Cf. Aristotle, op. cit. 6.9. 1142b16–28; G. Lawrence, 'The Rationality of Morality', op. cit. note 14, 127–8, 133.

general or in this particular instance—perhaps there is some other end I should rather be pursuing); or I may be wrong about the means to that end (in fact my visit will only depress them further). Now in so judging I am taking the fact that they need cheering up as a *reason* to visit them, (i) My taking it as a reason *shows* that I suppose this *end*—cheering them up—is good and good for me to pursue[17]; I would be acting well in doing something about it—at least so far as the *end* is concerned, (ii) The judgment also shows that I suppose *visiting* them a good way to realize this end[18]. (The course of my deliberations to this judgment will in reverse constitute the justification I offer post hoc, presuming I stand by the action: for it provides the account of why I thought the action good to do, as regards both end and means.)

Now this is a tight notion of practical reason, as comes out when we consider the calculating akratic. Take the akratic seducer. Let us suppose him to judge (rather lamely):

> 'She must fall in love with me: how can I achieve this? Flowers would do it; so, I should send flowers'.

Then in so judging the akratic would be taking this end of making her fall in love with him as a reason to send flowers.

[17] The reason—that they need cheering up—speaks for visiting them as being *the* good thing to do.

[18] This is open not only to technical assessment but also to criticism on other grounds. For other ends and concerns—both those the agent has, and those he should have—are relevant to the correctness of his choice of means. Cf. G. E. M. Anscombe, 'Von Wright on Practical Inference', reprinted in *Virtue and Reason,* op. cit. note 14, 32; G. Lawrence, 'The Rationality of Morality' op. cit. note 14, 134–5.

But, on the above view, this would have the akratic showing that he took the seduction as among the good ends for him to pursue, and that he would be acting well, and wisely, in pursuing it. Yet (*pace* Davidson) our akratic doesn't think this: in fact he thinks this end not good to pursue, not good to do something about attaining—not good to take any means, however effective, to encompass this end he supposes he shouldn't pursue. He doesn't make the above judgment; and so doesn't take the end of seduction as a *practical reason* for sending flowers. Perhaps what he judges is:

> 'She must fall in love with me: etc., so *I'll send* flowers'.

That would show that he accepts that he is going to pursue this end—that this is his aim or intention; and it shows he supposes that such an action is a way to attain that end. But it shows nothing about whether he views the end as good. So 'she must fall in love with me' is not, at least on the above view, being represented as a practical reason—as a reason that supports the action as the one he *should* do, that would be his acting well. And in fact our akratic thinks that it is *not* such a consideration.

But then what is going on? If the seduction is *a* reason for the akratic's acting—for sending flowers—then it is so in some qualified, or different, sense than what, on this view, counts unqualifiedly as a practical reason.

This 'Traditional' conception takes the High Road. By contrast, we can, I think, view Anscombe as offering a deflated—Low Road—version of a good-dependent conception, as follows:

(Al) *Practical Reasoning and the Role of Wanting* At least in cases involving practical reasoning[19], there is something the agent wants— and this in a certain sense of wanting that Anscombe distinguishes from wishing, hoping and the feeling of desire, and which 'cannot be said to exist in a man who does nothing towards getting what he wants' (36.3): a sense of wanting that we could view as a kind of *going for,* or primitive decision to act—'primitive' in the sense of simply being expressed in the action of going for. ('The primitive sign of wanting is *trying to get*' (36.4—5)). This wanting does not come into the reasoning as a premise[20]; rather its role is

> 'that whatever is described in the proposition that is the starting-point of the argument must be wanted in order for the reasoning to lead to any action'. (35.5)[21]

[19] Or where there is the practical syllogism—'which means the same thing' (*Intention* 33.1, pp. 57–8).

[20] Cf. 'Von Wright on Practical Inference', reprinted in *Virtue and Reason,* op. cit. note 14, 6–7. Here Anscombe repeats the point that 'the wanting *or intention of the end'* ought not to figure in the premises (note the gloss). (She adds a qualification about a way in which a desire may come in as a premiss, attributed to Anselm Müller).

[21] Thus an initial putative example of practical reasoning

> 'I want a Jersey cow; there are good ones in the Hereford market, so I'll go there '(*Intention* 34.1)

is seen to be incorrect ('formally misconceived', 35.5). It should run simply:

> 'They have Jersey cows in the Hereford market, so I'll go there' (35.5).

(**A2**) *The Proper First Premise: The Desirability Characterization of the Object Wanted* Now sometimes one can ask 'What do you want x for?' (37.1; 38.4; 40.4; cf. 34.3), or 'What for?', or 'What's the good of it?' (39.2; 40.4). Thus if I reason 'They have Jersey cows in Hereford market, so I'll go there', this shows *that* I want one or more Jersey cows, but not *why;* and so it naturally raises—*gives place for*—the question: 'what do you want Jersey cows for?'. The chain of 'Why's' in answer to this will come to an end when we reach what we can regard as strictly a 'proper first premise' (37.6). For this proper first premise characterizes the thing wanted as in some way desirable (37.1)—i.e. as falling under a *desirability characterization,* and this 'makes an end of the questions "What for?"' (38.1).[22] So:

> 'Any premise if it really works as a first premise in a bit of "practical reasoning", contains a description of something wanted; but with the intermediary premises, the question "What do you want that for?" arises—until at last we reach the desirability characterization, about which "What do you want that for?" does not arise, or if it is asked *has not the same point,* as we saw in the 'suitable food' example.'[23] (38.4, pp. 73–4)

And here the question 'What for?' is in place: for we do not have a proper first premise with a desirability characterization (cf.35.6; 38.4)—but only 'an intermediate premise'.

22 Presumably there are also undesirability characterizations, although Anscombe does not, I think, mention them.

23 The reference is back to 35.6 where Anscombe contrasts the two propositions, 'They have some good Jerseys in the Hereford market' and 'Dry food suits any man' on the ground, in effect, that the former is

> 'Aristotle would seem to have held that *every* action done by a rational agent was capable of having its grounds set forth up to a premise containing a desirability characterization; and as we have seen, there is a reasonable ground for this view, *wherever* there is a calculation of means to ends, or of ways of doing what one wants to do.' (38.2, pp. 72—3, my emphases)

And here Anscombe thinks, as she says in the next paragraph (38.3), Aristotle's only mistake is a failure 'to cover the case of "I just did, for no particular reason"'. But in such cases 'there is no calculation, and therefore no intermediate premises. . .about which to press the question "What for?"'; this kind of action exists yet, 'here of course there is no desirability characterization' (38.3). This suggests, then, that *wherever* there is a purpose at all, the demand for a desirability characterization is correct (cf. 38.3.fin):

> '. . ."What's the good of it?" is something that can be asked until a desirability characterization has been reached and made intelligible.' (39.2)

—i.e. a proper first premise (cf. 40.4).

an intermediate premise—one for which the question 'What for?' can sensibly be raised, while the latter is a proper first premise where the question can't sensibly be raised: if it *is* raised, it

> 'means, if anything "Do give up thinking about food as suitable or otherwise"—as said e.g. by someone who prefers people merely to enjoy their food or considers the man hypochondriac'

Let me append to this general point about the proper first premise and *the role* of desirability characterizations, three others:

(a) First, the chain up to a desirability characterization is not plausibly to be thought of as an actual mental process, but rather as revealing a rational order, 'an order which is there whenever actions are done with intentions' (42.2).

(b) Second, what sort of things are desirability characterizations? Generally speaking, these are things where the enquiry, 'What's the good of it?', 'is not a sensible one' (39.2; 35.6; 37.5; 38.4; 40.4) ('or if it is asked has not the same point'). That is, they purport to make a want intelligible. Anscombe gives as examples of such desirability characterizations Aristotle's terms '"should" [*dei*], "suits" [*sumpherei*], "pleasant" [*hedu*]' (37.5; 35.1; 35.2.); 'befits' (38.1.);[24] she generalizes from this: 'or some other evaluative term' (35.2); and gives as other examples 'digestible and wholesome' (37.6), 'fun' (38.2; 40.4).

I think it is *mistaken* to suppose that 'should' and 'fun' belong in the same list here[25]. In fact I think it a mistake

[24] By 'suits' Anscombe seems to mean Aristotle's '*sumpheron*', which may be equally be translated 'beneficial' or 'advantageous'. By 'befits' Anscombe perhaps intends Aristotle's '*prepei*'.

[25] I wonder whether Anscombe's (mis-)treatment of 'should' here isn't connected with her distance from the Traditional conception—where

to regard 'should' as a desirability characterization at all: it hardly seems a form or aspect of goodness! More apposite is Aristotle's remark in *NE* 2.3

> 'There are three things with a view to takings [*haireseis*], and three with a view to avoidances [*phugas*]—noble [*kalon*], beneficial ["suitable": *sumpheron*], pleasant, their opposites, ugly/ignoble, harmful, painful,. . .' (1104b30–2).[26]

It is 'noble' that goes along with 'beneficial' and 'pleasant'. 'Should', like 'ought', I regard as 'incomplete' in this sense that their form is rather 'X should/ought to ϕ: R' where R gives the reason[27]. 'Should' indicates that there is reason, but not what the reason is.

This point about 'should' is important, because there is a different way to look at Aristotle's view of practical deliberation and the practical syllogism: this is to take proper practical reasoning (*bouleusis*) as reasoning that issues in *Praxis* in a narrow sense of *chosen action,* to which we shall turn in a moment. For this is marked by

'should' (or similar locutions) play a distinctive role as characterizing unqualified, or proper/strict, practical evaluations.

[26] Cf. *NE* 3.4.1113a31ff; 8.2.1155bl8–27, *'trion d' onton di' ha philousin,. . .'.*

[27] Cf. 'The Rationality of Morality', op. cit. note 14, 115; 125 (cf. also my 'Reflection, Practice, and Ethical Scepticism' *Pacific Philosophical Quarterly* **74**, No. 4 (December 1993), 341-2). Equally we could say: with a 'should' claim, the question '*Why* should I?' is always in place (except when the answer is already obvious): cf. P. Geach, 'Goodness and Evil', reprinted in *Theories of Ethics,* P. Foot (ed.) (Oxford: Oxford University Press, 1967), 70.

the presence of a 'should' ('*dei*') in the conclusion (e.g. *NE* 1.2.1094a24; 7.8.1151a20–4).[28]

(c) Third, the agent can of course be mistaken about whether the thing conceived to fall under some desirability characterization actually does so, but nonetheless

> 'the good. . .conceived by the agent to characterize the thing must *really* be one of the many forms of good.' (*Intention* 40.1)

This strikes me as a hard remark—since some of the candidate desirability characterizations (some would-be forms of good) are controversial in themselves, and not simply in their applications: the Puritans mightn't think much of 'fun', nor Thrasymachus of 'just'; indeed for Thrasymachus 'unjust' is rather the desirability characterization.[29]

(A3) *Wanting sub specie boni (Under the aspect of* **some** *good)* As the question 'What's the good of it?' indicates, we are to think of the various desirability characterizations as *forms of good*;

[28] On this view, the so called 'syllogism of appetite' at *NE* 7.3.1147a31–35 is not a practical syllogism—a piece of *practical* calculation: cf. the contrast with akrasia of anger at 7.6.1149a32–5.

[29] What may be a desirability characterization for one person may not be for another—and so what may be a proper first premise for one might be an intermediate premiss for another. This seems clearer in 'On Promising and its Justice', op. cit. note 1, Vol. III, 19–20, with its distinction between premise and principle of inference.

> '*Bonum est multiplex*: good is multiform, and all that is required for our concept of 'wanting' is that a man should see what he wants *under the aspect of some good*'. (39.2, p. 75[30])

[30] 'should see what he wants *under the aspect of some good*' seems to be ambiguous at least between:

(1) the agent in wanting must conceive the object, or action, wanted as being good in *some* respect or other (e.g. pleasant, etc);
(2) the agent in wanting must conceive the object or action wanted as desirable under some aspect—e.g. pleasant—that is in fact a form of goodness. (Cf. 40.1 (pp. 76–7), quoted above: '. . .the good (perhaps falsely) conceived by the agent to characterize the thing must *really* be one of the many forms of good.')

Under (2) the agent need not conceive that what they find attractive in this case is good in this case: e.g. the akratic in finding the proposed seduction pleasant need not think its pleasantness is *in this case* good, although pleasure is indeed a form of goodness.

(2) is weaker than (1); but both are stronger than:
(3) the agent in wanting must conceive the object or action as desirable or attractive in some way—but not in a way that need either be thought good by them, or be a form of goodness (or be falsely thought to be).

So, for instance, someone might say:

> 'After what they did to my child, I just want to make them suffer—I want them to feel excruciating pain, to know what it's like to be on the receiving end. And I am going to take steps to see that they do. But I don't think there's anything good about my objective. The thought gives me *no* pleasure or satisfaction of any kind—I just want them to suffer and am going to see that they do. Call it a form of destructiveness if you like.'

Indeed, given this example, (3) also might be too strong depending on how exactly we understand 'desirable or attractive'.

I am suspicious of (1) and (2) myself.

Not all reasons for action give the intention (or objective) with which the action was done (cf. remark (d) at 12.6). Some reasons are backward-looking motives, as in the above cases of revenge and

And, as is indicated by the fact that Anscombe takes the question 'What's the good of it?' to be equivalent to 'What do you want X for?', there is a conceptual connexion between 'wanting' ('in the sense which we have isolated...')

gratitude (cf. 13; 14). Others are motives-in-general which in effect offer an interpretation of the action: 'see the action in this light' (13.2; 13.4), as in the example of admiration (or perhaps 'I was really angry, so I left the room'). (However motives, if they are forward-looking, are intentions: 13.5). I take it that it is sometimes clear, sometimes grey, whether a motive-in-general offers a reason or not (consider for example the reply 'I was bored').

So not only are there intentional actions where there is no reason for action, there are reasons for action—*positive* answers to the Anscombian 'Why?'—which, while revealing the action to be intentional, are not themselves intentions with which the action is done.

Two further complexities.

First, what of replies like 'I just feel/felt like it' or 'I just want/wanted to'? One might assimilate them to cases of offering an interpretation of the action (motive-in-general)—'see it in the light of a whim or impulse' (cf. 17.4); or else to cases like 'I just thought I would' (44.2. case (a)), which Anscombe seems to view as a variant on 'I just did, for no particular reason'. There may be cases of both; or we may think rather of a sliding scale, from cases where we take such a reply as a *positive* response, giving us the agent's reason, and to ones where we take it as accepting the question but claiming there was in effect no reason, passing through a range of 'grey' cases. (See further 51).

Second, how does Anscombe suppose these cases stand with regard to desirability characterizations? Do all positive reasons involve desirability characterizations? It would seem not. Wherever there is a *purpose* the demand for a desirability characterization is correct (38.3); but not all reasons are purposes, as is clear from the cases considered above (21.1 is a bit misleading on this point).

But these complexities need their own discussion.

and 'good' (Sec 40.1): what you want X for is a matter of what good you conceive it as being.

(A4) So, to sum up, Anscombe

(i) allows that there are intentional actions done for no reason, and 'here of course there is no desirability characterization' (38.3);

(ii) but at least for those intentional actions that involve practical reasoning, she holds a form of *sub specie boni* conception—for she holds that the agent must be conceiving of their goal (the thing wanted) as falling under some form of good.[31] But this is a deflationary form of that conception not simply in its scope (viz. that there are intentional actions that fall outside it)[32]. It is deflationary also in taking the *'boni* of the Latin tag as

[31] Anscombe countenances other cases besides (i) and (ii). That is, (iii) there are intentional actions for which the agent has a reason—i.e. Anscombe's 'Why?' gets a *positive* answer—but where the action does *not* involve practical reasoning or practical calculation ('not everything that I have described as coming in the range of "reasons for acting" can have a place as a premise in a practical syllogism.' 35.3): see 35.3–5 (cf. 5.2; 14.1; 14.5). Some examples: 'He killed my father, so I shall kill him'; 'he was very pleasant, so I shall visit him'; 'I admire him so much, <so> I shall sign the petition' (or 'X did such-and-such, so I shall sign the petition', 13.2); 'I want this, so I'll do it'. ('The conjunction "so" is not necessarily a mark of calculation').

[32] The Traditional Conception, as I interpret that, equally allows that there are such cases of intentional action. (See e.g. J. McDowell 'The Role of *Eudaimonia* in Aristotle's Ethics', in *Essays on Aristotle's Ethics*, Rorty, A. O. (ed.) (Berkeley: University of California Press, 1980), 360–1.)

governed by the indefinite rather than the definite article: 'under the aspect of *some* good' rather than 'under the aspect of *the* good'.[33]

On this 'deflationary'—Low Road—conception of the *sub specie boni* view of practical reason, the case of the calculating akratic is not, I think, so obviously problematic, at least not in the way it was on the full 'Traditional Conception'. We can ask 'why do you want X?' all the way presumably to a proper first premise of 'well, eating an ice cream would be pleasant—or rather naughty' (an English desirability characterization). What I cite in answer to this Anscombian 'Why?' are the intentions with which I act—and aren't they my reasons for acting as I do?[34] There only has to be something I think good about it—I don't have to think of it as the good thing to do, or as acting well.

This seems a very thinned down, minimal, view of practical reasoning and rationality, constructed, it seems, out of the elements of wanting, a desirability characterization ('under the form of some good'), and the 'A *in order to* B' relation (i.e. having an end, wanting something, *at a distance).*

33 Do not be misled by the question 'What's *the* good of it?'. Anscombe could equally have phrased the question she is asking as: 'What good is it?', 'What's it good for?' or 'What's its point?'.

34 A problem could be still be raised however over the possibility of a gap between the notion of a desirability characterization and that of 'some form of good'. Can I not be attracted by some aspect (e.g. 'fun') that I think of as not good at all: a Puritan whose feet want to dance? (cf. note 30).

Now it is possible of course for someone to have what Anscombe calls, in *Intention*, 'a principal aim' (39.2, p. 75), and, in 'On Promising and its Justice', 'a main purpose' (pp. 19—20)—such as health or pleasure, or happiness (or rather some 'substantive' conception of that[35]). But this appears just as *one case* among all the others of a wanted end giving rise to reasons.

> 'But when a man aims at health or pleasure, then the enquiry 'What's the good of it?' is not a sensible one.'

—not sensible because these are desirability characterizations—

> 'As for reasons against a man's making one of them his principal aim; and whether there are orders of human goods, e.g. whether some are greater than others, and whether if this is so a man need ever prefer the greater to the less, and on pain of what; this question would belong to ethics, if there is such a Science.' (*Intention* 39.2, pp. 75—6)

A footnote is added to 'prefer the greater to the less', viz.

[35] 'It may be that in some sense everyone wishes for happiness; but that is not enough to make it true that everyone has a main purpose. For, firstly, what people wish for they do not necessarily try to get [cf. *Intention* 36.1–2], and secondly, if one is trying to get happiness this may consist in trying to get something the possession of which one believes will be happiness, and *only in having such a substantive aim can one be said to have a main purpose.'*
('On Promising and its Justice', op. cit. note 1, Vol. III, 20, my emphasis).

> 'Following Hume, though without his animus, I of course deny that this preference can be as such "required by reason", in any sense.' (p.76)

So it belongs to ethics to evaluate and criticize the various substantive targets that people take as their principal aims. But it is also suggested that the question whether one even should have a principal aim also belongs to ethics—and is not something that can be required by reason, or be matter of practical rationality. This contrasts with the Traditional Conception where the rational need for a structuring of this sort is taken as among 'the logical features' of practical reasoning.

Anscombe's deflationary, Low Road, account of having a reason is, I believe, of a piece with her attack on 'ancient and medieval philosophers' in *Intention* 21 (pp. 33—4).

> '[A] Ancient and medieval philosophers—or some of them at any rate—regarded it as evident, demonstrable, that [**TI**] human beings must always act with some end in view, and [**T2**] even with some one end in view. The argument for this strikes us as rather strănge. [1] Can't a man just do what he does, a great deal of the time? He may or may not have a reason or a purpose; and [2] if he has a reason or purpose, it in turn may just be what he happens to want; why demand a reason or purpose for *it*) and [3] why must we at last arrive at some *one* purpose that has an intrinsic finality about it? [B] The old arguments were designed to show that the chain could not go on for ever; they pass us by, because we are not inclined to think it *must* even begin; and it can surely stop where it stops, no need to stop at a purpose that

> looks intrinsically final, one and the same for all actions. [C] In fact there appears to be an illicit transition in Aristotle, from "all chains must stop some-where" to "there is somewhere where all chains must stop".' (my numbers and letters added)

Anscombe here claims against **TI** and **T2** that:

(1) chains need not even begin—we sometimes do things for no particular reason (cf. 21.2)
(2) they can stop where they stop, where this may be with something the person merely happens to want—as, for example, if I go to the kitchen in order to make a cup of tea, just because I feel like drinking some;
(3) the chains need not stop with anything intrinsically final; thus I might put the kettle on in order to make myself a cup of tea, where that was my end; but that is not intrinsically final—I might have made myself a cup not because I felt like one but with some further intention, say, in order to keep myself awake.
(4) And *a fortiori* it need not be the case that the chains all end at one and the same intrinsic final end (whether this single ultimate goal is viewed as one that can differ from individual to individual, or supposed one and the same in the case of all agents, or of all human agents).

As I said, I want to ignore the 'lower end' question, **TI**—of whether Aristotle thinks all intentional actions are for an end, and so fails to acknowledge the class of actions done 'for no particular reason'" (cf. 21.2; 38.3). What I am interested in is the second thesis, **T2**—that human beings must always act with some one end in view— at least under a certain interpretation of that. On this interpretation

(1) Aristotle's claim is not that *all,* or all intentional, actions are for some one end—the calculating akratic's action is after all for an end that the agent thinks they should not be pursuing. The claim concerns all *chosen,* or *prohairetic,* actions—*Praxeis* in that tighter sense of action made explicit in *NE* 6.2 but that runs through *NE* Bk. 1.[36] Aristotle's idea is the idea of an overarching rational order to human actions in this tight sense. That is, fully rational actions exhibit such a structure. They are 'united' under a single end—the end of all being cases of what the agent considers *acting well* (or acting wisely).
(2) Secondly, the sense in which human beings 'must' so act is not any causal or logical necessity, but rather a rational one—must on pain of irrationality.[37] That is, because of what practical rationality is, human beings must so act if they are to be (fully) practically rational.

[36] Cf. J. McDowell, 'The Role of *Eudaimonia* in Aristotle's Ethics', op. cit. note 32, sections 1–6, especially 4; G. Lawrence 'The Function of the Function Argument', *Ancient Philosophy* 21 (2001), 459; and Scott MacDonald op. cit. note 6, in connection with Aquinas.

[37] Cf. 'The Rationality of Morality', op.cit. note 14, 131–2. Anscombe perhaps opposes the 'ancient and medievals' both because she is thinking that the claims are about *all* actions and so obviously false, and because the 'must' they have in mind is a logical necessity ("demonstrable").

> If you fail to do what you think would be acting well, then you look to be acting irrationally.[38]

Now I think it is in line with, or part of, her rejection of the High Road of reason that Anscombe criticizes Aristotle's conception of *prohairesis.* And to this criticism I now turn, in order eventually to come back to the notion of the High Road of reason.

Part 2

Aristotle's 'choice'—or preferential choice—is a taking of one thing before, or rather than, another for the sake of an end, where that end is the unconditionally final end of practical reason, the good of man. This end Aristotle takes to be identified at least nominally as *eudaimonia,* or, synonymously, living well (*euzoia*), or doing well (*eupraxia*),[39] This interpretation of *prohairesis* is controversial[40]. But it is

[38] That chosen actions aim at some one end—the human good, or acting or living well, as the agent conceives that—is a definitional thesis stemming from the account of choice. It has a role as a normative principle.

[39] This is a matter of living or doing well *in general* (*to eu zen holos*), and not merely in some specific aspect of life, such as health or fitness (cf. *NE* 6.5.1140a25–31; 6.9.1142b28–33).

[40] David Charles, for example, argues against it, in favour of no such limitation on the end that is in question in 'choice' (*Aristotle's Philosophy of Action* (London: Duckworth, 1984), 151–55.

the one to which Anscombe subscribes[41]. She casts it in the following terms: Aristotle's choice is for the objects of a person's *will* (*boulesis*)[42], where Aristotle limits these objects to the agent's 'idea of good work' or the kind of life they want to lead; in short, choice is a decision where that has 'in view what one thinks of as a good way of proceeding in one's life'.[43]

This concept is, Anscombe thinks, an 'artificial' one (*Intention* 40.4, n2, p. 77). In 'Thought and Action in Aristotle', she remarks:

> 'The notion of "choice" as conceived by Aristotle, his *prohairesis,* is a very peculiar one. I used to think it spurious. If it had been a winner, like some other Aristotelian concepts, would not "prohairetic" be a word as familiar to us as "practical" is?' (p. 71)

But while she no longer thinks it 'spurious' (nor 'a misconception', 'Promising and its Justice', p. 20), yet nonetheless '"choice"' she complains, 'cannot do all the work Aristotle wants to make it do.' ('Thought and Action in Aristotle', p. 71); and in similar vein, in 'On Promising and its Justice', she objects that he

[41] See 'Thought and Action in Aristotle', op. cit. note 1, Vol. I, 69–70; also 'On Promising and its Justice', op. cit. note 1, Vol III, 20:

> 'Aristotle's conception of "choice" is one according to which a man chooses to do only those actions which are governed by a main purpose;. . .'

She is followed by John McDowell, op.cit. note 32, 361 and footnote 6.

[42] Not a translation I agree with, for instance because of *NE* 3.2. 1111b 19-26. 'Wish' or 'rational wish' is better.

[43] 'Thought and Action in Aristotle', op. cit. note 1, Vol. I, 70.

> 'tried to make this concept of choice occupy the place in the analysis of action that ought to be occupied by the concept of intention.' (p.20)[44].

The nub of her complaint is exhibited in the case of the *calculating akratic* who occurs in Aristotle's discussion of *euboulia,* goodness at deliberation, in *NE* 6.9. *Euboulia,* Aristotle says, is a kind of correctness of deliberation, but not just every kind of correctness (1142b16–18); 'for', he goes on,

> 'the akratic and the bad man [*phaulos*] will as a result of calculation [*ek tou logismou*] hit on what they propose [*ho protithetai*] *if they are clever*[45], so that they will have deliberated correctly, but have obtained a great evil.'

The kind of correctness of deliberation at issue in *euboulia* is one where *to have deliberated well* or correctly is a good because it hits on something good (*'agathou teuktike')*. By contrast, in the cases of the calculating akratic and the bad man, their having deliberated 'well' or 'correctly' is not something good: it just succeeds in delivering something bad. (This kind of 'correctness of deliberation' Aristotle calls cleverness, '*deinotes*'[46].) Aristotle

[44] Cf. *Intention* 40.4, n2, p. 77. 'Aristotle's use of an artificial concept of "choice", where I use "intention", in describing "action", . . .'

[45] Reading *'ei demos'* with Ross at 1142bl9: cf.7.10.1152alo.

[46] Compare *NE* 6.12.1144a23–6:

> 'So there is a power/faculty which they call cleverness; and this is such as to be able to do those things that conduce to the target that has been proposed [*ton hupotethenta skopon*], i.e. to hit on them.'

(Reading *'autōn'* with the codd and Burnet, rather than Bywater's *'autou'*.)

here portrays a bad person and a kind of akratic as *parallel* in their calculations: each sets up some same end as one to achieve, and calculates how to attain it. How then are they distinct? They differ in that the bad person conceives of the end he sets up as being constitutive of the way to live, of his living well, whereas the akratic precisely does not: on the contrary he supposes that it is not at all the thing to do.[47] And so in doing what they do for this end, the one thinks he is doing what he *should* (*dei*) do, the other does not. In line with this difference, Aristotle holds that the bad person acts on choice—acts *kata prohairesin*—whereas the akratic does *not* (e.g. *NE* 3.2.1111b13–15): on the contrary the akratic acts 'in the

[47] If impulsive, the akratic would think he should not, if he stopped to think; if weak, the akratic does think he shouldn't. Whether Aristotle supposes the weak akratic is fully cognisant of this at the moment of action or has his judgment 'clouded', we can set aside. What is important is that Aristotle does *not* suppose that the akratic's judgment is clouded *in such a way* that he comes to believe—even if only for a short while—that attaining this end *is* after all the way to live; the akratic does not at the moment of action act on a *choice* even if only a temporary or fleeting one. Aristotle explicitly denies that the akratics act on a choice, or hold they should ('*dei*') so act. And this is, I take it, also the point of his remark, in agreement with Socrates, that their knowledge proper is 'not dragged around like a slave'—that is, their values, their general views of what is good and bad in life, are not dragged around, or changed to accommodate their temptations. (Compatibly with this Aristotle could have allowed for self-deception—for cases where the agent does take himself to be acting as he *should* because of the way his perception of the relevant features of the current situation has been (self) manipulated.)

grip of an appetite' (*epithumon*), and so acts on a fit of emotion, *kata pathos*'[48].

Anscombe describes it as follows:

> 'If <the akratic> had been a licentious man, an *akolastos,* the decision to seduce her [some woman] would have been a "choice", and the volition to perform each of the steps that he reckoned would enable him to succeed would in turn each have been a "choice" too. For the decision to seduce this woman was simply the particular application of his *general policy* of pursuing sensual enjoyment. But although the uncontrolled man perhaps reckons how to proceed—once he has given way to the temptation to go after this woman—*in exactly the same way as the licentious man,* his volitions in performing the steps he calculates will enable him to succeed are not "choices". (Aristotle, of course, does not set up a word for "volition" as I have been using it). So we have to say that the uncontrolled man carries out a deliberation how to execute what would have been a 'choice' if he had been an *akolastos*', . . .'

Now Anscombe's complaint is that:

> 'this, however, is something for which Aristotle has no regular name—for he has no general use of a psychological verb or abstract noun corresponding to "*hekousion*" (usually translated "voluntary") as "*prohairesthai*" ("choose"), "*prohairesis*" ("choice") correspond to "*prohaireton*" ("chosen"). Of course he

[48] Cf. *NE* 1.3.1095a4-11,etc.; cf.3.2.111 1b13–15, etc.

> regards the uncontrolled man as acting voluntarily. When he describes this man as calculating cleverly, he says he will get what he "proposes" (*protithetai*); and this verb expresses a volition, or perhaps rather an intention. Aristotle ought, we may say, to have seen that he was here employing a key concept in the theory of action, but he did not do so; the innocent unnoticeable verb he uses receives no attention from him.' ('Thought and Action in Aristotle', op. cit. n1, Vol. I, 68–9)

Or as she puts it later:

> 'The uncontrolled man who has further intentions in doing what he does, whose actions are deliberate, although the deliberation is in the interests of a desire which conflicts with what he regards as doing well—to describe his action we need a concept (our "intention") having to do with will or appetition: not just *epithumia*, "desire", for that may be only a feeling.' (op. cit, 71–2)

Let us try and unpack her complaint.

In a case of immediate, or non-calculating, akrasia, I may see an eclair, crave it, and eat it, before even so much as thinking about what I am doing and whether I should or should not[49]. (If asked even whether I had *decided* to eat it, I may say 'no, I just saw it, wanted it, and ate it'.) There are complexities in the description of this. But for present purposes we may think of it as a case of acting in the light of, or in reaction to, a felt desire (an appetitive desire or craving). When I am asked why I ate it and say 'well, I just had a

49 NB. this is not a case of mindless snacking.

sudden craving for it', I am putting my action in a certain light, as a response to a felt desire.[50]

Now the case of the calculating akratic is very different.[51]

[50] I am here (i) connecting Anscombe's remark that '*epithumia* may be only a feeling' with her remarks about 'wanting' as feelings of desire in *Intention* 36.2–3; and (ii) connecting that with some of the things she says about motives (Section 13). The felt desire may give the context, or light, in which my action occurred.

epithumia, an appetite, 'may be only a feeling'. But is it then sometimes something more? And if so, what? (Is Anscombe thinking that the expression of wanting in the sense of trying to get can sometimes be the expression of an appetite? Might the example of 'I want this, so I'll do it' (*Intention* 35.5, p. 66)—which is not a form of practical reasoning—be the expression of an appetite? But how are we to think of this? Is the 'wanting' here a motive in the light of which, as a response to which, we are to view my action? I feel cold, and so move closer to the fire; I feel parched, and so reach for the glass on the desk. The whole topic of *epithumia* is, I think, extremely difficult.)

[51] The distinction between immediate, or non-calculating, and calculating akratic is not the same as Aristotle's distinction between impulsive and weak akratic. In the former, the distinction turns on whether the akratic act itself is immediate or eise at a distance and so needs to be set up as an end whose attainment requires calculation. In the latter, the distinction turns on whether the akratic has or has not reached a conclusion about what, given their values, they *should* do. (The impulsive does not, the weak does, but then acts in violation of it.)

As a matter of human psychology it may be tempting to align the two distinctions—to suppose that, typically, impulsive akrasia will also be immediate, and immediate impulsive: for if time and calculation are involved in the akratic project then isn't it more likely that the akratic will think about what they are doing, and if they act akratically do so weakly rather than impulsively? But this need not be so. (i) An

(1) The end—the seduction—is set at *some distance* from what the agent can do here and now, and so there is need for practical calculation (cf. *Intention* 41.2). The particular actions that he does in the execution of his project may well not be ones for which he has an appetite (e.g. going out in the rain to buy the flowers and chocolates, perhaps even the calculating, the plotting, itself). They are actions he *decides* on in the light of his deliberation, and does with further intentions. He φ's *in order to* ψ.

(2) And as regards the seduction itself, this is something which he has set up as an end to be attained, something he has *decided on,* or *formed the intention* to bring about, to take steps to encompass: something that he has made his aim (p. 67). It is not enough to appeal to the presence of a desire or craving. To say 'he lusts' can report merely the presence of a feeling—'the prick of desire' (as Anscombe calls it, in *Intention* 36.2–3); one can lust and do nothing towards getting what one wants. The encratic can lust—and get the next plane out of

impulsive akratic could, I take it, set up an end at a distance—'I must have that'—and impulsively Start calculating how to achieve it, and set about doing so, all with-out stopping to think about what they should be doing. (ii) Again there are many cases of akrasia that are immediate yet weak: 'I really shouldn't', I murmur, as I accept your offer of yet another eclair or glass.

Anscombe's distinction turns on the presence or absence of calculation in the akratic project, Aristotle's on the presence or absence of calculation and conclusion about what the agent should do given their values. (Whether reaching this conclusion in fact always involves calculation is a complication we can set aside).

town! The mere presence of a desire does not determine itself as an end to be pursued[52]. There is then a difference between merely having an appetite or a desire, about which one may do nothing, and making its satisfaction an end of action (a decision or an intention). It may be that 'want' can be used to convey both[53]—both to convey that you find yourself with a desire, and to express a '*decided desire*' (or an intention or decision). But the roles at least are different.

So there are cases where an agent φ's with the intention of ψ'ing, or *in order to* ψ—but where they do not view ψ'ing as the way they should be going on: and so they do not act from choice. But then we need a concept 'having to do with will or appetition' (p. 71)—by 'appetition' here I think Anscombe has in mind that sense of 'wanting' she isolates in *Intention* 36.

Anscombe's complaint is, I think, double-barrelled.

One side of this is that the proper description of the calculating akratic's action requires a concept that Aristotle lacks, one 'having to do with will or appetition'. This suggests that there is something that Aristotle lacks the resources to say. Yet Anscombe also claims that in his use of 'propose' (*protithetai*) he is 'here employing a key concept in the theory of action' (p. 69), but failing to appreciate it. This suggests, on the contrary, that Aristotle can say it all

[52] Cf. also the discussion in my 'The Rationality of Morality', op. cit. note 14, pp. 126–7

[53] Cf. *Intention* 36.

right, but doesn't have his attention drawn to the importance of it.[54] Perhaps the idea is that the grammatical configuration of certain Greek concepts in this area—the facts, for example, that Aristotle's Greek does not provide him with, nor does he invent, a verb and abstract noun going with *'hekousion'*, or that *'prohairesis'* has ordinary overtones of 'policy', and so invites Aristotle's delimitation of it to the choice of means to the agent's conception of living well—perhaps the idea is that such facts mean he lacks a ready, or 'regular', means of seeing the proper connections between various cases—cases which he can in a certain way properly describe, but not so as to reveal their unity or family interdependencies. The surface of his language hides these, so to speak. *Prohairesis* covers something of the area of intention—but its limitation only to practical calculation for the end of doing well (as the agent conceives that) is too narrow a focus. Aristotle is left just to describe the calculating akratic's action as *'hekousion'* (voluntary or intentional), which is the same description as for the non-calculating akractic, but this masks their important difference.

We are here in very difficult territory.[55] But let us suppose Anscombe is correct in this first side of her

[54] In fact related talk of 'hypothesizing—or setting up—the end' also occurs elsewhere, and in connection with *demotes:* cf. *NE* 6.12.1144a23–26. Cf. also7.8.1151a15–19.

[55] Not only are these concepts difficult enough in English, but we are trying to compare and criticize across languages, where the languages do not obviously divide up the area along the same fault lines. Thus *'hekousion'* might perhaps characterize actions as 'intentional' (so D. Charles op. cit. note 40, 61–62, 256–61: for reasons against,

criticism, that Aristotle lacks a needed concept—and Aquinas too perhaps thought so[56]. Yet there is a *second* side to her criticism. This is her claim that Aristotle tries to make *choice* fill in this role, that he tries to make it 'occupy the place in the analysis of action that ought to be occupied by the conception of intention', but that it 'cannot do all the work that *Aristotle wants to make it do'*. This accusation is hard to unravel. After all one might have expected her to say: 'it *can* do all the work, if only Aristotle hadn't tied it to the end of doing well'. Her idea seems to be that Aristotle sees something of the need for a concept like 'intention' (or decision), but because he ties his conception of 'choice' to the end of living well, he hobbles it, and there still remains a conceptual need that *prohairesis* cannot, so hobbled, satisfy.

see S. Broadie, *Ethics with Aristotle* (Oxford: Oxford University Press, 1991), p. 174. n 10). Yet there are no ways of expressing an intention for the future or the intention with which an action is done in terms employing *'hekousion'*. Given Anscombe's claims about the unity of the concept of intention and the essential dependence of the characterization of actions as intentional on these other uses of the concept *(Intention* 20), are we to suppose that this means *'hekousion'* is not to be tied to the 'intentional'—or are we to suppose that it is, but depends on the availability of these others uses of intention, which the Greek language indeed makes available, but not in a way that makes this unity explicit on the surface of the language? The conceptual division that a language offers may cover the area but divide it very differently—yet we need not suppose that they 'fail to realize what we realize' (Wittgenstein *Zettel* 380—quoted by Anscombe, 'Linguistic Idealism', op.cit. note 1, Vol. I, 113).

[56] At any rate intention figures into his discussion alongside the voluntary/involuntary and choice: *Summa Theologicae* Ia2ae 6–13

Prohairesis has not now quite the right conceptual shape to fit the whole need.

Now this side of Anscombe's criticism appears to presuppose a view about 'what work' Aristotle does want the concept of *prohairesis* to do. But perhaps there is more philosophical motivation to the shape Aristotle gives *prohairesis* than mere hobbling! One could agree with the first side of Anscombe's complaint without going along with the second.

Aristotle—rightly or wrongly—is approaching things from a very different direction than Anscombe[57]. Anscombe talks as though Aristotle's interest is that of philosophy of action; but his interest— the direction from which he is approaching these issues—is that of *practical philosophy,* philosophy of action maybe but in an already loaded sense of *Praxis.* The fact that Aristotle assimilates the calculating akratic in a certain way to the immediate or non-calculating akratic—rather than to the bad or the wise person (the *phaulos* or *phronimos)*—indicates where Aristotle sees the important fault-line *for his purposes:* that the latter are realizing their values (good or bad) in their lives or shaping their lives by their values, while the former are not. (And we should note that in any case the 'assimilation' does not in fact prevent him from finding the vocabulary to

[57] As she herself admits in *Intention* 42.2, p. 80: but there she supposes there is a basic identity. ('The interest of the account <Aristotle's account of the practical syllogism> is that it describes an order which is there whenever actions are done with intentions. . .'.)

distinguish and up to a point to describe the different cases of non-calculating and calculating akratic). The proper, or formal, aim of practical deliberation is to achieve the human good—a life of action—of *Praxis* in the full-blooded sense: of action that realizes, or is shaped by, the agent's sense of value (of what they take to be good and bad in life). The kind of practical reasoning, or syllogizing, that Aristotle is interested in here is that leading to a conclusion about what the agent *should* do—should do *haplos,* i.e. if they are to be acting or living well. Aristotle, as I read him, marks such Practical conclusions by the presence of 'should' (*dei*)—although there is, I shall suggest, no need to exclude a kind of use of it in the calculating akratic's judgment.

So what I am proposing is this. The distinction that Aristotle wants to use *prohairesis* to mark—the 'work' he wants it to do—is that between *praxis* and *Praxis*—between action that is merely intentional (or action considered merely as intentional) and action that is not only intentional (*hekousion*), but is *valued* by the agent— or expresses, or is shaped by, the agent's values[58]: that is, Proper Human Action, that is chosen by the agent as being what he considers to be acting well or living well in the Situation, as what he *should*—unqualifiedly should—be doing (given his beliefs about how best, or most wisely, to live). These are

[58] A description or judgment of character is primarily one concerning the agent's stance re values—a characterization of the condition of their will. (Animals don't have character in this way, but only natural dispositions.)

the actions which the agent Stands behind, and holds justified.[59]

One could say this is an 'artificial' concept to this extent perhaps, that while there is an ordinary use of the question 'but did you *choose* to do it?' in the sense of 'were you doing what you thought you *should* be doing, what you took to express your values?', there are also other ordinary but looser uses of 'choice': so there is, in Aristotle, a somewhat technical or artificial delimitation of the notion of 'choice'. It is being reserved to mark this distinction between *praxis* and *Praxis.* But the distinction that it marks seems ordinary and intuitive. (That is not to say that it is ultimately sound, nor even that as it stands it is unproblematic.)

[59] One could see in this difference between Anscombe and Aristotle a 'battle of wills'. That is, there are conflicting pressures on how to conceptualize the will.

(1) One pressure is to connect the will with a decison to act, or the agent's setting themselves an end to pursue.
(2) A different pressure connects the will with the pursuit of an end that the agent 'stands behind'—sees *as* good, as the thing they should pursue, as expressing themselves and their values.

The case of the calculating akratic exposes the tension between these pressures.

If one views 'the will'—not psychologically but grammatically—as a matter of certain kinds of question being in place, and certain conversations, then there need not be any problem about allowing for different conceptions of 'the' will.

Part 3

The difference between Low and High Roads of the *sub specie boni* conception—between Anscombe's deflationary version and the Traditional Conception itself—can be framed as one of whether 'a reason for acting' properly attaches to intentional action (at least where the answer to the Anscombian 'Why?' is positive), or to Aristotelian chosen action (*Praxis* in the tight sense).

3.1. Three Options

There are at least three options here.

(1) *The Low Road Dominant* One could try and argue that the High Road of reason is an artificial, philosophically induced, product, and that really all there is—at least at the level of philosophy of psychology and action, as against ethics—is the Low Road. This seems to be Anscombe's position. Of course some people do have main purposes, and some have main purposes that are ethical (in the sense of moral)—but discussion of how things ought to be in this area seems a matter for ethics 'if there is such a science'—something to be approached only when we are armed with the basic under-standing of action provided by *Intention*.[60]

[60] Cf. note 2. That is, one may be leery of the inclination to build in more structure—to suppose that it is for a human always to act with some one end in view—sensing in this a wishfulness to secure ethics by writing it into philosophy of psychology (cf. *Intention* 39.1).

(2) *Two Different Roads* One could abandon any notion of dominance, and think simply that what we have here are just different issues—different perspectives of interest. There are many questions 'Why?', many puzzles, many kinds of reason—of '*ratio*' (of accounts or explanations). You could be interested in whether an action is *intentional* or not: in *what,* if anything, is going on, in *what* someone is after or up to. Alternatively, you could be interested in whether it is *rational or* not, and take the Standards of its rationality to be what the agent, *qua* rational, *should* do: i.e. whether in so acting they would be *acting well,* taking this to be success in practical rationality.[61]

Thinking on this line, one may suppose that we are not faced with rival accounts of conditions for being a reason for action. Rather these are different questions 'Why?', Anscombe's and Aristotle's, and two associated notions of reasons for action (and two associated kinds of action—all intentional actions, and then the subset of

[61] Crudely, there are two main kinds of error in practical rationality.

(1) There are mistakes (culpable or not) *in* the agent's practical reasoning—where their conclusion about what they should do is false, because it is not the end they ought to be pursuing, or not the means they ought to be taking, or both.
(2) There are errors *against* rationality—where the agent acts against what they take it—correctly or incorrectly—they should do (as in akrasia or tiredness or depression), or fail to utilize their rationality where they should.

(Cf. 'The Rationality of Morality', op. cit. note 14, 121–2).

chosen actions[62]). To Anscombe's 'Why?' the answer, where positive, yields a reason for action, in the sense of an explanation, or wider description, in terms of what someone is pursuing (its point)—and which can, at least in cases of practical calculation, be pushed back to a proper first premise which reveals the end—what is wanted—under a desirability characterization, i.e. under the aspect of *some* good. On Aristotle's 'Why?,' the 'Why?' is that of 'Why did you *choose* that?—or 'Why did you do that?', 'Why did you think that the thing to do?' (thus presupposing that the agent acted *fully rationally,* in the tight sense of chosen action that expresses or connects to their conception of acting, or living, well, or wisely). If this question is not rejected—as it will be by an akratic—then it will be answered with a reason or reasons, that are considerations the agent took to establish that action as one that he *should* do, as being what would constitute his acting well—an account that reveals why the agent thought that action *the* good action to do: i.e. under the aspect of *the* good.[63] (Note that in making these remarks we have *not* yet been engaged in ethics—at least if that is considered as arguing about what values are the correct ones, or what actually is acting well etc.).

(3) *The High Road Dominant* Finally, whether or not one supposes there are two rather different questions here,

[62] Cf. NE 3.2.1111b6–10.

[63] A rejection of this question can be equally informative—in claiming of some action that was obviously intentional that it was not done 'in character', and did not represent what the agent valued.

one could still think that the High Road is in a certain sense primary. It captures what is distinctive of *human action* in its primary application; that it is for a Rational Creature to live a Rational Life, composed of fully Rational Doings[64]—and this it will do unless it fails through certain defects. This is thus a normative principle of human practical rationality. It is of an adult human to have developed views of what is good and bad in human life—in general and in their particular circumstances; and to seek to make their actions conform to and express their values—to realize their values in acting well and thus live in a way they take to be wise. This is the form of human action. If they do things counter to this, then these are failures as 'actions'—they lack something they ought to have as human actions, and are thus far defective as *actions*: they do not achieve success as human actions. Thus, an akratic action is a kind of thing—a *failure* in a *kind* of *doing*—that a brute couldn't be guilty of.

3.2. Akrasia again

But, as we saw earlier, the High Road has trouble with akrasia: for on that view taking R as your reason to φ shows that you suppose the end in question good to pursue.[65]

[64] One moral of Aristotle's Function Argument in *NE* 1.7.

[65] In what follows I retrace the steps I offered in 'The Rationality of Morality', op. cit. note 14, section 5.3, pp. 135–9.

Anscombe says of Aristotle's calculating akratic that he 'reckons how to proceed—*once* he has given way to the temptation to go after this woman—*in exactly the same way* as the licentious man'—it's just that his volitions aren't to be called choices. But we can equally say: 'the akratic, at least if he is weak rather than impulsive, reckons how to proceed—*before* he has given way to temptation—in exactly the same way as the *practically wise man*'. Is this akratic's change then a change of mind about '*how to proceed*'? This phrase masks an important distinction. The licentious man in reaching conclusions about 'how to proceed' is reaching conclusions about what he *should* do—about how he *should* proceed, say:

> 'I need to make her fall in love with me: (so) I should send flowers'; or
>
> 'I should send her flowers: that will enamour her of me',

where this 'should' is the *unqualified* 'should' of full *practical evaluation*—stating what the agent (supposes he) is to do, or how he is 'to proceed', *if he is to act well unqualifiedly* (and not merely in some particular area). It is dependent for its truth on both the end and means at issue being correct (so in this case of licentiousness it is, we may suppose, in fact false). But *this* judgment the calculating akratic cannot reach (his full practical evaluation about what he *should* do, or how he *should proceed,* being quite other and similar to the wise person's[66]). So when, in yielding to temptation, he

[66] It need not be exactly the same. For someone who has correct values, yet knows that he is susceptible to temptations, may see the need to

calculates 'how to proceed' in this akratic project, this is not in his case a calculation addressed to how he *should,* unqualifiedly, proceed. So what is it? (A) We might claim that the akratic's calculation doesn't yield a 'should' judgment at all, wishing to reserve 'should' to mark the reasoning of full practical evaluation.[67] (B) Alternatively we may think that 'should' marks the presence of rational calculation, and so allow that the calculating akratic reaches some 'should' judgment, but then claim that this 'should' judgment is *qualified* or shielded in its truth assessment: e.g.

> 'Given I am going to pursue what I should not, viz. the seduction, I should send flowers (or it's best/there is reason for me to send flowers)'.

Here the qualifying concession shields assessment of the truth of the claim from evaluation of the correctness or incorrectness of the end in question (the seduction): that is set outside the truth assessment of the judgment. What the truth assessment of this judgment depends on would then need to be made clear. It may be claimed that the concession itself simply establishes the falsity of the judgment that one should send flowers: such a response, I suspect, stems from the inclination in (A) to take 'should' as essentially sensitive to the conditions of *unqualified* practical evaluation. But if

make a more cautious decision than the fully wise (e.g. to drink only one glass, or to refuse the invitation to the party). Of course this may not succeed in averting his eventual akratic act.

[67] That seems to be the line Aristotle takes (e.g. *NE* 7.9.1152a4–6, etc.). See earlier, Part 1 pp. 270–1; p. 275.

we think that the truth assessment *can* be shielded—that 'should' judgments can be qualified—then there is a real question of in what way. And this will surely be various. Thus the claim above may be advanced as truth assessable

(i) simply as a 'technical' claim that sending flowers is, in the circumstances, a suitably effective Step to the end of seduction (cf. 'I should, technically speaking'; 'it is best from a technical point of view'; 'there is a *technical reason* to. . .'). (And that may be correct: sending an asp, or a brick, would show a form of technical incompetence).[68]

(ii) Alternatively it may be a judgment sensitive to the akratic's other ends, and to its success in limiting or minimizing the damage he (supposes he) is doing. Thus he may think some other means than sending flowers more 'efficient', yet one that would more intensely hurt the feelings of another he cares about. (E.g. 'Why did you send flowers': 'to encompass the seduction, although jewellery would have been more effective, but *that* would have been extra hurtful to my wife. . .'). If so, then for this reason too, the akratic is unlikely to calculate 'in exactly the same way as the licentious'.

(iii) Or it may be supposed sensitive not only to the akratic's actual other ends, but also to other ends he should have, even if actually he does not. (He should have cared about his wife sufficiently not only not to have

[68] One may doubt whether this is strictly speaking a skill—a *techne*—but that needs another discussion.

attempted the seduction in the first place, but, given he did, not to have done it with jewellery!).

So what the akratic's shielded judgment would be sensitive to can vary: much depends on how the conversation would go—as to what room for criticism the akratic allows to be in place. And this depends on how the akratic frames 'the problem' he now takes himself to be addressing, once he has yielded to temptation.[69]

But it is clear that the akratic's *practical problem* in this bit of calculation is not that of working out *what to do bare and simple'*, i.e. of what he should—unqualifiedly—do, of what it is for him to act well or wisely; whereas *that* is the licentious person's problem, and is what his deliberation is addressing, and what his conclusion is about.

The mere fact that you intend, or have decided to pursue some end, does not, on this view unqualifiedly rationalize taking the technically appropriate means. If there is reason for you not to pursue the end, there is reason for you not to take the means. A reason unqualified is a reason why you *should* φ—it speaks for φ'ing being *the* thing to do.[70] And if we are tempted to say that, for example, the

[69] One may of course see a progression from the akratic's making a judgment of the second sort to his making one of the first sort—and see in that progression further akrasia (as more of the agent's ends and values get compromised by his pursuit of the akratic project).

[70] Contrast the notion of being unqualifiedly good-at-deliberation (*haplos euboulos*) with that of being qualifiedly (*pos*) so—good with respect *to a specific end* (*NE* 6.7.1141b12–14; cf. 6.5. 1140a25–31; 6.9.1142b28–31.

akratic agent has a reason for acting as they do, this is only in some qualified, or different, sense of having a reason.

This way of looking at things goes hand in hand with viewing practical reason as concerned with the problem of what the agent is to do, in the sense of *should* do—what it is best for them to do, where their acting well or wisely is a matter of getting both the end and the means (constitutive and/or instrumental) correct. So we can see that the licentious man and the calculating akratic are addressing *different* problems in their calculations: the one is addressing the question of what he should do (of how acting he would be acting well, *haplos*); the other has abandoned that, at least in its unconditional, unqualified, form.

And practical reason, so viewed, involves not merely calculating what action the agent should do, if they are to act well, but also their doing it: that they aim to do it *as a result* of their deliberation. Here one might think there is a natural home for a concept of (rational) choice—that demarcates an important difference between the licentious and the calculating akratic seducer: that the one acts as they suppose they *should,* as a result of their deliberations about what it is best to do; the other fails to act as they suppose they should—as they would choose to act; they fail to do what they suppose is the good thing to do.

Moreover, by contrast, on the Low Road the sense in which the akratic's action is *irrational* is left, it seems to me, under-addressed, in being viewed simply as an ethical matter. The akratic reasons: 'They have flowers in Hereford market: so I'll go there'. We ask 'what for?', and eventually get some proper first premise which characterizes the seduction as, say, pleasurable. That makes his pursuit of this end intelligible in a way. But in so acting he is acting irrationally. And this doesn't seem to be just an 'ethical' criticism. In this case the end is one a human should not be pursuing: that's ethical in a sense. But there is also something wrong with the *form* of the action—or, if that sounds metaphysical, with its *grammar*. It is not how the human acts when the human is acting in the way it is for a human to act—it is rather a defective form of acting.

3.3. The High Road of Reason again

Anscombe has little to say about the having of main purposes; they are not, I think, for her in any way requirements of reason.[71] It seems just one possibility among others, of subordinating some ends to others: some humans do this, some do not. In contrast to this Stands the possibility of a more complex picture of practical rationality: that, *qua* practically rational, we act with some one end in view (i.e. **T2**): that—formally speaking—of acting well, of achieving that kind of success in our actions that is proper to human action.

Thus, roughly speaking, it is part of being practically rational:

(1) to develop views of the goods and bads in human life, to develop a sense of what is worth pursuing in life and what not;

[71] Cf.Part 1 pp. 278–9.

(2) then to determine in the light of this what action one should do—what action will express or conform to these values. For that will be *human action proper*—that behind which the agent stands fully.

By contrast, with her rejection of **T2** in *Intention* 21, the picture Anscombe leaves me with is that many of my actions are just things that I do—for no particular reason, or for things I just happen to want; some will be actions for more distant ends, and so have longer chains. I may have a main purpose; but I may not. My whole life could consist simply in a series of little unconnected, independent, forays for things at some 'distance' from me that I happen to want, (which I conceive of under some desirability characterization or other, and which I calculate how to get)—amid a sea of 'just doings for no particular reasons'. This seems very close to Aristotle's view of someone living *kata pathos*—living at the beck and call of succeeding emotions and desires—hurried this way and that by whatever it is they happen to find they want at the moment—and where some of the things they want may be set at a distance and require cleverness (*deinotes*) on their part to attain.[72]

[72] They do not have any overarching purpose or end: they are adrift on a sea of wants, buffetted by the happenstance current of their desires. Even if, from habit, this started to take certain shapes—certain patterns of behaviour emerged—this would not be enough really to sustain talk of their having values. This drifting is different from coming to the view that nothing much is worth going for, or to conceiving of acting well as just going with the flow—that what is valuable in life is to take it

And of course this is right: my whole life *could* so consist. And perhaps Anscombe thinks of the 'ancient and medieval philosophers' as denying that this is so much as possible: in which case she is right. But can't we say that someone living as described above exhibits a *failure of practical rationality* ? Living like that they are not acting as it is human to act: and so cannot attain some of the good it is human to attain. (It is living more like a child.) For it is of an adult human to act and live, not *kata pathos,* but 'by choice', by their values (*kata prohairesin*): that is, in accord with a developed conception of how best to act and to live.[73] There seems more to the *structure* of practical rationality—and **T2**, when taken as normative principle of practical rationality, points to that. And I do not see that Anscombe gives us reason to resist it.

One could perhaps attempt to make such a conception of practical rationality and of action seem natural by considering the possibilities it opens up. Thus the basic unit of 'φ-ing in order to ψ (as it occurs in reasoning) constitutes a *rational* order or pattern[74]— the possibility of doing one thing in order to do (or be doing) another that is at a

as it comes. This latter is a much more complex attitude—one that is cognisant of the possible demands of reason.

[73] How we are to think of this is a further complex issue. (On avoiding the blue-print model, see John McDowell, 'Deliberation and Moral Development in Aristotle's Ethics', *Aristotle, Kant and the Stoics,* S. Engstrom and J. Whiting (eds.) (Cambridge: Cambridge University Press, 1996), 19-35.)

[74] And in this it contrasts, say, with a cat's skulking in order to catch a bird—where its doing one thing for the sake of another (or *in order to*

distance.[75] It is a 'unit' of ordering or structuring. This invites us to think about the *potential* for such Organization and structuring—it offers the possibility of ordering one's entire living around the attainment of some spatially or contextually distant goal: and why not organize it around making a success of one's *life?*—or making *a whole* out of one's life, of making a life?[76] And what could be better than that?[77]

Moreover this possibility of so doing may, viewed from another angle, seem rather a *requirement* of reason—as a Standard, or norm, of rational agency. Or so I have claimed. One who fails to exploit this possibility fails thus far to be fully exercising their powers of human rationality, and in this respect is defective. And, as I suggested earlier, one could appeal to the following principle as a constitutive principle of practical rationality:

> 'of goods the greater is ever the more takeable/choosable' (*NE* 1.7.1097M9–20).

achieve another) reveals a *natural* order, or natural pattern (centred around natural goods), (cf. *Intention* 42.2).

75 The distance, as Anscombe says (41.2; cf. 22.1), can be one of wider description, as well as temporal or spatial distance.

76 The 'unity' of life and person can be seen an achievement of integration. But it is very hard to get thoughts about such unities correct.

77 This exploration of the limits of 'organization' is reinforced by the possibility of the rational assessment or critique of ends (both in general and in particular). (I find myself wanting to say: ' "good" is an organizing concept').

That is, it is *irrational*—flying counter to the very point of practical rationality—to pursue what you suppose is the lesser of two available goods, a worse action rather than a better. For the point of practical rationality is to work out what is best for one to do so as to do it. And if the greatest human good is acting well, or living well, then in each action one should be concerned to be acting well— doing what is called for, what is wise, what one should. (Of course one can only do that as one conceives it.)[78] In a way then the end of acting well is the proper (though formal) end of human action.

As I said earlier, in *Intention* 20 Anscombe argues that

> The occurrence of other answers to the question '"Why?" besides ones like "I just did", is essential to the existence of the concept of an intention or voluntary action' (*Intention* 20.9)

There must be answers that (a) express intention for the future, and (b) express further intentions in acting—as when you say you are φ'ing *with the intention of*, or *for the sake of*, or *in order to*, ψ, revealing the rational order or structure of your actions. What an advocate of the dominance of the High Road may suspect is that there is a further stage to this argument: that it is essential to the existence of the concept of such a rational pattern (of intentions with which) that there must be the possibility of answers that reveal a *fully* rational structure—of action done because it is taken by the

[78] See Aristotle *NE* 3.4.

agent to be *the* thing—the good thing—to do: to be their *acting well.*

3.4. Conclusion

In conclusion. Perhaps one way to put my worry is this.

It seems distinctive of *human* action that it is *ethical—in an old sense* of having to do with matters of character and value, of what ways of going on the agent conceives as good and bad. Mere brutes cannot so act: their patterns of action are natural, and their ends set by nature. By contrast, the human, as Aquinas notes, pursues things *as* good; what ends they take it they should pursue is a matter of judgment and vulnerable to rational criticism and assessment. Now in thus saying that human action is *ethical* I do *not* mean two things at least. First, I do not mean that *all* human actions are so, or succeed in being so: for the akratic does not do what he considers expresses, or is fully shaped by, his values. And for that he is criticizable. For his action is not as human action should be—and is defective in this respect.[79] Second, I do not mean 'ethical' in the sense of 'correctly ethical', having the *correct* values and a *good* character—(*that* I could agree is the matter of *ethics*): in the sense I am concerned with, the actions of the wicked, expressing what they take to be the fine way to live and act, are 'ethical'.

[79] A fuller discussion would have to discuss the challenge that the High Road is overly intellectualistic, and distorts the nature of 'light' actions, like making oneself a cup of tea, and of sudden actions.

That human action is ethical in this sense strikes me as a grammatical remark. For it means that certain questions are in place about human action—that we can ask someone:

(a) 'Did you really mean to do that?' not in the sense of contrasting intentional with accidental, but in the sense of 'Did you really take that to be the thing to do?'.
(b) Or we can ask 'Is that what you choose to do?' in the sense of 'Is that what you think you *should* be doing?—is that what expresses what you think is *acting well*?'.

The applicability of these questions also is part of the grammar of our talk of action. Indeed their applicability is (part of) what is *distinctive* of human action as against that of mere brutes. Someone who couldn't understand, or was puzzled by, such questions would be revealed as lacking in mastery of the notion of human action.

The will, I should like to say, is just the possibility of this kind of conversation.

Modern Moral Philosophy and the Problem of Relevant Descriptions

ONORA O'NEILL

Anscombe's indictment of modern moral philosophy is full-blooded. She began with three strong claims:

> The first is that is not profitable to do moral philosophy... until we have an adequate philosophy of psychology, in which we are conspicuously lacking. The second is that the concepts of obligation and duty... and of the moral sense of 'ought', ought to be jettisoned... because they are derivatives... from an earlier conception of ethics... and are only harmful without it. The third thesis is that the differences between the well-known English writers on moral philosophy from Sidgwick to the present are of little importance.[1]

The connections between these three thoughts are not immediately obvious, but their influence is not in doubt. Many exponents of virtue ethics take Anscombe's essay as a founding text and have endorsed all three thoughts. Many contemporary consequentialists and theorists of justice, who may reasonably be thought the heirs of the 'modern moral

[1] G. E. M. Anscombe, 'Modern Moral Philosophy', *Collected Philosophical Papers of G. E. M. Anscombe,* Vol. III, *Ethics, Religion and Politics* (Oxford: Blackwell, 1981), 26.

philosophy' that Anscombe criticized, have disputed or disregarded all three. Yet I believe that Anscombe's essay is neither as reassuring for contemporary virtue ethics, nor as damaging to other strands in contemporary moral philosophy as this snapshot account of its influence could suggest.

1. Anscombe's Diagnosis and Virtue Ethics

Anscombe diagnoses many modern attempts to do moral philosophy as failing for lack of an adequate philosophy of psychology. As she sees it, we still use a moral vocabulary that once had sense and resonance, but we now have no adequate grip on the philosophy of psychology that supports that vocabulary. Consequently we use it to say things that are deeply confused, and sometimes morally corrupt. We cannot, on Anscombe's view, substitute 'modern', naturalistic psychology for an adequate philosophy of psychology since it offers no adequate basis for an account either of obligation or of virtue.[2]

This diagnosis of the failings of modern moral philosophy initially had limited influence, but has been widely accepted since the early eighties. Its widening acceptance can perhaps be traced to Alasdair MacIntyre's much discussed restatement of many of Anscombe's thoughts some twenty-five years after she wrote, in which he acknowledged a deep debt to her essay. In *After Virtue* he accused not only the 'modern' moral philosophers whom Anscombe names, but

[2] Ibid.

their Enlightenment predecessors of engaging in 'an inevitably unsuccessful project'.[3] They fell into confusion by discarding' *teleological accounts of human-nature-as-it-could-be in* favour of naturalistic accounts of human-nature-as-it-actually-is.[4] This left them unable to make coherent ethical claims, since ethics is about making a transition from human-nature-as-it-is to human-nature-as-it-would-be-if-fully-realized. Ethics, MacIntyre writes,

> presupposes some account of potentiality and act, some account of the essence of man as rational animal and above all some account of the human *telos*. The precepts that enjoin the various virtues and prohibit the vices, which are their counterparts, instruct us how to move from potentiality to act, how to realize our true nature and to reach our true end.[5]

MacIntyre adds that this scheme is

> . . .complicated and added to, but not essentially altered when it is placed within a framework of theistic beliefs. . . and the precepts of ethics. . . have to be understood not only as teleological injunctions but also as expressions of divinely ordained law.[6]

Apparently neither Anscombe nor MacIntyre saw any difficulty in combining Aristotelian teleological accounts of human beings and law conceptions of ethics *provided that the law concerned was divine law*. This view is easily read as a familiar Thomist fusion of Natural Law theory with

[3] A. MacIntyre, *After Virtue* (London: Duckworth, 1983), 53.
[4] Ibid., 50. [5] Ibid. [6] Ibid., 51.

Aristotelianism. A theological framework integrates the claims that God determines the end of man and that the principles He prescribes can guide their pursuit of that end. Anscombe puts her conclusion boldly:

> To have a *law* conception of ethics is to hold that what is needed for conformity with the virtues failure in which is the mark of being bad *qua* man... is required by divine law. Naturally it is not possible to have such a conception unless you believe in God as a lawgiver; like Jews, Stoics and Christians.[7]

In her view, any law conception of ethics collapses unless it is set in a theological framework.

So she sees the proponents of modern moral philosophy as attempting the impossible in putting forward a law conception of ethics that was detached from divine law. Anscombe comments on their ambition:

> Those who recognize the origins of the notions of 'obligation' and of the emphatic, 'moral' ought, in the divine law conception of ethics but who reject the notion of a divine legislator sometimes look about for the possibility of retaining a law conception of ethics without a divine legislator[8]

She sees this ambition as understandable but unrealizable:

> ...if such a conception is dominant for many centuries, and then is given up, it is a natural result that the concepts of 'obligation', of being bound and required as

[7] G. E. M. Anscombe, 'Modern Moral Philosophy', 30. [8] Ibid., 37.

> by a law, should remain although they had lost their root. . .
>
> It is as if the notion 'criminal' were to remain when criminal law and criminal courts had been abolished and forgotten.[9]

In failing to grasp this point, the proponents of modern moral philosophy fail to see that the 'moral' use of the notion of 'ought' 'has no reasonable sense outside a law conception of ethics'[10] and that the only coherent possibility here is a divine law conception of ethics. She concludes that if we reject a version of 'Aristotelian' ethics that dispenses with the notion of obligation, we must accept a divine law view of ethics.

Many who accept Anscombe's diagnosis have gone for the first option. They have rejected divine law accounts of ethics, but have argued for supposedly Aristotelian ethical visions, in which obligation and the moral 'ought' play no part. Most contemporary virtue ethics detaches virtue from any account of divine law. Its proponents say little about this element in Anscombe's criticisms of modern moral philosophy. They simply reject a morality of obligations, or of moral rules and see a life of virtue as constitutive of human flourishing. However, neo-Aristotelians differ widely in their views of human flourishing and the true end of man. Some take a relativized or quasi-relativized view of the human good, seeing it as varying in differing societies; others identify the human good with a comprehensive and supposedly

[9] Ibid., 30. [10] Ibid., 32.

universal list of desirable states of being and capacities, whose status and derivation may be hard to establish without a theological framework.[11]

Anscombe herself held to the divine law view of ethics, but left room for those unwilling to follow her to settle for Aristotelianism without divine law. Yet is this a stable position? Many, indeed most, contemporary virtue ethicists reject the thought that conformity with the virtues is or could be even *law-like*. They distinguish sharply between an *ethics of rules* and an *ethics of virtue*, and insist that virtue cannot be set out in rules of laws. If they are right, does it follow that Anscombe and MacIntyre were mistaken in supposing that virtue ethics was compatible with divine law? If they are mistaken, should they distance themselves from Anscombe's polemic against forms of moral philosophy that appeal to principles or rules, and that use the vocabulary of obligation without the backing of a divine law conception of ethics? I shall add a speculative postscript on this striking gap between Anscombe and her more recent followers and at the end of the lecture.

2. Modern Moral Philosophy and Relevant Descriptions

We can perhaps see a little more accurately what Anscombe has in mind by asking what a more adequate 'philosophy of psychology' was supposed to contribute to moral philosophy.

[11] Martha C. Nussbaum, *Women and Human Development: The Capabilities Approach* (Cambridge: Cambridge University Press, 2000).

She certainly was not lamenting the lack of an adequate scientific or naturalistic psychology. She was markedly hostile to experimental psychology when she taught me in the early 60's; she had no doubt been equally hostile to it a few years earlier; and I suspect that she would have been equally hostile to subsequent empirical work in psychology.

Her use of the term 'philosophy of psychology' is best illustrated by the philosophy of action that we find in Aristotle's *Nichomachean Ethics*, to which she repeatedly refers both in 'Modern Moral Philosophy' and in *Intention* (published a year earlier). An adequate philosophy of psychology would cover topics such as action, intention, voluntariness, wanting, pleasure, weakness of will and self-control—and might even embrace accounts of virtue and of flourishing.[12] I have occasionally seen the term *moral psychology* used to refer to more or less this cluster of topics,[13] but that term now seems to have been pressed into new and narrower duties in the discussion of psychological features of moral education, of the sort discussed by Jean Piaget, Laurence Kohlberg or Carol Gilligan. So I shall stick with Anscombe's term *philosophy of psychology*.

Perhaps the deepest thought linking the many topics that Anscombe would group under the rubric 'philosophy of psychology' is the thought that *action is propositional.* Acts fall under many descriptions; act-descriptions

[12] G. E. M. Anscombe, 'Modern Moral Philosophy', 38 and 41.

[13] For example, in Owen Flanagan and Amélie Oksenberg Rorty, (eds.), *Identity Character and Morality: Essays in Moral Psychology* (Cambridge, Mass.: MIT Press, 1993).

may have many instances. Although individual acts—act tokens—are events in the world, we both think about action and act *under certain descriptions.* We consent to action as described in certain ways, but not others;[14] we hold people responsible for what they do under certain descriptions, but not under others;[15] we classify acts under certain descriptions, but not others. How does this make a difference to the way we do moral philosophy?

In 'Modern Moral Philosophy' Anscombe views the fact that we think of action under descriptions as fatal to ethical positions that aim to provide accounts of moral *rules* or *principles.* She criticizes both Kantian and Utilitarian ethics—the central versions of 'modern moral philosophy'—on these grounds. She writes of Kant that

> ...it never occurred to him that a lie could be relevantly described as anything but just a lie... His rule about universalizable maxims is useless without stipulations as to what shall count as a relevant description of an action with a view to constructing a maxim about it.[16]

And she writes that

> Mill, like Kant, fails to realize the necessity for stipulation of relevant descriptions, if his theory is to have content. It did not occur to him that acts of murder and theft could be otherwise described. He holds that where a proposed

[14] G. E. M. Anscombe, 'Two Kinds of Error in Action', in *Collected Philosophical Papers of G. E. M. Anscombe*, Vol. III, *Ethics, Religion and Politics* (Blackwell, Oxford, 1981), 3.

[15] Ibid., 4-5.

[16] G. E. M. Anscombe, 'Modern Moral Philosophy', 27.

> action is of such a kind as to fall under some one principle established on grounds of utility, one must go by that.

The so-called 'problem of relevant descriptions' is the basis of Anscombe's condemnation of Utilitarian and Kantian positions, and is presented as a central source—perhaps the central source—of the alleged failure of modern moral philosophy. The problem can appear both profound and intractable. Any act-token will fall under many true descriptions, hence also under many possible principles of action. Absent a proper philosophy of psychology, how can we tell which act description is relevant for moral assessment? We will not, for example, know whether to assess an action under the descriptions that an agent intends it, or under descriptions others think salient, or under descriptions that nobody has noted. Both Kantian and Utilitarian ethics may have other defects, but if Anscombe is right they founder on this point alone: the many different act descriptions and principles under which any act falls may point to differing moral assessments, and so to incoherence.

I believe, although Anscombe's text does not make this explicit, that this is why she supposes that 'modern moral philosophy' so readily lapses into some form of consequentialism. For if we have no way of determining under which descriptions we should judge action, we cannot judge acts for their *intrinsic* character—which we cannot know. So we must end up judging acts by their extrinsic features, such as their (expected) consequences. This will lead us away from what Anscombe calls 'the Hebrew—Christian ethic', which prohibits certain acts 'simply in virtue of their description as such-and-such identifiable kinds of action'.[17] She points to examples of types of action that are intrinsically unacceptable, regardless of consequences:

> . . .it has been characteristic of that ethic to teach that there are certain things forbidden whatever *consequences* threaten, such as choosing to kill the innocent for any purpose, however good; vicarious punishment; treachery; idolatry; sodomy; adultery; making a false profession of faith.[18]

There are several oddities to these claims. How, in the first place, if the problem of relevant descriptions is so intractable, has 'the Hebrew—Christian ethic' managed to avoid it, whereas modern moral philosophy has not? I presume that Anscombe's answer to this point would be that the former has an adequate philosophy of psychology, while the latter does not. However, this is by and large an inference from her comments on the moral corruption of modern moral philosophy, and not (I think) something she establishes.[19] Equally, why did Anscombe think that the problem of relevant descriptions was a weakness—a fatal weakness indeed—in Kantian ethics and more generally in 'modern moral philosophy' but not fatal for Aristotelian

[17] Ibid., 34. [18] Ibid., 34; cf. 39–40.

[19] For example, she upbraids Sidgwick for his simplistic claim that we are responsible for *all* foreseen effects of action, and his failure to distinguish good action that has foreseen but unintended bad effects from bad action, Ibid., 35—6; she concludes with splendid certainty that 'it is a necessary feature of consequentialism that it is a shallow philosophy', Ibid., 36.

ethics? The problem of relevant descriptions— *if* it is a problem—will surely affect *all* approaches to ethics except those forms of radical particularism that (purportedly) do not view acts in terms of descriptions under which they fall. Mere claims that some approaches to moral philosophy have access to a philosophy of psychology that resolves the problem, and mere assertion that other approaches do not, are not enough.

3 Relevant Descriptions in *Intention*

These issues can be clarified to some extent by considering Anscombe's more systematic and extensive discussion of the problem of relevant descriptions in *Intention.* There she asks, 'how I am to select from the large number of true statements that I could make about a person?'[20]. And she suggests that any of us could 'say what would immediately come to your mind as a report to give someone who could not see and wanted to know'.[21] But if there are large numbers of distinct descriptions of a given action—large numbers of true descriptions—why should *just one* immediately come to mind? Might not a number come to mind? Might not the wrong one(s) come to mind?

In fact both problems seem to arise quite often. We may find that we are torn between a number of competing descriptions of an action. In *Intention* Anscombe provides an example that later became well-known; a man is moving

[20] G. E. M. Anscombe, *Intention*, (Oxford, Blackwell, 1957), 8. [21] Ibid.

his arm up and down, thereby pumping water into a cistern, thereby poisoning a water supply, thereby poisoning the inhabitants of a villa, thereby despatching a group of war criminals. Action can be correctly described in many distinct ways, whose ethical significance may differ: multiplicity of true descriptions is ubiquitous.

Does this raise a problem for *all* ethical judgment? Even if in a given case we settle with conviction on one description of what is done, and that description is true of the case, there will always be other true descriptions. If others think that one or other of the competing true descriptions is more compelling or ethically significant, how are we to reply? We have only to think about the competing act descriptions that have figured in debates about abortion, civil war or other political disputes to realize that a choice of one rather than another act description *might* have momentous ethical implications, and that there are no simple or general ways of choosing which is the most appropriate or relevant description of a given act.

So does the multiplicity of true descriptions of any given act create an intractable difficulty for *all* attempts to do ethics? How are we to tell which are the morally significant or most significant descriptions of a given act? How are we to judge the action of somebody who, as it seems to us, fails to see morally significant descriptions of what he does or of what others do? How are we to know that we are not overlooking morally significant descriptions of what we or others do? Won't any account of practical reasoning, *a fortiori* of ethical reasoning, be stymied at the very start if we have to resolve these problems? To many later writers

Anscombe's concerns seem to raise a central problem, perhaps the central problem, for any adequate account of ethical judgment. The worry is acknowledged and addressed both in work in the tradition of 'modern moral philosophy' *and* in the work of those who follow Anscombe in aspiring to virtue ethics.

For example, the leading Kantian writer, Barbara Herman, views the problem of relevant description as a serious issue for Kantian ethics, and also proposes a solution for it. She writes:

> . . .The CI [Categorical Imperative] cannot be an effective practical principle of judgment unless agents have some understanding of their action before they use the Cl procedure. . . It is useful to think of the moral knowledge needed by Kantian agents (prior to making moral judgments) as knowledge of a kind of moral rule. Let us call them 'rules of moral salience'.[22]

Both where do these 'rules of moral salience' come from, and how are they to be justified? Herman argues that these rules do not themselves have moral weight, but that

> Typically they are acquired in childhood as part of socialization; they provide a framework within which people act. When the rules of moral salience are well internalized, they cause the agent to be aware of and attentive to the significance of 'moral danger'. They are not learned as bits of information about the world, and

[22] Barbara Herman, *The Practice of Moral Judgement* (Cambridge Mass.: Harvard University Press, 1993), 77.

> not as rules of guidance to use when engaged in particular sorts of activities... They constitute the structure of moral sensitivity... They may indicate which actions should not be undertaken without moral justification...[23]

The 'rules of moral salience', it seems, are not *moral rules,* but a sort of *moral early warning system.* As such they are not (on Herman's view) essential to moral judgment, in that an early warning system is not *essential* for applying the Categorical Imperative. But these rules 'enable an agent to appreciate what is at issue in hard cases by making perspicuous the morally significant features that make them hard',[24] although they 'do not themselves generate duties'.[25] The rules of moral salience supposedly provide some answer to the problem of relevant descriptions because they 'alter our idea of how an agent perceives situations that require moral judgment'.[26]

Herman acknowledges that the rules of moral salience, which she sees as 'pre-procedural moral rules'[27] need some foundations (sic) that connects them to Kant's moral philosophy. Without such connection she would find herself

[23] Ibid., 78. [24] Ibid., 79. [25] Ibid., 79.

[26] Ibid., 81. Cf. also 'To be a moral agent one must be trained to perceive situations in terms of their morally significant features (as described by the RMS)', 83; 'The role of the RMS in moral judgment is to provide the descriptive moral categories (sic) that permit the formulation of maxims suitable for assessment by the Cl procedure', 84; They 'guide the normal moral agent to the perception and description of the morally relevant features of his circumstances', 78.

[27] Ibid., 86.

ascribing an internally incoherent account of practical reasoning to Kant.[28] It seems to me that Herman is torn between the thought that rules of moral salience are an indispensable presupposition of any use of the Categorical Imperative, and an account that makes them not just a *preliminary* but an *independent* basis for moral judgment, and so threatens to make the Categorical Imperative redundant. Once we have 'rules of moral salience' how much work remains for the Categorical Imperative?

Other writers, who share more of Anscombe's views, have suggested that any solution to the problem of relevant descriptions would be a matter not of *rules* of moral salience but of *capacities* to appreciate the salient features of situations, which we internalize, making any appeal to ethical principles redundant. On such views, we can reach ethical judgments without appeal to principles or rules, guided simply by our sensitized, attentive perception or judgment of the case at hand that calls for ethical response. For example, John McDowell writes of moral judgment or deliberation as 'a capacity to read the details of

[28] Ibid., 85. She locates this foundation in the Moral Law itself, and draws on the Fact of Reason passages in the *Critique of Practical Reason* to support her reading. This is not the occasion in which to query Herman's reading of those difficult passages; in my view they are about the status of practical reason and not about judgment. For a different reading of the passages see Onora O'Neill, 'Autonomy and the Fact of Reason in the *Kritik der praktischen Vernunft*', *30—41*, in Otfried Hoffe, (ed.), *Immanuel Kant, Kritik der praktischen Vernunft* (Berlin: Akademie Verlag, Klassiker Auslegen Bd. 26, 2002), 81–97.

situations'[29] or a 'capacity to read the details of situations in the light of a way of valuing actions'[30] or a 'capacity to read predicaments correctly.'[31]

If either 'rules of moral salience' or 'capacities to read situations' can provide this much, it may seem tempting to cast the weight of moral judgment on them, if at the price of flirting with forms of relativism. Yet it is quite unclear to me how either of these approaches could resolve the problem of relevant descriptions. What shows that 'rules of moral salience' or 'capacities to read situations' fasten on the (morally) relevant descriptions of the acts being considered?

4. Reflective and Determinant Judgment

I think that Herman was right to hold that Kant needs an account of capacities to judge the nature of cases. I also think that he wrote extensively on the topic. The most relevant texts are his discussions of *determinant* and *reflective* judging in the *Critique of Judgment.* Kant there divides theoretical judgments (note: theoretical, not practical or ethical judgments) into *determinant* and *reflective* judgments:

> If the universal (the rule, principle, or law) is given, then the judgment, which subsumes the particular, *is determinant*... If, however, only the particular is given

[29] See John McDowell, 'Deliberation and Moral Development' in S. Engstrom and J. Whiting, (eds.) *Aristotle, Kant and the Stoics,* (Cambridge: Cambridge University Press, 1996), 23.

[30] Ibid. [31] Ibid., 26.

> and the universal has to be found for it, then the judgment is simply *reflective*,[32]

Both sorts of judgment begin with a case to hand, for example with a particular object, or situation, or an act. Our judgment of a particular is *determinant* if we merely ask whether some 'given' description or category or principle applies. I see a bird and determine whether it is a chaffinch; I find four people playing cards and determine whether they are playing bridge; I write a cheque and determine whether my account will be overdrawn. Determinant judgment *subsumes*. Subsuming may not be philosophically thrilling, but is surely cognitively indispensable. Determinant judging does not offer an answer to the problem—or supposed problem—of relevant descriptions; it is blind to the problem, since it assumes that 'the universal (the rule, principle or law) is given'. However, it is not on Kant's view the only way to judge objects, situations or acts.

Reflective judging is more interesting, and resembles the ways in which both Herman and McDowell approach the task of finding relevant descriptions. Here 'only the particular is given' and 'the universal has to be found for it'. I see a bird, but rather than simply determining that it is or is not a chaffinch, I try to work out what sort of bird it is. If in the course of that task I conclude that it is not a chaffinch, the task is not at an end, as it would be in determinant judgment: there are further possibilities to

[32] Immanuel Kant, *Critique of Judgement*, tr. Meredith, (Oxford: Clarendon Press, 1973) 18/179.

consider, and the possibilities are open ended. In reflective judging we do not simply test whether the card players are playing bridge or not, but more ambitiously try to work out what sort of game they are playing. It may be a game that I do not know, and if so I will have to work out how it is played by grasping the rules being followed, and may need to find a new name for it. Or again, if I subject my financial affairs to reflective judging I may consider many matters other than being or not being overdrawn: I may take many different views of a particular payment and its implications for my own and others' financial situations.

When we judge reflectively we consider—or explore—ways in which we *might* describe an object, a situation or an act. There may be some gap between Barbara Herman's idea of (a list of) rules of moral salience or John McDowell's' picture of a capacity to read situations, and the more open ended view of reflective judging of cases that Kant proposed. But they are clearly on the same track. However, none of these approaches offers a particularly convincing way of determining which descriptions are 'relevant' in particular cases.

5. Practical Judgment

Both determinant and reflective judging, as Kant explicates them, and the proposals that Herman and McDowell set out, are types of theoretical judging. These types of judging are possible only when a particular case is *there to hand*, as material to be judged; or when some hypothetical case has been adequately specified to be an object of hypothetical theoretical judgment. The outcomes of determinant and reflective judging alike are judgments about what is the case, or is hypothetically the case. The difference between the two is that in determinant judgment the person who makes the judgment also has a specific rule, principle or law in mind, and seeks to determine whether the instance (actual or hypothetical) falls under it or not, whereas in reflective judging the person who makes the judgment doesn't have any specific rule, principle or law in mind, so has to search for ones that might apply to the instance (actual or hypothetical).

But in *practical* judging we are not judging a particular act. The task in practical judgment is to shape action *that is not yet done.* There is no particular act to be judged. The aim of practical judgment is to shape the world (in small part), not to identify some way in which the world is shaped. Action yet to be done can be shaped by ensuring that it satisfies a range of standards, rules, principles or laws that are taken into account in deliberating. There will, of course, often be many ways of satisfying any set of standards, rules, laws or principle, indeed many ways of satisfying a single standard, rule, principle or law. For example, a rule such as 'always check your petrol before driving onto the motorway' could be satisfied by many different acts. I might check the petrol the night before my trip, or as I get into the car, or as I pass a pump—or, alas, as I drive onto a long stretch of motorway without service stations. A principle such as 'keep in touch with your friends' can be satisfied by innumerable different sorts of action. Practical judgments, whether technical or legal, financial or managerial, political or ethical, aim *to guide action* rather than to pass judgment on *acts already done.* Practical judgment, including ethical judgment, does not encounter the problem of relevant descriptions because it is not directed at individuable act-tokens. Whereas determinant and reflective judgment aim to *fit the world* or *some possible world*; practical judgment aims in some measure to *shape the world*, or to *specify how it should be shaped.* The different direction of fit shields practical judgment from the problem of relevant descriptions.

Yet it may seem that practical judgment escapes the problem of relevant descriptions only to encounter one of its near relatives. Granted that practical judgment does not start with a particular act, so agents do not have to work out how a (non-existent) act should be described. Still, since practical reasoning starts with some rule, principle or law it seems doomed to reach no more than indeterminate recommendations. Yet in the end any act we do has to be fully determinate. For example, starting with the thought that it would be a good idea to buy enough groceries for the weekend, what am I to do when I go into a supermarket and see that there are literally countless ways in which I could act to satisfy this aim or principle? Practical judgment may not leave us unsure about how to describe a case, as reflective judging does; but doesn't starting with any rule, principle or law leave us unsure what to do?

I think that this problem is in large measure an artefact that arises from considering specific practical rules, principles and laws in isolation. But, of course, that is not how life is. If the sole rule or principle that I sought to satisfy were that of leaving a supermarket with enough food to last the weekend I would indeed feel (and perhaps behave) like Buridan's ass—or worse. However, even in this case selecting *any* bundle of goods that would last the weekend would resolve my asinine problem. But, of course, in what we call real life I enter the supermarket not with a single aim in mind but also with many other aims and various rules, principles and laws. I not only try to get enough food to last until Monday, but also to do so quickly, without overspending, and without buying food that is unhealthy, or monotonous, disliked by those who will eat it, or produced by methods of which I disapprove. And I will also have regard to legal rules such as refraining from shoplifting, or to ethical requirements such treating the staff with courtesy or refraining from queue jumping.

Practical judgment is typically a matter of finding some way—at least *one* way—of acting that satisfies *a large number of distinct aims, standards, rules, principles and laws.* The overwhelming indeterminacy that seemed to threaten when we considered the artificially simplified task of choosing an act that satisfies a single rule or principle reduces when we consider the more realistic task of satisfying a plurality of aims, standards, rules, principles and laws. Just as equations can often be solved only when we know a sufficient number of constraints, so questions about how to act are often resolved only by taking account of a number of constraints. (Of course, sometimes some groups of rules or principles may make demands that cannot all be simultaneously satisfied; and others may make demands that cannot all be satisfied in certain types of situations. I set aside questions about conflicts between principles of differing types, including conflicts between principles of duty.)

However, even when we can specify the action to be performed to a reasonable degree, the problem of indeterminacy will persist. Even when I meet *all* the constraints set by ethics, law, custom, family budget and food preferences, my supermarket choices do not point to a fully determinate basket of goods. Yet this seems to me to be unproblematic. *Any* basket of goods that meets all these constraints will be an acceptable basket of goods—no matter whether its acquisition reflects obsessive hours of calculation or a flurry of impulse buying. Since practical judgment aims to guide action, it is enough if it does so—and probably illusory in most cases to think that when all demands are met, further calculation to identify some more narrowly specified 'optimal' act is needed or possible. There is no reason for imagining that any ethical rules or principles must be (quasi) algorithms that lead us to a very tightly specified act-types—and no possibility that rules or principles of action will lead us to an individual act token. Those who imagine otherwise are probably suffering from unfulfillable Utilitarian hankerings.

If these considerations are convincing, the difficulty of identifying relevant act descriptions does not tell *for* an ethics of virtue or *against* the positions that Anscombe groups under the heading 'modern moral philosophy'. The problem of relevant descriptions arises in describing or judging a given particular, but not in shaping future action. Describing the world we confront in adequate ways is a demanding task—and every bit as demanding for

Aristotelians as for Utilitarians, for Kantians as for Rawlsians. But it is only the background for ethical and other practical reasoning. Those who conflate the appraisal of particular situations with practical judgment take a spectator view of the moral life.

6. Postscript: Divine Law and Lawlikeness

None of this shows that 'modern moral philosophy' escapes Anscombe's other criticisms. In fact, I think that at some points Anscombe comes close to acknowledging that the problems of relevant descriptions cannot be the *basic* problem for ethical judgment. For example, she remarks at one point that 'things have to exist to have predicates'[33]—and that simple thought is enough to show that no problem of relevant descriptions can arise for acts not yet performed.

If we set aside the problem of relevant descriptions, what is the most serious of Anscombe's criticisms of modern moral philosophy? It might be her thought that modern moral philosophy has been drawn to ethical terms that are excessively abstract ('Morally wrong' rather than 'untruthful', 'unchaste' or 'unjust'[34]). It might be her thought that modern moral philosophers say too little about intention, or about other topics in the philosophy of psychology, and consequently place too much faith in the project of justifying action by its (expected) results.

[33] G. E. M. Anscombe, *Modem Moral Philosophy*, 33. [34] Ibid.

However, I think that, judging by the amount she says, Anscombe's deepest objection was to the persistent use of the vocabulary of moral requirement, of moral obligation and moral prohibition by those who do not accept a divine law conception of ethics.

As noted, she is not opposed to law conceptions of ethics as such. She believes that Aristotelian ethics, an ethics of virtue, can be reconciled with a divine law conception of ethics. Yet a divine law conception ethics would have to be expressed in principles: if it were not, divine law would not be law-like. (How abstract the act descriptions contained in these principles are or should be is a further consideration.)

It seems to me uncontroversial that any law conception of ethics, including a divine law conception of ethics, must represent ethics as *law-like.* Disagreements between different law conceptions of ethics will be about the *source* and *authority* of the supposed laws, but all will assume that laws must be *law-like*—that they prescribe for all cases within their scope. Yet I am not sure whether Anscombe accepts this point. Her objections to those who advance law conceptions of ethics without accepting divine law appears to be only about their views on the *sources* of law. She stated that 'you cannot be under law unless it has been promulgated to you'[35] and notes that various alternative sources of law, such as positive law or social norms cannot provide a basis for ethical law. She casts scorn on a certain reading of the Kantian idea of self-legislation, insisting that

[35] Ibid., 37.

'the concept of legislation requires superior power in the legislator'.[36]

I find it hard to resist the thought that in speaking of *law* conceptions of ethics Anscombe in fact had in mind *command* conceptions of ethics, and overlooked the formal structure of laws. If I am right—the comments are scattered—then I think we can see why she simply swept aside non-theological law conceptions of ethics with so little consideration. There are easy objections to deriving ethics from non-divine legislators; some (for example, Plato in *Euthyphro)* even think that there are problems in deriving ethics from divine legislators, although Anscombe dismisses those worries.[37] I think she may have dismissed them because her view of a divine law conception of ethics far from being Thomist was *radically antinomian.* Divine Law is seen as fiat.[38] Starting from that standpoint, laws are decrees, and what is referred to (rather misleadingly) as Divine *legislation* need not have even the form of law.[39] On this approach it is not at all surprising that Anscombe rejects all use of the vocabulary of moral obligation that is not divinely promulgated. Nor is it surprising that she objects to rules and principles without divine backing. Nor therefore is it surprising that she thought that it was possible to

[36] Ibid., 27. [37] Ibid., 41.

[38] Consider the startling remark 'What obliges is the divine law—as rules oblige in a game', Ibid., 41. It seems clear that it is the *source,* not the *form* or the *content* of law that is viewed as authoritative.

[39] Ibid., 37.

reject positions that argue for ethical rules—and the moral ought—with so little consideration. If this is indeed the background to her blanket criticism of the positions she groups together as 'modern moral philosophy', there may be a lot more to be said.

INDEX

Printed in the United States
by Baker & Taylor Publisher Services